T0212488

Communications in Computer and Information Science 657

Commenced Publication in 2007
Founding and Former Series Editors:
Alfredo Cuzzocrea, Dominik Ślęzak, and Xiaokang Yang

Editorial Board

Juan Carlos Figueroa-García
Eduyn Ramiro López-Santana
Roberto Ferro-Escobar (Eds.)

Applied Computer Sciences in Engineering

Third Workshop on Engineering Applications, WEA 2016
Bogotá, Colombia, September 21–23, 2016
Revised Selected Papers

 Springer

Editors
Juan Carlos Figueroa-García
Universidad Distrital Francisco José
 de Caldas
Bogotá
Colombia

Roberto Ferro-Escobar
Universidad Distrital Francisco José
 de Caldas
Bogotá
Colombia

Eduyn Ramiro López-Santana
Universidad Distrital Francisco José
 de Caldas
Bogotá
Colombia

ISSN 1865-0929   ISSN 1865-0937 (electronic)
Communications in Computer and Information Science
ISBN 978-3-319-50879-5   ISBN 978-3-319-50880-1   (eBook)
DOI 10.1007/978-3-319-50880-1

Library of Congress Control Number: 2016960314

Printed on acid-free paper

This Springer imprint is published by Springer Nature
The registered company is Springer International Publishing AG
The registered company address is: Gewerbestrasse 11, 6330 Cham, Switzerland

Preface

The Workshop on Engineering Applications (WEA) was born as a forum focused on different applications of all sciences in engineering. Its main goal is to open a space to show applications of all kinds of scientific theories in engineering coming from both academia and industry, as one of the flagship conferences of the Faculty of Engineering of the Universidad Distrital Francisco José de Caldas, in Bogotá, Colombia.

In the last two editions, the conference has turned to computer science topics such as software engineering, computer informatics, computational intelligence, intelligent computing, simulation systems, systems dynamics, systems modeling, IoT, among others. In this third edition, the conference unified itself to computer sciences and simulation systems with some miscellaneous applications, which give a clear idea of the trends in applied computer science, applied computational intelligence, applied simulation methodologies, and other applications. Therefore, the main topic of our conference was "Applied Computer Sciences in Engineering."

WEA 2016 received 128 submissions from eight countries and regions. All submissions were rigorously peer-reviewed and 49 papers and five posters were accepted for presentation at WEA 2016. The Program Committee finally selected 35 high-quality papers to be included in this volume of *Communications in Computer and Information Sciences* (CCIS) proceedings published by Springer.

The Faculty of Engineering of the Universidad Distrital Francisco José de Caldas, the Corporación Unificada Nacional (CUN), and the Faculty of Engineering of the National University of Colombia in Bogotá made significant efforts to guarantee the success of the conference. We would like to thank all members of the Program Committee and the referees for their commitment to help in the review process and for spreading our call for papers. We would like to thank Alfred Hofmann and Jorge Nakahara from Springer, for their helpful advice, guidance, and their continuous support in publishing the proceedings. Moreover, we would like to thank all the authors for supporting WEA: Without all their high-quality submissions, WEA 2016 would not have been possible. Finally, we are especially grateful to the IEEE Universidad Distrital Francisco José de Caldas and National University of Colombia Student branches, the Institute of Industrial and Systems Engineers Chapter 985 (IISE) of the Universidad Distrital Francisco José de Caldas, the Laboratory for Automation and Computational Intelligence (LAMIC), the Expert Systems and Simulation (SES), the Laboratory for Development and Research in Networks and Electronics (LIDER) research groups of the Universidad Distrital Francisco José de Caldas, and the Algorithms and Combinatory (ALGOS) research group of the National University of Colombia.

September 2016

Juan Carlos Figueroa-García
Eduyn Ramiro López-Santana
Roberto Ferro-Escobar

Preface

The Workshop on Engineering Applications (WEA) was born as a forum focused on different applications of all sciences in engineering. Its main goal is to open a space to show applications of all kinds of scientific theories in engineering coming from both academia and industry, as one of the flagship conferences of the Faculty of Engineering of the Universidad Distrital Francisco José de Caldas, in Bogotá, Colombia.

In the last two editions, the conference has turned to computer science topics such as software engineering, computer informatics, computational intelligence, intelligent computing, simulation systems, systems dynamics, systems modeling, IoT, among others. In this third edition, the conference unified itself to computer sciences and simulation systems with some miscellaneous applications, which give a clear idea of the trends in applied computer science, applied computational intelligence, applied simulation methodologies, and other applications. Therefore, the main topic of our conference was "Applied Computer Sciences in Engineering."

WEA 2016 received 128 submissions from eight countries and regions. All submissions were rigorously peer-reviewed and 49 papers and five posters were accepted for presentation at WEA 2016. The Program Committee finally selected 35 high-quality papers to be included in this volume of *Communications in Computer and Information Sciences* (CCIS) proceedings published by Springer.

The Faculty of Engineering of the Universidad Distrital Francisco José de Caldas, the Corporación Unificada Nacional (CUN), and the Faculty of Engineering of the National University of Colombia in Bogotá made significant efforts to guarantee the success of the conference. We would like to thank all members of the Program Committee and the referees for their commitment to help in the review process and for spreading our call for papers. We would like to thank Alfred Hofmann and Jorge Nakahara from Springer, for their helpful advice, guidance, and their continuous support in publishing the proceedings. Moreover, we would like to thank all the authors for supporting WEA: Without all their high-quality submissions, WEA 2016 would not have been possible. Finally, we are especially grateful to the IEEE Universidad Distrital Francisco José de Caldas and National University of Colombia Student branches, the Institute of Industrial and Systems Engineers Chapter 985 (IISE) of the Universidad Distrital Francisco José de Caldas, the Laboratory for Automation and Computational Intelligence (LAMIC), the Expert Systems and Simulation (SES), the Laboratory for Development and Research in Networks and Electronics (LIDER) research groups of the Universidad Distrital Francisco José de Caldas, and the Algorithms and Combinatory (ALGOS) research group of the National University of Colombia.

September 2016

Juan Carlos Figueroa-García
Eduyn Ramiro López-Santana
Roberto Ferro-Escobar

Organization

General Chair

Juan Carlos Figueroa-García   Universidad Distrital Francisco José de Caldas, Bogotá, Colombia

Finance Chair/Treasurer

Roberto Ferro-Escobar   Universidad Distrital Francisco José de Caldas, Bogotá, Colombia

Program Chair

Germán Jairo Hernández-Pérez   Universidad Nacional de Colombia, Campus Bogotá

Publication Chair

Eduyn Ramiro López-Santana   Universidad Distrital Francisco José de Caldas, Bogotá, Colombia

Track Chairs

Edwin Rivas   Universidad Distrital Francisco José de Caldas, Bogotá, Colombia

Germán Andrés Méndez-Giraldo   Universidad Distrital Francisco José de Caldas, Bogotá, Colombia

Javier Arturo Orjuela-Castro   Universidad Nacional de Colombia, Campus Bogotá

Organizing Committee Chairs

Yesid Díaz   Corporación Unificada Nacional (CUN), Colombia

Germán Jairo Hernández-Pérez   Universidad Nacional de Colombia, Campus Bogotá

Organizing Committee

July Díaz-Barriga   Universidad Distrital Francisco José de Caldas, Bogotá, Colombia

Rafael Ropero-Laytón   Universidad Distrital Francisco José de Caldas, Bogotá, Colombia

| Catleen Natalia Lozano-Reina | Universidad Nacional de Colombia, Campus Bogotá |
| Juan David Solanilla-Mora | Universidad Nacional de Colombia, Campus Bogotá |

Program Committee

DeShuang Huang	Tongji University, Chinese Academy of Sciences, China
Jair Cervantes-Canales	Universidad Autónoma de México, Mexico
Guadalupe González	Universidad Tecnológica de Panamá, Panama
Adil Usman	Indian Institute of Technology, Mandy, India
Rafael Bello-Pérez	Universidad de las Villas, Santa Clara, Cuba
Román Neruda	Czech Academy of Sciences of the Czech Republic, Prague, Czech Republic
Martin Pilat	Charles University, Prague, Czech Republic
Mabel Frías	Universidad de Camagüey, Cuba
Yurilev Chalco-Cano	Universidad de Tarapacá, Chile
Francisco Ramis	Universidad del Bío-Bío, Chile
Heriberto Román-Flores	Universidad de Tarapacá, Chile
I-Hsien Ting	National University of Kaohsiung, Taiwan
Ivan Santelices Manfalti	Universidad del Bío-Bío, Chile
Martha Centeno	University of Turabo, Puerto Rico
Aydee Lopez	Universidade Estadual de Campinas (UNICAMP), Brazil
Germán Jairo Hernández-Pérez	Universidad Nacional de Colombia, Campus Bogotá
Dusko Kalenatic	Universidad de La Sabana, Chía, Colombia
Yesid Díaz	Corporación Unificada Nacional (CUN), Colombia
Jairo Soriano-Mendez	Universidad Distrital Francisco José de Caldas, Bogotá, Colombia
Juan Pablo Orejuela-Cabrera	Universidad Nacional de Colombia, Campus Bogotá
Miguel Melgarejo	Universidad Distrital Francisco José de Caldas, Bogotá, Colombia
Alvaro David Orjuela-Cañon	Universidad Antonio Nariño, Bogotá, Colombia
Javier Arturo Orjuela-Castro	Universidad Nacional de Colombia, Campus Bogotá
Alonso Gaona	Universidad Distrital Francisco José de Caldas, Bogotá, Colombia
Carlos Osorio-Ramírez	Universidad Nacional de Colombia, Campus Bogotá
Elvis Eduardo Gaona	Universidad Distrital Francisco José de Caldas, Bogotá, Colombia
Ignacio Rodríguez-Molano	Universidad Distrital Francisco José de Caldas, Bogotá, Colombia
Elkin Muskus-Rincón	Universidad Central de Colombia, Bogotá, Colombia

Adolfo Jaramillo-Matta   Universidad Distrital Francisco José de Caldas, Bogotá,
                              Colombia
Javier Moncada   Universidad Distrital Francisco José de Caldas, Bogotá,
                              Colombia
Carlos Franco-Franco   Universidad Católica de Colombia, Bogotá, Colombia
Diana Ovalle   Universidad Distrital Francisco José de Caldas, Bogotá,
                              Colombia
Henry Diosa   Universidad Distrital Francisco José de Caldas, Bogotá,
                              Colombia
Egdda Patricia   Universidad Nacional de Colombia, Campus Bogotá
    Vanegas-Escamilla
Lindsay Álvarez-Pomar   Universidad Distrital Francisco José de Caldas, Bogotá,
                              Colombia
Gustavo   Universidad Distrital Francisco José de Caldas, Bogotá,
    Puerto-Leguizamón   Colombia
Frank Alexander   Universidad Nacional de Colombia, Campus Bogotá
    Ballesteros-Riveros
Sergio Rojas-Galeano   Universidad Distrital Francisco José de Caldas, Bogotá,
                              Colombia
Feizar Javier   Universidad Distrital Francisco José de Caldas, Bogotá,
    Rueda-Velazco   Colombia

Contents

Simulation Systems

Fuzzy Sets and Systems

Power Systems

Miscellaneous Applications

Computer Science

A Model for Knowledge Management in Software Industry

José Sergio Ruiz-Castilla$^{(\boxtimes)}$, Yulia Ledeneva, Jair Cervantes, and Adrián Trueba

Universidad Autónoma del Estado de México,
Toluca, Estado de México, Mexico
jsergioruizc@gmail.com, yledeneva@yahoo.com,
chazarra17@gmail.com, atruebae@yahoo.com

Abstract. In Micro and Small Companies for Software Development (MSCSD) of Mexico, the knowledge is generated in each software project. So, it is possible to transform tacit knowledge into explicit, to have some strategy and data storage device. Note that, when the knowledge exists only in the brains of developers there is the disadvantage that, when a developer leaves the organization, knowledge is lost. Therefore, it is possible to transform the tacit knowledge into explicit, if exist some strategy and data storage device. Developers need to generate and storage knowledge in any device and format to process, storage and exploit. In this paper, it has been called knowledge asset to an idea or solution processes or software development activities, which may be embodied as text, images, audio or video.

A novel model for knowledge management is proposed that defines how must obtain, process, store and exploit knowledge resulting in the México's MSCSD. The conclusion is that it is necessary to implement politics and processes in MSCSD to promote knowledge management and that must change the culture in organizations.

Keywords: Knowledge management · Software industry · Software project

1 Introduction

Davenport [1] defines the knowledge as *"a fluid mixture of structured experience, values, contextual information and expert internalization that originates and is applied in the minds of connoisseurs. In organizations, it is reflected in the processes routines, practices and institutional rules"*.

The Organization for Economic Cooperation and Development (OECD) classifies knowledge into public and private [2]. Since 1999, it was determined that tacit knowledge can be when it is into people's mind, while it becomes explicit knowledge when it takes the form of text, diagrams or models among other formats [3].

Knowledge management is responsible for management of asset knowledge in organizations. The International Organization for Standardization (ISO) in paragraph 12207 states that the human resources of the organization are responsible for ensuring that the knowledge, information and individual skills can be stored, reuse and improve over time [4].

© Springer International Publishing AG 2016
J.C. Figueroa-García et al. (Eds.): WEA 2016, CCIS 657, pp. 3–14, 2016.
DOI: 10.1007/978-3-319-50880-1_1

The OECD proposed a seven-step model for knowledge management: production, validation, collation, dissemination, adoption, implementation and institutionalization [2]. While in the software industry, the Software Engineering Institute (SEI) has taken the premise of process management and quality of a system or product [5].

On the other hand, the life cycle Rational Unified Process (RUP) starts with the business model and initial planning. In RUP can be repeated six disciplines: Requirements, Analysis and Design, Implementation, Testing and Unfolding. While considering the configuration management, change management, project management and the environment. In addition to using phases: Start, Development, Construction and Transition for each discipline. At the end of each iteration, the implementation of a module is obtained. The proposed model is based on RUP.

The objective of this work is to create a model of knowledge management that allows the collection and storage of knowledge of the processes of software development in a knowledge base to transfer knowledge from expert developers to inexpert developers, in a methodology as RUP or any other.

The proposed model is different to a Wiki because the users cannot edit from the browser, but users can only access knowledge for consultations. While that the developers are experts who have privileges to incorporate new knowledge assets and update existing ones. The advantage vs. a wiki is that knowledge is reviewed and validated by knowledge workers, who are also skilled developers. This seeks only keep valuable and useful knowledge for the organization.

Knowledge management applied development of software projects in [6–9], education [10], in areas of health [11], in small and medium enterprises [12, 13] and in the petrochemical sector [14]. This paper proposes MSCSD of Mexico to manage existing knowledge generated during the development of software projects. The MSCSD can be more productive and competitive advantage using the tacit and explicit knowledge.

2 Knowledge Management

2.1 Knowledge

There are data, information and knowledge in organizations, which relate according to the following:

Data. They are letters, numbers and other symbols. They are described as structured transaction records, described facts and all the persons and organizations using them.

Information. They are meaningful data, with matter and purpose. The data is transformed into information when purchasing one or more of the following characteristics: contextualized, categorized, calculated, corrected and condensed.

Knowledge. It is derived from the minds as a series of experiences, values, contextual information and internalization. We can generate new knowledge.

2.2   The Experience

The dictionary defines it as the set of knowledge acquired with practice. All is learned by the senses [15]. The experience is the event or phenomenon exists when the experience is created, it is perceived by any of the senses or by several of them, learned is etched in the minds of people.

From the point of view of Aristoteles senses perceive environmental effects carting memory situations, and when these effects are repeated often experience develops [3]. People listen, observe, learn, make new things or making repeated under different contexts accumulate experience.

2.3   Tacit Knowledge

The tacit knowledge is a very personal and difficult to describe through the formal language knowledge and, therefore, difficult to transmit and share with others. It has origin in the depths of individual experience, as well as the ideals, values and emotions of each person [3].

2.4   Explicit Knowledge

The explicit knowledge can be expressed through the formal language; that is, with words and numbers, and can be easily shared and transmitted in the form of data, scientific formulas, codified procedures or universal principles, usually expressed in a physical device [3].

2.5   Knowledge Measurement

Metrics for knowledge management are measures of the activity of knowledge management in an organization, some metrics may be Knowledge Assets (KA): existing, stored, viewed, reused and transferred among others.

3   Proposed Model

A model using a layered architecture is proposed. Through the layers knowledge is obtained, reviewed and validated, then stored to finally allow their exploitation. The following sections describe the elements of the model KMSI. The proposed model and its components are presented in Fig. 1.

The model is proposed as a means to transfer existing knowledge and generated in MSCSD. Developers will be experts who provide knowledge.

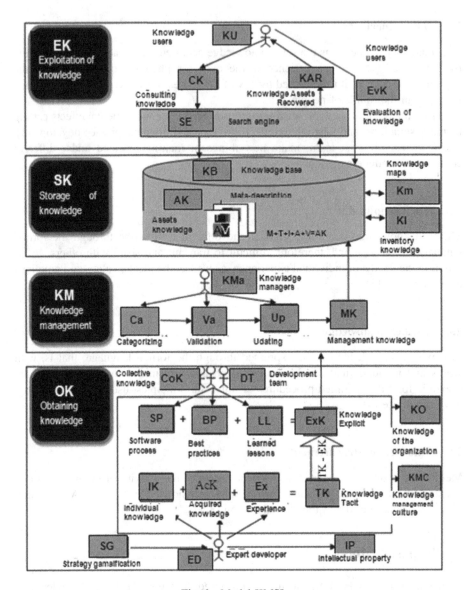

Fig. 1. Model KMSI.

3.1 Knowledge Obtaining Phase

Knowledge obtaining is the first model layer where the knowledge for further processing is obtained. It describes and explains each item in Table 1.

Table 1. Knowledge extraction.

Elements	Definition
Expert developer (ED)	It is a member of the organization who has knowledge and experience that can be shared to other non-expert developers of the organization
Strategy Gamification (SG)	It is a strategy designed to seek motivate developers to participate in knowledge management They have identified the following elements for gamification: (a) Bronze medals, silver and gold (virtual medals), (b) Appointments for accumulated points y, (c) Exchange of points for cash bonuses
Intellectual Property (IP)	Each asset knowledge provided by an expert developer take their responsibility and has its authorization for the use of knowledge assets within the organization
Individual Knowledge (IK)	Individual knowledge refers to the set of tacit knowledge possessed by a developer and acquired during their training and years of experience
Acquired knowledge (AcK)	It is the knowledge that the developer has acquired during the stay in the organization. This acquired knowledge can be caused by: Training courses, Developer, Self-taught
Ex (Experience)	Experience is the result after performing tasks and has solved problems in the organization related to software development processes
TK (Tacit Knowledge)	Tacit knowledge is in the minds of developers They can be seen in the skills and competencies developer and is difficult to convey
SP (Software Processes)	The software processes the organization established or adopted from some methodology, model or international standard Processes can be in print or digital format, developers formally know and use
BP (Better Practices)	Best practices are established by national and international organizations and that the organization has decided to apply
LL (Learned Lessons)	The lessons learned are having solved a problem. They are all strategies that were successful and those that fail during the project and documented post-mortem
ExK (Explicit Knowledge)	Explicit knowledge is available in some way. It may be in the form of text, images, audios or videos and can be shared by their availability
TK - ExK	It refers to the conversion of tacit to explicit knowledge. When an expert developer to achieve capture the tacit knowledge in some text, audio, image (model, diagram, diagram) or video; It is transformed into explicit knowledge
DT (Development Team)	It refers to a group of developers has integrated them and charge a single target so they coordinate and support to achieve the set goal

(*continued*)

Table 1. (*continued*)

Elements	Definition
CoK (Collective Knowledge)	It refers to the tacit knowledge of the entire development team of the organization
KO (Knowledge of the Organization)	It refers to all the tacit and explicit knowledge that exists in the organization The knowledge of the organization has increased productivity and competitiveness
KMC (knowledge Management Culture)	It is the result of the activities carried out daily in organizations that have become habits and good practice for the organization

3.2   Knowledge Management Phase

It refers to the second layer model that deals with the treatment of knowledge assets so that they can add to the knowledge base then the elements are defined in Table 2.

Table 2. Elements of knowledge management.

Elements	Definition
Ca (Categorization)	It is a process to classify knowledge assets into categories according to the procedures established by the RUP has been chosen as a framework
Va (Validation)	It is a process carried out by knowledge workers in order to validate the knowledge asset in form and content
Up (Update)	It is a process for the contents of knowledge assets can be updated with new texts, images, audios or videos that determine the authors. The new content may be added or replaced. When the upgrade occur the knowledge asset changes state
MK (Managed knowledge)	It is the result after the processes applied to knowledge assets. It is an important task to ensure that the knowledge base remains orderly and updated

3.3   Storage Knowledge Phase

It refers to the strategy for storing knowledge assets with the aim of knowing that knowledge exists and where it resides. In Table 3, the elements are listed.

3.4   Knowledge Exploitation Phase

The exploitation of knowledge layer allows users to seek and obtain knowledge assets more accurate knowledge according to their needs or problems to solve. The elements are listed in Table 4.

Table 3. Storage elements of knowledge

Elements	Definition
AK (Assets knowledge)	Knowledge assets are a collection of texts, images, audio or videos. They refer specifically to an issue or problem
KB (Knowledge base)	It is the set of knowledge assets that through knowledge management organization has accumulated and available for members of the development teams
KI (knowledge inventory)	It allows the organization to meet the amount of assets existing knowledge and seek some method of measuring the accumulated knowledge
Km (Knowledge map)	It allows the organization to know where the knowledge to access it in an effective and timely manner
Meta-description	It is the set of asset knowledge's data in order to facilitate processing, storage and search

Table 4. Elements of knowledge exploitation.

Elements	Definition
SE (Search engine)	It is the algorithm designed to find and show knowledge assets according to some search criteria for a user
CK (Consulting knowledge)	It refers to a request for knowledge by a user. You can search according to the categories of RUP processes or using a word or phrase to search the meta-description of knowledge assets
KAR (Knowledge assets recovered)	Is the set of knowledge assets that the tool found after a search? The result may be 0 if there is no knowledge and n when there are one or more knowledge assets that meet the search criteria
KU (Knowledge users)	It is any developer organization has decided to consult the knowledge management tool to expand your knowledge or to solve a problem that has been presented
EvK (Evaluation of knowledge)	It allows the user to issue a rating of knowledge to active knowledge according to their content and degree of utility and application

3.5 Asset Knowledge

The asset knowledge could be a text, but not always. It is possible to retain knowledge in audio because it is a conversation or interview. Also, it is possible to capture knowledge through images, because they show different shapes, sizes and colors, among other features. Finally, it is possible to obtain knowledge through a video with high impact because it has audio and displays the "how" some task or process is done. It was decided that an AK should be able to have text, images, audio or video (TIAV). An AK can have a single format or all four. Figure 2 shows the structure of an AK.

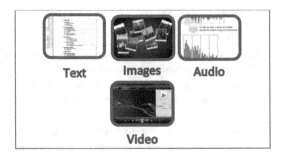

Fig. 2. Structure the asset knowledge

3.6 Metrics Proposed for Knowledge Management

1. The TK is a kind of difficult to measure knowledge, however metric the next.
2. You can measure the amount of tacit knowledge in the organization at any time.
3. To determine the AK of TK should follow the following strategy:
4. IK (individual knowledge). By entering a developer you should apply a test that will result in the AK has.
5. AcK (acquired knowledge). When the developer takes courses of internal and external training must show new TK.
6. Ex (Experience). Every six months accumulated in a position or role will apply an instrument to know that new AK has learned.
7. Take into account the AK of points 1, 2, and 3 for inventory TK developer.
8. The TK of all developers will be integrated.
9. Finally common knowledge will be subtracted to avoid duplication.

Therefore Eq. 1 is proposed to obtain the tacit knowledge of a developer:

$$TKD = \sum_{i=1}^{n} IK_i + \sum_{i=1}^{n} AcK_i + \sum_{i=1}^{n} Ex_i \tag{1}$$

where *TKD* is tacit knowledge developer, *IK* is the individual knowledge, *AcK* is the knowledge gained, and *Ex* is the knowledge as result of experiences developer.

The organization consists of developers, so the Formula 2 is necessary to obtain the TK of the organization. Note that it is necessary to subtract the common AK, to avoid duplication when two or more developers have the same knowledge.

$$TKO = \sum_{i=1}^{n} TKD_i - \sum_{i=1}^{n} CKA_i \tag{2}$$

where *TKO* is the tacit knowledge of the organization, *TKD* is the tacit knowledge developer, and *CKA* are common knowledge assets.

3.7 Metric Proposals for Explicit Knowledge

For the organization to achieve to have explicit knowledge is required to be managed and stored on any media. The procedure should be as follows:

- The organization must have properly documented the software development processes according to some standard software development.
- The organization must have best practices that developers know and apply in everyday activities.
- The organization must have documented lessons learned after each project.

For which the organization has explicit *AK* is necessary to consider the knowledge embodied in a printed medium, audio, images or videos. Explicit knowledge is grouped in software processes, best practices and lessons learned. Therefore Formula 3 can obtain the *ExK* organization.

$$ExKO = \sum_{i=1}^{n} SP_i + \sum_{i=1}^{n} BP_i + \sum_{i=1}^{n} LL_i \tag{3}$$

where *ExKO* is the explicit knowledge of the organization and *SP* software processes are documented and implemented and *BP* the best known and applied practices and *LL* lessons learned are documented.

3.8 Metric Proposals for Organizational Knowledge

Knowledge of the organization includes the tacit and explicit knowledge. In the organization has knowledge can be more effective and efficient when developing software. To measure the knowledge of the organization Formula 4 is necessary.

$$KO = \sum_{i=1}^{n} TKO_i + \sum_{i=1}^{n} ExKO_i \tag{4}$$

where *KO* is the organization's knowledge and *TKO* is the tacit knowledge of the organization and *ExKO* is the explicit knowledge of the organization and Metrics proposed for the inventory of knowledge.

The knowledge managed by the organization at the base of knowledge can be measured to determine the inventory of knowledge. This is important to know the behavior over time. It can be expressed in Eq. 5:

$$IK = \sum_{i=1}^{n} AK_i \tag{5}$$

where *IK* is the inventory of knowledge and *AK* is asset knowledge.

3.9   Metric Proposals for Consultation of Knowledge

Consultation of knowledge becomes very important, so its measurement is necessary. It is also important to know who has consulted the knowledge that is required for the technique to be added strategies to motivate users to make use of *KMSI*. Equation 6 is required to measure knowledge consulting.

$$CK = \sum_{i=1}^{n} CKA_i \qquad (6)$$

where *CK* is the consultation of knowledge and *CKA* are consulted knowledge assets.

4   Results

The first contribution of the research is the Model proposed for Knowledge Management KMSI for MSCSD for the Software Industry in Mexico Fig. 1.

4.1   Application of KMSI

The contribution is the tool created for knowledge management, which has been called KMSI. In Fig. 3 shows the view in the catalog of knowledge assets.

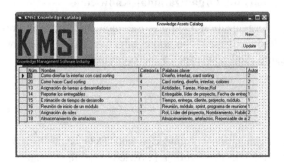

Fig. 3.   KMSI - AK catalog.

The main view shows the catalog KMSI Asset knowledge where experts Developers can add and modify these knowledge assets Fig. 3.

When a user enters any query knowledge, a word or phrase must be typed and KMSI seeks knowledge assets with them. A query is generated with AKs that contain the word or phrase, so the user can choose an AK for consultation, as shown in Fig. 4.

Once the user chooses an Active knowledge the user can view all text, images, audio and video, as shown in Fig. 5.

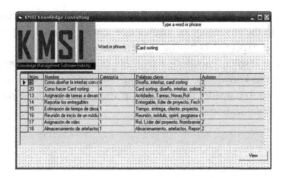

Fig. 4. AK view seeker

Fig. 5. View of the components of an AK

To display the elements TIAV knowledge, simply check an item and go to the next or return to the previous. The contents can be complementary or present knowledge differently.

5 Conclusions

It is concluded that the developers themselves perform knowledge management activities despite the MSCSD not have processes, policies and tools for knowledge management.

It is also concluded that the solution of the problem is not possible with technology alone, but through a change of culture in knowledge management. Therefore the following recommendations:

1. Include knowledge management processes in your company.
2. Allocate resources and trained personnel with roles for knowledge management.
3. Define a method and techniques for the conversion of tacit to explicit knowledge.
4. Have knowledge management tools to capture, store and share knowledge.
5. Measure the impact of knowledge management once implemented.

It is necessary that organizations define and implement metrics to measure knowledge assets and follow up the inventory of knowledge assets. If measured periodically it is possible to know the expected behavior is increasing.

According to the results, knowledge workers in MSCSD have practiced showing willingness to carry out knowledge management. Therefore it is more important to raise awareness of the need to consider this activity as important and incorporate it into their processes of these organizations.

References

1. Silveira, B., De Almeida, R.: Managing Software Process Knowledge. Revista Computer Science Department, Federal University of Espírito Santo (2010)
2. Rimawi, Y., Cuevas, G., San Feliu, T., García, J.: A knowledge base for software process improvement. In: The Second International Conference on Innovation in Information Technology (IIT 2005) (2005)
3. IEEE/EIA 12207 1-1997 Industry Implementation of ISO/IEC 12207:1995-Standard for Information Technology-Software Life Cycle Process 01-05-1997. IEEE Standards Association (2013)
4. Fidalgo, Á., sein-Ecahluce, M.L., Leris, D., García-Peñalvo, F.J.: Knowledge management system to implement innovate educational experiences in education. Credos Universidad de Salamanca **755**, 750 (2013)
5. Muñoz, M.E., Loyola, J., Caballero, P., Huaillani, S.: Virtual coordination center of knowledge on HIV/AIDS: knowledge management experience in public health policies (2015)
6. Acosta, J.C., Fisher, A.L.: Conditions of knowledge management, innovation (2013)
7. Linares, N., Piñero, Y., Rodríguez, E., Pérez, L.: Design of a knowledge management model to improve IT project teams. Revista española de Documentación Científica **37**(2) (2014)
8. Grant, R.M.: The development of knowledge in the oil and gas industry. Universia Bus. Rev. **6**, 92–98 (2013)
9. Capote, J., Llanten, C., Pardé, C., Collazos, C.: Management knowledge in improvement process software program inn MiSyMCs: KMSPI Model. Grupo de investigación y desarrollo en ingeniería de Software **1**(50), 205–216 (2009)
10. Chrissis, M.B., Konrad, M., Shrum, S.: CMMI Guíde of Procces Integration and Improvement Products. Pearson-Addison Wesley, Madrid (2009)
11. Davenport, T., Pruzak, L.: Who Management the Knowledge the Organizations?. McGraw Hill, Buenos Aires (2001)
12. Larousse. Larousse ilustred. Dictionary enciclopedic. Ediciones Larousse, México (2009)
13. Nonaka, I., Takeuchi, H.: The Organization as Maker of Knowledge. Oxford University Press, México D.F. (1999)
14. F.-M. OCDE. Knowledge management in knowledge society. Mayol Ediciones, Bogota-Colombia (2006)
15. Ruiz, B., Javier, F., Dolado, J.: A ontology for management knowledge for software proyects. REICIS Magaz. Sp. Innov. Qual. Softw. Eng. **4**(1) (2008)
16. Zapata, L., Adriensénes, M., Cardenas, B., Franke, L., Gómez, M., Manrique, L.: Organizational Learning. McGraw Hill, México D.F. (2008)

PintArq: A Visualizer of Architectural Execution Flow for Component-Based Software Architectures

Jorge Alejandro Rico García and Henry Alberto Diosa[✉]

ARQUISOFT Research Group, Engineering Faculty,
Universidad Distrital Francisco José de Caldas, Bogotá, Colombia
hdiosa@udistrital.edu.co
http://arquisoft.udistrital.edu.co

Abstract. Formal effort required to specify and analyze architectures using formal languages is high. This has motivated us to build a software tool that allows the interpretation of component-based software architecture described using ρ_{arq} calculus. This tool offers the display facility to architects on a graphic way the structure and the architectural execution flow described in the formal expressions under study. For the development of this software tool some different modules were considered, altogether, they interpret expressions in accordance with the syntax and the operational semantics of the ρ_{arq} calculus; in addition, the tool maps the formal expressions to UML 2.x notation graphic elements. In this way, the application displays the architectural configuration using a visual modeling language(UML components) while showing the architectural execution flow by highlighting the provision interfaces when a ρ_{arq} calculus rewriting rule is executed. The ρ_{arq} calculus use is simplified with this. The architectural analysis tasks will be easier and the architect could focus on the architectural behavior and not on the calculus itself.

Keywords: ρ_{arq} calculus · Component-based software · Architectural execution flow · UML

1 Introduction

Software architecture has received plenty attention in the last decade because it allows better comprehension, reuse levels, control and management capabilities of software development projects [18]. This software engineering's knowledge-area emerged at end of the past century [10]. Subsequently, several architectural description languages has been proposed with less or more formal approach (See Table 1 for a not exhaustive list of related work).

Some approaches have proposed UML as the basis to describe software architectures [11,22]. Although UML has been a popular modeling language for many years [30,33], this modeling language is still semiformal. However, nowadays it supports component-based software models that include the essential concepts

© Springer International Publishing AG 2016
J.C. Figueroa-García et al. (Eds.): WEA 2016, CCIS 657, pp. 15–26, 2016.
DOI: 10.1007/978-3-319-50880-1_2

Table 1. Related work about structural and dynamic modeling in several ADLs.

ADL	¿STRUCTURAL MODELLING?	¿DYNAMIC MODELLING?
WRIGHT [1]	Connector types were used to describe the interaction between components	The interaction was modelled with Hoare's CSP [16]
UNICON [36]	Compositional design of software architectures. This ADL use conector types	It doesn't propose a formal model for this aspect
RAPIDE [19]	Module specifications were used to describe the wired components, connection rules and restrictions to identify legal and illegal assembly patterns of modules	Use Partially Ordered Set of Events (POSET model)
SYNTACTIC APPROACH [4]	Set theory was used to model node types and connections at software architectures. It can model partially architectures or static perspective of sub-architectures	It doesn't propose a formal model for this aspect
UML [22]	From UML 2.x this language provides the component, provide and require interfaces as architectural abstractions. Assembly connectors and composite structures allow complex architectural configurations	The interaction diagrams and state machines provide semiformal modelling possibilities. Meta-modelling extensions can be used to support analysis of dynamic properties
AO-ADL [34]	It supports the definitions of component, connector and functional restrictions on connections. The restrictions on interfaces should be satisfied	Temporal Logic (TL) and other tools that
ACME [9]	It uses annotations to specify structural properties or additional restrictions	The last versions have the ACMELib library. It allows to programme the behavior of architectures. ACME is inherently extensible and it allows architects to associate an external formal model. This model could specify the dynamic aspects of software architectures
DARWIN [20]	It supports hierarchical models. It uses canonical textual representations. These representations describe the components and their interfaces	It uses the $\pi - calculus$ as formal tool. It models dynamic architectures (i.e. architectures changing on execution time)
xADL [3]	It defines the basic structures of prescriptive software architectures: Components, connectors, interfaces, links and groupings	It doesn't propose a formal model for this aspect
Weaves [13]	It uses directed bipartite multigraphs to model interconnected networks of components. It can be seen as a variant of the architectural style Pipe-and-Filter	It doesn't propose a formal model for this aspect
CHAM [17]	The syntax models structures and configuration. This syntax uses the analogy of chemical solutions and molecules	It has an expressions rewriting system based on chemical reaction concept
KOALA [28]	It describes structures, configuration and component interfaces within the domain of electronic devices. It inherits properties of Darwin language	Idem to Darwin language
ADML [40]	It specializes ACME with meta-properties	Analogous to ACME
ASDL [35]	It uses Z language to specify structure and static restrictions	It adds Hoare's CSP expressions to specify dynamic aspects on the interfaces
AADL [8]	Quality attributes driven design is supported. It uses compliance static analysis and data consistency	It accepts extensions to formal methodsde trabajo
π-ADL [29]	It provides graphical and textual syntax in accord with UML 2.x profile. This profile models software architectures	π-calculus typed of high order
SAM [15]	It can use a graphical and textual syntax. It allows horizontal and vertical hierarchical partitioning	It allows graphical simulation. Formal techniques as Petri nets and Temporal Linear Logical can be used

of software architecture [27]. Extending UML with a formal tool allows exploiting the analysis possibilities that formal tools offer while the software architects stays within the same design framework. We propose PintArq, a tool allowing software architects to visualize the architectural execution flow.

The PintArq tool uses a built-in interpreter that transforms ρ_{arq} calculus expressions [5,6] into Tex format [12] to visual representation of software architectures as wired components in concordance with UML 2.x notation [27]. Additionally, the tool enables users to show the execution flow in accordance with ρ_{arq} calculus rewriting rules (Operational semantics).

To begin with we show an overview of the ρ_{arq} calculus. Then, the methodology to develop the PintArq tool is explained step by step. Third section analyses results from three points of view: Transformation tools, logical architecture and technological aspects. The last sections discuss some conclusions and future work.

2 ρ_{arq} Calculus Overview

The ρ_{arq} calculus is a formalism to specify component-based software architectures; this calculus models dynamic and structural aspects with the possibility to control architectural executions based in boolean guards. As all formal calculus it comprises a syntax and semantics. Table 2 summarizes the syntactic entities with their meanings and interpretations of ρ_{arq}.

Replacements of any expression by other is governed by structural congruence rules (Table 3).

The semantic of ρ_{arq} calculus is based on rewriting rules. These operational semantic rules are shown in Table 4.

For illustration purposes, some basic examples of several architectural configurations and architectural execution flow are shown at Table 5[1].

3   Method

The first version of PintArq project involved the following steps:

3.1   The Study of the ρ_{arq} Calculus

For the purpose of representing ρ_{arq} calculus expressions using the extended BNF [25,32], the TEX format [12] was used. This activity was crucial in order to specify the formal source language that the interpreter transforms to other visual language. The Table 6 shows the equivalence between ρ_{arq} expressions against TEX expressions.

---

[1] For more details about syntax, semantics and examples of architectural execution control (i.e. architectural control flow) see [6,7].

Table 2. Syntax of ρ_{arq} calculus. Source: $[6, 23, 26, 38, 39]$

SYMBOLS			MEANING
$x, y, z, \ldots$		variables	Variables only hold names.
$a, b, c, \ldots$		names	Names and variables are named references.
$u, v, w, \ldots ::= x \mid a$		references	
EXPRESSIONS			**INTERPRETATION**
$E, F, G ::=$	$\top$	Null component	Component that doesn't execute any action.
	$E \wedge F$	Composition	It represents concurrent execution of E and F.
	$E^{(int)}$	Interior of component E	No observable part of E
	$if(C_1 \cdots C_n)$ else G Committed choice combinator		This representation of components with alternative executions in the $\rho_{arq} - Calculus$ is a derivation of the **Guarded Disjunction** proposed in the early extended versions of $\gamma - Calculus$ [38] [39] is a useful generalization of conventional conditional[a].
	$x :: \overline{y}/E$	Abstraction	It represents receiving a symbolic entity by means of x, it can replace $\overline{y}$ in E, as long as this entity is free in the scope of component E.
	$x\overline{y}/E$	Application	The **Application** $x\overline{y}/E$ expresses sending $\overline{y}$ by means of x and continuing with the execution of E.
	τ/E	Internal reaction	It is represented with τ/E, this term doesn't have its explicit counterpart in the original $\rho - Calculus$. It might demand specifying many transitions as internal reactions to limit the quantity of observations [2].
	$\exists w E$	Declaration	The **Declaration** $\exists w E$ introduces a reference w with scope E.
	$x : \overline{y}/E$	Replication	The replication $x : \overline{y}/E$ can be expressed as: $x : \overline{y}/E \equiv x :: \overline{y}/E \wedge x : \overline{y}/E$ It produces a new abstraction, ready for reaction and it allows of replicating another when necessary.
	$E^\top$	E's succesful execution	Observable succesful execution of E
	$E^\perp$	E's non succesful execution	Observable non succesful execution of E
	$OSO(E)$ do F else G On Success Of		If E executes with succes then it redirects to execute architectural expression F else it redirects to execute the architectural expression G.
	$!OSO(E)$ do F else G Replication of OSO rule		Consecutives observations of "On Succes Of " rule on the same component.
$\phi, \psi ::=$	$\top$	Logical truth	Constraints as ϕ, ψ can resolve to true ($\top$).
	$\perp$	Logical false	Constraints as ϕ, ψ can resolve to false ($\perp$).
	$x = y$	Equational restriction	Constraints can correspond to equational constraints ($x = y$) with logical variables. The information about values of variables can be determined by means of equations that can be seen as constraints. The equations can be expressed as total information (i.e.: $x = a$) or partial information(i.e.: $x = y$); taking into account that the names are only values loaded to variables. [39].
	$\phi \wedge \psi$	Conjunction of constraints	Constraints can correspond to conjunction ($\phi \wedge \psi$); the conjunction is congruent to constraints' composition. This leads to constraints that must be explicitly combined by means of reduction [26]:
	$\exists \phi$	Existential quantifier	The existential quantification over constraints is congruent to the variables declaration over constraints ($\exists x \phi$).

[a]Where $C_k ::= \exists \overline{x}(\phi_k \text{ then } E_k)$ with $k = 1 \ldots n$ are arguments. Clauses $(C_1) \cdots (C_n)$ contains guards, if the guard of a clause is satisfied its body E_k is liberated for reaction; otherwise, this clause is ignored.

Table 3. Structural congruence rules of ρ_{arq} calculus. Source: [6,26]

$(\alpha - conversión)$	Cambio de referencias ligadas por referencias libres
(ACI)	$\wedge$ es asociativa, conmutativa y satisface $E \wedge \top \equiv E$
$(Interchange)$	$\exists x \exists y E \equiv \exists y \exists x E$
$(Scope)$	$\exists x\ E \wedge F \equiv \exists x (E \wedge F)\ \ if\ x \notin \mathcal{FV}(F)$
$(Equivalence\ of\ Constraints)$	$\phi \equiv \psi\ \ if\ \phi \not\models_\Delta \psi\ y\ \mathcal{FV}(\phi) = \mathcal{FV}(\psi)$
$(Observable\ replication)$	$!OSO(E)\ do\ F\ else\ G \equiv OSO(E)\ do\ F\ else\ G \wedge !OSO(E)\ do\ F\ else\ G$
$(Observable\ Succesful/Failure)$	$[v/w]E^{(int)} \equiv \top \wedge if\ [\ (\top\ then\ E^\top)\,,$ $(\top\ then\ E^\perp)\ ]$ $else\ (\top)$

Table 4. Rewriting rules of ρ_{arq} calculus. Source: [6,26]

$(A_{\rho_{arq}})$	$\phi \wedge x : \overline{y}/E \wedge x'\overline{x}/F \longrightarrow \phi \wedge x : \overline{y}/E \wedge [\overline{x}/\overline{y}]E^{(int)} \wedge F\ \ si\ \phi \models_\Delta\ x = x', \mathcal{V}(\overline{z}) \cap \mathcal{BV}(E^{(int)}) = \emptyset$
$(C_{\rho_{arq}})$	$\phi_1 \wedge \phi_2 \longrightarrow \psi\ \qquad\qquad\qquad\qquad\qquad\qquad\qquad if\ \phi_1 \wedge \phi_2 \not\models_\Delta \psi$

$(Comb_{\rho_{arq}})\quad \phi \wedge if\ (C_1)\dots(C_n)\ else\ F\ fi \longrightarrow \begin{cases} E_k, & if\ \phi \models_\Delta\ \psi_k \\ F, & if\ \phi \models_\Delta\ \neg\psi_k\ \forall k = 1, 2, \dots, n \end{cases}$

$Donde\ C_k ::= \exists \overline{x}(\psi_k\ Then\ E_k)\ ;\ k = 1, 2, \dots, n$

$(Ejec_T)$

(a) $[OSO(E)\ do\ F\ else\ G] \wedge E^\top \longrightarrow F, Because\ succesful\ execution\ of\ E\ component$

(b) $[OSO(E)\ do\ F\ else\ G] \wedge E^\perp \longrightarrow G, Because\ non\ succesful\ execution\ of\ E\ component$

3.2   Transformation Technology: Review and Selection

Three alternatives were evaluated in order to transform from formal textual expressions to UML graphical notation: Model Driven Architecture (MDA) tools [14,37,41], DUALLY [21] and ANTLR [31].

Based in the possibilities and the capabilities of each tool, ANTLR was the selected tool to implement PintArq because it is extensible by using a programming language that supports the tasks derived to accomplish the rewriting calculus and the transformation to UML 2.x.

3.3   Analysis, Design and Implementation of Software

Four subactivities were conducted:

1. Definition of prescriptive architecture.
2. Analysis and design.
3. Programming of the "web enabled" application.
4. Specification of ρ_{arq} *Calculus* grammar and basic architectural expressions proposed in [5,6] for the testing phase.

3.4   Concept Testing

Once the application was developed, a set of tests was executed to verify the appropriate interpretation of expressions and rewriting rules of architectures defined using ρ_{arq} calculus. The objective of these tests were:

- Verify operational semantics in action.
- Test mapping from ρ_{arq} calculus to UML's component-based diagrams.
- Review of visualization for architectural execution flows.

Table 5. ρ_{arq} calculus in action: a sample

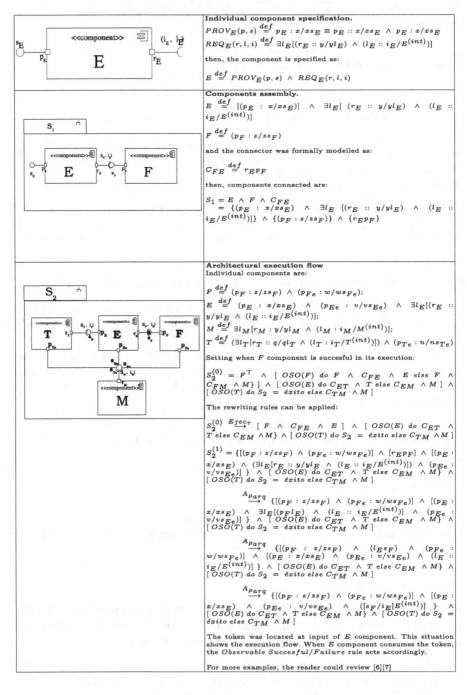

Individual component specification.

$$PROV_E(p,s) \stackrel{def}{=} p_E : x/xs_E \equiv p_E :: x/xs_E \wedge p_E : x/xs_E$$

$$REQ_E(r,l,i) \stackrel{def}{=} \exists l_E[(r_E :: y/yl_E) \wedge (l_E :: i_E/E^{(int)})]$$

then, the component is specified as:

$$E \stackrel{def}{=} PROV_E(p,s) \wedge REQ_E(r,l,i)$$

Components assembly.

$$E \stackrel{def}{=} [(p_E : x/xs_E)] \wedge \exists l_E[(r_E :: y/yl_E) \wedge (l_E :: i_E/E^{(int)})]$$

$$F \stackrel{def}{=} (p_F : z/zs_F)$$

and the connector was formally modelled as:

$$C_{FE} \stackrel{def}{=} r_E p_F$$

then, components connected are:

$$S_1 = E \wedge F \wedge C_{FE}$$
$$= \{(p_E : x/xs_E) \wedge \exists l_E [(r_E :: y/yl_E) \wedge (l_E :: i_E/E^{(int)})]\} \wedge \{(p_F : z/zs_F)\} \wedge \{r_E p_F\}$$

Architectural execution flow
Individual components are:

$$F \stackrel{def}{=} (p_F : z/zs_F) \wedge (p_{Fe} : w/ws_{Fe});$$

$$E \stackrel{def}{=} (p_E : x/xs_E) \wedge (p_{Ee} : v/vs_{Ee}) \wedge \exists l_E[(r_E :: y/yl_E \wedge (l_E :: i_E/E^{(int)})];$$

$$M \stackrel{def}{=} \exists l_M[r_M : y/yl_M \wedge (l_M : i_M/M^{(int)})];$$

$$T \stackrel{def}{=} (\exists l_T[r_T :: q/ql_T \wedge (l_T : i_T/T^{(int)})]) \wedge (p_{Te} : n/ns_{Te})$$

Setting when F component is succesful in its execution:

$$S_2^{(0)} = F^\top \wedge [OSO(F) \, do \, F \wedge C_{FE} \wedge E \, else \, F \wedge C_{FM} \wedge M \}] \wedge [OSO(E) \, do \, C_{ET} \wedge T \, else \, C_{EM} \wedge M] \wedge [OSO(T) \, do \, S_2 = éxito \, else \, C_{TM} \wedge M]$$

The rewriting rules can be applied:

$$S_2^{(0)} \stackrel{Ejec_T}{\longrightarrow} [F \wedge C_{FE} \wedge E] \wedge [OSO(E) \, do \, C_{ET} \wedge T \, else \, C_{EM} \wedge M \} \wedge [OSO(T) \, do \, S_2 = éxito \, else \, C_{TM} \wedge M]$$

$$S_2^{(1)} = \{[(p_F : z/zs_F) \wedge (p_{Fe} : w/ws_{Fe})] \wedge [r_E p_F]\} \wedge [(p_E : x/xs_E) \wedge (\exists l_E[r_E :: y/yl_E \wedge (l_E :: i_E/E^{(int)})]) \wedge (p_{Ee} : v/vs_{Ee})] \} \wedge [OSO(E) \, do \, C_{ET} \wedge T \, else \, C_{EM} \wedge M \} \wedge [OSO(T) \, do \, S_2 = éxito \, else \, C_{TM} \wedge M]$$

$$\stackrel{A_{\rho arq}}{\longrightarrow} \{[(p_F : z/zs_F) \wedge (p_{Fe} : w/ws_{Fe})] \wedge [(p_E : x/xs_E) \wedge \exists l_E[(p_F l_E) \wedge (l_E :: i_E/E^{(int)})] \wedge (p_{Ee} : v/vs_{Ee})] \} \wedge [OSO(E) \, do \, C_{ET} \wedge T \, else \, C_{EM} \wedge M \} \wedge [OSO(T) \, do \, S_2 = éxito \, else \, C_{TM} \wedge M]$$

$$\stackrel{A_{\rho arq}}{\longrightarrow} \{[(p_F : z/zs_F) \wedge (l_E s_F) \wedge (p_{Fe} : w/ws_{Fe})] \wedge [(p_E : x/xs_E) \wedge (p_{Ee} : v/vs_{Ee}) \wedge (l_E :: i_E/E^{(int)})] \} \wedge [OSO(E) \, do \, C_{ET} \wedge T \, else \, C_{EM} \wedge M \} \wedge [OSO(T) \, do \, S_2 = éxito \, else \, C_{TM} \wedge M]$$

$$\stackrel{A_{\rho arq}}{\longrightarrow} \{[(p_F : z/zs_F) \wedge (p_{Fe} : w/ws_{Fe})] \wedge [(p_E : x/xs_E) \wedge (p_{Ee} : v/vs_{Ee}) \wedge ([s_F/i_E]E^{(int)})] \} \wedge [OSO(E) \, do \, C_{ET} \wedge T \, else \, C_{EM} \wedge M \} \wedge [OSO(T) \, do \, S_2 = éxito \, else \, C_{TM} \wedge M]$$

The token was located at input of E component. This situation shows the execution flow. When E component consumes the token, the *Observable Succesful/Failure* rule acts accordingly.

For more examples, the reader could review [6][7]

4   Results

4.1   ¿How ANTLR Was Applied?

Table 6 shows the correspondence between the ρ_{arq} calculus expressions and the TEX expressions:

Table 6. Equivalence of ρ_{arq} expressions to TEX expressions

ρ_{arq} expression	Typography	TEX
Composition	$A \wedge B$	A \wedge B
Null component	$\top$	\top
Interior of component	$A^{(int)}$	A^{(int)}
Committed choice combinator	$if(C_1...C_n)\,else\,A$	$if(C_1)(C_2)...(C_n)\,else\,A$
Abstraction	$x :: \overline{y}/E$	x::y/E
Application	$x\overline{y}/E$	x\overline{y}/E
Declaration	$\exists w E$	\exists w E
Abstraction replication	$x : \overline{y}/E$	x::y/E
Successful execution	$E^{\top}$	E^{\top}
Non-successful execution	$E^{\perp}$	E^{\bot}
On Success Of	$OSO(E)do\,F\,else\,G$	$OSO(E)\,do\,F\,else\,G$
Replication of OSO rule	$!OSO(E)\,do\,F\,else\,G$	$!OSO(E)\,do\,F\,else\,G$
Logic truth	$\dot{\top}$	\dot{\top}
Logic false	$\perp$	\bot
Equational restriction	$x = y$	x = y
Conjunction of constraints	$\phi\dot{\wedge}\psi$	$\phi\dot{\wedge}\psi$
Existential quantifier	$\dot{\exists}x\phi$	\dot{\exists}x\phi

Once the language definition was ready, the next step was to generate the API that let the manipulation and identification of each word in the architectural expressions. With this API it was possible to implement the Interpreter module by using the design patterns offered by ANTLR (Observer and Visitor) [31].

4.2   The Architecture of the Application

Figure 1 shows the architectural inception for PintArq. The component-connector diagram with stereotyped components as modules depicts the architectural configuration with assembly connectors; these lastly were labeled with the name of data-structures that flow between modules.

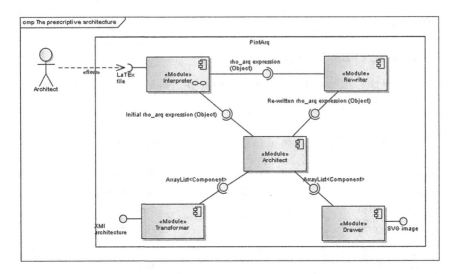

Fig. 1. The prescriptive architecture of PintArq

4.3 The Tool

The PintArq tool was built using the Java programming language, XML technologies (SVG and XMI) and ANTLR tool, the first version is web enabled. The tool is publicly available at: http://arquisoft.udistrital.edu.co/PintArq/Index. jsp. Some analyzable expressions can be downloaded from: http://arquisoft. udistrital.edu.co/documentos/EjemplosExpresionesArq.rar.

Figure 2 shows the PintArq's graphical user interface when the user loads an architectural configuration specified by ρ_{arq} calculus expressions[2]:

When the user presses the PLAY button, the visualizer shows the architectural execution flow that operational semantics in action produces and the user can see how a token passes between interfaces. In this case, the ρ_{arq} formal expressions are:

$$S = Arch \wedge Transf \wedge Drawer \wedge Rewriter \wedge Interp$$
$$\wedge\, (OSO\,(Interp)\,do\,(C_{IR} \wedge C_{IA} \wedge Rewriter^{\top})\,else\,\tau Interp) \wedge Interp^{\top}$$
$$\wedge\, (OSO\,(Arch)\,do\,(C_{AG} \wedge C_{AT})\,else\,\tau Arch)$$
$$\wedge\, OSO(Rewriter)do(C_{RA} \wedge Arch^{\top})else\tau Rewriter$$

where each component was specified as:

$$Interp = RLoad \wedge PArcInitial_{ANTLR} \wedge PArchitecture_{ANTLR}$$
$$RLoad = \exists l_{Interp}[(r_{Interp} : x/x\overline{l_{Interp}}) \wedge (l_{Interp} : File/Interp^{(int)})]$$
$$PArcInitial_{ANTLR} = (p1_{Interp} : y/y\overline{Architecture_{ANTLR}})$$
$$PArchitecture_{ANTLR} = (p2_{Interp} : y/y\overline{Architecture_{ANTLR}})$$

$$Rewriter = RArchitecture \wedge PRewriter$$
$$RArchitecture = \exists l_{Rewriter}[(r_{Rewriter} : x/x\overline{l_{Rewriter}}) \wedge (l_{Rewriter} : Architecture/Rewriter^{(int)})]$$
$$PRewriter = (p_{Rewriter} : y/y\overline{ArchitectureWritten})$$

---

[2] These expressions should be written in TeX format.

$$Arch = RArchitecture_{Arch} \wedge PArchitectTrans \wedge PArchitectGraf$$
$$RArchitecture_{Arch} = \exists l_{Arch}[(r_{Arch} : x/x\overline{l_{Arch}}) \wedge (l_{Arch} : Architecture/Arch^{(int)})]$$
$$PArchitectTrans = p1_{Arch} : y/y\overline{ObjectsArchitecture}$$
$$PArchitectGraf = p2_{Arch} : y/y\overline{ObjectsArchitecture}$$

$$Transf = RArchitecture_{Transf} \wedge PTransf$$
$$RArchitecture_{Transf} = \exists l_{Transf}[(r_{Transf} : x/x\overline{l_{Transf}}) \wedge (l_{Transf} : Architecture/Transf^{(int)})]$$
$$PTransf = p_{Transf} : y/y\overline{ArchitectureXMDrawerI}$$

$$Drawer = RArchitecture_{Drawer} \wedge PDrawer$$
$$RArchitecture_{Drawer} = \exists l_{Drawer}[(r_{Drawer} : x/x\overline{l_{Drawer}}) \wedge (l_{Drawer} : Architecture/Drawer^{(int)})]$$
$$PDrawer = p_{Drawer} : y/y\overline{ArchitectureSVG}$$

The assembly connectors are:

$$C_{IR} = {}^{r}Rewriter\overline{{}^{p2}Interp}$$
$$C_{RA} = {}^{r}Arch\overline{{}^{p}Rewriter}$$
$$C_{IA} = {}^{r}Arch\overline{{}^{p1}Interp}$$
$$C_{AT} = {}^{r}Transf\overline{{}^{p1}Arch}$$
$$C_{AG} = {}^{r}Drawer\overline{{}^{p2}Arch}$$

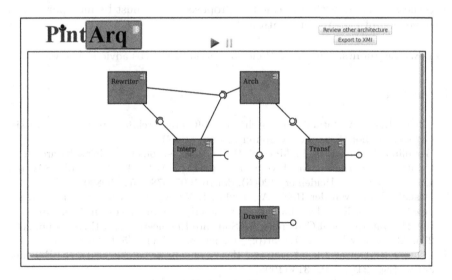

Fig. 2. The PintArq's graphic interface

5   Conclusions

In line with research works about languages that allow to simulate the execution of software architectures as Rapide [19], Archware ADL [24], Pi-ADL [29];

a visualizer of architectural execution flow for software component-based was described in this paper. In this work, the interpreter of ρ_{arq} expressions identifies the structural elements and it transforms the architectural expressions to UML component-configuration [27]. Then, the PintArq tool visualizes the execution flow according to ρ_{arq}'s operational semantics [5,6]. The interpretation engine was based in ANTLR [31] and the expressions were wrote in Tex format [12]. The prescriptive architecture was shown in the Fig. 1 and the concise description was done in the Sect. 4.

The research group ARQUISOFT is committed to the *Open Models* initiative. In consequence, the prescriptive architecture, functional models, structural models and dynamic models can be found in the ARQUISOFT's web portal: http://arquisoft.udistrital.edu.co/modelos/modelPintArqHTML/, for any interested reader.

6 Future Work

Since software architects may not know the complexities of formal calculus and prefer to concentrate their efforts on analysis tasks. A second phase of PintArq project will develop an interpreter from component-based visual models to ρ_{arq} expressions and this result will be integrated to actual version. Additionally, the correctness checking with ρ_{arq} calculus proposed in [7] must be incorporated in a new version of PintArq at a future.

Acknowledgements. Thanks to Professor Sergio Rojas. His advices were worthy.

References

1. Allen, R.J.: A formal approach to software architecture. Ph.D. thesis, Carnegie Mellon, School of computer Science (1997)
2. Bertolino, A., Inverardi, P., Muccini, H.: Formal methods in testing software architectures. In: Bernardo, M., Inverardi, P. (eds.) SFM 2003. LNCS, vol. 2804, pp. 122–147. Springer, Heidelberg (2003). doi:10.1007/978-3-540-39800-4_7
3. Dashofy, E.M., van der Hoek, A., Taylor, R.N.: An infrastructure for the rapid development of XML-based architecture description languages. In: Proceedings of the 24th International Conference on Software Engineering (ICSE 2002), pp. 266–276. ACM, New York (2002). http://doi.acm.org/10.1145/581339.581374
4. Dean, T.R., Cordy, J.R.: A sintactic theory of software architecture. IEEE Trans. Softw. Eng. **21**(4), 302–313 (1995)
5. Diosa, H.A.: Especificación de un Modelo de Referencia Arquitectural de Software A Nivel de Configuración, Estructura y Comportamiento. Ph.D. thesis, Universidad del Valle- Escuela de Ingeniería de Sistemas y Computación, Febrero 2008
6. Diosa, H.A., Díaz, J.F., Gaona, C.M.: Cálculo para el modelado formal de arquitecturas de software basadas en componentes: cálculo ρ_{arq}. Revista Científica. Universidad Distrital Francisco José de Caldas (12) (2010)
7. Diosa, H.A., Díaz, J.F., Gaona, C.M.: Especificación formal de arquitecturas de software basadas en componentes: Chequeo de corrección con cálculo ρ_{arq}. Revista Científica. Universidad Distrital Francisco José de Caldas (12) (2010)

8. Feiler, P.H., Gluch, D.P.: Model-Based Engineering with AADL: An Introduction to the SAE Architecture Analysis and Design Language. Addison-Wesley, Boston (2013)
9. Garlan, D., Monroe, R., Wile, D.: ACME: an architecture description interchange language. In: Proceedings of the 1997 Conference of the Centre for Advanced Studies on Collaborative Research (CASCON 1997), p. 7. IBM Press (1997). http://portal. acm.org/citation.cfm?id=782010.782017
10. Garlan, D., Shaw, M.: An introduction to software architecture. Technical report CMU-CS-94-166. Carnegie Mellon University, Enero 1994
11. Gil, S.V.H.: Representación de la arquitectura de software usando UML. Sistemas y Telemática 1, 63–75 (2006)
12. Goossens, M., Mittelbach, F., Samarin, A.: The LaTeX Companion. Addison-Wesley, Reading (1994)
13. Gorlick, M., Razouk, R.: Using weaves for software construction and analysis. In: 13th International Conference on Software Engineering, Proceedings, pp. 23–34, May 1991
14. Guerra, E., de Lara, J., Kolovos, D., Paige, R.: A visual specification language for model-to-model transformations. In: IEEE Symposium on Visual Languages and Human-Centric Computing (VL/HCC), pp. 119–126 (2010)
15. He, X., Yu, H., Shi, T., Ding, J., Deng, J.: Formally analyzing software architectural specifications using SAM. J. Syst. Softw. 71, 11–29 (2004)
16. Hoare, C.A.R.: Communicating sequential processes. Commun. ACM 21, 666–677 (1978). http://doi.acm.org/10.1145/359576.359585
17. Inverardi, P., Wolf, A.: Formal specification and analysis of software architectures using the chemical abstract machine model. IEEE Trans. Softw. Eng. 21(4), 373–386 (1995)
18. Bass, L., Paul Clements, R.K.: Software Architecture in Practice, Chap. 2. SEI Series in Software Engineering. Addison Wesley, Boston (2013)
19. Luckham, D.C.: Rapide: a language and toolset for simulation of distributed systems by partial orderings of events. Technical report, Stanford, CA, USA (1996)
20. Magee, J., Dulay, N., Eisenbach, S., Kramer, J.: Specifying distributed software architectures. In: Schäfer, W., Botella, P. (eds.) ESEC 1995. LNCS, vol. 989, pp. 137–153. Springer, Heidelberg (1995). doi:10.1007/3-540-60406-5_12
21. Malavolta, I., Muccini, H., Pelliccione, P., Tamburri, D.A.: Providing architectural languages and tools interoperability through model transformation technologies. IEEE Trans. Softw. Eng. 36(1), 119–140 (2010)
22. Medvidovic, N., Rosenblum, D.S., Redmiles, D.F., Robbins, J.E.: Modeling software architectures in the unified modeling language. ACM Trans. Softw. Eng. Methodol. 11, 2–57 (2002). http://doi.acm.org/10.1145/504087.504088
23. Milner, R.: Communicating and Mobile Systems: The π-Calculus. Cambridge University Press, New York (1999)
24. Morrison, R., Kirby, G., Balasubramaniam, D., Mickan, K., Oquendo, F., Cimpan, S., Warboys, B., Snowdon, B., Greenwood, R.: Support for evolving software architectures in the ArchWare ADL. In: Fourth Working IEEE/IFIP Conference on Software Architecture (WICSA 2004), pp. 69–78 (2004)
25. Naur, P.: Revised report on the algorithmic language ALGOL 60. Commun. ACM 6(1), 1–17 (1963)
26. Niehren, J., Müller, M.: Constraints for free in concurrent computation. In: Kanchanasut, K., Lévy, J.-J. (eds.) ACSC 1995. LNCS, vol. 1023, pp. 171–186. Springer, Heidelberg (1995). doi:10.1007/3-540-60688-2_43

27. Object Management Group: OMG Unified Modeling Language (OMG UML). Version 2.5, September 2013

28. van Ommering, R., van der Linden, F., Kramer, J., Magee, J.: The Koala component model for consumer electronics software. Computer **33**(3), 78–85 (2000)

29. Oquendo, F.: Dynamic software architectures: formally modelling structure and behaviour with Pi-ADL. In: Software Engineering Advances (ICSEA 2008), pp. 352–359, October 2008

30. Pandey, R.K.: Architecture description languages (ADLs) vs UML: a review. SIGSOFT Softw. Eng. Notes **35**, 1–5 (2010). http://doi.acm.org/10.1145/1764810.1764828

31. Parr, T.: The Definitive ANTLR 4 Reference. The Pragmatic Bookshelf, Dallas (2012)

32. Pattis, R.E.: Extended Backus-Naur Form. Disponible en (1980). http://www.cs.cmu.edu/~pattis/misc/ebnf.pdf

33. Robbins, J., Medvidovic, N., Redmiles, D., Rosenblum, D.: Integrating architecture description languages with a standard design method. In: Proceedings of the 1998 International Conference on Software Engineering, pp. 209–218, April 1998

34. Rong, M.: An aspect-oriented software architecture description language based on temporal logic. In: 2010 5th International Conference on Computer Science and Education (ICCSE), pp. 91–96, August 2010

35. Seidman, S.B.: Computer Science Handbook, Chap. 109. Chapman & Hall/CRC (2004)

36. Shaw, M., DeLine, R., Klein, D., Ross, T., Young, D., Zelesnik, G.: Abstractions for software architecture and tools to support them. IEEE Trans. Softw. Eng. **21**(4), 314–335 (1995)

37. Singh, Y., Sood, M.: Models and transformations in MDA. In: International Conference on Computational Intelligence, Communication Systems and Networks, pp. 253–258 (2009)

38. Smolka, G.: A calculus for higher-order concurrent constraint programming with deep guards. Technical report, Bundesminister für Forschung und Technologie (1994)

39. Smolka, G.: A foundation for higher-order concurrent constraint programming. Technical report, Bundesminister für Forschung und Technologie (1994)

40. Spencer, J.: Architecture description markup language (ADML) creating an open market for IT architecture tools. Disponible en, Septiembre 2000. http://www.opengroup.org/architecture/adml/background.htm

41. Zuo, W., Feng, J., Zhang, J.: Model transformation from xUML PIMs to AADL PSMs. In: International Conference on Computing, Control and Industrial Engineering (CCIE), pp. 54–57 (2010)

A Metaprocesses-Oriented Methodology Based on RAS (Software Assets Reuse)

Javier Darío Fernández[1,2(✉)], María V. Hurtado[1], José Luis Garrido[1],
Manuel Noguera[1], and John Freddy Duitama[3]

[1] Department of Software Engineering, E.T.S.I.I., University of Granada,
c/Saucedo Aranda s/n, 18071 Granada, Spain
{jfernandez_9,mhurtado,jgarrido,mnoguera}@ugr.es
[2] Faculty of Industrial Engineering, University Pontificia Bolivariana,
cir. 1 N.70-01, Medellin, Colombia
javier.fernandez@upb.edu.co
[3] Department of Systems Engineering, University of Antioquia,
calle 70 No. 52-21, 1226 Medellin, Colombia
freddy.duitama@udea.edu.co

Abstract. Software reuse in the early stages is a key issue in rapid development of applications. Recently, several methodologies have been proposed for the reuse of components, but mainly in code generation as artifacts. However, these methodologies partially consider the domain analysis, the business modeling, and the reuse through of components. This paper introduces a metaprocess-oriented methodology based on reuse it as software assets starting from specifications and analysis of the domain. The approach includes the definition of a conceptual level to adequately represent the domain, a reuse process to specify the metaprocess as software assets, and an implementation level which defines the rules for conceptual level and reuse of metaprocess. The methodology has been applied successfully to the first phase, i.e. at the specification of the conceptual level in the field of e-health, in particular in monitoring system of patients with cardiovascular risk, but our work has advances in reuse of models for implementation in other contexts contributing to productivity in software development.

Keywords: Metaprocess · Processes · Reuse · e-health

1 Introduction

The software reuse in the early stages allows a rapid development of applications. It contributed to increasing the productivity and quality in software development. Our proposal is based into reuse of models thought the metaprocesses.

There are several proposals about metaprocesses definition in the context of software development. However, a metaprocess can be defined as a complete process metamodel that serves as benchmarks to be instantiated including different cases or situations for the same domain. This metamodel contribute to the generalization of processes through its metamodeling, specification of methods, decomposition of tasks, and rules of consistency. Rolland

© Springer International Publishing AG 2016
J.C. Figueroa-García et al. (Eds.): WEA 2016, CCIS 657, pp. 27–38, 2016.
DOI: 10.1007/978-3-319-50880-1_3

and Prakash [19] conceive metaprocesses as artifacts with general features, for instantiation, customization and gradual refinement of processes and models.

Metaprocesses are generic specifications of activities, tasks, roles, and behaviors supporting the execution of processes with the main objective of obtaining an abstraction of the domain.

There are several proposals about metaprocesses in the context of software development, for example, metaprocesses as metamodeling-based models [5] and metaprocesses as methodologies for process-oriented software development [7]. However, none of them provide the reuse of the metaprocess specification as software assets for instantiation and customization in the early stages.

Metaprocess metamodeling and its specification as software assets for reuse in the early stages is a field requiring a great effort to standardize software processes in the context of software industrialization.

Greenfield and Short [8] define *"[...] metaprocess-oriented methodology can contribute to raise productivity and quality in the software construction process "*. In particular, a methodology that takes into account the abstraction of the domain specification and process modeling, as well as its specification as software assets for reuse in the early stages can ensure lower development times in the release of applications. This can also reduce costs in areas with strong demand for the development of rapid applications in domains as e-health.

The purpose of this article is to present a metamodeling-based approach intended to provide a conceptual perspective for a domain and it specification as software assets to improve metaprocess reuse in early stages of software development.

This approach includes the elements proposed in the use of standards for software development as software and business process modeling (such as UML (Unified Modeling Language) [3, 12] and BPMN (Business Process Management Notation) [13]), adding a conceptual elements to the business domain metamodeling. In the same way, the approach proposed incorporates elements of the OMG (Object Management Group) specification - RAS (Reusable Asset Specification) [14], which provides an integrative methodological approach. To illustrate the applicability of our proposal, this article presents a real application currently running on the e-health domain: a monitoring system for patients with cardiovascular risk.

The remainder of the article is organized as follows. In Sect. 2 we discuss related work. Section 3 provides a description to the proposed approach. Section 4 analyzes the proposed methodology for the specific application mentioned above. Finally, we present the conclusions and future work in Sect. 5.

2 Related Works

Nowadays, there are several approaches that deal with the use of metaprocesses, but, in general, reusability is not taken into consideration from the early software development stages. Acuña and Ferré [1] define Metaprocesses as *"[...] generic building environments that support domain-oriented software development, and its mechanisms of specification and validation."* Our objective is to consider metaprocesses, as part of a generic environment that integrally support model-oriented software development taking into consideration the specific domain.

Ramsin and Paige [17] incorporate the use of metaprocess as an oriented methodology towards model driven software development. It collects what has been accomplished in terms of components reuse, but it is not based on reuse of models from the early stages of software development. Ouyang et al. [15] present a methodological proposal which is oriented to business processes with applications geared towards the use of metaprocesses.

Several works have proposed a systematic approach to the modeling that accompanying the use of metaprocesses in all phases of software development from the early stages to understand and analyze the domain, to design the software solution and build its implementation, but they does not take into account the issue of reuse specification and its formalization in the early stages of software development. Kühne [9] incorporates the concept of metaprocesses to evolution of software processes. Asikainen and Männistö [2] consider the need to semantically formalize the software development processes by the metamodel processes. Levendovszky et al. [10] incorporate the use of process metamodel patterns as a first step to formalize specifications. These approaches use independent platform models and their implementation from the domain, but none of them include the problem of instantiation and customization through the metaprocesses reuse.

Cechticky et al. [4] proposes to reuse code components for real time applications. This proposal is based on the reuse of code but does not cover models and metaprocesses. Park et al. [16], use code components as software assets to facilitate the reuse, which is done independently from models. De Freitas [6] incorporates flexibility by the reuse of application code, without addressing the issues of models and metaprocesses reuse to generate applications. Finally, Rodriguez et al. [18] propose reuse design knowledge, reducing costs and difficulties in software development as a contribution to the methods developed in collaborative systems such as groupware design patterns, pattern languages and frameworks. [4, 6, 16, 18] does not include the theoretical and conceptual articulation of metaprocesses usage in software development through the fostering of reuse, the instantiation and customization using platform independent architectures, and the use of models and metamodels as a contribution to software industrialization.

3   A Methodogical Proposal for the Reuse of Metaprocesses

This section introduces a methodology that consists of a multi-level design for the description of metaprocesses: *conceptual level, reuse process and implementation level* (see Fig. 1). Based on the concept of instantiation and customization of the domain model, this approach enables the reuse of metaprocesses. The representation and construction of metaprocesses begin from a generic metamodel refined in different models to fully represent the domain, this leads to the possibility of applying customization at different development stages, from requirements specification to the design, and software applications.

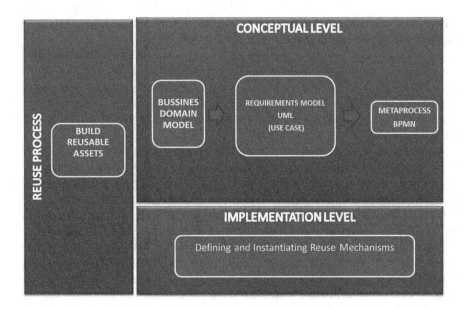

Fig. 1. Metaprocesses specification levels as software assets through models

Likewise, the metaprocesses should be sufficiently expressive and complete in order to cover a domain with elements which facilitate the reuse in the software development.

The *conceptual level* is a generic abstraction of the domain, which is represented through business domain, requirements, and process models. It is consistent with the Model-Driven Development (MDD) paradigm, through transformation of models between the early stages of the software development process. The business domain model specifies the business cycle: mission, policies business and process elements. The requirements model is based on the utilization of use case diagrams. The metaprocess is based on the use of the standard BPMN; it provides from defining the business requirements captured through use cases and process elements of the domain and their relationships.

The *conceptual level* is specified through steps: the first step encompasses the representation of the domain through the *Business Domain Model (BDM)*. It specifies the business activities, the business tasks and business roles. BDM contains diagrams as business diagram and processes flow diagrams.

The processes flow diagram specifies the process activities and process roles. In this sense a business activity is conducted through one or more activities of the process.

The second step is to build the *Requirement Model (RM)* includes use case diagrams.

The third step is to build the *Process Definition Model (PDM)* that includes the business process functionality from a domain perspective and from the system support implementation at this software component.

Once the business model, process model and requirements model diagrams have been built, a relationship analysis amongst its elements takes place, conceptually to verify consistency between diagrams and models proposed. For the construction of a first Conceptual Relationship Activities; which refers to all conceptual elements that identify Business Activities and roles, Process Activities and roles and Use Cases and actor at a system requirements, the relationship analysis use the relational elements: *(AN) Activity Business, (RN) Rol Business, (AP) Activity Process, (RP) Rol* Process, (UC) Use Case, (A) Use Case Actor's.

Finally, having verified the consistency between the previous models we proceed to specify items metaprocess generic, so that this is made up of activities and roles of metaprocess. The activities of metaprocess (MA) will correspond according to the specification of business activities and process activities. The roles of metaprocess will correspond based on specification business and process roles.

Then follows the metaprocess construction based on information provided on the *Domain Analysis*, using the BPMN Notation. In which are clearly identified the activities (task in BPMN) and roles (Lines in BPMN) of *Metaprocess* well as the use cases and applications or systems that support the execution of metaprocess.

There are therefore activities–applications relationship in the Metaprocess. It is through such relationship where the metaprocess implementations can be visualized to the extent that each defined element from the domain will make up a metaprocess element and will be implemented through each application independent of the platform. Thereby the consistency of building systems from the early stages of software development is guaranteed.

The *reuse process* allows represent the metaprocess as reusable asset software. It represents the metaprocess architecture with its constituent elements specificated as software artifacts. The reuse process uses the OMG-AS,OMG's RAS standard and a reuse-software asset repository to enable assets storage and search with packed files that contains the assets and an XML manifest (XML Schema) to facilitate management of its (reusable assets software) (see Fig. 2).

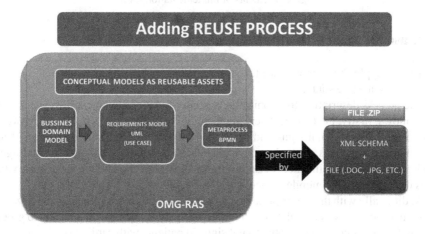

Fig. 2. Elements of reuse

The *implementation level* uses the reuse rules and well-formed rules for the reusable assets software. The implementation is based on the rules definition for the build meta-process correctly that consists to define well-formed rules to metamodeling of metaprocess and reuse rules specified in OMG-RAS standard.

The well-formed rules to metamodeling of metaprocess help maintain consistency between domain models. The reuse rules facilitate to search and recovery elements of the metaprocess as software assets (models, components, artifacts) into repositories (see Fig. 3):

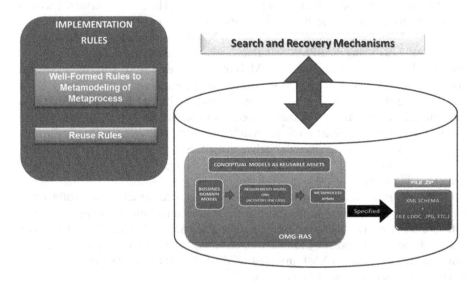

Fig. 3. Elements of implementation level

4   Case Study in e-Health Domain

In order to apply the proposal, we take a monitoring system for patients with cardio-vascular risk as case study.

The process description for monitoring system for patients with cardiovascular risk is as follows: firstly, the technical personnel configure the device. A body area network gathers the patient's vital signs and sends this information to a mobile device. If an abnormal event happens, the mobile device sends the alert and a set of historic vital signs to telephone exchange. In other occasions, the medical staff can retrieve the historic vital signs directly from the mobile device.

Additionally with this description, the process description was refined in the develop with others activities as calculate multivariate analysis as a statistical analysis to group data by factors or components about vital signs in patients with cardiovascular risk and activate the emergency medical system. Figure 4 depicts an overall view of the system.

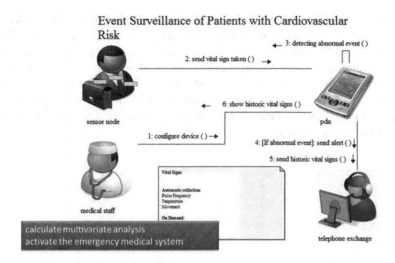

Fig. 4. Elements of domain: event surveillance of patients with cardiovascular risk

A monitoring system also involves the use of metaprocesses to specify the medical guideline and protocols to be followed during an emergency by the medical staff. The telephone exchange uses the medical guidelines and protocols when the monitoring system triggers an alert.

In this article, we only focus on the metaprocesses specification at a conceptual level.

In the next subsection the methodology phases to conceptual level, the architecture and other technological issues are described.

4.1 Methodology Phases

4.1.1 Conceptual Level Specification

The *Business Domain Model (BDM)* specifies how the monitoring e-health service is provided as well as the macroprocesses documentation along the lines of the methodology to support the understanding of the domain. It specifies the business activities as configure medical data system, check periodically patients, monitoring vital signs and other activities; the business tasks as exchange information, customize, provides information and other tasks and business roles as patients, medical doctor, teleoperator and other roles. BDM of case study contains diagrams as business diagram and processes flow diagrams.

The processes flow diagram specifies the process activities as configure remote monitoring system, verification patient board, activation service of emergency and other activities and process roles as medical doctor, teleoperator and other roles to gathered vital sign, device configurations and trigger of alerts.

The *Requirement Model (RM)* includes use case diagrams (with actors as medical staff, technical staff and patients and use cases as configure the system, display historical of vital signs, activate alerts, acquire vital signs and others).

The *Process Definition Model (PDM)* is showed in Fig. 5 through a BPMN diagram. It provides elements of metaprocess as activities. The activities of metaprocess defined by the analyst and domain expert, in study case, are the following: Enter Patient Information, Monitoring System Configuration, Patient Monitoring through Monitoring System, Patient Behavior Analysis through Monitoring System, Manage System Alerts, Patient Assistance and Emergency System Activation. In the case of the roles of metaprocess were the following: Patients, Monitoring System, Tele-Operator, Doctor, Care Unit and Emergency System.

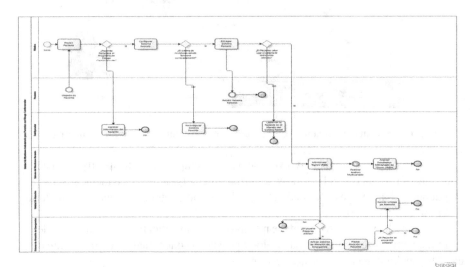

Fig. 5. Metaprocess model

The metaprocess model (see Fig. 6) allows identifier the activities (MA) and roles (MR) of *Metaprocess*, use cases (UC) and applications or systems (S).

These applications are the following: Patient Information System, Monitoring System Configuration, Monitoring System, Multivariate Calculation System, Alert Management System, Event Care System and Emergency Care System.

4.1.2   Reuse Process and Implementation Level

In the *reuse process*, the metaprocess elements defined above are being specified as reuse software assets for the case application, based on the RAS-OMG specification to provide a *Ras Metamodelled Metaprocess*.

In the implementation *level*, the rules are being defined for the reuse of reuse software assets from the repository by search mechanisms whether through keywords that identify the assets or through the storage logic route of the assets in the repository. Also, efforts continue on the specification of a first evolutionary instantiation mechanism via XML-Schema.

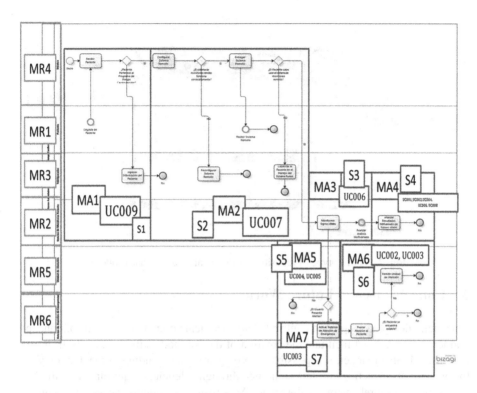

Fig. 6. Activities, roles and applications in metaprocess

4.1.3   A Repository for Reuse

As technological support to the previous levels and reuse process the software assets repository for e-health domains is being constructed to facilitate the reuse tasks of e-health oriented application development. It constituted a first step to accomplish higher productivity and quality as well as the decrease of error and time to release applications.

Consequently a knowledge base and artifacts will be available to e-health users. Additional to this we follow in developing applications for the domain of e-health, reusing models with metaprocess specified in conceptual level based on the proposed methodology as well as in the develop of an integrated repository development tools through Eclipse (see Fig. 7):

The repository will be integrated development environment to build and reuse software artifacts in e-health and other domains, taking also into consideration the reuse level and implementation levels of the proposal.

In terms of building the metaprocess and its specification in conceptual level for the proposed application case, the work that has been completed up to this point has allowed the building of software to remotely monitor patients with cardiovascular risk as represented on the following architecture and the technical elements of the developed system.

The elements specified in conceptual level in monitoring systems of patients with cardiovascular risk are used to specified and build other systems as home care patients system or patients in a medical emergency system.

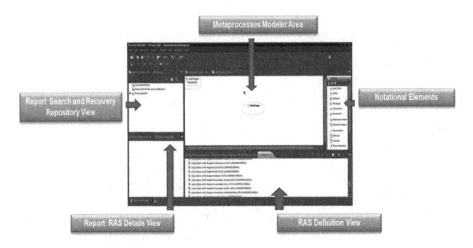

Fig. 7. A prototype of repository for software assets reuse proposed

5   Conclusions and Future Work

This methodological approach contributes to specificate domains by means of conceptual level. These level facilitate the creation of design models independently from the platforms. In this manner, it is possible to obtain an under-standing of the domain with the purpose of correcting problems inherited through a deficient requirements gathering or a lack of comprehension of the same. As a result, we obtain specific elements in conceptual level that can be reused in the development of future applications.

The methodology proposed for the metaprocess at the conceptual specification level as software assets for reuse in the early stages of software development is intended to make easier the development of domain process oriented applications, in this case for e-health. It facilitates the software development process for one case, in which guided models contributed to the development of applications from the domain, independently from the development platforms. In turn, this proposal in conceptual level has been validated and tested. Now, models, metaprocess, components and artifacts are being used to develop others systems like an interoperability platform for pre-hospitalary domain.

The monitoring system of patients with cardiovascular risk and interoperability platform for pre-hospitalary domain has been implemented in IPS University Hospital (Medellín, Colombia) and this is being required in other countries and regions in Colombia.

Presently, the system has been evaluated by measuring their impact on the indicators; briefly the statistics and analysis on its implementation indicate that there is a significant improvement in the allocation of hospital resources and times of patient care.

As future work we think of the formalization of the methodology through the use of logic languages with a formal definition [11] and testing the use of patterns and mechanisms metaprocesses instantiation and reuse process as part of software reuse assets not specified in the OMG standard.

Acknowledgment. We thank ARTICA research of Colciencias, TICs Ministery (Colombia) and COOPEN research European Community and University of Granada.

References

1. Acuña, S., Ferré, X.: Software process modelling. In: Proceedings of the 5th World Multiconference on Systemics, Cybernetics and Informatics (SCI 2001), Orlando, Florida, USA, pp. 1–6 (2001)
2. Asikainen, T., Männistö, T.: Nivel: a metamodelling language with a formal semantics. Softw. Syst. Model. **8**(4), 521–549 (2009)
3. Baisley, D., Björkander, M., Bock, C., Cook, S., Desfray, P., Dykman, N., Ek, A., Frankel, D., Gery, E., Haugen, Ø., Iyengar, S., Kobryn, C., Møller-Pedersen, B., Odell, J., Övergaard, G., Palmkvist, K., Ramackers, G., Rumbaugh, J., Selic, B., Weigert, T., Williams, L.: OMG Unified Modeling Language (OMG UML), Superstructure v 2.2. Object Managment Group (OMG), February 2009
4. Cechticky, V., Egli, M., Pasetti, A., Rohlik, O., Vardanega, T.: A UML2 profile for reusable and verifiable software components for real-time applications. In: Morisio, Maurizio (ed.) ICSR 2006. LNCS, vol. 4039, pp. 312–325. Springer, Heidelberg (2006). doi:10.1007/11763864_23
5. Conradi, R., Nguyen, M.: Classification of metaprocesses and their models. In: Software Process, pp. 167–175 (1994)
6. De Freitas, J.: Model business processes for flexibility and re-use: a component-oriented approach. IBM Dev. Works J., 1–11 (2009)
7. Finkelstein, A., Gabbay, D., Hunter, A., Kramer, J., Nuseibeh, B.: Software Process Modeling and Technology. Research Studies Press Ltd., Londres (1994)
8. Greenfield, J., Short, K.: Software Factories: Assembling Aplications with Patterns, Model, Frameworks and Tools. Wiley, New York (2004)
9. Kühne, T.: Editorial to the theme issue on metamodelling. Softw. Syst. Model. **8**(4), 447–449 (2009)
10. Levendovszky, T., László, L., Mészáros, T.: Supporting domain-specific model patterns with metamodeling. Softw. Syst. Model. **8**(4), 501–520 (2009)
11. Noguera, M., Hurtado, M., Rodríguez, M., Chung, L., Garrido, J.: Ontology-driven analysis of UML-based collaborative processes using OWL-DL and CPN. Sci. Comput. Program. **75**, 726–760 (2010)
12. OMG. Software & Systems Process Engineering Meta-Model Specification doc.ormsc/ (2008-04-01)
13. OMG: Business Process Model and Notation (BPMN) v1.2. Object Managment Group (OMG) (2008)
14. OMG. Reusable Asset Specification. OMG Available Specification Version 2.2. (2005)
15. Ouyang, C., Dumas, M., Van der Aalst, W., Ter Hofstede, A., Mendling, J.: From business process models to process-oriented software systems. ACM Trans. Softw. Eng. Methodol. **19**(1), 2 (2009)
16. Park, S., Park, S., Sugumaran, V.: Extending reusable asset specification to improve software reuse. In: Proceedings of the 2007 ACM Symposium on Applied Computing (SAC 2007), pp. 1473–1478 (2007)
17. Ramsin, R., Paige, R.: Process-centered review of object oriented software development methodologies. Computing **40**(1), 1–89 (2008)

18. Rodríguez, J., Ochoa, S., Pino, J., Herskovic, V., Favela, J., Mejía, D., Morán, A.: Towards a reference architecture for the design of mobile shared workspaces. Future Gener. Comput. Syst. **27**, 109–118 (2011)
19. Rolland, C., Prakash N.: On the adequate modeling of business process families. Université Paris1 Panthéon Sorbonne, Francia (2000)

User Experiences in Virtual Reality Environments Navigation Based on Simple Knowledge Organization Systems

David Martin-Moncunill[1(✉)], Paulo Alonso Gaona-García[2],
Kevin Gordillo-Orjuela[2], and Carlos Enrique Montenegro-Marin[2]

[1] Computer Science, University of Alcalá, Alcalá de Henares, Spain
d.martin@uah.es
[2] Faculty of Engineering, Universidad Distrital Francisco José de Caldas,
Bogotá, Colombia
{pagaonag, cemontenegrom}@udistrital.edu.co,
k.gordillo@correo.udistrital.edu.co

Abstract. During last decades, there has been concern on organizing the information in order to make it more understandable. Many organizations are focused on providing a better classification in such a way that information will be understood by humans and allow a rapid access to resources. This article is intended to present a proposal to strengthen the uses of virtual reality based on simple knowledge representation schemes, in order to provide an environment for navigation through concepts of a given knowledge area that will enable a virtual learning environment. Finally, outcomes from this survey are presented by TAM testing in order to perform validation mechanisms for the proposal.

Keywords: 3D navigational interfaces · SKOS · Simple knowledge organization systems · TAM · Virtual reality · Visual interfaces

1 Introduction

The SKOS (Simple Knowledge Organization Systems) are systems that allow organizing the information in schemes that are navigable by human beings. These may be mental maps, ontologies, taxonomies, thesauri, etc. Specially, the ontologies have the peculiarity that they group terms corresponding to some grouping or characteristic in addition to establish semantic relationships between concepts; for example, a mammalian ontology shall group all the animals that are mammals. On the other hand, it may include subcategories like felines and a semantic relationship that indicates that felines are mammals, in such a way that if felines include an animal like a tiger, it may be inferred that a tiger is a mammal.

SKOS have been used in areas such as key words extraction in order to take advantage of them in repositories [1], as well as knowledge domains associated to mathematics and life sciences [2]. However, it has been barely explored to carry out interoperability of different KOS (Knowledge Organization Systems) in several languages under knowledge domains such as humanities, arts or culture. The SKOS

© Springer International Publishing AG 2016
J.C. Figueroa-García et al. (Eds.): WEA 2016, CCIS 657, pp. 39–49, 2016.
DOI: 10.1007/978-3-319-50880-1_4

represent a big opportunity to be used as mechanisms for navigational searches in Web environments in order to access resources in digital repositories. However, they have been barely explored in virtual reality environments [3] as a medium to access resources.

One of the benefits of the SKOS is that it is possible that they will be simple knowledge organization schemes to link a series of terms with semantic relationships. This does not only provide a big possibility to enrich terms but also to use them for carrying out navigation activities that will ease learning processes in education areas [4–6] in order to: (1) facilitate concepts relationship, (2) improve concepts retention in various knowledge areas and (3) relate concepts to resources on open-use repositories [6, 7]. Thanks to these features SKOS become strategic elements to interact with as navigation mechanisms from several knowledge areas, as it is presented in various proposals by authors like [1–4] and meet different needs, purposes and contexts of use by final users.

Virtual reality is a technology in growth that facilitates 3D spaces to represent said structures. It also allows displaying interactive contents that provide information in addition to the concepts that are being consulted; i.e., besides having information due to the semantic relationships between concepts, it is possible to have virtual resources that help the learning process.

The motivation of this paper is to analyze the possibilities of using Virtual Reality based on Simple Knowledge Organization System to develop a navigational interface to associate concepts that are defined in a taxonomical structure. This study provides a complementary usability study that contrasts preliminary results made by [3] in order to apply the outcomes in an educational context.

2   Background and Related Work

Each data structure has advantages and disadvantages to represent different types of knowledge; therefore, as [8] indicates, there is not a representation method of generic knowledge that allows to structure data and work on any application type in a standardized way. In order to go by these knowledge representation structures, each user performs a navigation process. This process is essential within the information display area [9].

Virtual and augmented reality technologies present big challenges regarding their use within training processes. In this way, immersion has been one of the choices used to develop tourism applications [10–12], clinical treatment management [13–15], and also in virtual learning environments from technological tools like SecondLife [16–18].

By using immersing environments we may find the Ezzell's proposals [19] based on an ontology display in a 3D simulation environment as a tool for managing variables and parameters. The simulation on which tests were carried out was a hypovolemic shock (condition that results when there is a severe blood loss making it impossible for the heart to pump a sufficient amount of blood to the body). They built an ontology about the arterial connections that are involved in a hypovolemic shock,

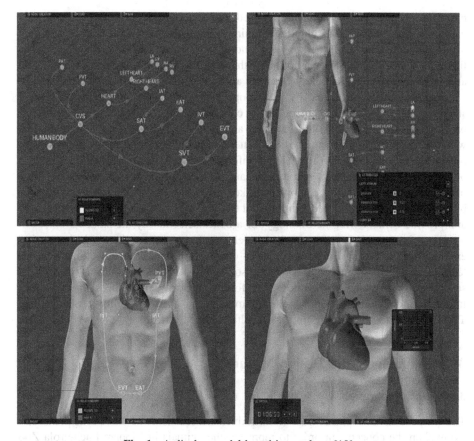

Fig. 1. A display model based in ontology [19]

and the Beneken model, which is a differential equation that molds the way the heart retains and pumps blood. They basically used this ontology to specify and handle all the variables that are involved in the simulation model. This model is showed in Fig. 1.

Wang [20] proposes an educational approach, to use ontologies for organizing knowledge and academic resources as graphs, audio, video images, etc. They are divided by knowledge areas, such as Philosophy, Engineering or Economy. Said ontology works by connecting database repository resources and showing them to students or teachers; the proposed structure allows maintenance and scalability. Synonyms and antonyms are used to create relationships among each one of the related resources. The information display is not explicit. But a kind of scheme representing how ontologies would be assembled for educational resources is presented.

A recent survey carried out by [21] addresses the implementation of a virtual laboratory that will allow students to interact and know about the safety procedures that they shall have when working with laboratory machines; for example, they show a machine to polish metals that requires that the person is at a given distance for preventing accidents. So, simulation is used to ask questions in the form of a test by using pop-up windows that submit an inquiry to the participant, for example, at which distance the polisher shall stand or what kind of tools he/she shall use, etc. The authors finally conclude that these scenarios allow the students to understand in a more suitable and safe way how to wear safety elements and take all the caution in given scenarios.

Finally, studies performed by [22] propose to create an ontology that allows a student to choose which kind of studies or courses he/she may attend based on his/her previous knowledge and skills in a given area. For example, an Engineering student who is in pre-grade studies and has had better competence in informatics may access a post-grade in something that is related to informatics or any other skill he/she has. The ontology was constructed with Protegé 4.0 and each one of the objects that make up the ontology has bi-directional relationships like "it has passed by", "it has been selected by" and others. Basically, it is a simple tool to show the courses offered by a university and provide context with the ontology for a better selection by the student.

From these guides, so few works are related to navigation schemes in immersion environments by using SKOS in order to carry out processes that facilitate student learning in education areas, the concept association and improve concepts retention in several knowledge areas. Therefore, the following survey introduces the outcomes from using this kind of navigation environment, by means of usability techniques like TAM in order to contrast preliminary results obtained in [3].

3 Methodology and Design Methods

3.1 Test Preparation

The purpose of this phase was: (i) introduce the concepts to the participants and (ii) explain the concepts in order to represent the animals in Bioparc Fuengirola Zoo (Malaga, Spain). This preparation phase took place without actual interaction with the 3D navigational environment so that the data collected helped in capturing the desires and pre-conceptions of the participants. This phase had three principal aims:

1. To introduce the 3D navigational environment and interfaces to the participants, so the learning curve of the environment and client application will be stepped.
2. To explain the concept of the 3D navigational environment and the concepts related to the animals.
3. To get initial data on the participants' perception and their preferences.

This preparation phase took place without actual interaction with the 3D navigational environment so that the data collected helped in capturing the desires and pre-conceptions of the participants. In Fig. 2a and b the 3D environment is presented.

In summary, this phase consisted on a training session in a face-to-face setting. The session organizer gave a short speech about the historical background of the Malaga Zoo. In order to avoid problems arising from the use of existing KOS, which were not built according to these principles, we decided to create a simple SKOS, aiming to ensure the use of a proper sample for the experiment. This SKOS was constructed

Fig. 2 (a) 3D Environment by area. (b) 3D Environment of the scenario

to represent the animals in Bioparc Fuengirola Zoo (Malaga, Spain), which allowed us to build a thesaurus, where broader/narrower relationships were established according to the animal's habitat. The interface was built using a Unity 3D engine. Figures 3 and 4 show different views of the thesaurus.

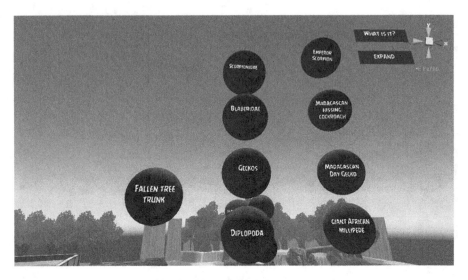

Fig. 3. 3D navigational structure

Fig. 4. A broader view of the navigational structure in the Bioparc's zoo

3.2   Method of Evaluation

We used the Technology Acceptance Model (TAM) to conduct a survey as a method of evaluation with the purpose of obtaining subjective impressions for the use of immersive navigational search and to demonstrate the potential value of this approach in order to use it in academic environments. The purpose of this evaluation was to obtain values to analyze the user satisfaction and the relevance of 3D navigational environment, which are two predominant aspects of these types of studies for applications' performance in information systems.

We add some factors of related research in digital libraries [23, 24] like *ease of use*, *navigational search*, and *aesthetic* defined by [25] as a measure of system performance in digital libraries. For *learnability*, we use aspects related with *understanding*, *taxonomy classification*, and *location*; which were used in related research on repositories [4] in order to evaluate visual search interfaces.

We developed a questionnaire with 12 questions based on these two aspects (*user satisfaction* and *learnability*). To carry out the user satisfaction assessment, 8 questions were designed based on user satisfaction; and the other questions, according to *relevant* aspects of visual interfaces. The final statement questions are presented in Table 1.

Table 1. TAM questions used in the test

General aspects of 3D navigational environment	
I believe 3D navigational environments provide all levels of information (e.g. abstracts, descriptions, etc.) that I need for my information seeking tasks	Disagree 1 2 3 4 5 Agree
I believe that number of concepts in a 3D navigational environment is easy to see (It refers to the number of concepts presented by classification level)	Disagree 1 2 3 4 5 Agree
I believe that concepts, in a 3D navigational environment, are reliable to support my job tasks when identifying an animal in a Zoo	Disagree 1 2 3 4 5 Agree
I believe that the sources' form in the 3D navigational environment is suitable for job tasks. (forms: text, sound, image, videos)	Disagree 1 2 3 4 5 Agree
In general, I find the 3D navigational environment as a useful system for my job tasks	Disagree 1 2 3 4 5 Agree
I believe that the 3D navigational environment has a pleasant aesthetic appearance	Disagree 1 2 3 4 5 Agree
I believe that the 3D navigational environment offers easy methods to navigate in the system	Disagree 1 2 3 4 5 Agree
I believe that the 3D navigational environment uses understandable terminology. (Terminology refers to concepts and terms in a navigation structure)	Disagree 1 2 3 4 5 Agree
I believe that the 3D navigational environment is a learnable system	Disagree 1 2 3 4 5 Agree
I believe that the 3D navigational environment is a useful system for searching resources associated to the concept	Disagree 1 2 3 4 5 Agree
In general, I believe that the 3D navigational environment responds very quickly to my search	Disagree 1 2 3 4 5 Agree
In general, I find the 3D navigational environment as a well performing system to find animals in a Zoo	Disagree 1 2 3 4 5 Agree

Based on the questions proposed in Table 1, the aims of the study are the following:

1. To investigate the general factors affecting the acceptability of an immersive 3D navigational search.
2. To evaluate the participants' acceptability in order to find animals and its features in a zoo.

Participants were 12 children ranging from 10 to 12 years who were invited to try the interface for fifteen minutes. Participants were randomly selected in order to obtain unbiased results.

4   Preliminary Results

This section presents the results from the questionnaire. A Likert scale is a psychometric scale commonly used in questionnaires. It is the most widely used scale in survey research. In literature related to the evaluation of digital libraries, the used Likert scales usually include five response levels [25–27]. Table 1 shows the survey results of the participants from our study, also using a five-point scale (1 = strongly disagree; 2 = disagree; 3 = neutral; 4 = agree; 5 = strongly agree). The five scale values represent the subjective satisfaction of the users in regards to the 3D navigational environment and the use of the interface in order to search animals in the navigational structure.

These results show that the majority of the participants in the test identified animals and their relationship with the habitat and the selected animal category according to the KOS classification defined for the zoo. Table 2 presents these results based on Likert Scale.

Table 2. Statistical description of visual perception based on Likert Scale

	1		2		3		4		5		Mean	Standard Deviation (SD)
User satisfaction	n	(%)	n	(%)	n	(%)	n	(%)	n	(%)	n	(%)
Navigational search	0	0	0	0	2	8.3	4	33.3	6	58.3	4.39	0.601
Aesthetic	0	0	0	0	0	0	6	50	6	50	4.7	0.728
Ease of use	0	0	0	0	2	16.7	6	50	4	33.3	4.26	0.649
Learnability	n	(%)	n	(%)	n	(%)	n	(%)	n	(%)	n	(%)
Understanding	0	0	0	0	3	25	6	50	3	25	4.	0.722
Location	0	0	0	0	2	16.7	8	66.7	2	16.7	3.89	0.627
Classification	0	0	0	0	2	8.3	7	66.7	3	25	4.17	0.565

Table 3 shows these results in a detailed statistical description of visual perception.

Table 3 present results of the participants' visual perception. This aspect was based on the questionnaire of the 3D navigational environment. Participants in general found

Table 3. Statistical description of visual perception

Evaluation criteria	N	Mean	Standard deviation
Location	12	3.89	0.627
Navigational search	12	4.39	0.601
Classification	12	4.17	0.565
Understanding	12	4.00	0.722
Ease of use	12	4.26	0.649
Aesthetic	12	4.70	0.728

that immersive interface is a good tool in order to navigate and find animals in a zoo (Mean = 4,9; SD = 0,601). The same way, the participants agreed on the ease of using the navigation structure in order to find concepts in the navigation structure (Mean = 4,26; SD = 0,649); also, they agree in the aesthetic qualities of design (Mean = 4,70; SD = 0,728). However, participants found that the navigational interface has problems in terms of locating animals' concepts in a navigational structure (Mean = 3,89; SD = 0,627). This was possibly due to the concepts visibility within the selected node. Nevertheless, the majority of the participants were able to conduct animals' location in their habitat based on its classification (Mean 4,17; SD = 0,565) and issues related to ease to learn for potential users in different knowledge areas (Mean 4,00; SD = 0,702).

5 Conclusions and Future Work

Results obtained from the Technology-Acceptance-Model questionnaire were adapted to our setting, allowing participants to describe frustrating experiences with concrete aspects and provide suggestions for additional features. The results of this questionnaire were then contrasted with subjective impressions of the participants in order to analyze potential limitations of usability or navigational structure mechanics regarding the original expectations about the whole 3D navigational interface.

According to the results for learnability, the study shows a potential use of Simple Knowledge Organization Systems for (1) applying them as a mechanism to navigate and relate concepts, (2) a better understanding of concepts associated to the selected category, and (3) locating animals' concepts based on a navigational structure.

There are still relevant usability aspects to explore in order to perform 3D navigational scenarios. In our results for usability, we found some problems related to: (1) distractions in the proposed scenario to search terms within the navigation structure, (2) dizziness when surfing between different depth levels, and (3) confusion when moving horizontally within the navigation structure.

As a future work, we think to analyze methods and techniques for integrating ontological representations in 3D environments, with linked open resources like Linked Open Data (LOD). We expect to take advantage of LOD functionality to get relevant and detailed information that will allow linking to the selected ontology concept and a further resource's graphical depicting in 3D models in order to provide searching choices that will facilitate the users' interaction, specifically for students.

Acknowledgments. Authors are grateful to the Universidad Distrital Francisco José de Caldas, for supporting these results through research projects call 11/2016, by CIDC Research Center.

References

1. Martín-Moncunill, D., García-Barriocanal, E., Sicilia, M.-A., Sánchez-Alonso, S.: Evaluating the practical applicability of thesaurus-based keyphrase extraction in the agricultural domain: Insights from the VOA3R project. Knowl. Organ. **42**, 76–89 (2015)
2. Chen, S.-J., Chen, H.-H.: Mapping multilingual lexical semantics for knowledge organization systems. Electron. Libr. **30**(2), 278–294 (2012)
3. Gaona-García, P.A., Martin-Moncunill, D., Gordillo, K., Gonzalez-Crespo, R.: Navigation and visualization of knowledge organization systems using virtual reality glasses. IEEE Latam., vol. 14, no. 6 (2016, in press)
4. Gaona-García, P.A., Martín-Moncunill, D., Sánchez-Alonso, S., Fermoso, A.: A usability study of taxonomy visualisation user interfaces in digital repositories. Online Inf. Rev. **38**(2), 284–304 (2014). doi:10.1108/OIR-03-2013-0051
5. Martín-Moncunill, D., Sánchez-Alonso, S., Gaona-García, P.A., Marianos, N.: Applying visualization techniques to develop interfaces for educational repositories: the case of Organic. In: Lingua and VOA3R, Paper presented at the Proceedings of the Learning Innovations and Quality: The Future of Digital Resources, Rome (2013)
6. Gaona-García, P.A., Sánchez-Alonso, S., Montenegro, C.E.: Visualization of information: a proposal to improve the search and access to digital resources in repositories. J. Ingeniería e Investigación **34**(1), 83–89 (2014)
7. Gaona-García, P.A., Stoitsis, G., Sanchez-Alonso, S., Biniari, K.: An exploratory study of user perception in visual search interfaces based on SKOS. Knowl. Org. **43**(4), 217–238 (2016)
8. Gaševic, D., Djuric, D., Devedžic, V.: Model driven engineering and ontology development, 2nd edn. Springer, New York (2009)
9. Graham, M., Kennedy, J., Benyon, D.: Towards a methodology for developing visualizations. Int. J. Hum Comput Stud. **53**, 789–807 (2000)
10. Guttentag, D.A.: Virtual reality: applications and implications for tourism. Tour. Manag. **31**(5), 637–651 (2010)
11. Minucciani, V., Garnero, G.: Available and implementable technologies for virtual tourism: a prototypal station project. In: Murgante, B., Misra, S., Carlini, M., Torre, C.M., Nguyen, H.-Q., Taniar, D., Apduhan, B.O., Gervasi, O. (eds.) ICCSA 2013. LNCS, vol. 7974, pp. 193–204. Springer, Heidelberg (2013). doi:10.1007/978-3-642-39649-6_14
12. Neuhofer, B., Buhalis, D., Ladkin, A.: A typology of technology-enhanced tourism experiences. Int. J. Tour. Res. **16**(4), 340–350 (2014)
13. Ghanbarzadeh, R., Ghapanchi, A.H., Blumenstein, M., Talaei-Khoei, A.: A decade of research on the use of three-dimensional virtual worlds in health care: a systematic literature review. J. Med. Internet Res. **16**(2), e47 (2014)
14. Wiecha, J., Heyden, R., Sternthal, E., Merialdi, M.: Learning in a virtual world: Experience with using Second Life for medical education. J. Med. Internet Res. **12**(1), e1 (2010)
15. Barak, A., Grohol, J.M.: Current and future trends in internet-supported mental health interventions. J. Technol. Hum. Serv. **29**(3), 155–196 (2011)
16. Boulos, M.N.K., Hetherington, L., Wheeler, S.: Second Life: An overview of the potential of 3-D virtual worlds in medical and health education. Health Info. Libr. J. **24**(4), 233–245 (2007)

17. De Lucia, A., Francese, R., Passero, I., Tortora, G.: Development and evaluation of a virtual campus on Second Life: the case of SecondDMI. Comput. Educ. **52**(1), 220–233 (2009)
18. Jarmon, L., Traphagan, T., Mayrath, M., Trivedi, A.: Virtual world teaching, experiential learning, and assessment: an interdisciplinary communication course in Second Life. Comput. Educ. **53**(1), 169–182 (2009)
19. Ezzell, Z., Fishwick, P.A., Cendan, J.: Linking simulation and visualization construction through interactions with an ontology visualization. In: Proceedings - Winter Simulation Conference, pp. 2921–2932 (2011)
20. Wang, S., Cheng, J.: Research on organization technology of education resource based on ontology. In: 2008 International Conference on Wireless Communications, Networking and Mobile Computing, WiCOM 2008 (2008)
21. Jin, G., Nakayama, S., Virtual reality game for safety education. In: 2014 International Conference on Audio, Language and Image Processing (ICALIP), pp. 95–100. IEEE (2014)
22. Ayesha, K.U.R., Khan, B.P.: Creation of ontology in education domain. In: 2012 IEEE Fourth International Conference on Technology for Education, pp. 237–238. IEEE (2012)
23. Jeng, J.: Usability assessment of academic digital libraries: effectiveness, efficiency, satisfaction, and learnability. Libri **55**, 96–121 (2005)
24. Tsakonas, G., Papatheodorou, C.: Analysing and evaluating usefulness and usability in electronic information services. J. Inf. Sci. **32**, 400–419 (2006)
25. Tsakonas, G., Papatheodorou, C.: Exploring usefulness and usability in the evaluation of open access digital libraries. Inf. Process. Manag. **44**, 1234–1250 (2008)
26. Garibay, C., Gutiérrez, H., Figueroa, A.: Evaluation of a digital library by means of quality function deployment (QFD) and the Kano model. J. Acad. Librariansh. **36**(2), 125–132 (2010)
27. Quijano-Solís, Á., Novelo-Peña, R.: Evaluating a monolingual multinational digital library by using usability: an exploratory approach from a developing country. Int. Inf. Libr. Rev. **37**(4), 329–336 (2005)

Technological Mediations in the Educational Event of the Information and Knowledge Society: Training of Engineers

Claudio Gonzalez[1(✉)], Vanessa Nieto[2], José Lopez[2], and Yesid Diaz[2]

[1] Universidad Nacional Abierta y a Distancia, Bogotá, Colombia
claudio.gonzalez@unad.edu.co
[2] Corporacion Unificada Nacional de Educacion Superior CUN, Bogotá, Colombia
yurivane89@hotmail.com, {jose_lopezq,Yesid_diaz}@cun.edu.co

Abstract. The present paper seeks to socialize the understanding brought about by the investigation of the processes of appropriation and use of information and communication technologies in the educational field of engineering, at a private University that offers in-class education in Latin America. This study is carried out in a context of complexity called "information society and knowledge", interweaving related fields (called dimensions), such as education, communication, information technologies and subjectivity. The article presents results of the imaginaries of the information society that the actors (students and teachers of a Faculty of Engineering) have of the appropriation, recognition and measurement of the information and communication technologies in its educational events. The analyzed results correspond to the relationships between information society, knowledge and education.

Keywords: Information society · Technological environments · Information and Communication Technology (ICT) · Appropriation of ICTs

1 Introduction

The training in engineering has been experiencing a significant drop in demand, against which arise reasons, arguments and various proposals. Within the more frequently referenced causes is the rejection of many students, from secondary education, of the study of natural and exact sciences and their applications. Already in the universities, some studies [1] and reflections [2] have shown that the highest rate of subject failure and repetition occurs in those who have basic science as the core components of their studies, especially mathematics and physics. Such a situation has implications for the productive sectors and society to reduce the capabilities to meet developmental needs or meet humanity's challenges, such as climate change [3]; A case in point is that of Siemens, which in 2001 introduced some 64% of the board as engineers, reduced to 25% in 2010 [4].

On the basis of a general principle, which places engineering as a profession that studies and includes the advances of science to develop technological innovations that

© Springer International Publishing AG 2016
J.C. Figueroa-García et al. (Eds.): WEA 2016, CCIS 657, pp. 50–61, 2016.
DOI: 10.1007/978-3-319-50880-1_5

generate improvements in the quality of life, the University is facing a crucial moment in the training of engineers and in the development of engineering.

The strategies implemented to try to overcome the difficulties are different, in particular those that pose the solution in the field of didactics, in particular the use of technological mediations, under the assumption that this generation of students feel very comfortable with the activities carried out through digital devices and the capacity to connect to data traffic through 3G–4G and Wireless technologies [5]. It is therefore not only a problem of education, but also a problem of their position as thinking subjects in the dimension of their contribution to the society that we want, built from singularities under a single global society that is based on the information and whose greatest asset is the knowledge.

This research is conceived within the construct of a trans-disciplinary field in which converge fields of knowledge such as information and communication technologies, education, communication and sociology, in the context of a globalized society, known as the information society and knowledge, seeking not only to question and to propose, by and in context, but also highlight places and possibilities in two scenarios that are crucial for the conception of society that beckons us: engineering and education.

Finally, the guiding question throughout the research was: "What are the correlations and feelings that are perceived in students and teachers of a Faculty of Engineering, compared to the technological mediations which form part of its educational events? This question leads to more specific ones, such as: What is considered learnable in the unidirectional logic of the educational binomen teaching-learning? Or, to what extent does the inclusion of information and communication technologies (TIC's) in the processes of student formation guarantee the learning of that which is teachable? Furthermore, does the method ensure that that which is teachable is learnt? Still more emerged, which enlivened and invigorated the research process [6].

The results of this research provide elements that allow to understand the characteristics of the use of the technologies that make up the mediations in the community, the relationships generated and possible meanings for and in the accomplishment of education, from complex epistemic understandings conceived in the meeting of education and technology as fields of knowledge framed in a major event called the information society and knowledge.

The first paragraph covers the context and impacts on education, technology and engineering in the framework of an information and knowledge society, the second paragraph refers to the methodological process that is carried out within the investigation framework, in order to check its effectiveness. The analysis of the results obtained is displayed in the third paragraph, as well as the similar studies carried out prior to the present research. Finally, the conclusions and recommendations are presented for any future work to be carried out on the subject of this investigation.

First of all there is an explanation of Context and impacts on education, technology and engineering in the framework of an information and knowledge society, then there is a description of Methodological procedure where Design and Validation of the instruments, definition of population and samples, information collecting techniques and data analysis techniques are specified, subsequently there is a description of result and analysis in four categories, in addition similar studies and finally conclusions and future work.

2   Context and Impacts on Education, Technology and Engineering in the Framework of an Information and Knowledge Society

The knowledge society, is given by the continuous innovation in scientific and technological areas which human beings have had to face and adapt to, this due to the fact that technology has become a relevant factor in the everyday life, living in a historical moment where the volume of information is increasing exponentially every day [7].

Society has been going through many changes on its path to consolidating features that characterize information and knowledge, and they are inexorably extended to all areas and social aspects including education. There are many demonstrations of this, but perhaps one of the most important is the use of computer networks to access information that, by mediating policies and organizational processes and personal, become knowledge. As a consequence, the present work focuses more on understanding and characterizing feelings and interests that guide the actions of the individuals and the organizations involved in the educational event, regardless of the level of formality that they have.

Although education with technological mediations is not a matter only of the current times, indeed various technologies have always been available, today we can associate it with, to mention but a few, devices, platforms, databases, documents, search engines, to all of which we implement and benchmark to expand coverage and *"teach"* [8].

3   Methodological Procedure

This study uses two elements of two complementary methodological approaches: the quantitative and the qualitative. By applying the quantitative approach in the first phase established a description or characterization of technological mediations; it also established which mediations the students and teachers had access to, as well as the uses (in terms of frequency and time of dedication) that they gave them. Table 1 sets out the categories, sub-categories and defined variables.

Complimentarily, the second phase was carried out using the qualitative approach, with an understanding of demonstrations and appraisals of subjectivity around the technologies and their uses, in addition to the relationships between individual learners and educators. The method contemplated the socialization of quantitative results to energize the dialogs.

Table 1. Categories, sub-categories and variables

Category	Sub-category	Variables*
Subject	Student	Gender, age, engineering program, semester
	Teacher	Gender, Age, Profession
Hardware	Machines	Various physical media recognized as computers, hard-drives, memories, among others.
	Connection Means	Means of access to the network
Software	Operating Systems	Most commonly used operating system
	Utility Packages	Most commonly software packages used
	Specialized Software	Specialized software Packages
	Software origen	Availability of licensed software
Uses	Frequency/Use -Service/Location	Frequency and preferred place for use of devices and access to contents
	Time/Use -Service/Location	Time allocated for device use and content consumption

3.1 Design and Validation of the Instruments

The information collection instrument was designed on the basis of the categories, sub-categories and variables set, configuring a deductive structure. The validation was carried out with pilot tests in sample groups (teachers and students), with the purpose of measuring: clarity of the questions, understanding of the terms, levels of empathy with the instrument and response time. For this purpose we used an additional instrument to inquire about the elements to measure; the information gathered allowed to make the final adjustments, to finally submit the instrument to the concept of an investigator and proceed to digitize and locate the survey in the selected electronic platform (e-survey).

3.2 Definition of Population and Samples

The study was conducted with the communities of students and teachers of a faculty of traditional engineering, with a random sampling by participation. For the community of students (97) persons were signed up ninety-seven in phase 1, a figure that corresponds approximately to 11% of the student population belonging to six undergraduate programs in engineering; in phase 2 twelve students participated. The community of teachers thirty-four persons took part, a figure equivalent to 35% of the teachers of the Faculty; in phase 2 8 teachers were signed up. The following table shows the technical sheet for the study (Table 2):

Table 2. Sampling information

Population	880 students of the Faculty of Engineering 97 teachers of the Faculty of Engineering
Geographical Coverage	Santiago de Cali, Faculty of Engineering with classroom methodology
Sample type	Random
Information collection	Survey delivered and completed through an electronic platform Talking Sessions

3.3 Information Techniques Collection

For phase 1 several surveys were designed, organized by categories, sub-categories and quoted variables. The implementation of the instrument was made through a web platform application (e-survey), with links sent to the emails of members of the communities mentioned (based on institutional mailing lists), establishing a date of expiry of the survey. Subsequently, the records were exported to an Excel file, where they gave a data structure that could also be exported to statistical analysis software, in this case SPSS 16.

For phase 2 the qualitative information was obtained from two processes which, although independent, complement each other to allow one to view the subjects' perceptions. Demonstrations were obtained of the subjects involved, related with signifiers, uses, relationships and perceptions of the incursion of ICT's in their lives. At the same time, strategies of observation and reflection on formative processes, past and present, were coordinated – processes in which ICT's interfere and have interfered. All this information was systematically transcribed and incorporated into working documents.

3.4 Data Analysis Techniques

Once preprocessed in SPSS, quantitative data were processed and plotted regarding each one of the variables to later be interpreted in terms of percentage values and finally to establish links by means of context indicators.

On the other hand, the qualitative data permitted to achieve a greater sense of understanding than the quantitative data, especially in relation to the use and frequency of use, from the signifiers and relationships of the subject, in their interaction with technological mediations linked to their formative processes.

4   Results and Analysis

Our main goal is to present the obtained results in a category related to education and technology. The above notwithstanding, there is a statistical framework for categories, sub-categories and variables in each one of the dimensions.

4.1 Category: Subject

The vast majority of the student subjects were born when two of the digital technology elements that characterize the information and knowledge society had already reached an important place: personal computers (from the 1980's) and the internet [9]. However, a large part of their activities, many of their decisions, as well as the perception of the world around them, are influenced by the technologies of information and communication, and one can consider that the vast majority of students participating in the study are digital natives and that all participating teachers are digital migrants [10].

Figure 1 shows that youngest students who participated are 16 years old and oldest are 37 with an average of 20. Most of them (53.1%) are between 17 and 19 years old.

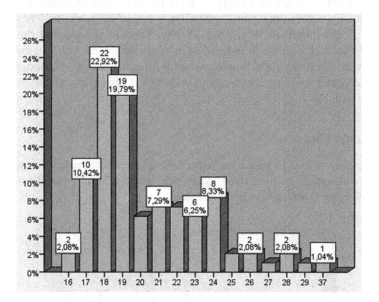

Fig. 1. Percentage participation by student age

4.2 Category: Hardware

As a means of establishing the position in the socio-economic context, it is considered important to the relationship of some figures, to highlight that university students, especially those in the Faculty of Engineering, were located mainly in the social stratas 3 and 4 (middle class), although cases are found in strata 2 and 5.

High penetration of mobiles is clear where a special interest lies between the difference of almost 20 percentage points between students and teachers who used mobile communication devices. The figures of connectivity in both cases exceeded the 95% that in comparison with the national and international indices, positioning these communities at a much higher level, surpassing the indicators posed by recent studies.

4.3 Category: Software

Considering that training in engineering requires developing abilities and skills for analysis, design and product innovation, only 34% used tools that allow them to design graphics and/or program computers and only 23.7% use simulation tools. 41% of the students used tutorial, from which a 19.2% came from Google; followed by Oracle with 15.4% (a platform for databases, whose use is targeted at engineering students directly related to information systems). Then there were the educational videos on Youtube with 11.5%; other software related to computer programming followed with 14%. This places the students of systems engineering and multimedia engineering as those who use ICT the most as a support to their independent learning.

Digital databases were used by only 51.5% of the students; they manifested their use in their formation process, but even more telling is that of those who said they used the databases, 24.2% related to Wikipedia, 18.2% related to Google and the 9.1% to 'Encarta', all tools that are far from being specialized databases. 64.9% of the students used electronic platforms for education. Moodle (institutionalized platform administered by the Center for Virtual Education) with 58%, CourseCompass, with 16% and Mymathlab with 8%.

4.4 Category: Uses

The internet sites related to education (virtual libraries, educational platforms, among others) were visited daily, from their households, by only 21.6% of students; furthermore, 22.6% entered four or five times per week.

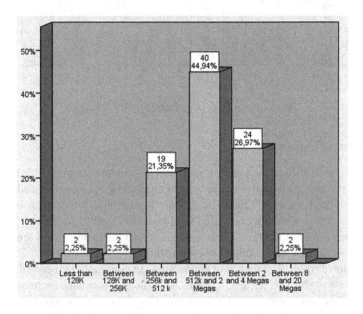

Fig. 2. Internet access speed from students' residences

The internet sites related with social networks or virtual communities were visited every day, from their residences by some 51.6% of students and only by 17.7% of the teachers. Utilitarian software (text processors, spreadsheets, among others), was used daily from home by 30.9% of students, 10.3% used it between 4 and 5 times per week, 15.5% between 1 and 2 times per week.

Figure 2 shows that the 44.9% of students believed that internet speed from their residence was between 512 Kb and 2 Mb; 26.9% believed that it was between 2 and 4 Mb; 21.3% believed that it was between 2256 and 512 Kb; 2.2% thought that it was between 128 and 256 Kb; 2.2% believed that it was between 128 and 256 Kb and the 2.2% believed that it was between 8 and 20 Mb.

Figure 3 shows that only thirty-three (33) students, equivalent to 34.0% of the total, used special software on their computers. Of them, 24.2% used Adobe; 15.1% Used Eclipse, Netbeans and Derive; the 9.0% used Netbeans. The reminder tools were used for computer programming, internet browsing, and simulation.

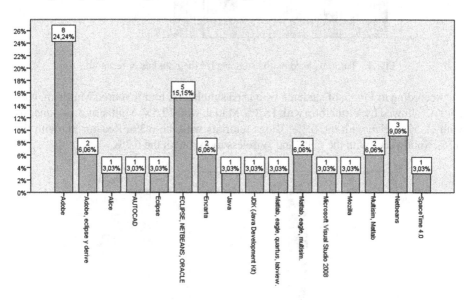

Fig. 3. Special software used by students on their computers.

Figure 5 shows that of the students who used tutorials, five stated that they used Google, with 19.2%, the source to find tutorials, without establishing any preference for one in particular. It was followed by the on line tutorials of Oracle (databases), with 15.4%; Video tutorials was next with 11.5% and then other aimed at computer programming: Java with 7.7%, Programming with 7.7%; on line tutorials with the 7.7%. Investigative journalism with 3.8%, the Visual Basic library with 3.8%, Multisim with 3.8%, Matlab with 3.8%, data structures with 3.8%, online oracle-linex with 3.8%, youtube with 3.8% and youtube/wikipedia with 3.8%. (Figure 4)

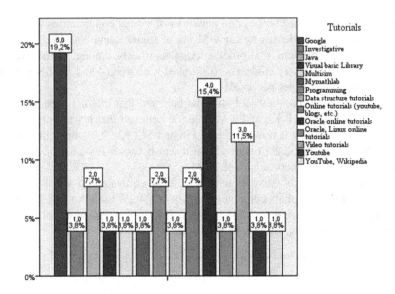

Fig. 4. Tutorials used by the students for their studies or research.

According to Fig. 5, of students who used simulators, four favoured Multisim, with 25.0%, followed by Virtualbox with 18.8%, Matlab with 12.5%, Multisim-eagle-quartus with 12.5%, Alice with the 6.3%, Blogs tutorials with the 6.3%, Reactor 3D with the 6.3%, Solidworks with the 6.3% and Wireless toolkit with the 6.3%.

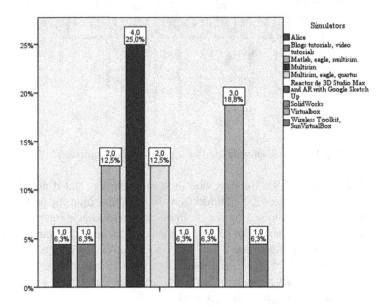

Fig. 5. Simulators used by the students for their studies or research.

According to Fig. 6, most of the teachers opt for computers of the brands that have greater market penetration (Hewlett Packard, Dell), which made up 43.0% of the sample. There were also a considerable number of teachers (20%) which possessed the computers denominated *"clone"*. The access to information and the interest in knowledge is not within the priorities of the majority of participants (teacher-students).

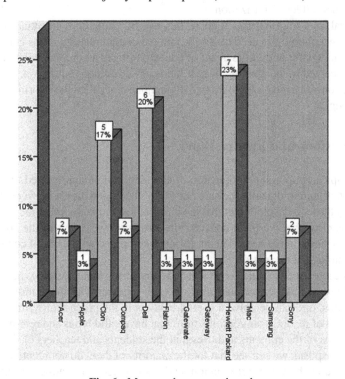

Fig. 6. Most used computer brands

Considering the amount of time devoted to the processes of study-research-training with respect to the time devoted to other activities, study groups perceive, that TIC´s do not constitute a scenario that differentiates the development of the subjects' autonomy in a trance overcoming models imposed by the media for the purposes of consumption, and are not reflected traits of significant self-determination in the processes of training.

5   Similar Studies

The educational institution in the present: An analysis of the role of the technologies in the processes of subjectivation from the Universidad Autónoma de Barcelona with objective of determining the influence of the technologies (all kinds of technologies) in the generation of subjectivities in learners [11].

Characterization of knowledge and use of the specialized tools for the Internet between the academic community, scientific, professional and cultural life of the

University of Antioquia in Medellin [12]. Its objective is to create a data model to determine what the most used tools of the internet are by the academic community.

Technological tools for improving university teaching. A reflection from the experience and research in Salamanca, Spain from the Universidad de Salamanca (Spain) to learn the use that teachers make of those tools and the specific skills that teachers should acquire for their effective utilization.

In general, as a trait that sets it apart, this research aims to understand the characteristics of the technologies used by an educational community, relations generated and possible meanings for and in the event of education, from a complex epistemic understanding conceived in the meeting of four fields of knowledge (education, subjectivity, communication and technologies) framed in a major event called the information society and knowledge.

6   Conclusions and Future Work

In both groups an important conjunction of elements can be appreciated, which allow us to assert that technologically they are not part of the digital divide between developed societies and those in development that the information and knowledge society has been formed. It is clear that we must consider the structural weakness in the speed of the broadband channels implemented in our country, compared with those of countries with greater technological capacity.

Given the low use of productivity tools and considering that nowadays the production of texts is done in this type of platforms, brought together with the demonstrations of the participants, one can perceive a great weakness in the process of writing texts that are the product of readings and/or reflections that have valid bases and reference points.

On the basis of the contents and uses that the students and teachers of the study are have at their disposal, we can see that for the majority of them do not identify the distinguishing features between information and knowledge circulating in information networks, therefore having a means of access doesn't represent any advantage in the development of creative and innovative capacities, nor in subjectivities to transcend the determinism of the mere consumption of information.

While as educators we give meaning to the technologies in terms of their potential as mediation of the educational process, students do so in terms of the relationship with the world that surrounds them, both near and distant. This then produces distortions and gaps in the communicative processes between communities of meanings. While the meaning to one, in terms of the main objective of the mediations, is troubleshooting specific didactic problems and improving competencies, to the other it means to have access to the information, be interconnected and count with the latest devices with better functionality.

We also recommend establishing a regular process of replication of the study to establish variations and trends in relation to the movements of the technological and educational scenarios.

To facilitate the process of analysis it is recommended that a technological tool be implemented to allow registration and data recovery, by setting filters and functionality to compare information between different versions of the study.

In order to obtain qualitative information spaces should be implemented in electronic platforms such as forums or blogs, to obtain a greater quantity of information from the more extensive periods of time. This involves linking students together to structure the information in accordance with the categories addressed.

References

1. Bravo, Mario, Gonzalez, D.: Retraimiento poblacional en educación superior. Editorial San Buenaventura. Cali **43**, 1 (2009)
2. Ulloa, G.: Qué pasa con la ingeniería en Colombia? Ingeniería y sociedad., Ingeniería y Sociedad, 2 (2010)
3. UNESCO: Engineering: Issues, Challenges and Opportunities for Development. UNESCO Publishing (2010)
4. Garcia Gonzalez, F.: Una Mirada a La Formación En Ingenieria En El Contexto Internacional, ACOFI (2013)
5. Vazquez-Cano, E.: El reto de la formación docente para el desarrollo de una metodología ubicua en la educación superior. Perspectiva Educacional de Formación **54**(1), 149–162 (2015)
6. Sunkel, G.: Las tecnologías de la información y la comunicación (TIC) en la educación en América Latina, Desarollo social de Santiago de Chile (2006)
7. Dominguez Alfonso, R.: La Sociedad Del Conocimiento Y Los Nuevos Retos Educativos, pp. 1–19 (2009)
8. Escobar, A.: Bienvenidos a cyberia. Notas para una antropología de la cultura, Revista de Estudios Sociales, **22** (2010)
9. Rubio Moraga, A.: Historia de internet: aproximación al futuro de labor investigativa. La Comunicación Audiovisual en la Historia, 1 (2001)
10. Prensky, Marc: Digital Natives, Digital Immigrants, Part II: Do They Really Think Differently, On the Horizon. NCB University Press, p. 6 (2001)
11. Muñoz-Repiso, A.G.-V.: Herramientas Tecnológicas Para Mejorar La Docencia Universitaria. Una Reflexión Desde La Experiencia Y La Investigación. RIED, Revista Iberoamericana de Educación a Distancia, **10,** 2 (2007)
12. Vanegas Arrambide, Guillermo: La Institución Educativa En La Actualidad. Un Análisis Del Papel de Las Tecnologías En Los Procesos de Subjetivación, Universidad de Barcelona, 2002

Computational Intelligence

Induction of Rules Based on Similarity Relations for Imbalance Datasets. A Case of Study

Yaima Filiberto[1], Mabel Frias[1(✉)], Rafael Larrua[1], and Rafael Bello[2]

[1] Department of Computer Sciences,
Universidad de Camagüey, Camagüey, Cuba
{yaima.filiberto,mabel.frias,
rafael.larrua}@reduc.edu.cu
[2] Department of Computer Sciences,
Universidad Central "Marta Abreu" de Las Villas, Santa Clara, Cuba
rbellop@uclv.edu.cu

Abstract. In this paper, the performance of the IRBASIR-Imb algorithm (Induction of Rules Based on Similarity Relations for Imbalance datasets) is used in a classical task in the branch of the Civil Engineering: predict if structural failure depends on the connector (canals) or concrete capacity of connectors. The use of similarity relations allows applying this method in the case of mixed data (features with discrete or real domains). The experimental results show a satisfactory performance of the IRBASIR-Imb algorithm in comparison to others such as C4.5.

Keywords: Classification rules · Similarity relations · Imbalanced data sets

1 Introduction

Learning classification rules is a classic machine learning problem. The construction of classifiers is one of the techniques commonly used in data mining (Wu and Kumar [20]). Most methods try to generate rules following a sequential covering strategy. These methods learn from a training set consisting of objects described by attribute conditions and the decision feature (class) (Mitchell [17]). Among the classical algorithms for solving this problem is the ID3 and its extension, called C4.5, to the case of features with continue domains which induce decision trees.

Rough sets have proven to be effective for data analysis; hence, the machine learning is one of the areas where they have aroused great interest. The Rough Set Theory (RST) was introduced by Z. Pawlak [18].

Different algorithms have been developed for the discovery of classification rules (decision rules) based on rough sets. Among the best known are LEM2 (Learning from Examples Module v2), this algorithm is part of the data mining system LERS (*Learning from Examples based on Rough Sets*) (Grzymala [11]) and IRBASIR (Filiberto, Bello et al. [10]).

© Springer International Publishing AG 2016
J.C. Figueroa-García et al. (Eds.): WEA 2016, CCIS 657, pp. 65–73, 2016.
DOI: 10.1007/978-3-319-50880-1_6

This article presents a study of the method for discovering classification rules for decision systems with mixed data, i.e., for the case of imbalance datasets, IRBASIR-Imb. Imbalance datasets are those where the quantity of examples in the classes has a high difference. Classical learning methods do not work properly in the case of imbalance training set, the classifiers are biased towards the majority classes and they usually have problems to classify correctly new unseen objects from the minority class. Among the methods reported in the literature with better results in the pre-processing of these data types found: SMOTE (Chawkla [4]), SMOTE-Tomek Links (Batista [2]), SMOTE-ENN (Batista [2]), Borderline-SMOTE1 (Han [12]) and Safe-Level-SMOTE (Bunkhumpornpat [5]).

2   The Quality of Similarity Measure in the Rough Set Theory for Imbalanced Data

The measure quality of similarity computes the degree to which the similarity between objects according to the condition features is similar to the similarity according to the decision feature. The measure of quality of similarity of a decision system (DS) with a universe of M objects is defined in (Filiberto, Bello et al. [11]) in (1):

$$\theta(DS) = \left\{ \frac{\sum_{i=1}^{m} \varphi(x)}{M} \right\} \tag{1}$$

The goal is to maximize the value of θ. The term $\varphi(x)$ is defined by expression (2):

$$\varphi(x) = \frac{|N_1(x) \cap N_2(x)|}{0.5 * |N_1(x)| + 0.5 * |N_2(x)|}; \quad 0 \leq \varphi(x) \leq 1 \tag{2}$$

This denotes the degree of similarity between the sets $N_1(x)$ and $N_2(x)$, for the object x. Sets N_1 and N_2 are defined by the expressions (3) and (4):

$$N_1(x) = \{y : xR_1y\} \tag{3}$$

$$N_2(x) = \{y : xR_2y\} \tag{4}$$

where similarity relations R_1 and R_2 are defined in the following form:

$$xR_1y \; if \; and \; only \; if \; F_1(x,y) \geq \varepsilon_1 \tag{5}$$

$$xR_2y \; if \; and \; only \; if \; F_2(x, y) \geq \varepsilon_2 \tag{6}$$

The function F_1 is defined by expression (7) taking into account the conditions features of the decision system; and F_2 is a function that allows comparing the values of the decision feature. In the case of classification problems, the function F_2 is defined by the expression (9):

$$F_1(x, y) = \sum_{i=1}^{n} w_i * \partial_i(x_i, y_i) \tag{7}$$

$$\partial_i(x_i, y_i) = \begin{cases} 1 - \frac{|x_i - y_i|}{max(D_i) - min(D_i)} & \text{if } i \text{ is continuous} \\ 1 & \text{if } i \text{ is discrete and } x_i = y_i \\ 0 & \text{if } i \text{ is discrete and } x_i \neq y_i \end{cases} \tag{8}$$

$$F_2(x, y) = \begin{cases} 1 & \text{if } x = y \\ 0 & \text{other case} \end{cases} \tag{9}$$

Equation (1) is modified for imbalanced datasets (see (10), (11)). The purpose is to modify the measure quality of similarity in order to make more sensitive it to the objects in the minority class. These changes affect the set of weights, because this measure is used as the function for evaluating the quality of the particles in the search method.

$$\theta(DS) = \left\{ \frac{\sum_{\forall x \in U} \varphi * (x)}{|U|} \right\} \tag{10}$$

$$\varphi * (x) = \begin{cases} \varphi(x) & \text{if } x \in C+ \\ \varphi(x)^2 & \text{if } x \in C- \end{cases} \tag{11}$$

where $C+$ *and* $C-$ are the sets of objects belonging to the majority minority classes.

3   An Algorithm to Generate Classification Rules Based on Similarity Relations

IRBASIR (Filiberto, Bello et al. [9]) is an algorithm for inducing classification rules that allows discovering knowledge from decision systems with mixed data, because the difference between discrete and continuous domains only lies in the function of comparison to be used for each feature; therefore, it does not require making any discretization process, before the learning process or during the learning process such as C4.5. This algorithm finds a set of rules following a sequential covering strategy, which builds similarity classes of objects in the decision system. The similarity classes group together similar objects, not identical, according to a similarity relation R. Similarity relations do not induce a partition of universe U, but generate similarity classes to any object. The similarity class of x, according to the similarity relation R is denoted by R(x) and is defined as $R(x) = \{y \in U : xRy\}$. This is read as "the set of objects in the universe U that are similar to object x according to the relation R".

The algorithm induces rules of the form *If P then Q*, but in this case the condition part P has the form $\sum w_i * \partial_i \geq \varepsilon$, where wi is the weight of the feature i, $\partial_i()$ is the comparison function for the features i, and ε is a threshold.

4 Experimental Results

The experimental framework, including the benchmark data-sets and the statistical tests, used to carry out the comparison of the performance of the IRBASIR-Imb algorithm and the algorithm C4.5. We have considered 22 data-sets from the UCI repository, with low imbalanced rate. The description of these data-sets appears in Table 1.

Table 1. Description of the data-sets used in the experiments

Data-sets	# Ex	#Attributes	%Class(min., maj.)
Glass1	214	9	(35.51, 64.49)
Ecoli0vs1	220	7	(35.00, 65.00)
Wisconsin	683	9	(35.00, 65.00)
Pima	768	8	(34.84, 66.16)
Iris0	150	4	(33.33, 66.67)
Glass0	214	9	(32.71, 67.29)
Yeast 1	1484	8	(28.91, 71.09)
Vehicle 1	846	18	(28.37, 71.63)
Vehicle 2	846	18	(28.37, 71.63)
Vehicle 3	846	18	(28.37, 71.63)
Haberman	306	3	(27.42, 73.58)
glass0123vs456	214	9	(23.83, 76.17)
vehicle0	846	18	(23.64, 76.36)
ecoli1	336	7	(22.92, 77.08)
new-thyroid2	215	5	(16.89, 83.11)
new-thyroid1	215	5	(16.28, 83.72)
ecoli2	336	7	(15.48, 84.52)
segment0	2308	19	(14.26, 85.74)
glass6	214	9	(13.55, 86.45)
yeast3	1484	8	(10.98, 89.02)
ecoli3	336	7	(10.88, 89.12)
page-blocks0	5472	10	(10.23, 89.77)

The sets were divided in order to perform a 5 folds cross validation, 80% for training and 20% for testing, where the 5 test data-sets form the whole set. For each data-set we consider the average results of the five partitions. Partitions were carried out in such a way that the quantity of elements in each class remained uniform (Fernández [8]), available at KEEL webpage (http://www.keel.es/datasets.php, (Alcalá [1])).

The performance of machine learning algorithms is typically evaluated using predictive accuracy. However, this is not appropriate when the data is imbalanced and/or when the costs of different errors vary markedly (Chawla [6]).

The error rate of the classification of the rules of the minority class is 2 or 3 times greater than the rules that identify the examples of the majority class and that the examples of the minority class are less likely to be predicted than the examples of the majority one. Because of this, instead of using the error rate (or accuracy), in the context of imbalanced problems more appropriate metrics are considered.

An appropriate metric that could be used to measure the performance of classification over imbalanced data-sets is the Receiver Operating Characteristic (ROC) graphics (Bradley [4]) where the tradeoff between the benefits (TPrate) and costs (FPrate) can be seen, and shows that the capacity of any classifier cannot increase the number of true positives without also increasing the false positives. The Area Under the ROC Curve (AUC) (Huang and Ling [14]) is the probability of correctly identifying which of the two stimuli is noise and which is signal plus noise. AUC provides a single-number summary for the performance of learning algorithms and it has been used in the context of imbalance datasets such as has shown in (Tong and Y.C. [19]).

In this experimental study, we have used the data-sets resulting from preprocessing mechanisms based on SMOTE (Synthetic Minority Over-sampling TEchnique), a well acknowledged over-sampling method (Chawla [7]) (Tong and Y.C. [19]), (Khoshgoftaar [16]); that is, the SMOTE algorithm and some hybrid approaches: SMOTE-TomekLinks, SMOTE-ENN, Borderline- SMOTE1 and Safe-Level-SMOTE. The results of the experimental study is shows in Tables 2, which presents the AUC's results for C4.5 algorithm applied to edited data sets and IRBASIR-Imb algorithm for the original imbalances data-sets.

Table 2. Results of Friedman's statistical test

Algorithms	Ranking
Smote	3.6364
Smote-TomekLink	3.6591
Smote-ENN	3.7955
Borderline-SMOTE1	3.9318
SafeLevel-SMOTE1	3.9773
IRBASIR-Imb	2

In order to compare the results, we use a multiple comparison test to find the best preprocessing algorithm, in Table 3 we can observe that the best ranking is obtained by our proposal (IRBASIR-Imb). A Iman–Davenport test [15] is carried out (employing F-distribution with 5 and 105 degrees of freedom) in order to find statistical differences among the algorithms, obtaining a p-value near to zero. In this manner, Table 4 shows the results of the Holm procedure (Holm [13]) for comparing our porposal (IRBASIR-Imb) with the remaining ones.

Table 3. AUC's results for: C4.5 after edit the data-sets with different edition methods and IRBASIR-Imb's results over original data-sets

Data-sets	Smote	Smote-TomekLink	Smote-ENN	Borderline-SMOTE1	SafeLevel-SMOTE	IRBASIR-Imb
Glass1	0.74	0.77	0.72	0.75	0.71	**0,82**
Ecoli0vs1	**0.98**	**0.98**	**0.98**	**0.98**	**0.98**	**0,98**
Wisconsin	0.96	0.96	0.94	0.96	0.95	**0,98**
Pima	0.71	0.69	0.71	0.71	0.73	**0,74**
Iris0	0.99	0.99	0.99	0.99	0.99	**1,00**
Glass0	0.78	0.80	0.81	0.77	0.77	**0,86**
Yeast 1	**0.71**	0.68	**0.71**	**0.71**	**0.71**	0,67
Vehicle 1	0.68	**0.76**	0.75	0.71	0.75	0,68
Vehicle 2	0.96	0.95	0.95	0.96	0.94	**0,98**
Vehicle 3	0.71	**0.73**	0.72	0.69	**0.73**	**0,73**
Haberman	0.64	0.59	0.65	0.62	0.64	**0,66**
glass0123vs456	0.89	0.89	0.92	0.87	0.90	**0,95**
vehicle0	0.94	0.92	0.93	0.94	0.93	**0,97**
ecoli1	0.89	0.89	0.87	0.89	**0.91**	**0,91**
new-thyroid2	0.93	0.94	0.92	0.95	0.93	**0,99**
new-thyroid1	0.94	0.96	0.95	0.96	0.95	**0,99**
ecoli2	**0.94**	0.89	0.88	0.89	0.89	0,93
segment0	**0.99**	**0.99**	**0.99**	0.98	**0.99**	**0,99**
glass6	0.89	0.88	0.92	0.91	0.87	**0,95**
yeast3	0.90	0.91	0.91	0.89	0.88	**0,91**
ecoli3	0.86	0.85	0.84	0.79	0.86	**0,90**
page-blocks0	**0.94**	0.94	0.94	0.94	0.90	0,90

Table 4. Holm's test for $\alpha = 0.05$, IRBASIR-Imb is the control method

i	Algorithms	z = (R0 − Ri)/SE	p	Holm	Hypothesis
5	SafeLevel-SMOTE1	3.50533	0.000456	0.01	Rejected
4	Borderline-SMOTE1	3.424748	0.000615	0.0125	Rejected
3	Smote-ENN	3.183001	0.001458	0.016667	Rejected
2	Smote-TomekLink	2.941254	0.003269	0.025	Rejected
1	Smote	2.900963	0.00372	0.05	Rejected

As we can observe the method imbalance-IRBASIR shows results statistically superiors to the methods C4.5 + Borderline-SMOTE1, C4.5 + Smote, C4.5 + Smot-ENN, C4.5 + SafeLevel-SMOTE and C4.5 + Smote-TomekLinks.

5   Applications of the Method in the Solution of a Real Problem

In this section a real problem related with the branch of the Civil Engineering is solved, using the following procedure:

Step 1:   Build the decision system for the application domain

Step 2:   Determine the function of global similarity (it was used the expressions 7 and 9) and the local comparison functions for the features (it was used the expression 8)

Step 3:   Establish the thresholds of wanted similarity (values recommended $\varepsilon_1 = 0.85$)

Step 4:   Calculate the quality of similarity measure (using PSO + RST)

Step 5:   Apply the method IRBASIR-Imb

The steel-concrete composite structures have been widely used in the construction of bridges and buildings from the last Century to date; in them the benefits of each material are exploited, which makes them very efficient and economical.

An essential component of a composite beam is the connection between section steel and reinforced concrete slab. This connection is secured by connectors that are installed on the top flange of the steel beam, usually by welding, before concreting of the slab. The connectors ensure that the various materials constituting the composite section act together.

A remarkable number of experimental studies have been developed to deepen in the study of the behavior of the connections. Specifically, the rehearsals of connectors of the push-out type have been an important way for the evaluation of the influence of different parameters in the behavior of the same ones, as well as obtaining the formulations that allow predicting their resistant capacity.

The problem is to predict if structural failure is by the connector (canals) or concrete; the conector is responsible of ensuring the connection between compound steel-concret structures. The description of the dataset is shown in Table 5, which was formed from the results of the research reported in (Bonilla [3]). The output variable is the structural failure that may be effected by the concrete or the connector used.

Table 5. Description of the data-set used in the experiment

Dataset	# Ex	%Class (min, maj)	Input variable	Output var.
Canals	27	(37.04, 62.96)	Thickness of the soul (w) Thickness of the wing (t) Longitude of the connector (L) Height of the connector (H) Resistance of the concrete to the compression (fc)	structural failure (connector or concrete)

To solve this problem, the IRBASIR-Imb algorithms will be used with the quality of similarity measure in the rough set theory for imbalanced data proposed in (Yaima and Bello [21]) and explained previously. An experimental study for the data-set canals is performed. (Table 6)

Table 6. AUC's results for: C4.5 after edit the data-set with different edition methods and IRBASIR-Imb's results over original data-set.

Data-set	Smote	Smote-TomekLink	Smote-ENN	Borderline-SMOTE1	SafeLevel-SMOTE	IRBASIR-Imb
Canals	78.33	75.00	66.66	78.33	78.33	**82.66**

6 Conclusions

In this article has been studied the IRBASIR-Imb algorithm for the generation of classification rules from imbalanced data-sets. The similarity relations are computed using the measure quality of similarity, thus, allowing dispense of preprocessing mechanisms on data sets. According to results presented in this work, the proposal is statistically significant to the methods C4.5 + Smote, C4.5 + Smote-TomekLink, C4.5 + Smote-ENN, C4.5 + Borderline-SMOTE1, C4.5 + SafeLevel-SMOTE, in terms of classification accuracy.

This method could be applied in the case of discrete and continue decision feature. Its application to solve a classification problem of branch of the Civil Engineering has shown satisfactory results.

References

1. Alcalá, J., et al.: KEEL data-mining software tool: data set repository, integration of algorithms and experimental analysis framework. J. Multi.-Valued Log. Soft Comput. **17**, 255–287 (2010)
2. Batista, G.E., et al.: A study of the behaviour of several methods for balancing machine learning training data. SIGKDD Explor. **6**(1), 20–29 (2004)
3. Bonilla, J.D.: Estudio del comportamiento de conectores tipo perno de estructuras compuestas de hormigón y acero mediante modelación numérica. Ph.D., Universidad Central "Marta Abreu" de Las Villas Santa Clara
4. Bradley, A.P.: The use of the area under the ROC curve in the evaluation of machine learning algorithms. Pattern Recogn. **30**(7), 1145–1159 (1997)
5. Bunkhumpornpat, C., Sinapiromsaran, K., Lursinsap, C.: Safe-Level-SMOTE: safe-level-synthetic minority over-sampling TEchnique for handling the class imbalanced problem. In: Theeramunkong, T., Kijsirikul, B., Cercone, N., Ho, T.-B. (eds.) PAKDD 2009. LNCS (LNAI), vol. 5476, pp. 475–482. Springer, Berlin, Heidelberg (2009). doi:10.1007/978-3-642-01307-2_43
6. Chawla, N.V., et al.: Editorial: special issue on learning from imbalanced data sets. SIGKDD Explor. **6**(1), 1–6 (2004)

7. Chawla, N.V., et al.: SMOTE: synthetic minority over-sampling technique. J. Artif. Intell. Res. **16**, 321–357 (2002)
8. Fernández, A., et al.: A study of the behaviour of linguistic fuzzy rule based classification systems in the framework of imbalanced data-sets. Fuzzy Sets Syst. **159**(18), 2378–2398 (2008)
9. Filiberto, Y., Bello, R., et al.: Algoritmo para el aprendizaje de reglas de clasificación basado en la teoría de los conjuntos aproximados extendida. Revista DYNA **78**, 62–70 (2011)
10. Filiberto, Y., Bello, R., et al.: A method to built similarity relations into extended Rough set theory. In: Proceedings of the 10th International Conference on Intelligent Systems Design and Applications (ISDA2010), Cairo, Egipto (2010)
11. Grzymala-Busse, J.W.: A new version of the rule induction system LERS. Fundamenta Informaticae **31**, 27–39 (1997)
12. Han, H., Wang, W.-Y., Mao, B.-H.: Borderline-SMOTE: a new over-sampling method in imbalanced data sets learning. In: Huang, D.-S., Zhang, X.-P., Huang, G.-B. (eds.) ICIC 2005. LNCS, vol. 3644, pp. 878–887. Springer, Berlin, Heidelberg (2005). doi:10.1007/11538059_91
13. Holm, S.: A simple sequentially rejective multiple test procedure. J. Stat. **6**, 65–70 (1979)
14. Huang, J., Ling, C.X.: Using AUC and accuracy in evaluating learning algorithms. IEEE Trans. Knowl. Data Eng. **17**(3), 299–310 (2005)
15. Iman, R., Davenport, J.: Approximations of the critical region of the friedman statistic. Commun. Stat. Theor. Method, Part A **9**, 571–595 (1980)
16. Khoshgoftaar, T.M., Van Hulse, J.: Comparing boosting and bagging techniques with noisy and imbalanced data. IEEE Trans. Syst. Man Cybern. Part A Syst. Hum. **41**, 552–568 (2010)
17. Mitchell, T.: Machine Learning. McGraw Hill, New York (1997)
18. Pawlak, Z.: Rough Sets. Int. J. Comput. Inf. Sci. **11**, 341–356 (1982)
19. Tong, L., Chang, Y.C.: Determining the optimal resampling strategy for a classification model with imbalanced data using design of experiments and response surface methodologies. Expert Syst. Appl. **38**, 4222–4227 (2011)
20. Wu, X., Kumar, V.: The Top Ten Algorithms in Data Mining. Data Mining and Knowledge Discovery Series. Chapman & Hall/CRC, Boca Raton (2001)
21. Yaima., F., Bello, R., et al.: Método para el aprendizaje de reglas de clasificación para conjuntos de datos no balanceados. Revista Cubana de Ciencias Informáticas (RCCI) **5**(4)

Price Direction Prediction on High Frequency Data Using Deep Belief Networks

Jaime Humberto Niño-Peña[(⊠)] and Germán Jairo Hernández-Pérez

Universidad Nacional de Colombia, Bogotá, Colombia
{jhninop, gjhernandezp}@unal.edu.co

Abstract. This paper presents the use of Deep Belief Networks (DBN) for direction forecasting on financial time series, particularly those associated to the High Frequency Domain. The paper introduces some of the key concepts of the DBN, presents the methodology, results and its discussion. DBNs achieves better performance for particular configurations and training times were acceptable, however if they want to be pursued in real applications, windows sizes should be evaluated.

Keywords: Deep Belief Networks · Stocks forecasting · High frequency data

1 Introduction

Financial Markets are part of the financial system and they facilitate the recording, clearing and settlement of financial transactions of traded instruments between corporations, governments and individuals [1, 2]. Financial markets facilitates to their participants: transaction cost reductions while exchanged a financial asset; improvements in liquidity provision, which means the availability of funds to either buy or sell any traded financial instrument at any given time; facilitates price discovery, resulting in narrowing spreads between sell and buy prices [2].

Market agents intentions are recorded in the Limit Order Book (LOB). For any financial instrument, LOB registers buy and sell intentions as they are generated from traders. A record contains a timestamp, a quantity of the instrument offered (bided) and a price of the offer (bid). LOB data is ordered by price and timestamp. On the offer side ascendingly, the opposite for the bid size. To equal prices, time determines which go first. A graphic representation of LOB data is shown in Fig. 1.

In addition to LOB data, transaction data, also known as tick by tick data, is the other major source of financial data. Transactions are agreements in price which ends up in the exchange of an asset for a price. The quantity exchange is usually quoted as volume within the financial community. Any transaction has a timestamp, a quantity and a price [3, 4]. Both LOB data and tick by tick data are discrete in time, and not uniformly distributed. However, they can be aggregated on equal time intervals as we do in this paper (periods of fifteen seconds as shown in Sect. 3).

On the other hand, High Frequency Trading (HFT) refers to the activity conducted by automated markets agents (algorithms) to perform trades. It is characterized by the speed that is usually in order of seconds to microseconds. HFT does not have an standard definition around the world, by now is one of the key factors [5, 6].

© Springer International Publishing AG 2016
J.C. Figueroa-García et al. (Eds.): WEA 2016, CCIS 657, pp. 74–83, 2016.
DOI: 10.1007/978-3-319-50880-1_7

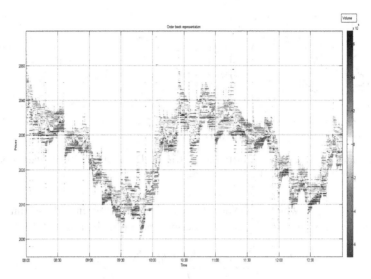

Fig. 1. Illustration of LOB data, taken from [7]

Predicting Financial Time Series remains a difficult task, due to the complexity of this kind of data [8–10]. Different approaches have been using while modelling Financial Time Series, including both stochastic and machine learning techniques. Deep Learning has emerged recently as a superior technique when dealing with classification problems in different domains [11–13]. Given its performance some works has been developed to target time series modelling in general and FTS in particular [10, 14–18]. As a result, the goal of this project is to build and test a prediction model based on Deep Belief Networks (DBN), having as an entries the two time series illustrated before.

The paper continues as follows, Sect. 2 will introduce key concepts on DBNs, then the methodology is presented, to be followed by the results, their discussion and the conclusions.

2   Deep Belief Networks

A DBN is a probabilistic generative model composed by an input layer, an output layer and in between, multiple stacked layers of Restricted Boltzmann Machine (RBM). Where each RBM is compose of two layers, one visible, and other hidden. This model was proposed by Hinton [12] and graphically can be described in Fig. 2.

Training of this network is done in two steps, one called unsupervised pre-training and the second called supervised fine tuning. In [12], Hinton presents an efficient approach to train this network in a greedy layer by layer manner.

Hidden layers of this networks are compose of RBMs, which are bipartite graphs, with one set called visible units and the other hidden units. It is restricted because there are no connections between units of the same layer (visible, hidden) [19, 20]. The standard RBM is binary valued for both hidden and visible units, having a weight

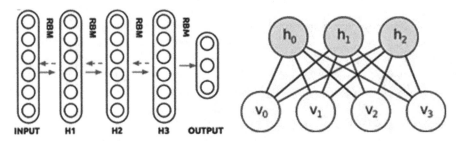

Fig. 2. DBN with 3 hidden layers of RBM and out output layer, taken from [18]

Fig. 3. Diagram of a RBM, taken from [18]

matrix $W_{mxn} = (w_{i,j})$, which associates the connections between hidden units h_j and visible ones v_i, as shown in Fig. 3. The energy function is defined as [19, 20]:

$$E(v,h) = -\sum_i a_i v_i - \sum_j b_j h_j - \sum_i \sum_j v_i w_{i,j} h_j \tag{1}$$

Due to the restriction in the graph, the hidden unit activations are mutually independent, given the visible unit activation and vices versa, as a result:

$$P(v|h) = \prod_{i=1}^{m} P(v_i|h)$$
$$P(h|v) = \prod_{j=1}^{n} P(h_j|v) \tag{2}$$

The individual activation probabilities are given by:

$$P(h_j = 1|v) = \sigma\left(b_j + \sum_{i=1}^{m} w_{ij} v_i\right)$$
$$P(v_i = 1|h) = \sigma\left(a_i + \sum_{j=1}^{n} w_{ij} h_j\right) \tag{3}$$

where σ is the activation function (sigmoid, tanh).

These networks learn to extract a deep hierarchical representation of the training data, by modelling the joint distribution between observed vector x and the ℓ hidden layers h^k, as shown in [12, 13, 19]:

$$P(x, h^1, \ldots, h^\ell) = \left(\prod_{k=0}^{\ell-2} P(h^k|h^{k+1})\right) P(h^{\ell-1}, h^\ell)(1), \tag{4}$$

where $x = h^0$, $P(h^k|h^{k+1})$ is the conditional probability of visible on hidden units at level k, and $P(h^{\ell-1}, h^\ell)$ is the visible hidden joint distribution in top level RBM.

The training process is done in the following way:

1. Train the first layer as an RBM that models the raw input $x = h^0$ as its visible layer
2. Use the first layer to obtain a representation of the input that will be used for the second layer
3. Train the second layer as a RBM, taking the transformed data (samples or mean activations) as training samples
4. Iterate 2 and 3 for the number of layers. Each layers should propagate upward either samples or mean activations values
5. Fine tuning all the parameters (W matrix for each layer) with respect to a proxy for DBN log like hood or with respect to a supervised training criteria, for example a linear classifier at the top of the DBN architecture

In this work, the fine tuning was done using gradient descent, using a logistic regression classifier on the top of the DBN. Unsupervised pre-training allows the model to get better values for W, which results in finding a better local optima. The supervised fine tuning phase allows the model to adjust better the initial weights (W) found on the pre-training phase [18].

3 Methodology

3.1 Dataset

The dataset was constructed using Facebook stock data. Dataset includes dates from 2015-08-25 to 2015-10-30, with the tick by tick data and LOB data (first 5 lines for each side)[1], both sampled every 5 s. Data was aggregated every 15 s. Tick by tick data was transformed to a candlestick representation[2], which is a time series of open, high, low and close prices. For each timestamp, the volume[3] was represented as a boxplot series, that is minimum, quantile 25, median, quantile 75 and maximum volume exhibit during the time frame.

On the order hand, the order book was represented as follows: minimum, median and maximum values for both ask and bid sides. For entries with the same price, the maximum volume was chosen. In the case of the selling orders (ask side of the book), the volume was multiplied by one. In addition, two variables were added, the returns, measured between closing prices of the candlestick series, and the volatility measured as the difference between the higher and lower prices traded in the time frame.

The prediction column (label) was composed of 1 when the return for the $X_{t-1} > 0$, 0 otherwise. Finally the dataset was limited in time from 2015-09-09 13:50:00 to 2015-10-28 10:43:00, since there was some missing data outside this period, as shown in Fig. 4. The dataset contains nearly 43,283 periods of 15 s. Since the input of the

---

[1] It means five sell intentions and five buy intentions, recorded every five seconds. If something changed in the LOB within the 5 s interval it is not registered.

[2] Candlestick is an ancient representation from rice Japanese traders in the 1700's. Widely used by technical traders to analyze price formations (Luca, 2000).

[3] Traded quantity of Facebook stock for each 15-seconds interval.

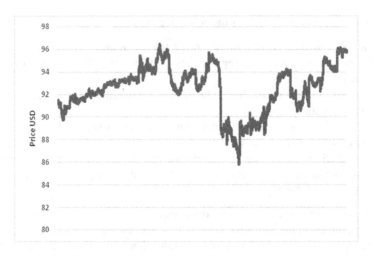

Fig. 4. Closing prices evolution for the FB stock within 15 s time series

Table 1. Binary Vector representation of the raw data

90 pos	60pos	90 pos	60 pos	80 pos	150 pos	20 pos	20 pos
Ask vol	Ask price	Bid vol	Bid price	Traded price	Traded vol	Volatility	Returns

DBN is binary (not limited to), each row was converted to a binary vector with 570 elements. The total size of the input dataset was 43,283 × 570 (Table 1).

4 Experiment Setup

Network architecture: two different network architectures were tested. One five layer (570-190-100-50-25) (A), and the other was a 4 layers (570-390-195-98) (B), all with one output. Package Darch[4] for R was used to conduct the experiments. Batch sizes, epochs were set up at 10, and parameter K (Contrastive Divergence for Fine Tuning) was changed to 1.

Experiments were conducted on Win Server 2008 56 GB RAM 4 Cores. During experimentation K parameter was detected as an important factor for long training times. $K = 1$ is a good setup following recommendation from Hinton's paper. 20000 observations were used as validation data and testing data (10,000 each) and the other part of the dataset as training data. Targets or labels correspond to the real direction of the time series in time $t + 1$ given prices in time t.

---

[4] https://cran.r-project.org/web/packages/darch/index.html.

5   Results

5.1   Training Times

There are several parameters that impact training times, including architecture deep, training sizes among others included within the training algorithms. Along these, K parameter of training of the RBM increases training times, following by epochs and batch sizes. For the three different architectures, Table 2 illustrates time consumption per architecture, along with MSE measures for both training and validation sets.

Table 2. Training times and training errors for different architectures and training sizes

DBN	Pre-training	Fine tuning	Data set training size	Pre training error last epoc	MSE on training set	MSE on validation
5-layers-A	4'18"	4'39"	23,283 × 570	0.005	0.2510	0.2427
4-layers-B	12'01"	16'38"	23,283 × 570	0.0106	0.2501	0.2405

5.2   Classification Performance Measures

Given the fact that we are presenting a classification problem for a predicted direction (1: long, price going up; 0: short, price going down), it is important to state the measures to evaluate, which are shown in Table 3.

Table 3. Source [21, 22]

Measure	Formulation
Accuracy (ACC)	$\frac{TP+TN}{TP+TN+FP+FN}$
True Positive Rate (TPR)	$\frac{TP}{TP+FN}$
True Negative Rate (TNR)	$\frac{TN}{FP+TN}$
Positive Predictive Value (PPV), for our case long predictions	$\frac{TP}{TP+FP}$
Negative Predictive Value (NPV), for our case short predictions	$\frac{TN}{TN+FN}$

TP stands for True Positives, TN for True Negatives, FP for False Positives and FN for False Negatives. Table 4 shows the results for the one-step ahead prediction

Table 4. Summary of results for the one-step-ahead prediction

	DBN 5-Layers-A	DBN 4-Layers-B	Linear model
ACC	**0.465**	**0.501**	**0.508**
TPR	0.666	0.487	0.573
TNR	0.326	0.578	0.411
PPV	0.405	0.407	0.592
NPV	0.586	0.590	0.392

Overall results are not really encouraging, since the overall accuracy is near by 50%. However on individual bases (up-only/down-only) prediction, there are a better results. Many different configurations were tested, including direction forecast for different steps ahead. Variations also include drastic changes in the training size dataset, because changes in prices (returns) in high frequency data exhibit a behavior similar to data

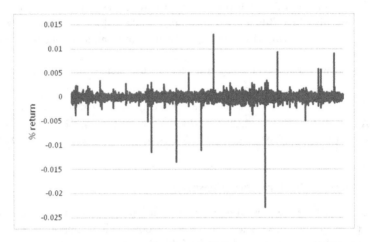

Fig. 5. Returns evolution for the FB stock within the selected time frame. Calculated over 15 s closing prices.

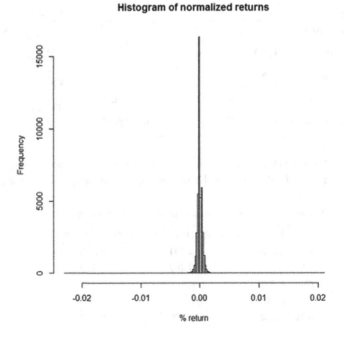

Fig. 6. Histogram of normalized returns over closing prices each fifteen seconds.

normally distributed (see Fig. 5). Most of the drastic changes in return among prices occur between different trading days, when some news may affect stock prices.

As seen in Fig. 6, normalized returns fit very well to a normal distribution with mean zero and a small variance. Under this fact it is possible to experiment with small training datasets, since most of the dynamics may be already capture with smaller datasets, rather than larger ones. This dynamic is valid within the high frequency domain but not necessarily in the low frequency one (minutes, hours, days, months), where more notable changes in closing prices could be seen.

Table 5 illustrates the best prediction for each DBN configuration, and some of the setups tested, including direction prediction up to 5 steps ahead, it means 5 periods of 15 s each. This kind of setup produces better results in the overall accuracy of the classifier, with the constraints of a more frequent retrain of the model as new data is becoming available.

Table 5. Summary of best measures for testing errors among different setups

DBN	Training size	Down		Up		Total precision	
		Step ahead	TNR	Step ahead	TPR	Step ahead	ACC
5-layers-A	50	1	0.48	3	**0.75**	3	**0.62**
	75	3	0.54	3	0.67	3	0.61
	100	**4**	**0.62**	4	0.59	4	0.60
	125	2	0.56	2	0.45	2	0.51
	150	3	0.52	3	0.50	3	0.51
4-layers-B	50	4	0.52	4	0.52	4	0.52
	75	5	0.51	5	0.50	5	0.50
	100	5	0.59	5	0.50	5	0.55
	125	4	0.54	4	0.54	4	0.54
	150	2	0.52	5	0.61	5	0.57

6   Discussion

Given the setups, experiments produced, dataset, there are many different angles to examine the results. The first one is related to the dataset itself. As observed in Fig. 4 prices as moving-up trend, therefore our expectation was to get better results while predicting an up direction. In general, results evidence that, however for the general 4-layers configuration (B) that was not the case. Any model should be designed to work in any condition, for our case trending markets (up or down) as well as not trending ones. Having said that it is necessary to include such dynamics within the training dataset, in order to avoid or reduce any bias on the model's output.

Another interesting fact is related to the training dataset size. Our intuition of reducing the size of the training dataset given the distribution of the returns did in fact improve the results of both classifiers (A and B). As mentioned previously, this fact could be valid in the high frequency domain, generating another interesting point for future works: how often should be re-trained the model?

Regarding to data representation, it is important to take into account two different factors:

1. The binary characteristic of the DBN used that is it works with binary data. There are continuous implementation of DBN that could be worth to test in order to evaluate performance.
2. Converting all of the characteristic to binary format (returns, volatility, volume, LOB and tick by tick data) create a big sparse matrix something desirable for the Deep Learning paradigm, but not necessarily useful, particularly when working with nominal prices as shown in a [4]. A better approach to represent nominal prices should be taken for both LOB and tick by tick data.

7 Conclusions

DBNs training times are very sensitive to parameters of the training algorithm, as well as dimensionality of the data representation (570). For the high frequency domain, experimental evidence of this work suggest small sizes for training datasets, which implies a more often re-training of the model, therefore training time became an important issue to work with, particularly for any real implementation of this technique.

Results taken the traditional approach of large training dataset looks discouraging, however working with smaller datasets appears to yield better overall performance, regardless the bias of the dataset (up in our case). High Frequency Domain data exhibit different dynamics from Low Frequency Domain. As a result, it is important to work in how to better represent these data, including training dataset sizes.

For this particular dataset, DBN over perform results of the linear model when using small datasets. When using the large dataset, DBN do as good as the Linear Model. This finding supports the idea of small dataset training sizes for High Frequency Data in finance, which implies very frequent re-training procedures of the model, as new data became available.

References

1. Bank for International Settlements, Settlement Systems Technical Committee of the International Organization of Securities Commissions Principles for financial market infrastructures, Basel, Switzerland, March 2011
2. Darskuviene, V.: "Fininical Markets." Leonardo Da Vinci Transfer of Innovation Program, pp. 1–140 (2010)
3. Sandoval, J.: High Frequency Exchange rate prediction using dynamic bayesian networks over the limit order book information. Universidad Nacional de Colombia (2015)
4. Arévalo, A., Niño, J., Hernández, G., Sandoval, J.: High-frequency trading strategy based on deep neural networks. In: Huang, D., Han, K., Hussain, A. (eds.) ICIC 2016. LNCS, vol. 9773, pp. 424–436. Springer, Heidelberg (2016). doi:10.1007/978-3-319-42297-8_40
5. ESMA, "High-frequency trading activity in EU equity markets" (2014)

6. UK's Gov Office, "The Future of Computer Trading in Financial Markets An International Perspective" (2012)
7. Sandoval, J., Nino, G., Hernandez, G., Cruz, A.: Detecting informative patterns in financial market trends based on visual analysis. Procedia Comput. Sci. **80**, 752–761 (2016)
8. Ohlsson, S.: Stellan Ohlsson: deep learning: how the mind overrides experience. Sci. Educ. **21**, 1381–1392 (2012). Cambridge University Press, New York
9. Tay, F.E.H., Cao, L.: Application of support vector machines in financial time series forecasting. Omega **29**, 309–317 (2001)
10. Ortega, L.F.: A neuro-wavelet method for the forecasting of financial time series. In: Proceedings of the World Congress on Engineering and Computer Science, vol. I (2012)
11. Schmidhuber, J.: Deep Learning in Neural Networks: An Overview, vol. 61, pp. 1–66. arXiv Preprint arXiv1404.7828 (2014)
12. Hinton, G.E., Osindero, S., Teh, Y.-W.: Communicated by Yann Le Cun a fast learning algorithm for deep belief nets. Neural Comput. **18**, 1527–1554 (2006)
13. Hinton, G.: A practical guide to training restricted Boltzmann machines. Comput. (Long Beach Calif.) **9**, 1 (2010)
14. Zhu, C., Yin, J., Li, Q.: A stock decision support system based on DBNs⋆. J. Comput. Inf. Syst. **2**, 883–893 (2014)
15. Längkvist, M., Karlsson, L., Loutfi, A.: A review of unsupervised feature learning and deep learning for time-series modelling. Pattern Recogn. Lett. **42**(1), 11–24 (2014)
16. Kuremoto, T., Kimura, S., Kobayashi, K., Obayashi, M.: Time series forecasting using a deep belief network with restricted Boltzmann machines. Neurocomputing **137**, 47–56 (2014)
17. Dalto, M.: Deep neural networks for time series prediction with applications in ultra-short-term wind forecasting (2015)
18. Lai, A., Li, M.K., Pong, F.W.: Forecasting Trade Direction and Size of Future Contracts Using Deep Belief Network (2012)
19. Salakhutdinov, R., Hinton, G.: Deep Boltzmann machines. In: Artificial Intelligence and Statistics, vol. 5, no. 3, pp. 448–455 (2009)
20. Bengio, Y.: Learning deep architectures for AI. Found. Trends Mach. Learn. **2**(1), 1–127 (2009)
21. Fawcett, T.: An introduction to ROC analysis. Pattern Recogn. Lett. **27**(8), 861–874 (2006)
22. Powers, D.: Evaluation: from precision, recall and F-measure to ROC, informedness, markedness & correlation. J. Mach. Learn. Technol. **2**(1), 37–63 (2011)

Search Techniques for Automated Proposal of Data Mining Schemes

Roman Neruda[✉]

Institute of Computer Science Academy of Sciences of the Czech Republic,
Pod Vodárenskou věží 2, 18207 Prague, Czech Republic
roman@cs.cas.cz

Abstract. Data mining schemes, or workflows, are collections of inter-connected machine learning models, including preprocessing procedures, and ensembles methods combinations. The proposal of data mining schemes for a task at hand has always been a task for experienced data scientists. We will study generating and testing workflows by automated procedures. Two representations of data mining schemes are used in this paper – a linear one, and a one based on direct acyclic graphs. Efficient procedures for generating schemes are presented and evaluated by testing the generated schemes on real data.

1 Introduction

While most of data mining tools provide collections of methods for building machine learning models, it is usually a task of an experienced human expert to set them up into suitable schemes to solve a data mining task at hand. For non-trivial tasks, these schemes usually include one or more methods of preprocessing, ways of collecting the models into ensembles, post-processing, etc. The task has to be done for every new problem encountered, which is based both on empirical experience as well as on theoretical results, such as implications of the no-free-lunch theorem [1]. Many of the machine learning models are based on non-linear optimization techniques that are sensitive to the data as well as to proper settings of their parameters.

Current meta-learning approaches utilize previous experience with many results of experiments with the pairs of (data set, model) for data dependent method recommendation [2]. However, it has been noted that many data mining tasks [3] often include data-sets which are not suitable for the direct application of a particular machine learning method. The data can express several relations, can be noisy, or contain irrelevant, redundant or correlated information.

Naturally, each machine learning model has a bias, an implicit assumptions about the task at hand, that would influence its performance on given data sets. To recommend a good model, or better a collection of models, would deal with the problem of fixed (and maybe even incompatible) bias. It has also been noted that machine learning models need different pieces of information based on their properties or empirical behavior. Some methods, like a decision tree, need

© Springer International Publishing AG 2016
J.C. Figueroa-García et al. (Eds.): WEA 2016, CCIS 657, pp. 84–90, 2016.
DOI: 10.1007/978-3-319-50880-1_8

attributes characterizing the decision problem well. On the other hand, models like deep neural networks can learn complex tasks, but the learning process for large data would take unreasonable amount of time.

Thus, it makes sense to try to search for workflow schemes incorporating the combinations of machine learning methods together with feasible preprocessing methods [4].

In this paper we will demonstrate two possible solutions of a problem how to find optimal combinations of a certain type of data mining processes. We focus on classification tasks only, and test our approaches on several classification datasets from the UCI machine learning repository [5]. The simpler approach deals with short linear workflow schemes [6] combining several preprocessing methods with a machine learning method. The latter approach works with general representations of workflows by means of direct acyclic graphs (DAGs), containing machine learning methods together with preprocessing algorithms and various methods of combining them into ensembles.

2   Generating Workflow Schemes

Our first approach searches for good data-dependent combinations of linearly ordered preprocessing methods with a machine learning procedure. It is worth noting that the quality criteria for the system performance present another level of complexity, since there is an obvious trade-off between error-rate and run-time performance indicators. The data mining classification processes have two natural performance criteria: the percentage of misclassifications on testing data (i.e. *error-rate*) and the *execution-time*. The effort is put to minimize both criteria. However, these conditions are partly in contradiction. In this sense, the problem belongs to a class of *multi-objective optimization*. In order to measure a quality of the whole model in terms of error-rate, we employ the cross-validation method. It will include the generalization ability of the data mining process. The optimal solution is such a solution which is not dominated (superior in both criteria) by any other on the data-sets. These solutions form the so-called non-dominated front. Thus we will use the algorithm generating all possible combinations of preprocessings and classifiers up to certain size (in our case it is 2 preprocessing methods and one classifier). After cross-validation of the data mining process the average values of error-rate and execution-time will be recorded. From these configurations, the non-dominated solutions are chosen as the optimal for the data-sets.

In the second approach we aim to systematically generate general schemes of workflows in the form of direct acyclic graphs (DAGs) representing syntactically correct model compositions. In our previous work [4], we have proposed a solution based on formal descriptions of models and schemes by means of mathematical logic. The approach utilized the description logic, a well defined subset of first-order logic with predicates of arity of one and two only, as well as the agents and multi-agent systems framework. The logical description of models contained conditions under which particular agents could be connected into a part of the scheme, together with ways how to connect them into a complete workflow (cf. Fig. 1 left). A description logic reasoner was used to generate all valid schemes for evaluation. In order to enhance the system for additional constraints, a stronger expressive power was needed, thus, we have utilized a prolog-like rules to allow for very general conditions about the relationships of models (cf. Fig. 1 right). Overall, the procedure was complete and exhaustive, but it was not very efficient for dealing with bigger schemes.

```
comp_MAS(MAS) ←
    type(CAC, computational_agent)∧
    instance(CA, CAC)∧
    has_agent(MAS, CA)∧
    type(DSC, data_source)∧                  trusted_MAS(MAS) ←
    instance(DS, DSC)∧                           findall(X, has_agent(MAS,X), A))∧
    has_agent(MAS, DS)∧                          all_trusted(A)
    connection(CA, DS, G)∧               all_trusted([]) ← true
    type(TMC, task_manager)∧             all_trusted([F|R]) ←
    instance(TMC, TM)∧                       instance(F,FC)∧
    has_agent(MAS, TM)∧                      type(FC, trusted) ∧
    connection(TM, CA, GC)∧                  all_trusted([R])
    connection(TM, DS, GD)
```

Fig. 1. An example of description logic based scheme definition (left) and a prolog-like constraints (right) for the logical description of schemes within a multi-agent framework.

In order to overcome the time complexity of exhaustive search procedure, we decided to use more efficient search heuristics while still aiming for general DAG schemes. Our current approach is utilizing tree representation of workflow DAGs using typed genetic programing initialization designed for polymorphic and parametric types. Terminal nodes of a tree correspond to the nodes of the DAG, where each node contains a computational intelligence method. Function nodes of a tree represent higher-order functions combining several DAGs in a serial or parallel manner. We use types to distinguish between input data (D) and predictions (P) so the generated trees represent meaningful workflows. The generating method systematically produces workflow DAGs from simple ones to more complex and larger ones, working efficiently with symmetries.

The nodes of the workflow DAG contain three types of nodes; they can be *preprocessing* nodes – k-Best (it selects k features most correlated with the target) or principal component analysis (PCA), or *classifier* nodes – gaussian naïve Bayes (gaussianNB), support vector classification (SVC), logistic regression (LR) or decision trees (DT). The last type of nodes implements *ensemble* methods – there is a copy node and a k-means node, which divides the data into clusters by the k-means algorithm, and two aggregating nodes – simple voting to combine the outputs of several methods, and merging for k-means node.

3   Experiments

For the linear workflows we generate all possible configurations of the data mining processes up to the size of 2 preprocessings and execute five times with

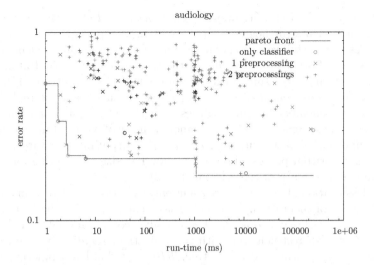

Fig. 2. Performance of linear workflow processes on audiology data-set with respect to time and error.

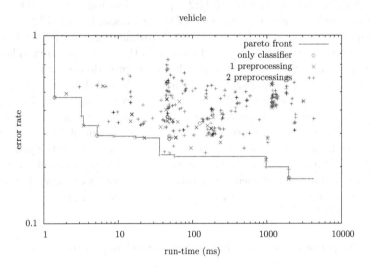

Fig. 3. Performance of linear workflow processes on vehicle data-set with respect to time and error.

different splits between training and testing data in order to perform the 5-fold cross-validation. Every time all computations are performed with a process, the sum of execution time of training methods of both preprocessing and classification methods is recorded. In this experiment we have focused on 30 classification data-sets obtained from the UCI Machine Learning repository [5], we demonstrate the performance on two selected date sets – audiology and vehicle.

We have used the following preprocessing methods: *PCA* – the algorithm of principal components (orthogonal transformation of input space) is performed so as to preserve the full variation of data. The feature selection is not performed and it is a goal of other preprocessing methods. *EMmember* – expectation maximization clustering algorithm is executed on non-class attributes with number of clusters set to dimensionality of input space. Each instance is replaced by vector of cluster-membership probabilities. *ReliefF* – the number of attributes is shrunk to a half of original. *Resample* – random choice of data instances with bias towards uniform class distribution. *K-means* – the output instances are centroids of K-means algorithm processed on each class. The size of resulting data-set is approximately one tenth of the original (Fig. 2).

The classification algorithms were agent encapsulations of algorithms present in the Weka implementation. To simplify the search-space we have used only implicit values of classifier options. The classifier computational agents are as follows: *NNge* – Nearest-neighbor with generalization, *RandomTree* – an implementation of an unpruned decision tree, *RBF* – Radial-basis function neural network, *J48* – implementation of C4.5 decision tree algorithm, *MLP* – Multilayer Perceptron, *1R* – rule-based classification algorithm which takes only one attribute from the whole data-set, *PART* – partial decision trees, *SMO* – sequential minimal optimization algorithm of SVM with linear kernel (Fig. 3).

To demonstrate the performance of DAG workflows generating we have chosen the winequality-white and wilt datasets from the UCI repository. They both represent medium size classification problems. To provide a baseline, we tested each of the four classifiers separately on the two selected datasets. The parameters of the classifiers were set using an extensive grid search with 5-fold cross-validation; the classifiers were compared using the quadratic weighted kappa metric. Next, we generated more than 65,000 different workflows using the proposed approach, and evaluated all of them. All computational intelligence methods used the default settings, or the tuned settings of the individual methods (denoted as 'default' or 'tuned' in Table 1). The best workflows for the two datasets are presented in Figs. 4 left and right, and their numerical results are presented in Table 1.

Table 1. Comparison of κ metric from the cross-validation of the classifiers and the workflows.

Dataset	Winequality		Wilt	
Params	Default	Tuned	Default	Tuned
SVC	0.1783	0.3359	0.0143	0.8427
LR	0.3526	0.3812	0.3158	0.6341
GNB	0.4202	0.4202	0.2916	0.2917
DT	0.3465	0.4283	0.7740	0.8229
Workflow	**0.4731**	**0.4756**	**0.8471**	**0.8668**

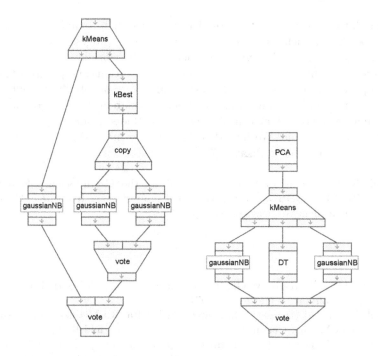

Fig. 4. Best workflow for the winequality (left) and wilt (right) datasets

4 Conclusion

We have demonstrated two approaches that utilize search techniques in order to recommend schemes of data mining workflows. The generation procedures are rather simple, yet they might serve as an important meta-learning algorithm useful for recommending more complicated workflows that go beyond traditional method recommendation approaches, and resemble more realistic workflows used by human investigators for real-world data mining problems.

The linear workflows are quite limited in their power, but they enable faster generation (such as hours of processing time for smaller schemes. That is why we were able to perform multi-objective evaluation in terms of classification error and training time. The DAG-based generation requires a more complex algorithm to provide the correct solutions, nevertheless the valid workflow DAGs can be easily generated by a typed genetic programming initialization method. This method is superior to our previous work where we have utilized description logics based definitions of syntactically correct ways to compose DAGs of models, together with more expressive prolog-like rules for handling additional constraints.

The generated workflows beat the baseline obtained by the hyper-parameter tuning of single classifier by a grid search, which is not surprising, as the single method is also among the generated DAGs. On the other hand the workflow generation requires thousands of hours of processing time.

In our future work, we will extend this approach to a more sophisticated search procedures, such as applying the full genetic programming algorithm, which will also optimize the hyper-parameters of the workflows. The GP procedure has to be modified to start with minimalistic solutions and progress towards more complex schemes, since the search space grows exponentially fast with number of models used. Also, some additional heuristics about feasible combinations should enhance the search algorithms, as was concluded from our previous work with logical desrciptions. We intend to include the method in our multi-agent system for meta-learning – Pikater [7].

Acknowledgment. This work was supported by the Czech Science Foundation project no. P103-15-19877S. and the institutional support of the Institute of Computer Science, Czech Academy of Sciences RVO 67985807.

References

1. Wolpert, D.H., Macready, W.G.: No free lunch theorems for optimization. IEEE Trans. Evol. Comput. **1**(1), 67–82 (1997)
2. Brazdil, P., Giraud-Carrier, C.G., Soares, C., Vilalta, R.: Metalearning – Applications to Data Mining. Cognitive Technologies. Springer, Heidelberg (2009)
3. Clarke, B., Fokoue, E., Zhang, H.H.: Principles and Theory for Data Mining and Machine Learning. Springer Series in Statistics. Springer, Heidelberg (2009)
4. Neruda, R., Beuster, G.: Toward dynamic generation of computational agents by means of logical descriptions. Int. Trans. Syst. Sci. Appl., 139–144 (2008)
5. Bache, K., Lichman, M.: UCI machine learning repository (2013)
6. Kazík, O., Neruda, R.: Data mining process optimization in computational multi-agent systems. In: Cao, L., Zeng, Y., An, B., Symeonidis, A.L., Gorodetsky, V., Coenen, F., Yu, P.S. (eds.) ADMI 2014. LNCS (LNAI), vol. 9145, pp. 93–103. Springer International Publishing, Cham (2015). doi:10.1007/978-3-319-20230-3_8
7. Pešková, K., Šmíd, J., Pilát, M., Kazík, O., Neruda, R.: Hybrid multi-agent system for metalearning in data mining. In: Vanschoren, J., Brazdil, P., Soares, C., Kotthoff, L. (eds.) Proceedings of the MetaSel@ECAI 2014. CEUR Workshop Proceedings, vol. 1201, pp. 53–54. CEUR-WS.org (2014)

Comparison Between Neuronal Networks and ANFIS for Wind Speed-Energy Forecasting

Helbert Espitia[1(✉)] and Guzmán Díaz[2]

[1] Universidad Distrital Francisco José de Caldas, Bogotá, Colombia
heespitiac@udistrital.edu.co
[2] Universidad de Oviedo, Oviedo, Spain
guzman@uniovi.es

Abstract. The generation distributed systems are a good alternative for the reasonable use of energy. Moreover, neuronal networks are an appropriate option for modeling and control of nonlinear complex systems. The eolian energy has shown to be an alternative for electric power generation, even though it also presents limitations for proper management due to associated variations to weather conditions which affect wind speed. In this paper, considering the characteristics present in wind power, neuronal and neuro-fuzzy systems are suggested for the prediction of wind velocity associated whit wind power. The results show an adequate performance of neuro-fuzzy systems for forecasting of wind speed.

Keywords: Forecasting · Fuzzy systems · Neuro-fuzzy · Neuronal networks · Wind power

1 Introduction

Renewable energy is a promising source of alternative energy and it is useful as a complement for the generation of conventional electric energy generation [1]. Thus, systems of distributed generation become highly important for reasonable use of energy.

New alternatives for economic generation of continuous energy are required as demands of energy and associated costs increase. The Distributed Generation (DG) has become a very attractive method to supply power for both consumers and retailers. From this focus, the cost and installation of generators and generation of electricity can be cheaper. In addition, the electric efficiency can be improved if public services make use of cogeneration [1].

Conventionally, systems for electricity generation consist of large interconnected systems characterized by high tension centralized generators and long distances transmissions. In recent years the DG focus has served for new resources use and for diminishing energy waste. In general, technologies on DG can be classified as follows: generation of micro-turbine, wind, photovoltaic and diesel engines generation [2].

© Springer International Publishing AG 2016
J.C. Figueroa-García et al. (Eds.): WEA 2016, CCIS 657, pp. 91–102, 2016.
DOI: 10.1007/978-3-319-50880-1_9

Among different renewable energetic resources, the eolian energy has achieved a prompt development representing remarkable inputs in systems based on electricity [3,4]. Advances in eolian energy generation, both technically and economically have promoted an increasing use of this renewable energy in developed countries [5], showing accelerated growth as a source of clean energy [6].

Nonetheless, similar to other sources as solar energy, the eolian tends to be unstable as wind speed is affected by meteorological and nature conditions [7]. In this regard, it is relevant to remind that the fluctuant power of wind farms may affect the proper functioning of the interconnected networks [8]. In [9] is shown the output power may present straight up increases and abrupt descents during the day.

In order to avoid destructive impacts on electric networks stability, it is mandatory to have ability to manage both the intermittent nature of the eolian energy, and the large fluctuations generated by the stochastic behavior of meteorological conditions [7]. Thus, some measures may be required to soften the output fluctuations to keep a reliable system of energy [10].

Among these challenges is necessary to administrate the intermittent nature of eolian energy and the occasional large fluctuations for preventing both some undesirable effects and potential destruction on electricity networks stability [7].

Moreover, as output power of wind farms fluctuates, deviations of frequency and tension can be seen; this way the eolian energy generates challenges and technical issues including networks interconnection, quality of power, reliability, protection, control and dispatch generation [6].

In addition, according to [11] uncertainty in both the eolian generation availability and the lack of coincidence, including the system top demands let wind farms (WFs) as energy resources of difficult dispatch.

Firstly, the purpose of this paper is to show that a neuronal system or neuro-fuzzy system can be useful to predict the wind speed. Secondly, this paper aims to determine which of the two alternatives may be the most suitable.

Considering the characteristics present in wind power, neuronal and neuro-fuzzy systems are alternatives for wind velocity prediction associated with wind power. It is expected in future works that this forecasting system can be used in wind energy control systems.

2   Wind Energy Conversion System

In order to capture the maximal wind energy, it is necessary to install power electronic devices between the WTG and the grid where frequency is constant. The input of a wind turbine is the wind and the output is the mechanical power (generator rotor) [12,13]. For a variable speed wind turbine, mechanical power output from a wind turbine could be expressed as:

$$P_m = \rho A C_p(\lambda, \beta) V_w^3 \tag{1}$$

where ρ and A correspond to air density, and the area swept by blades, respectively. V_w is the wind velocity (m/s), and C_p is called the power coefficient, which is given as a nonlinear function of the tip speed ratio (TSR) λ with:

$$\lambda = \frac{w_r r}{V_w} \tag{2}$$

in this equation r is wind turbine blade radius, and w_r is the turbine speed. C_p is a function of λ and the blade pitch angle β.

In the previous equations it is noteworthy the remarkable influence of the wind speed which is given by specific weather conditions, characterized for the stochastic nature of the wind itself. Therefore, it is important to set a method that allows to estimate the wind speed associated behavior [14].

3   Forecasting Scheme

According to [15], the process of forecasting seeks establish predictions (trend analysis) of the future based on past and present data. The general equation for forecasting is:

$$y[n] = f(y[n-1], y[n-2], y[n-3], y[n-4], ..., y[n-k]) \tag{3}$$

where, k is the number of past data and f can be a nonlinear equation. In this paper f is given by both neuronal network and neuronal-fuzzy system. Figure 1 shows a representation of forecasting.

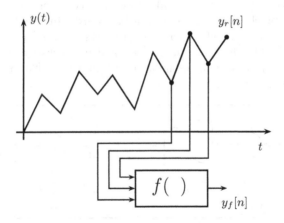

Fig. 1. Forecasting scheme.

In Fig. 1, $y_r[n]$ is the real data, $y_f[n]$ the forecasting data, and f the nonlinear function. In this way, artificial neuronal networks and neuro-fuzzy systems can be a good alternative to forecasting, due to the nonlinear relations among inputs and outputs [16,17]. About training algorithms for neuronal networks and neuronal-fuzzy systems is frequently used *Back Propagation* [18].

4   Neuronal Networks

Using computing resources, neuronal nets aim the emulation of human being processes made by brain neurons [19,20]. As seen in Fig. 2, those artificial neurons have inputs, connection weight and an output related to an activation function f.

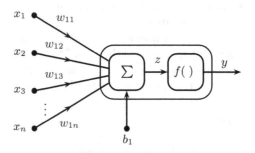

Fig. 2. Artificial neuron [19].

Each entry is assigned a weight which is later added up for a later evaluation using an activation function [21]. Among the advantages seen in neuronal networks, it is outstanding the flexibility in adaption and acknowledgement and patterns recognition. Those are trained and self-organized and are also fault-tolerant, a failure in a neuron does not mean a failure in the whole net [22].

There are several types of neuronal networks. According to the type of connection they can be classified as forward or backwards. In nets feed-forward the signals travel forward. For self-recurrent neural nets the connections allow backwards trajectories. On the other hand, neuronal networks can be classified in regard of its number of layers as monolayer and multilayer [23]. Figure 3 show a multilayer neuronal network.

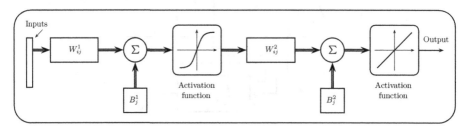

Fig. 3. Multilayer neuronal network.

5   Fuzzy Logic

Fuzzy logic allows to represent information in terms of fuzzy sets. These fuzzy sets are combined in rules to define actions. In this way the control systems based on fuzzy logic combine some input variables (defined in terms of fuzzy sets), through groups of rules that produce one or more output values [24].

5.1 Fuzzy Systems

Fuzzy systems allow modeling nonlinear processes; they also obtain information from a data set using learning algorithms. Systems based on fuzzy logic allow easy the use of a preliminary knowledge as a starting point for optimization [24, 25].

In the fuzzy rule-based systems, relationships between variables are represented by fuzzy rules like:

If the proposition of the antecedent X *then*, proposition of consequent Z.

An associated feature of X is called linguistic label and is represented by a fuzzy set in the universe of discourse X [25].

For fuzzy modeling (system) there are different categories as linguistic, relational, Takagi-Sugeno and singleton, which are primarily distinguished by their ability to represent information [26].

Linguistic Model. Based on *If-Then* rules where precedent and consequent are linguistic terms, e.g. Mandani model is a representative case of this type where the general output is established by means of output superposition of individual rules.

Relational Model. Involves a generalization of the Linguistic model; utilizing fuzzy relations this model encrypts combinations among linguistic terms defined in input-output system.

Singleton Model. Considered a especial case of the linguistic model where the consequent is a Singleton-type group. Practically, this group can be represented as of constant values.

Takagi-Sugeno Model. This model consists of logical rules which are made of fuzzy antecedents and functional consequents. This model integrates the capability of linguistic models to represent qualitative knowledge, and it is also a mechanism to manipulate quantitative information.

5.2 Takagi-Sugeno Fuzzy Systems

The Takagi-Sugeno Fuzzy model (TSK) was proposed to develop a systematic approach to generating fuzzy rules from a given input-output data set [27]. A typical fuzzy rule in a TSK fuzzy model has the form:

$$\text{if } X \text{ is } A \text{ and } Y \text{ is } B \text{ then } Z = f(X, Y)$$

where A and B are fuzzy sets in the antecedent and $Z = f(X, Y)$ is a function in the consequent.

In many applications $f(X, Y)$ is a polynomial of inputs X and Y, in this way some TSK systems are:

- Zero-order TSK fuzzy model: Function f is a constant value $f = c$.
- First-order TSK fuzzy model: Function f is a first-order polynomial like $f = ax + by + c$.

A zero-order TSK fuzzy model can be viewed as a special case of the Mamdani Fuzzy inference system, in which each rule at consequent is modeled by a fuzzy singleton.

Additionally a zero-order TSK fuzzy model is functionally equivalent to a radial basis function network under some considerations [27].

6   ANFIS

Artificial Neuro-Fuzzy Inference Systems (ANFIS) are a class of adaptive networks that are functionally equivalent to fuzzy inference systems. They are represented by Sugeno fuzzy models and use a hybrid learning algorithm.

Assume that fuzzy inference system has two inputs x and y and one output z. A first-order Sugeno fuzzy model has rules as the following:

- Rule1: If x is A_1 and y is B_1, then $f_1 = p_1 x + q_1 y + r_1$.
- Rule2: If x is A_2 and y is B_2, then $f_2 = p_2 x + q_2 y + r_2$.

In Fig. 4 is presented an example of TSK fuzzy system.

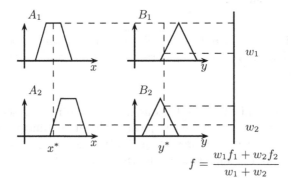

Fig. 4. Example of TSK fuzzy system.

An example of ANFIS system is presented in Fig. 5.

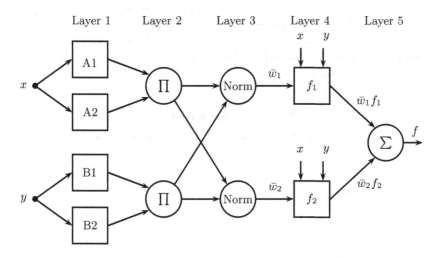

Fig. 5. Example of ANFIS system.

The layers of ANFIS are:

- **Layer 1:** In these layer the fuzzification process is performed, it is also an adaptive node. The output is the membership grade of a fuzzy set. In Fig. 5 are (A_1, A_2, B_1, B_2). Parameters of adaptation are referred to as premise parameters.
- **Layer 2:** Associated whit the fuzzy relation process between membership functions using a T-norm. The output is the product of all the incoming signals. Each node represents the fuzzy relation of the respective rule.
- **Layer 3:** In this layer is performed the normalization process. The outputs are called normalized firing strengths.
- **Layer 4:** Every node in this layer is an adaptive node with function $\bar{w}_i f_i$. Parameters of this node are $\{p_i, q_i, r_i\}$, are referred to as consequent parameters.
- **Layer 5:** In this layer is computing the overall output as the sum of all incoming signals. Layer associate to defuzzification process.

7   Results

Figure 6 shows the forecasting architecture. In these cases a maximum of 3 delays are used for inputs. Figure 7 shows the data used for identification. Each sample is taken at a 10 min intervals.

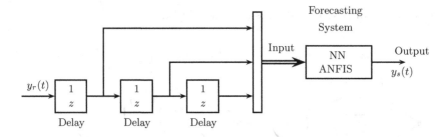

Fig. 6. Forecasting model.

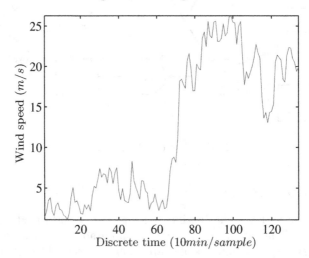

Fig. 7. Data used for identification.

For system identification it is considered the following neural networks configurations:

– Delays (inputs): 1, 2 and 3.
– Neurons in the hidden layer: 2, 3 and 4.

For ANFIS system is used the following configurations:

– Delays (inputs): 1, 2 and 3.
– Member functions for each input: 2, 3 and 4.

Due to that the initialization weights of the neural network is assigned randomly, then 30 training processes are performed for each configuration. Table 1 shows the results of the Root Mean Square Errors (RMSE) for each configuration. To establishing the final system, the configuration having the best result of RMSE is chosen. The RMSE is given by Eq. 4, where N is the total number of data taken, y_r real data and y_s simulated data.

$$\text{RMSE} = \sqrt{\frac{1}{N} \sum_{n=1}^{N} (y_r[n] - y_s[n])^2} \tag{4}$$

Table 1. RMSE values obtained from the training process using NN.

Delays: 1				
Neurons	Maximum	Minimum	Mean	Variance
2	1.685	1.684	1.684	0.02498
3	1.658	1.658	1.658	6.148×10^{-5}
4	1.683	1.67	1.672	0.1023
Delays: 2				
Neurons	Maximum	Minimum	Mean	Variance
2	1.684	1.684	1.684	2.125×10^{-8}
3	1.668	1.668	1.668	2.125×10^{-8}
4	1.682	1.672	1.673	0.09614
Delays: 3				
Neurons	Maximum	Minimum	Mean	Variance
2	1.589	1.589	1.589	4.251×10^{-8}
3	1.628	1.628	1.628	1.59×10^{-5}
4	1.592	1.586	1.587	0.06118

Performance for 30 training processes for each configuration processes using ANFIS the RMSE values are presented in table 2.

Table 2. RMSE values obtained from the training process using ANFIS.

Delays: 1				
M functions	Maximum	Minimum	Mean	Variance
2	1.645	1.645	1.645	1.129×10^{-15}
3	1.565	1.565	1.565	2.258×10^{-16}
4	1.555	1.555	1.555	4.517×10^{-16}
Delays: 2				
M functions	Maximum	Minimum	Mean	Variance
2	1.567	1.567	1.567	0
3	1.385	1.385	1.385	2.258×10^{-16}
4	1.217	1.217	1.217	2.258×10^{-16}
Delays: 3				
M functions	Maximum	Minimum	Mean	Variance
2	1.389	1.389	1.389	2.258×10^{-16}
3	0.8999	0.8999	0.8999	1.129×10^{-16}
4	0.3972	0.3972	0.3972	0

Best RMSE values are obtained for ANFIS system with three delays and four member functions (0.3972), therefore, this case is chosen for implementation. The best case for neuronal networks is for three delays and four neurons (1.586).

Figure 8 represents the system response after training using NN. Additionally, the simulation for neuro-fuzzy system is presented in Fig. 9. These figures show a better fitness for ANFIS. It is noteworthy, that neuro-fuzzy systems allow to have an initial configuration before the training process, this produces a very small variation of ANFIS system for training process.

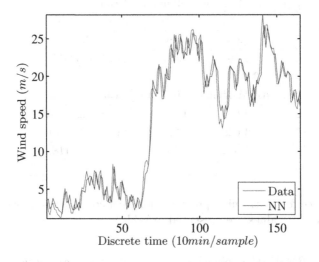

Fig. 8. Neuronal network simulation.

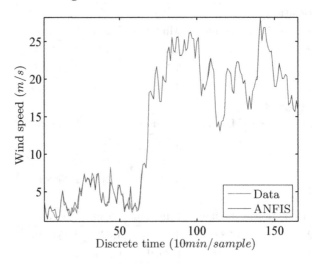

Fig. 9. Fuzzy simulation.

8   Conclusions

In this article was show that both, neuronal networks and neuro-fuzzy systems can be utilized to predict win-speed. Furthermore, this paper registers achievements in the identification of wind velocity using a scheme of neuronal networks and neuronal-fuzzy.

The group of experiments allows to establish the best configurations to be employed. Besides, it is seen that the neuro-fuzzy systems showed better performance in the wind speed prediction.

It was also observed that neuro-fuzzy systems allow the establishment of an initial configuration before the training process. Moreover, while having a random initialization of the parameters in neuronal networks a higher variation could be seen.

In future works it is expected to use this identification for implementing a closed loop control strategy with neuro-fuzzy systems.

References

1. Dugan, R., McDermott, T., Ball, G.: Planning for distributed generation. IEEE Industry Application Magazine (2001)
2. Tong, J., Yu, T.: Nonlinear PID control design for improving stability of microturbine systems. In: Third International Conference on Electric Utility Deregulation and Restructuring and Power Technologies DRPT, pp. 2515–2518 (2008)
3. Mathew, S.: Wind Energy, Fundamentals, Resource Analysis and Economics. Springer, Heidelberg (2006)
4. Heier, S., Waddington, R.: Grid Integration of Wind Energy Conversion Systems, 2nd edn. Wiley, Hoboken (2006)
5. Khatamianfar, A., Khalid, M., Savkin, A., Agelidis, V.: Improving wind farm dispatch in the Australian electricity market with battery energy storage using model predictive control. IEEE Trans. Sustain. Energ. 4(3), 745–755 (2013)
6. Teleke, S., Baran, M., Huang, A., Bhattacharya, S., Anderson, L.: Control strategies for battery energy storage for wind farm dispatching. IEEE Trans. Energ. Convers. 24(3), 725–732 (2009)
7. Wang, X., Vilathgamuwa, D., Choi, S.: Determination of battery storage capacity in energy buffer for wind farm. IEEE Trans. Energ. Convers. 23(3), 868–878 (2008)
8. Holttinen, H., Hirvonen, R.: Power system requirements for wind power. In: Ackermann, T. (ed.) Wind Power in Power Systems, pp. 143–167. Wiley, New York (2005)
9. Han, C., Huang, A., Baran, M., Bhattacharya, S., Litzenberger, W., Anderson, L., Johnson, A., Edris, A.: STATCOM impact study on the integration of a large wind farm into a weak loop power system. IEEE Trans. Energ. Convers. 23(1), 226–233 (2008)
10. Lundsager, P., Barring-Gould, E.: Isolated systems with wind power. In: Ackermann, T. (ed.) Wind Power in Power Systems, pp. 299–329. Wiley, New York (2005)
11. Abdullah, M., Muttaqi, K., Sutanto, D., Agalgaonkar, A.: An effective power dispatch control strategy to improve generation schedulability and supply reliability of a wind farm using a battery energy storage system. IEEE Trans. Sustain. Energ. 6(3), 1093–1102 (2015)

12. Borowy, B., Salameh, Z.: Dynamic response to a stand-alone wind energy conversion system with battery energy storage to a wind gust. IEEE Trans. Energ. Convers. **12**, 73–78 (1997)

13. Huang, C.: Modified neural network for dynamic control and operation of a hybrid generation systems. J. Appl. Res. Technol. **12**(6) (2014)

14. Dowell, J., Pinson, P.: Very-short-term probabilistic wind power forecasts by sparse vector autoregression. IEEE Trans. Smart Grid **7**(2), 763–770 (2015)

15. Hyndman, R., Athanasopoulos, G.: Forecasting: principles and practice. OTexts, Melbourne (2014)

16. Huarng, K., Yu, T.: The application of neural networks to forecast fuzzy time series. Physica A. Stat. Mech. Appl. **363**(2), 481–491 (2006)

17. Peng, H., Wu, S., Wei, C., Lee, S.: Time series forecasting with a neuro-fuzzy modeling scheme. Appl. Soft Comput. **32**, 481–493 (2015)

18. Singh, M., Singh, I., Verma, A.: Identification on non linear series-parallel model using neural network. MIT Int. J. Electr. Instrumen. Eng. **3**(1), 21–23 (2013)

19. Torres, N., Hernandez, C., Pedraza, L.: Redes neuronales y predicción de tráfico. Revista Tecnura **15**(29), 90–97 (2011)

20. Martinez, F., Gómez, D., Castiblanco, M.: Optimization of a neural architecture for the direct control of a Boost converter. Revista Tecnura **16**(32), 41–49 (2012)

21. Arrieta, J., Torres, J., Velásquez, H.: Predicciones de modelos econométricos y redes neuronales: el caso de la acción de SURAMINV. Semestre Económico **12**(25), 95–109 (2009)

22. Pérez, F., Fernández, H.: Las redes neuronales y la evaluación del riesgo de crédito. Revista Ingenierpias Universidad de Medellín **6**(10), 77–91 (2007)

23. Heaton, J.: Introduction to Neural Networks with Java. Heaton Research Inc. (2008)

24. Wang, L.: A Course on Fuzzy Systems and Control. Prentice Hall PTR, New Jersey (1997)

25. Del Brio, B., Sanz, A.: Redes Neuronales y Sistemas Difusos. Alfaomega, Segunda Edición (2006)

26. Babuska, R.: Fuzzy Modeling for Control. Kluwer Academic Publishers, Wiley, London, England (1998)

27. Jang, J., Sun, C., Mizutani, E.: Neuro-Fuzzy and Soft Computing: A Computational Approach to Learning and Machine Intelligence. Matlab Curriculum Series (1990)

Improving the Performance of Leaves Identification by Features Selection with Genetic Algorithms

Laura D. Jalili, Alfredo Morales, Jair Cervantes$^{(\boxtimes)}$, and José S. Ruiz-Castilla

Posgrado e Investigación, UAEMEX (Autonomous University of Mexico State), 56259 Texcoco, Mexico
lauradojali2@gmail.com, a9009.da@gmail.com, jcervantesc@uaemex.mx, jsergioruizc@gmail.com

Abstract. The development of vision systems to plant leaves identification from images is a very important current challenge. One of the main lines of research is the improvement in performance. The performance of automatic identification systems is directly linked to the extracted features. The extracted features allow to identify or classify the object. However, sometimes a high number of features introduces noise which affects the performance. In this research, a genetic algorithm is proposed to extract the most discriminative features. The proposed technique reduces the dimensionality of the data set and improves the performance to identifying plants. In the experimental results, the proposed method is compared with feature selection classic techniques. Experimental results show that the proposed technique obtains a significant improvement in the performance in comparison with other techniques.

1 Introduction

Nowadays, vision algorithms have been implemented in many research areas, one of these areas is the agronomy one. The development of vision systems that automatically detect and identify different plants is a current challenge that has several applications. These can range simple identification, pest detection, diseases detection, identification of plants by customs staff, identification of a plant for care and protection of pesticides, etc.

In recent years, development of automatic algorithms to leaves identification has been guided by several researchers. However, plants identification is not an easy job, because plants identification involve different problems, such as: leaf features; the huge amount of different plants; many plants possess and/or share one or more properties such as: shape, size, texture, color, even when they are different plants, some characteristics like color and texture in plants leaves are modified by the maturity of the leaves, humidity, diseases, etc. In last few years, researchers have developed different methodologies to identify plants from leaves. Most of these systems have focused on obtaining geometric, textural and chromatic, features to identify leaves.

© Springer International Publishing AG 2016
J.C. Figueroa-García et al. (Eds.): WEA 2016, CCIS 657, pp. 103–114, 2016.
DOI: 10.1007/978-3-319-50880-1_10

This research has been motivated of these disadvantages. The proposed algorithm uses a genetic algorithm to obtain the most helpful attributes for classification's accuracy. The proposed algorithm reduces the noise introduced to the classifier with the feature dimensionality. The proposed technique take advantage from the search capacity of the genetic algorithms, this search is guided using different performance metrics. Obtained experimental results show's that proposed algorithm can help to improve performance of the classifier. The Sect. 2 introduces the state of the art, Sect. 3 shows the proposed methodology, Sect. 4 are shown the experimental results and finally, the conclusions are shown in Sect. 5.

2   State of the Art

Plants play a very important role for the life and human development, in different research areas like: agriculture [10–12, 16], vegetable ecology [10, 14, 17], medicine based plants [9, 12, 14, 18], natural conservative and many others. In the world exists approximately 310,000 to 420,000 variety of plants species [9], without taking in account those that have not been classified. For this reason, identify a plant through leaves images is not a trivial job.

Currently pattern recognition techniques, involve techniques to measure the morphological features and textures of the objects contained in the image. The best way to extract valid features is obtaining them from the picture of the plant leaves. In modern literature is shown that external shape of leaf, provides a lot of information to classify them. Some other researches, have focused on the extraction of features and pattern recognition methods for the leaf, using four important features for classification: Shape [9, 13, 15, 16, 18], texture [8, 11, 12], color [10, 19], and leaf venation [17, 20, 21].

Leaf shape is one of the most important features of plant leaves, and the two basic approaches for these kind of analysis are the ones that are based on contour and region. The one based on region usually use moments descriptors, that includes Zernike geometric moments and Legendre moments.

On the other side, the one based on contour, usually gets the contour using methods based on the leaf curvature [10]. Other researches had used a combination of geometric and textural, allowing them to use dried, wet or even misshapen leaves [12]. Some authors use basic descriptors, such as perimeter, area, circularity and elliptical [8], or invariant descriptors like Hu moments and Fourier descriptors for leaf contour recognition [15]. Recently, some systems have been proposed to extract features describing edge variations of the leaf, using descriptors invariant to translation, rotation and size [18].

Texture of the leaves can be defined as the characteristics that the leaf has on its surface which is manifests as gray scale variations in the image. Some author added textural information to identify leaves [3, 4]. Other researches use color as a comparison feature of images, since a simple color similarity between two images can be measured by comparing their color histograms [10]. In [19] they use as an alternative color space L * a * b *, showing more consistent color and presents more or less the same axis for the entire leaf in opposite to RGB space. However, a recurring problem is that the chromaticity in the leaves of plants is not static, this is variable with on the time and commonly on the other factors. Although classification approaches such as shape, texture and color are valid, it has not been documented the influence of each type of features in the performance of classification algorithms.

On the other hand, genetic algorithms (GA) are heuristics widely used in recent years. GA were originally introduced in literature by John Hollan in the 70's. GA are popular algorithms based on the mechanics of natural selection and evolution optimization. In particular, they are heuristic search procedures that modify the value of individuals strings commonly encoded as binary strings. These have been applied widely in many fields such as bioinformatics, prediction [22], finance [23], bio-chemical control process [24], manufacture [25], autonomous vehicles [26], robotics [27], etc. Specifically in classification problems genetics have been used to obtain optimal parameters (tuning) [28], reduce the dimensionality of data sets [29], improve accuracy classification [30] and even generating sets of compact rules from input data [31].

3   Proposed Method

Methodology of proposed system is shown in Fig. 1. First steps are common in any system of recognition from characteristics. In experiments geometric, chromatic and textural features were obtained. Due to space conditions, it is briefly defined the steps that are common in classification systems and also are applied by proposed method.

First, the images are preprocessed and segmented. Autonomous segmentation is one of the most difficult tasks in image processing. In pictures of leaves, often they are surrounded by greenery in the background. However, the images used, were leaves totally in a controlled environment (images with only leaf and white background). Segmentation tests were done using adaptive border segmentation algorithms, Otsu and segmentation using a phase of principal component analysis (PCA) and no differences between them were obtained by the nature of the data set, so finally Otsu algorithm was used for segmentation.

3.1   Segmentation Techniques

In order to obtain a good segmentation even when there are changes in global brightness conditions, the region of the leave in each image was segmented using the following steps (1) Computation of high-contrast gray scale from optimal linear combination of RGB color components; (2) Estimate optimal border using cumulative moments of zero order and first order (Otsu method). (3) Morphological operations to fill possible gaps in the segmented image. By segmenting the image, the proposed system can use only the region of the leaf, determine its edges and calculate properties by extracting features.

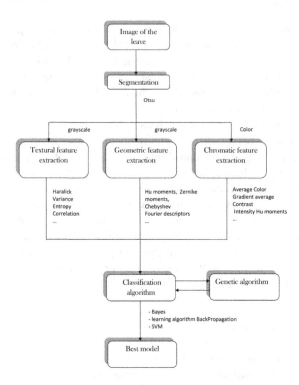

Fig. 1. Proposed methodology diagram

3.2 Features Extractors

Once the region has been segmented its features are extracted. Feature extraction allows us to represent the image using a set of numerical values with high discriminative power, eliminating redundant features and reducing the dimensionality of the image. The characteristics obtained are able to associate very similar ranges to similar images, associate different ranges to different images, the features obtained are invariant to scaling, rotation and translation, enabling the classifier to recognize objects despite having different size, position and orientation. All these features play an important role in the algorithm performance and allow the classifier to discriminate between different classes in an appropriate manner. Deeper information on the subject can be found in [3, 4, 7, 10, 13].

Geometric Features. Geometric features are the most important and used visual features to classify plants. The basic geometric characteristics describe the basic properties of the region to recognize, these are; area, roundness of the leaf edge, length of the leaf, elongation defined by the length and width of the leaf, x and y coordinates of the gravity center, density, defined by the length of the edges of the leaf. However, an efficient classification system should allow to recognize leaves regardless of their orientation, location and size, i.e. it must be invariant to scaling, rotation and transfer.

Textural Features. The extraction algorithms of textural features look for basic repetitive patterns with periodic or random structures in images. These structures give rise to a property that may be ruggedness, roughness, granulating, fineness, smoothness, etc. Because a texture repeats a pattern along a surface textures are invariant to displacement, this explains why the visual perception of a texture is independent of the position. In this article were used Haralick textural features. These extractors consider the distribution of intensity values in the region, by obtaining the mean and range of the following variables: mean, median, variance, smoothness, bias, Kurtosis, correlation, energy or entropy, contrast, homogeneity, and correlation.

Chromatic Features. Chromatic features provide information of the color intensity of a segmented region. These characteristics can be calculated for each intensity channel, for example, red, green, blue, grayscale, hue (Hue), Saturation (Saturation) and intensity (Value), etc. The used features were: standard intensity features, they describe the mean, standard deviation of intensity, first and second derivative in the segmented region, Hu moments with intensity information, Gabor features based on 2D Gabor functions. In experiments 122 characteristics were obtained for each channel. Since the experiments were performed in RGB only 366 chromatic features were used.

3.3 Feature Selection

In order to eliminate some features that do not contribute to the classifier performance, in this research a genetic algorithm was used to extract the best combinations of features.

In the proposed algorithm, each set of features per leaf, conforms a vector defined by the number of descriptors or features. The number of features of each data set defines the size of each binary string needed to implement the genetic algorithm. The relationship between each binary string with the feature set, is that 1 is taken as a used feature and 0 as the absence of that feature. The aptitude of each individual is taken from the accuracy obtained by classifying the set corresponding to that chain.

In the proposed methodology the individual with better aptitude is taken and it passes intact to the next generation, it was used two-point crosses and mutation probability of 0.08. Figure 2 shows an example of chromosomal chains used and the classifier performance when features labeled 1 are used.

The dimensionality of the data set is an important classifiers performance factor. Sometimes inappropriate attributes can affect the performance of the classifier. Features selection helps to improve the performance of a classifier. This problem has been addressed by several authors, this problem is common in pattern recognition and it is commonly called course of dimensionality. An important factor when reducing characteristics, is to eliminate those that are not important to the classifier or find the combination of attributes that optimizes the performance of the classifier.

[1, 0, 1, 1, 1, 0, 0, 1, 0, 1, 1, 1, 1, 0, 0, 0, 0, 0, 0, 1, 1, 1, 0, 0, 1, 1, 1, 0] 87.4213836
[0, 0, 0, 0, 1, 0, 1, 0, 1, 1, 0, 0, 0, 0, 1, 0, 0, 0, 1, 0, 1, 1, 1, 0, 0, 1, 0, 1] 86.7924528
[1, 0, 0, 1, 0, 0, 1, 0, 1, 0, 1, 1, 0, 0, 0, 0, 0, 0, 0, 1, 1, 1, 0, 0, 0, 0, 0, 0] 91.1949686
[1, 0, 1, 0, 1, 1, 0, 1, 1, 1, 0, 0, 0, 1, 0, 1, 0, 1, 1, 1, 1, 1, 1, 1, 0, 1, 0, 0] 86.163522
[1, 1, 1, 1, 0, 0, 0, 0, 0, 0, 0, 0, 0, 0, 0, 1, 1, 0, 0, 1, 1, 1, 1, 0, 1, 1, 1, 1] 90.5660377
[1, 1, 1, 0, 0, 1, 0, 1, 1, 0, 1, 1, 0, 0, 0, 0, 0, 1, 0, 1, 1, 0, 0, 0, 1, 1, 1, 0] 89.3081761
[0, 1, 1, 0, 0, 1, 1, 0, 1, 0, 1, 0, 0, 0, 0, 0, 0, 1, 1, 0, 0, 1, 0, 1, 1, 0, 0, 0] 88.0503145
[0, 0, 0, 1, 0, 0, 0, 1, 1, 1, 0, 0, 0, 1, 0, 1, 0, 1, 0, 0, 1, 0, 1, 0, 1, 0, 1, 1] 93.7106918
[0, 1, 0, 0, 0, 1, 1, 0, 0, 0, 0, 1, 1, 1, 1, 0, 0, 0, 0, 1, 1, 0, 1, 0, 1, 0, 1, 1] 87.4213836
[1, 1, 1, 1, 0, 0, 0, 1, 0, 0, 0, 1, 0, 1, 0, 0, 0, 1, 0, 0, 1, 1, 1, 0, 0, 1, 0, 0] 91.8238994

Fig. 2. Chromosomic chains and its aptitude

Feature selection or dimensionality reduction is regularly raised as an optimization problem. In recent years, genetic algorithms (GAs) have been used extensively to solve optimization problems. GAs are based on the premise of using the natural evolution as an optimization procedure. GA are characterized to represent the solutions of a problem in the form of binary strings.

Formally, given a n-dimensional patterns set, the GA task is to find a set of attributes in a k-dimensional space that maximizes an optimization criterion, where $k << n$. Obtained patterns are evaluated based on two conditions, dimensionality of the data set and spacing between classes or classification accuracy.

The general outline of a proposed genetic algorithm is described in more detail in the next subsections.

3.4   Initial Population

A GA require a population of individuals. Each individual is a candidate to be the solution of the problem that leads to the problem solution. Each individual in the population is represented by a binary string. Individuals of the initial population are usually strings of 0s and 1s completely randomly generated, this is important because it allows genetic algorithm to provide the population with enough variety to explore all areas of the search space. The chains are called individual's *genotype* and is analogous to the *chromosome* in the biological system. Each genotype represents a point x in the search space of the problem. At each point x is called *phenotype*. Term *gene* is used to refer to the codification of a particular characteristic of the individual. Each *gene* can take different values that are called *alleles*. To refer to a certain position of the binary string the term locus is used. In our case, the chromosome size depends on the number of features of the data set. The relationship between each chromosomal chain with the attributes set, is that 1 is taken as a used feature and 0 as the absence of that attribute.

3.5   Selection of Individuals

The basic idea of selection is to use a probability selection of a chain, where the probability is directly proportional to the fitness function of the individual. The fitness function of each individual is taken from the precision obtained by classifying the corresponding set. That is, the selection process should favor the number of copies of individuals that are more adapted. In this research only roulette selection technique was used.

3.6   Crossover

The crossover process, where both parents are involved, provides a mechanism for inherit traits to their offspring, this is a method of genetic information fusion of two individuals. The crossing mechanism used in the experiments was two-point crosses.

3.7   Mutation

The mutation is a process where the genetic material can be altered at random, due to an error in the reproduction or deformation of genes. The probability in a genetic algorithm is greater than the probability in human genetics and prevents that the algorithm get trapped in minimum local. The easiest way of mutation is changing the value of one of the positions of the chain. If the value is zero happens to one, and if one goes to zero.

3.8   Stop Condition

It is necessary to specify the conditions under which the genetic algorithm stops and the best solution found is presented. The simplest stop condition, is presented when is detected that most of the population has converged to a similar manner, lacking enough diversity that makes sense to continue the evolution. In the proposed method, the algorithm ends after 10 iterations where was no improvement. Chain with better accuracy is stored in a text file with the precision obtained.

3.9   Elitism

Of the entire population, the individual with the best qualifying result in the generation is taken and it passes intact to the next generation. Then a selection method is used and the crossing method is applied to the selected individuals for the new generation. The same procedure for the next generation is done, and if a better result than the previous one is obtained, it replaces the individual who had the best accuracy. If there was no chain that improve aptitude, the previous string still remains intact in the new generation.

3.10   Classification Techniques

Classification, consist is detect or recognize a pattern in terms of properties or traits. Pattern recognition is one of the most important tasks. However, it is also one of the most complex tasks. In experiments the results were compared with some classification techniques, Bayesian classifier, the Backpropagation learning algorithm and support vector machine (SVM).

4   Experimental Results

In this section, parameters selection technique is shown, also data normalization and experimental results obtained with the proposed system.

4.1   Data Set

ICL data set, which is a collection of leaves of Hefei University was used in these experiments. The data set contains 16,849 leaf images from 220 species. The images of the leaves were segmented using Otsu's method and the above mentioned features were extracted.

All the extracted features were normalized with the relationship:

$$f_{ij} = \frac{T_{ij} - \mu_j}{\sigma_j}$$

where $i = 1, \ldots, m$ and $j = 1, \ldots, n$, μ_j and $\sigma_j T_{ij} = \sigma_j$ represent the mean and standard deviation of the jth feature, T_{ij} represents the jth feature of the ith vector, m is the number of images and n the number of features. The normalized features have mean zero and standard deviation equal to 1.

4.2   Parameter Selection

Parameter selection is a very important step, because a good selection of parameters has considerable effect on the classifier performance. In all used classifiers optimal parameters were obtained by cross-validation and grid search. Cross-validation is a model validation technique for assessing how the results of a statistical analysis will generalize to an independent data set [5]. On the other hand grid search exhaustively search all parameter combinations obtaining the best parameter combination. More information about how to use grid search can be found in [2].

4.3   Results

In the experiments, all data sets were normalized and cross-validation was used with $k = 10$. Table 1 shows the results obtained with geometric features, textural and chromaticity, as each individual features. CH_i defines the used leaves data set. For each classifier used, accuracies obtained with each individual set of

Table 1. Performance with different feature selection techniques.

Classificador		ODS	RG	SFS	SBS
Bayes	Acc	88.84	94.08	92.31	91.78
	TP	0.888	0.941	0.923	0.918
	Recall	0.87	0.991	0.90	0.92
BP	Acc	90.72	94.32	92.73	92.27
	TP	0.91	0.943	0.93	0.92
	Recall	0.92	0.993	0.94	0.92
SVM	Acc	91.37	95.65	92.71	92.38
	TP	0.914	0.957	0.93	0.92
	Recall	0.90	0.999	0.95	0.91
LR	Acc	82.56	89.03	85.61	86.07
	TP	0.826	0.890	0.86	0.86
	Recall	0.827	0.871	0.84	0.87

characteristics are reported. The metric used to evaluate the performance of the classifier was precision and this is obtained from the classifier hits divided by the total of data set.

In the results, it is not possible to infer that the similarity between leaves significantly affect classifiers, performance of the classifiers that used very similar images of each other and dissimilar, are not contrasting. However, it is possible to appreciate that the textural features are little discriminative for most data sets, except for the set CH_6. One possible reason is that the size of the data set is very small (only three classes).

Table 1 shows the results obtained with different techniques. In the Table, ODS represents the results obtained with the original data set, RG represents the results obtained with the proposed Genetic, SFS means forward sequential selection technique and SBS backward sequential selection technique. Acc is the number of correct predictions made divided by the total number of predictions made, Recall is the number of positive predictions divided by the number of positive class values in the test data $Recall = TP/(TP + FN)$, where TP are the true positives and FN are the false negatives. Recall is also called Sensitivity or the True Positive Rate. Recall can be thought of as a measure of a classifiers completeness. A low recall indicates many False Negatives.

In the results it is possible to see an improvement in classification accuracy compared to the performances obtained with the original data set and compared with the other features selection techniques. In all tests with different classification techniques, the results with the proposed technique improves the results obtained with other techniques. These results highlight the utility of the proposed method. The obtained results accuracy was improved in all chains using genetic, it is important to note that even though the number of features significantly decreased in all the results the combination of the three types of features is very necessary.

5   Conclusions

In this article, a feature selection algorithm is proposed to improve the performance of classifiers for identifying plants from leaves. The proposed method helps improve the performance of the classifier removing attributes that introduce noise to the classifier. The proposed method uses a genetic algorithm to eliminate attributes using as aptitude a metric performance. The proposed method searches for the best attributes and/or best combination of attributes, eliminating those attributes that affect the performance. The experiments obtained show that the proposed method generates notable results by eliminating attributes that do not provide information. The main advantage of the proposed method is its ease of implementation and ease of use on small and medium size data sets. Characteristics reduction is important to improve the response time it takes for the system to recognize a new leaf. The results show that the used recognition system improves in all cases the obtained accuracy with all the features, removing individual features or combination of features that introduce noise to the classifier.

Acknowledgements. This research was funded by the Ministry of Research of the Autonomous University of the State of Mexico with the research project 3771/2014/CIB.

References

1. Cope, J., Corney, D., Clark, J., Remagnino, P., Wilkin, P.: Plant species identification using digital morphometrics: a review. Expert Syst. Appl. **39**(8), 7562–7573 (2012)
2. Bergstra, J., Bengio, Y.: Random search for hyper-parameter optimization. J. Mach. Learn. Res. **13**, 281–305 (2012)
3. Ma, W., Manjunath, B.: Texture features and learning similarity. In: Proceedings of the Conference on Computer Vision and Pattern Recognition, pp. 425–430 (1996)
4. Manjunath, B., Ma, W.: Texture features for browsing and retrieval of image data. IEEE Trans. Pattern Anal. Mach. Intell. **18**, 837–842 (1996)
5. Kohavi, R.: A study of cross-validation and bootstrap for accuracy estimation and model selection. In: Proceedings of the Fourteenth International Joint Conference on Artificial Intelligence, vol. 2(12), pp. 1137–1143. Morgan Kaufmann, San Mateo (1995)
6. BrandstÃdt, A., Le, V.B.: Structure and linear time recognition of 3-leaf powers. Inf. Process. Letters **98**(4), 133–138 (2006)
7. Hu, M.K.: Visual pattern recognition by moment invariants. IRE Trans. Inform. Theory **8**, 179–187 (1962)
8. Sampallo, G.: Reconocimiento de tipos de hojas. Inteligencia Artificial. Revista Iberoamericana de. Inteligencia Artificial **7**(21), 55–62 (2003)
9. Du, J.X., Wang, X.F., Zhang, G.J.: Leaf shape based plant species recognition. Appl. Math. Comput. **185**(2), 883–893 (2007)
10. Zhang, S., Lei, Y.K.: Modified locally linear discriminant embedding for plant leaf recognition. Neurocomputing **74**(14), 2284–2290 (2011)

11. Asraf, H.M., Nooritawati, M.T., Shah Rizam, M.S.B.: A comparative study in kernel-based support vector machine of oil palm leaves nutrient disease. Procedia Engineering **41**, 1353–1359 (2012)

12. Husin, Z., Shakaff, A.Y.M., Aziz, A.H.A., Farook, R.S.M., Jaafar, M.N., Hashim, U., Harun, A.: Embedded portable device for herb leaves recognition using image processing techniques and neural network algorithm. Comput. Electr. Agric. **89**, 18–29 (2012)

13. Hu, R., Collomosse, J.: A performance evaluation of gradient field HOG descriptor for sketch based image retrieval. Comput. Vis. Image Underst. **117**(7), 790–806 (2013)

14. Zhang, S., Lei, Y., Dong, T., Zhang, X.P.: Label propagation based supervised locality projection analysis for plant leaf classification. Pattern Recogn. **46**(7), 1891–1897 (2013)

15. Novotný, P., Suk, T.: Leaf recognition of woody species in Central Europe. Biosyst. Eng. **115**(4), 444–452 (2013)

16. Xia, C., Lee, J.M., Li, Y., Song, Y.H., Chung, B.K., Chon, T.S.: Plant leaf detection using modified active shape models. Biosyst. Eng. **116**(1), 23–35 (2013)

17. Du, J.X., Zhai, C.M., Wang, O.P.: Recognition of plant leaf image based on fractal dimension features. Neurocomputing **116**, 150–156 (2013)

18. Gwo, C., Wei, C.H., Li, Y.: Rotary matching of edge features for leaf recognition. Comput. Electr. Agric. **91**, 124–134 (2013)

19. Cerutti, G., Tougne, L., Mille, J., Vacavant, A., Coquin, D.: Understanding leaves in natural images - a model-based approach for tree species identification. Comput. Vis. Image Underst. **117**(10), 1482–1501 (2013)

20. Larese, M.G., Namías, R., Craviotto, R.M., Arango, M.R., Gallo, C., Granitto, P.M.: Automatic classification of legumes using leaf vein image features. Pattern Recogn. **47**(1), 158–168 (2014)

21. Larese, M.G., Bayá, A.E., Craviotto, R.M., Arango, M.R., Gallo, C., Granitto, P.M.: Multiscale recognition of legume varieties based on leaf venation images. Expert Syst. Appl. **41**(10), 4638–4647 (2014)

22. Mizas, C., Sirakoulis, G.C., Mardiris, V., Karafyllidis, I., Glykos, N., Sandaltzopoulos, R.: Reconstruction of DNA sequences using genetic algorithms and cellular automata: towards mutation prediction? Biosystems **91**(1), 61–68 (2008)

23. Rafiei, F.M., Manzari, S.M., Bostanian, S.: Financial health prediction models using artificial neural networks, genetic algorithm and multivariate discriminant analysis: Iranian evidence. Expert Syst. Appl. **38**(8), 10210–10217 (2011)

24. Caputo, A.C., Pelagagge, P.M., Palumbo, M.: Economic optimization of industrial safety measures using genetic algorithms. J. Loss Prev. Process Ind. **24**(5), 541–551 (2011)

25. Zhang, R., Chang, P.C., Wu, C.: A hybrid genetic algorithm for the job shop scheduling problem with practical considerations for manufacturing costs: Investigations motivated by vehicle production. Int. J. Prod. Econ. **145**(1), 38–52 (2013)

26. Breen, J., Souza, P., Timms, G.P., Ollington, R.: Onboard assessment of XRF spectra using genetic algorithms for decision making on an autonomous underwater vehicle. Nuclear Instrum. Methods Phy. Res. Sect. B. Beam Interact. Mater. Atoms **269**(12), 1341–1345 (2011)

27. Köker, R.: A genetic algorithm approach to a neural-network-based inverse kinematics solution of robotic manipulators based on error minimization. Inf. Sci. **222**, 528–543 (2013)

28. Mohideen, K.A., Saravanakumar, G., Valarmathi, K., Devaraj, D., Radhakrishnan, T.K.: Real-coded Genetic Algorithm for system identification and tuning of a modified Model Reference Adaptive Controller for a hybrid tank system. Appl. Math. Model. **37**(6), 3829–3847 (2013)

29. Zafra, A., Pechenizkiy, M., Ventura, S.: HyDR-MI: a hybrid algorithm to reduce dimensionality in multiple instance learning. Inf. Sci. **222**, 282–301 (2013)

30. Chou, J.S., Cheng, M.Y., Wu, Y.W.: Improving classification accuracy of project dispute resolution using hybrid artificial intelligence and support vector machine models. Expert Syst. Appl. **40**(6), 2263–2274 (2013)

31. Sarkar, B.K., Sana, S.S., Chaudhuri, K.: Selecting informative rules with parallel genetic algorithm in classification problem. Appl. Math. Comput. **218**(7), 3247–3264 (2011)

Impact of Weight Initialization on Multilayer Perceptron Using Fuzzy Similarity Quality Measure

Lenniet Coello[1(✉)], Yumilka Fernández[1], Yaima Filiberto[1], and Rafael Bello[2]

[1] Department of Computer Science, Universidad de Camagüey, Camagüey, Cuba
{lenniet.coello,yumilka.fernandez,yaima.filiberto}@reduc.edu.cu
[2] Department of Computer Science, Universidad Central de Las Villas, Santa Clara, Cuba
rbellop@uclv.edu.cu

Abstract. This paper presents an algorithm for initializing the weights in multilayer perceptrons based on the new metrics called Fuzzy Similarity Quality. The new metric used a binary fuzzy relation for quantify the strength of the similarity between two objects. This measure computes the grade of similarity in a decision system in which the features can have discrete or continuous values. Experimental results show that the proposed initialization method performs better than other previously reported methods to calculate the weight of features.

Keywords: Fuzzy Similarity Quality Measure · Multilayer perceptrons · Weight of features

1 Introduction

For the last decades, the size of machine-readable data sets has increased dramatically and the problem of data explosion has become apparent. These developments have created a new range of problems and challenges for the analysts, as well as new opportunities for intelligent systems in data analysis and have led to the emergence of the field of Intelligent Data Analysis (IDA), a combination of diverse disciplines including Artificial Intelligence and Statistics in particular. Inside the field of the Artificial Intelligence, the Rough Set Theory (RST) proposed by Pawlak in 1982 offers measures for the analysis of data. Rough Set Theory, (RST) proposed by Pawlak in 1982 offers measures for the analysis of data. The measure called classification quality (1) is applied when the RST is used to construct the evaluation function.

$$\gamma_B(Y) = \sum_{i=1}^{n} |B_* Y_i| / |U| \tag{1}$$

This measure allows calculating the consistency of a decision system. Its main limitation is being used only for decision systems where the features domain is discrete.

A new measure (named Similarity Quality Measure) for the case of decisions systems in which the features domain, including the decision feature, does not have to be necessarily discrete, is proposed in [1]. This measure has the limitation of using thresholds when constructing relations of similarity among the objects of the decision system.

© Springer International Publishing AG 2016
J.C. Figueroa-García et al. (Eds.): WEA 2016, CCIS 657, pp. 115–122, 2016.
DOI: 10.1007/978-3-319-50880-1_11

These thresholds are parameters of the method to be adjusted and parameters are aggravating factors recognized when analyzing any algorithm. The accuracy of the method is very sensitive to small variations in the threshold. Threshold values are also dependent on the application, so an exquisite adjustment process of the thresholds is needed to maximize the performance of the knowledge discovery process. Therefore, it is necessary to incorporate a technique that allows us handling inaccuracy. The Fuzzy Sets Theory, as one of the main elements of soft computing, uses fuzzy relations to make computational methods more tolerant and flexible to inaccuracy, especially in the case of mixed data [2].

Since the Similarity Quality Measure is quite sensitive to similarity values of thresholds, this limitation was tackled by using fuzzy sets to categorize its domains through fuzzy binary relations. It was shown how fuzzy sets facilitate the definition of similarity relations (since there are fewer parameters to consider) without degrading, from a statistical perspective, the efficiency of the mining tasks of subsequent data.

This new measure named Fuzzy Similarity Quality Measure based on Fuzzy Sets is less sensitive than the quality measure of similarity and methods derived too. The Fuzzy Similarity Quality Measure computes the relation between the similarity according to the conditional features and the similarity according to the decision feature.

The method proposed here as a weighing method of features is based on a heuristic search in which the quality of the fuzzy similarity measure of a decision system is used as heuristic value. We use PSO (Particles Swarm Optimization) to find the best set W; this method has showed good performance to solve optimization problems [1]. In the problem of features weighing, each particle represents a set of weights W with n component (one for each feature). The quality of the particles is calculated using the quality measure of similarity. At the end of the search process developed by the PSO method, the best particle is the weight vector w to be used in the similarity function and with this one the relation of similarity is constructed. The impact of a new method called PSO + RST + FUZZY, in the Multilayer Perceptron (MLP) algorithm is studied in this paper.

2   The Classification Problem with Multilayer Perceptron

The most popular neural network model is the Multilayer Perceptron (MLP) and the most popular learning algorithm is the Back-propagation (BP), which is based on correcting the error. The essential character of the BP algorithm is gradient descent, because the gradient descent algorithm is strictly dependent on the shape of the error surface. The error surface may have some local minimum and multimodal. This results in falling into some local minimum and appearing premature convergence [3].

BP training is very sensitive to initial conditions. In general terms, the choice of the initial weight vector W_0 may speed convergence of the learning process towards a global or a local minimum if it happens to be located within the attraction based on that minimum. Conversely, if W_0 starts the search in a relatively flat region of the error surface it will slow down the adaptation of the connection weights [4].

An MLP is composed of an input layer, an output layer and one or more hidden layers, but it has shown that for most problems it is sufficient with a single hidden layer. The number of hidden units is directly related to the capabilities of the network, in our case the number determine what follows $(i + j)/2$, where i is input neurons and j is the output. Each entry has an associated weight W, which is modified in the so-called learning process. The input layer is responsible for assigning weights Wij to inputs using the proposed PSO + RST + FUZZY method. From there, the information is passed to the hidden layer, and then transmitted to the output layer, that is responsible for producing the network response [5–8].

3   The Similarity Quality Measure with Fuzzy Sets

In [9] a fuzzy (binary) relation R was defined as a fuzzy collection of ordered pairs, then a fuzzy relation from x to y or, equivalently, a fuzzy relation in X ∪ Y, is a fuzzy subset of X × Y characterized by a membership (characteristic) function μR which associates with each pair (x,y) its "degree of membership" μR (x,y), in R. We shall assume for simplicity that the range of μR is the interval [0, 1] and will refer to the number μR (x,y) as the strength of the relation between x and y.

In Fuzzy Similarity Quality Measure, a membership (characteristic) function is defined by a similarity function (2) and (3). This function includes the weights for each feature and local functions to calculate how the values of a given feature are similar.

Given a decision system is a pair DS = (U, A∪ {d}) where U is a non-empty, finite set of objects called the universe, A is a non-empty, finite set of input attributes and d ∉ A is the decision (or class) attribute. These two granulations are built using the crisp binary relations R_1 and R_2 defined in Eqs. (2) and (3):

$$xR_1y = F_1(x, y) \tag{2}$$

$$xR_2y = F_2(x, y) \tag{3}$$

where R_1 and R_2 are fuzzy relations defined to describe the similarity between objects x and y regarding condition traits and trait decision respectively. Crisp binary relations R_1 and R_2 are defined by the following functions F_1 and F_2.

$$F_1(x, y) = \sum_{i=1}^{n} w_i *_i (x_i, y_i) \tag{4}$$

$$F_2(x, y) = \partial(d(x), d(y)) \tag{5}$$

$$\partial_i(x_i, y_i) = \begin{cases} 1 - \dfrac{|x_i - y_i|}{max(\alpha_i) - min(\alpha_i)} & \textit{if } i \textit{ is continuous} \\ 1 & \textit{if } i \textit{ is discrete and } x_i = y_i \\ 0 & \textit{if } i \textit{ is discrete and } x_i \neq y_i \end{cases} \tag{6}$$

where ∂_i is the similarity function of two objects X and Y with respect to the *i-th* attribute, W_i its associated weight and decision attribute d. (6) establishes a relationship of similarity between two objects (x, y) considering the similarity of the same with respect to traits in A (calculated as the F_1 function in relation R_1) and the target trait (calculated according to the function F_2 universe in relation R_2), the purpose is to find the relations R_1 and R_2 such that $R_1(x)$ and $R_2(x)$ are as similar as possible to any element of the universe. From fuzzy relations R_1 and R_2 can be constructed fuzzy sets $N_1(x)$ and $N_2(x)$. Based on this approach, the sets are constructed:

$$N_1(x) = \{(y, \mu R_1(x, y)) \, for \, \forall y \in U\} \tag{7}$$

$$N_2(x) = \{(y, \mu R_2(x, y)) \, for \, \forall y \in U\} \tag{8}$$

The problem is finding the functions F_1 and F_2 such that $N_1(x) = N_2(x)$, where the symbol " $=$ " the greatest possible similarity between $N_1(x)$ and $N_2(x)$ sets for every object in the universe U. The degree of similarity between the two sets for an object x is calculated as the similarity between fuzzy sets $N_1(x)$ and $N_2(x)$ can be calculated by expression (9). The expression (9) was presented in [10].

$$\varphi(x) = \frac{\sum_{i=1}^{n} \left[1 - |\mu R_1(x_i) - \mu R_2(x_i)|\right]}{n} \tag{9}$$

Using the expression (9) as the quality of a similarity decision system (DS) with a universe of objects $n = |DS|$ is defined by (10):

$$\theta(DS) = \left\{ \frac{\sum_{i=1}^{n} \varphi(x)}{n} \right\} \tag{10}$$

This measure represents the degree of similarity of a decision system.

3.1 Algorithm PSO + RST + Fuzzy

The following describes the operation of the PSO + RST + FUZZY algorithm based on the method proposed in [5–8]:

Step 1: Initialize a population of particles with random positions and velocities in a D-dimensional space

Step 2: For each particle, evaluate the quality of the similarity measure (11), D variables.

$$max \rightarrow \left\{ \frac{\sum_{\forall x \in U} \varphi(x)}{|U|} \right\} \tag{11}$$

Step 3: To compare the quality measure of the current similarity measure each particle with the quality of its best similarity *pbest* previous position. If the current value is better than *pbest*, then assign the current value *pbest* and $P_i = X_i$, i.e. the current location results to be the best so far

Step 4: Identify the particle in the neighborhood with the highest value for the quality of the similarity measure and assign its index to the variable g and assign the best value quality measure of similarity to m

Step 5: Adjust the speed and position of the particle according to the Eqs. (12) and (13) (for each dimension)

$$v_i(t + 1) = \alpha * v_i(t) + U(0, \varphi 1)\big(pbest(t) - x_i(t)\big) + U(0, \varphi 2)\big(gbest(t) - x_i(t)\big) \quad (12)$$

$$x_i(t + 1) = x_i(t) + v_i(t + 1) \quad (13)$$

Step 6: Check if the stop criterion (maximum number of iterations or takes five iterations without improving the overall quality measure similarity (m)) is satisfied if no, go to Step 2

4   Experimental Results

The MLP method with PSO + RST + FUZZY weights will be applied on a real dataset from the UCI Machine Learning repository. The variants for calculating the weights for k-NN are: the proposed method in [6] (called PSO + RST), and the weight obtained by Conjugated Gradient method (k-NN VSM), assigning the same weight to each feature (called Standard), Relief method, and weights calculated by the method proposed in this paper (PSO + RST + FUZZY).

Four different methods were used to initialize the weights in the MLP: random generation (MLP-Ram); calculation of the weights by the conjugate gradient method (KNNVSM); use of the same weight value for all traits (Stand = 1/numAtt); original method PSO + RST [6]; and weights calculated by the method proposed in this paper (PSO + RST + FUZZY).

They are the most referenced as standard patterns. In spite of the fact that every day new alternatives appear to solve the problem of calculating the weights, these sophisticated learning procedures are not capable yet of compensating the bad initial weight values (Table 1).

In order to compare the results, a multiple comparison test is used to find the best algorithm. In Table 2 the results of the Friedman statistical test are shown. There can be observed that the best ranking is obtained by our proposal. Thus, this indicates that the accuracy of PSO + RST + FUZZY is significantly better. Also the Iman-Davenport test was used [11]. The resulting p-value = 0.000000002666 < α (with 5 and 55 degrees of freedom) indicates that there are indeed significant performance differences in the group for both methods.

Table 1. Results of the general classification accuracy for MLP

Datasets	PSO + RST FUZZY	PSO + RST	KNNVSM	Estándar	MLP-AL	Relief
TAE	59.12	58.94	55.63	49.01	54.3	54.97
Diabetes	76.43	74.8	74.22	76.69	75.39	74.74
Iris	97.33	97.9	96.67	95.33	97.33	98
Hepatitis	84.45	82.01	81.29	78.06	80	79.35
Postoperative-patient-data	57.77	57.78	53.33	54.44	55.56	55.56
Zoo	97.66	96.04	40.59	73.27	94.29	75.25
Bridges-version1	68.03	71.43	41.9	41.9	69.52	60
Biomed	92.98	90.7	82.99	83.51	86.08	83.51
Schizo	69.54	68.27	62.5	63.46	65.38	63.46
Soybean-small	100	100	76.6	78.72	100	74.47
Cars	80.58	80.3	71.17	71.17	78.06	71.17
Heart-statlog	83.33	81.85	80.37	80.37	78.15	80.37

Table 2. Average ranks obtained by each method in the Friedman test for MLP

Algorithm	Ranking
PSO + RST + FUZZY	1.625
PSO + RST	2
MLP-AL	3.4167
RELIEF	4.2083
Estándar	4.7083
KNNVSM	5.0417

There is a set of methods to increase the power of multiple tests. These methods are called sequential methods, or post-hoc tests. In this case it was decided to use Holm [12] test to find algorithms significantly higher. PSO + RST + FUZZY - as the control method - conduct to pair wise comparisons between the control method and all others, and determine the degree of rejection of the null hypothesis.

Table 3. Holm´s table with $\alpha = 0.05$ for MLP, PSO + RST + FUZZY is the control method

i	Algorithm	z = (R0 − Ri)/SE	p	Holm	Hypothesis
5	KNNVSM	4.473467	0.000008	0.01	Reject
4	Estándar	4.037031	0.000054	0.0125	Reject
3	RELIEF	3.382377	0.000719	0.016667	Reject
2	MLP-AL	2.345842	0.018984	0.025	Reject
1	PSO + RST	0.49099	0.623433	0.05	Not rejected

The results reported in Table 3 reject all null hypotheses the p-value of which is lower than 0.025, hence confirming the superiority of the control method [5]. Since the PSO + RST vs. PSO + RST + FUZZY null hypothesis was NOT rejected, this is equivalent to saying that no significant performance differences were spotted between the two algorithms and therefore they can be deemed equally effective.

Although the experimental results don't demonstrate a crushing superiority of PSO + RST + FUZZY, it objectives were completed. PSO + RST + FUZZY is more flexible to imprecision than PSO + RST, especially in the case of mixed data, because it use fuzzy sets instead of thresholds to obtain methods less sensitive.

5 Conclusions

A new measure called Fuzzy Similarity Measure Quality which, using the approach of fuzzy relation based on Fuzzy Set Theory, has been presented in this paper. The main contribution is the use of similarity function of Rough Set theory as a membership function. This measure computes the grade of similarity in a decision system in which the features can have discrete or continuous values.

The paper includes the calculus of the features weights by means of the optimization of this measure. The experimental study for problems of classification shows a superior performance of the MLP algorithm when the weights are initialized using the method proposed in this work, compared to other previously reported methods to calculate the weight of features.

References

1. Filiberto, Y., Bello, R., Caballero, Y., Larrua, R.: A method to build similarity relations into extended rough set theory. In: 10th International Conference on Intelligent Systems Design and Applications, pp. 1314–1319 (2010)
2. Verdegay, J.L., Yager, R.R., Bonissone, P.P.: On heuristics as a fundamental component of soft computing. J. Fuzzy Sets Syst. **159**, 846–855 (2008)
3. Fu, X., Zhang, S., Pang, Z.: A resource limited immune approach for evolving architecture and weights of multilayer neural network. In: Tan, Y., Shi, Y., Tan, K.C. (eds.) ICSI 2010, Part I. LNCS, vol. 6145, pp. 328–337. Springer, Heidelberg (2010)
4. Adam, S., Karras, D.A., Vrahatis, M.N.: Revisiting the problem of weight initialization for multi-layer perceptrons trained with back propagation. In: Köppen, M., Kasabov, N., Coghill, G. (eds.) ICONIP 2008. LNCS, vol. 5507, pp. 308–315. Springer, Heidelberg (2009). doi: 10.1007/978-3-642-03040-6_38
5. Coello, L., Fernandez, Y., Filiberto, Y., Bello, R.: Improving the MLP learning by using a method to calculate the initial weights with the quality of similarity measure based on fuzzy sets and particle swarms. J. Computación y Sistemas **19**, 1–12 (2015)
6. Filiberto, Y., Bello, R., Caballero, Y., Larrua, R.: Using PSO and RST to predict the resistant capacity of connections in composite structures. In: González, J.R., Pelta, D.A., Cruz, C., Terrazas, G., Krasnogor, N. (eds.) NICSO 2010. SCI, vol. 284, pp. 359–370. Springer, Heidelberg (2010)
7. Fernandez, Y., Coello, L., Filiberto, Y., Bello, R., Falco, R.: Learning similarity measures from data with fuzzy sets and particle swarms. In: 11th International Conference on Electrical Engineering, Computing Science and Automatic Control, pp. 1–6. IEEE Press, Mexico (2014)

8. Filiberto, Y., Bello, R., Caballero, Y., Frias, M.: An analysis about the measure quality of similarity and its applications in machine learning. In: 4th International Workshop on Knowledge Discovery, Knowledge Management and Decision Support, pp. 130–139, Mexico (2013)

9. Zadeh, L.A.: Similarity relations and fuzzy orderings. Inf. Sci. **3**, 177–200 (1971)

10. Wang, W.: New similarity measures on fuzzy sets and on elements. J. Fuzzy Sets Syst. **85**, 305–309 (1997)

11. Iman, R., Davenport, J.: Approximations of the critical region of the Friedman statistic. Commun. Stat. Part A Theor. Meth. **9**, 571–595 (1980)

12. Holm, S.: A simple sequentially rejective multiple test procedure. J. Stat. **6**, 65–70 (1979)

A Genetic Optimized Cascade Multilevel Converter for Power Analysis

Jorge Luis Diaz-Rodriguez[(⊠)], Luis David Pabón-Fernández,
Edison Andres Caicedo-Peñaranda, and Aldo Pardo-G.

University of Pamplona, Pamplona, Colombia
jdiazcu@gmail.com, eacaicedo@gmail.com,
davidpabon@hotmail.es

Abstract. This work presents a power converter prepared to easy modify its electrical connections in order to obtain all configurations possibilities of the cascaded multilevel power converter with four H-bridges. Allows to implement both sub-topologies: single CD source and separate DC source, with symmetrical and asymmetrical configurations until 81 voltage levels. All the modifications can be performed using a graphical user interface develop in Matlab®. The modulations are optimized using a genetic algorithm and the system control is a FPGA. The power converter was developed mainly to performing power quality analysis.

Keywords: Power converter · Multilevel converter · PWM · FPGA · Optimization · Genetic algorithm · GUI · THD

1 Introduction

The study of power quality in power conversion is a very topical issue [1–3]. The power inverters play a leading role in power conversion, so its optimum design is required. The multilevel inverters stand as interesting solution, due to the fact that their output voltage have lower harmonic content comparing to conventional converters [4]. Another solution comes from a suitable selection of the control method [5, 6] the topology [7], the frequency variation method [8] or the modulation technique [9].

The current trend in multilevel converters point out to the use the H-bridges cascaded converters, due their considerable advantages compared with the multilevel classical topologies such as diode clamping or flying capacitors [4, 10]. The cascaded multilevel H-bridge converters have two sub-topologies: single CD source and separate DC source [11]. The first sub-topology requires only one voltage source for the entire converter and the galvanic isolation between stages is achieved with the use of transformers [12]. Instead of the second sub-topology who needs a voltage source for each H-bridge and all the voltage sources must be isolated [13].

For harmonic content optimization in multilevel converters, numerous techniques have been applied, depending on the topology and according to the specific goal and the nature of the search [14–16]. However, there are promising strategies with evolutionary algorithms mainly: particle swarm optimization (PSO) [17], ant colony optimization (ACO) [18] and genetic algorithms (GA) [19–21]. Genetic algorithms are

© Springer International Publishing AG 2016
J.C. Figueroa-García et al. (Eds.): WEA 2016, CCIS 657, pp. 123–137, 2016.
DOI: 10.1007/978-3-319-50880-1_12

suitable to describe the THD in terms of switching angles provides a clear criteria of evaluation of the function of optimization [9].

2   Cascaded Multilevel Converters

Figure 1 shows the general diagram of a H-bridge Cascaded Multilevel Inverter (CMLI). The output waveform is the addition of the outputs of every single H-bridge. The CMLI topology can be divided into two categories, depending on the relationship of the voltages at of each bridge. These categories are symmetrical and asymmetrical. Symmetrical if the voltages in all bridges are equal and asymmetrical if the voltages are different, are commonly used transformer ratios of 1:2 o 1:3.

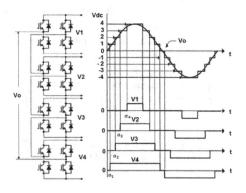

Fig. 1. H-bridge multilevel converter, waveforms and converter output.

Depending of the ways of obtaining the voltage of each bridge, two sub-topologies can be described: separate DC source, in which all bridges are powered from different voltage sources (see Fig. 2a) and single CD source, in which all bridges are powered from the same voltage source. The difference in voltages and the electrical isolation is achieved through the use of transformers (see Fig. 2b). Figure 2c shows an example of these sub-topologies in asymmetric form with transformer ratio of 1:2. In both the output voltage waveform is the same.

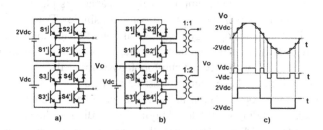

Fig. 2. Asymmetrical sub-topologies of the cascaded H-bridge multilevel converter. (a) Separate DC source, (b) Single DC source, (c) Output voltage.

3   Graphical User Interface

The software for the converter has been implemented by means of a Graphical User Interface (GUI) developed in Matlab® and essentially relies on five options at the main menu (see Fig. 3).

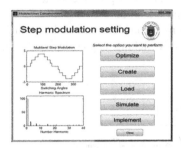

Fig. 3. Graphical User Interface main menu.

The first option is the optimization stage (using a genetic algorithm) used to *Optimize*, it is the one that allows finding a low harmonic content modulation. The second process allows to *Create* the modulation by means of the specification the switching angles at the first quarter of the output voltage waveform. The third option allows to *Load* the data in case you have one previously generated modulation. The fourth option is to *Simulate* the cascaded multilevel converter that allows to detail the relevant electrical parameters and its behavior. The last option is to *Implement* the modulation in the hardware, including the specified connection characteristics. The different options of the converter are described below.

3.1   Optimize Option

The optimization process is presented in Fig. 4.

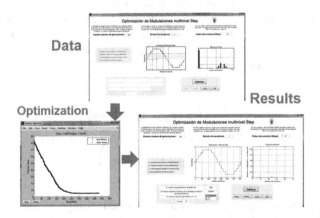

Fig. 4. Optimization process.

In order to obtain an optimized modulation, it is necessary to enter the following parameters: the number of voltage levels at the first quarter of the waveform, the maximum harmonic for the THD calculation and the maximum number of generations needed for genetic algorithm. Once the parameters were entered, the search starts in the least THDv modulation up to the selected harmonic. Finally, the genetic algorithm will find the optimum modulation and will give the switching angles, the waveform, the THD and the harmonic spectrum, so on.

The flowchart of the optimization algorithm is shown in Fig. 5, in which the vector L represents the number of switching angles by stage in the first quarter of the waveform.

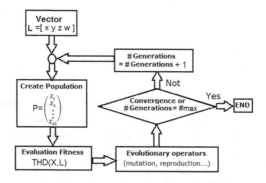

Fig. 5. Optimization algorithm flowchart.

For the Step modulation, the switching angle corresponds to 1 for each voltage level and each vector part indicates a voltage level [1 1 1 1 . .]. The algorithm begins with a random sample and continues mutating and crossing until it arrives at a convergence, evaluating the generations with a fitness function.

The genetic algorithm was carried out in Matlab® through the GA (Genetic Algorithm) Toolbox which evaluates each generation with the mathematic expression of THD, expressed in terms of the levels number and the number of switching angles per level, which corresponds to the fitness function (Eq. 1), explained in detail in [7]. The α_{ij} corresponds to the angle, j is the number of the angle, i is the number of the step, and L_i is the component i of the vector L.

$$THD = \frac{\sqrt{\sum_{n=2}^{50} \left[\frac{1}{n} \left(\sum_{i=1}^{4} \sum_{j}^{L_i} (-1)^{j-1} \cos \alpha_{ij} \right) \right]}}{\left(\sum_{i=1}^{4} \sum_{j}^{L_i} (-1)^{j-1} \cos \alpha_{ij} \right)} \cdot 100 \qquad (1)$$

The corresponding optimization was performed using a genetic algorithm, according [27]. The population size for the algorithm is consider of 20 individuals, each individual (X) formed by all switching angle in the first quarter of the output voltage waveform.

$$X = \begin{bmatrix} \alpha_{11}, \alpha_{12}, \cdots, \alpha_{1x}, \alpha_{21}, \alpha_{22}, \cdots, \alpha_{2y}, \alpha_{31}, \cdots, \alpha_{1z}, \cdots, \alpha_{4w} \end{bmatrix} \qquad (2)$$

The calculation ends when the values of the population converge or because the number of generations reaches the maximum assigned.

3.2 Create a Modulation

The option of create (a modulation) allows to obtain any modulation between the range of 3–81 stages, the GUI software requests the input of the switching angles for the first quarter of the voltage waveform. Each angle corresponds to a change in the voltage level of the output waveform. The THD value and the harmonic spectrum are updated with the change of any switching angle calculated to the selected maximum harmonic. This process is shown in Fig. 6. Finally, it is possible to store the modulation for later analysis, simulation or implementation.

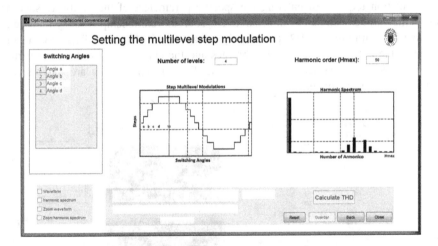

Fig. 6. Graphical User Interface for creating the modulation.

3.3 Load the Modulations

The GUI allows the user to store modulations; for its later recovering if it's necessary. In this option, the modulation waveform is loaded along with the THD harmonic spectrum and the switching angles (Fig. 7).

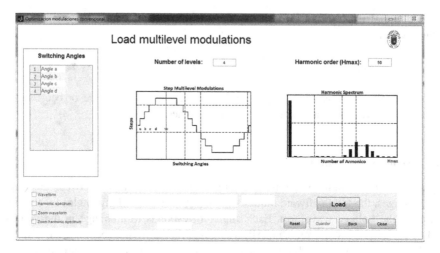

Fig. 7. Load multilevel modulations interface.

3.4 Simulation

The simulation requires of entering the specific parameters of the hardware such as voltage magnitudes (single CD or separate DC source), relationship type (symmetrical, asymmetrical with ratios of 1:2, 1:3), supply voltage and RMS value. These parameters determine the necessary number of H-bridges and the characteristics of the converter. The simulation was carried out in Simulink (Fig. 8). The results are the relevant electrical parameters for the converter.

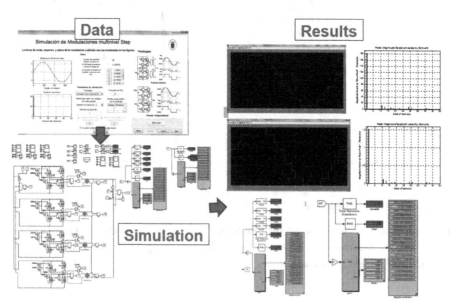

Fig. 8. Simulation process.

The simulation is only for the power stage and has the ability to modify the H-bridges numbers, the voltage sources magnitudes and the topology. The simulation includes the measurements of the input voltage, input current, output voltage of each H-bridge, converter output voltage, output current, display of the control signals, harmonic spectrum of voltage and current, and both THD (THDv and THDi).

3.5   Implementation

The implementation is the culminating process, in which the converter's parameters (of the hardware) are required, among those the topology (single CD or separate DC source) and the type of relationship of the sources (symmetrical, asymmetrical 1:2, 1:3). The software calculates the H-bridges numbers and the voltage magnitudes in order to implement the modulation. The process is divided into two stages; the first is the calculation of the electrical parameters (the drive signals of the H-bridges). The second stage is the coding to be transmitted to the FPGA that is responsible for sending the switching signals to the converter (hardware) (see Fig. 9).

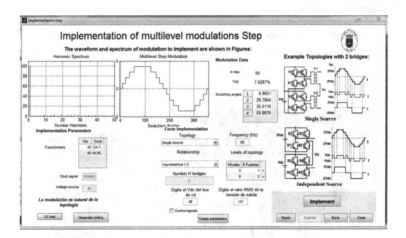

Fig. 9. Modulation implementation using the Graphical User Interface.

4   Hardware

4.1   General Circuit

The aim of the system is to achieve the desired flexibility with the lowest switches number, being the result the electronic diagram shown in Fig. 10. The system relies on four H-bridges that allows obtaining modulations from 3 to 81 voltage levels, in symmetrical or asymmetrical configurations. The highest level reached are 81 levels with asymmetrical sources with transformer ratios 1:3:9:27 in single CD sources or in separate DC source with the same ratio among the sources.

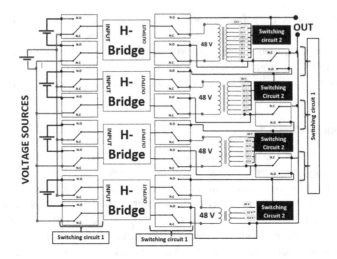

Fig. 10. Electrical diagram (hardware) of the converter.

4.2 Communication Stages

In order to commute the connections of the circuit's bridges, there are essentially two switching circuits. The first is in charge of the power connections and is made up of the switches (switching circuit 1) shown in Fig. 11.

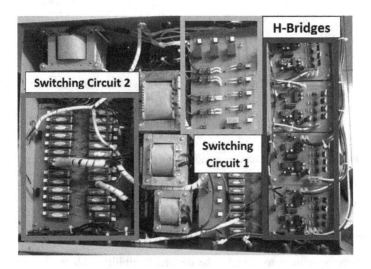

Fig. 11. Configurable converter up to 81 stages.

Its function is to connect the inputs and outputs of the H-bridge. At the input, it is necessary to select the H-bridges type of power supply, whether that is an isolated voltage source per bridge or that all H-bridges are connected to a single source.

At the output, it is necessary to select the connection or de-connection of the transformers in accordance with the H-bridges numbers. Additionally, it is necessary to connect outputs of the H-bridges in cascaded or series connection of the transformers' secondary windings. The second circuit is responsible for selecting the derivation of the transformer that is necessary to obtain the different voltage values of the asymmetry selected and maintain the waveform and the RMS level of the output voltage. This works only in single CD source configuration. There is an extra circuit that works simultaneously with the first and is in charge of connecting the control of the H-bridges in an equal configuration to the power level of the implemented circuits (Fig. 11).

4.3   Configurable Power Converter

This prototype consists of four H-bridges, four transformers and 32 relays that allow the configuration of deferential sub-topologies. The control was developed through an algorithm in Matlab® and the use of a FPGA XUPV5-LX110T, enabling the arrangement of the converter in order to obtain a separate DC source inverter. With 1 to 4 stages can achieve modulations between 3 and 81 levels with Step modulations and PWM modulations, the transformers are designed to avoid saturation facing square waveforms.

5   Communication

The overall diagram of communication is shown in Fig. 12. The characteristics of connection and drive control are coded in order to be sent to the graphical user interface in an organized way, and then to be sent to the FPGA via the RS-232 protocol. The FPGA decodes the information and sends it to the conditioning circuits which provide the precise values in terms of magnitude and time in order to commute the relays and transistors.

The FPGA was programmed in VHDL in such a way that it codifies the information and sends the switching signals to the conditioning circuits. For the reception of the data, the UART (Universal Asynchronous Receiver-Transmitter) is used to receive values with an input bit, 8 data bits and a stop bit. In the process, FIFO buffers were used to verify the data at a rate of 16X and a transfer speed of 115.200 bauds.

6   Test Run

6.1   Optimization

To verify the converter it's necessary to make a test beginning with the optimization of a modulation. The chosen modulation has 9 levels and its waveform is shown in Fig. 13, along with the harmonic content of THDv of 7.62%. The switching angles are shown in the simulation interface in Figs. 13 and 14.

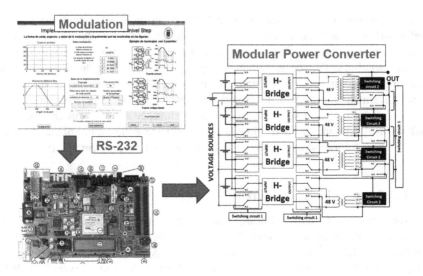

Fig. 12. General diagram of the process for the implementation.

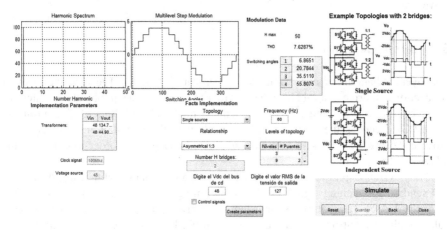

Fig. 13. Simulation interface.

6.2 Simulation

In the simulation, converter physical characteristics are selected to be implemented as shown in Fig. 15. For this test, the selection is the separate DC source sub-topology with asymmetry at the outputs of 1:3, for which the use of two H-bridges is required. The converter (in Simulink) is shown in Fig. 15, in which you can appreciate the hardware configuration.

The output of each of the H-bridges is presented in Fig. 15a. The addition of the two that correspond to the output of the simulated multilevel converter (Fig. 15b), in which can observe that correspond precisely with the theoretical waveform.

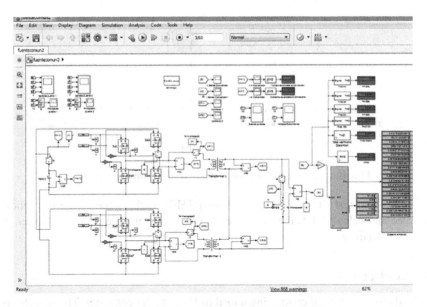

Fig. 14. Converter simulation using Simulink®.

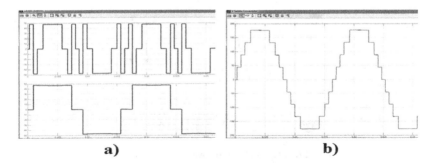

Fig. 15. Output (a) Individual H-bridges (b) Cascaded H-bridges.

6.3 No-Load Test

The implemented converter uses only two H-bridges, each one connected to a transformer at the output. The transformation ratios are of 48/127.2 V and of 48/42.42 V, calculated by the GUI and selected by the second circuit of the switching circuit.

In this way, the prototype must be powered by a DC source of 48 V and the result is an alternating voltage waveform with a 170 V peak. The nominal power of the converter is limited by the design of the transformers, which have a 200 VA. The measurements (Fig. 16a) with a calibrated Fluke 434 series II network analyzer. Can be noticed the similarity between the measured waveform and the simulation waveform (Fig. 15b).

The harmonic spectrum and the THDv of the implemented modulation correspond to the theoretical value of the optimized modulation, as can be observed in Fig. 16b.

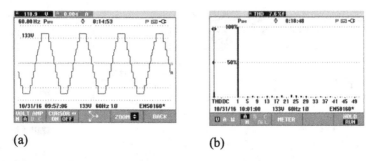

(a)   (b)

Fig. 16. (a) Step modulation waveform, (b) Harmonic spectrum.

The no-load test shows that the measured THDv is the same as the theoretically simulated and calculated THDv. Also verify the proper running of the converter, and show its versatility.

6.4   Load Test

The load test consisted of connecting a load of 60 W to the converter. The waveform is shown in Fig. 17.

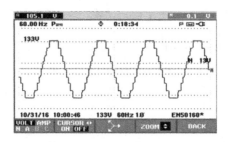

Fig. 17.   Step modulation waveform with load.

6.5   DC Bus

To acquire the voltage, the Fluke TP 120 sensor was used. For the current waveform, the Fluke 801–110 s sensor was used. A DAQ was developed with the National Instrument NI6211 and as data acquisition software used was Matlab® at a rate of 48 KSamples/s. In Fig. 18, can be seen the current waveforms and DC bus voltage waveforms of each converter using the step modulation.

6.6   Output Variables

The output variables measured are shown in Table 1. The THD of the 9 level separate DC source converters along with the power values in order to estimate the efficiency. The result of the no-load test differs slight from the load test, in which the THDv increases.

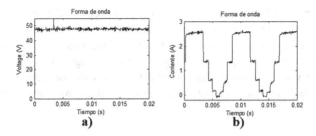

Fig. 18. DC buses with step modulation. (a) Voltage and (b) Current of the DC bus of the single CD source converter

Table 1. Experimental results

Modulation	Test	Parameter	Single CD source
Step	No-load test	RMS Voltage	118.9 V
		THDv	7.8%
	Load test	RMS Voltage	105.1 V
		RMS current	0.571 A
		Output Power	60.01 W
		THDv	7.6%
		THDi	7.6%
		Entrance Power	70.192 W

The step modulation demonstrates a greater performance due to lower losses as a result of the commutation of the converter.

7 Conclusions

The flexibility of the developed converter in the research of cascaded multilevel converters allows to obtain relevant electrical parameters in a matter of seconds for both sub-topologies in symmetrical and asymmetrical configurations. This was carefully verified by a precise hardware implementation, thus facilitating the comparison of the sub-topologies' functionalities in terms of power quality and performance.

The obtained THDv is the same to the theoretically calculated, verifying the successful functionality of the switching circuits, the communication system, the optimization process and the H-bridges, for the proper functioning of the converter. Considering that the measuring instrument was calibrated and complies with the IEEE 519 the THDv is therefore calculated considering the first 50 harmonics, so the optimization was carried out up to the 50th harmonic and the resulting error is insignificant.

The feasible possibilities of the converter with the aim of carrying out a thorough practical study are extremely vast, and increase with the use of PWM modulations. This doubles the modulations for analyzing the converter behavior with Step modulations and optimized PWM modulations.

The developed GUI facilitates the use of the power converter; only has to enter the converter's data and closely follow the instructions.

The developed converter is a powerful tool to analyze theoretically and practically, several multilevel sub-topologies in a range up to 81 voltage levels. The optimization process and the versatility for creating modulations in a simple way and easy way to implementing, facilitate the obtaining of the relevant electronic parameters.

References

1. Baier, C.R., Espinoza, J.R., Rivera, M., Munoz, J.A., Wu, B., Melin, P.E., Yaramasu, V.: Improving power quality in cascade multilevel converters based on single-phase nonregenerative power cells. IEEE Trans. Ind. Electron. **61**(9), 4498–4509 (2014)
2. Garrido Arevalo, V., Diaz-Rodriguez, J.L., Pardo Garcia, A.: Analysis of the power quality using intelligent techniques. WSEAS Trans. Power Syst. **10**, 46–54 (2015)
3. Diaz-Rodriguez, J.L., Pabón-Fernández, L.D., Contreras-Peña, J.L.: Low-cost platform for the evaluation of single phase electromagnetic phenomena of power quality according to the IEEE 1159 standard. DYNA **82**(194), 119–129 (2015)
4. Rodriguez, J., Lai, J.S., Peng, F.Z.: Multilevel inverters: a survey of topologies, controls, and applications. IEEE Trans. Ind. Elect. **49**(4), 724–738 (2002)
5. Hannan, M.A., Abd Ghani, Z., Mohamed, A., Uddin, M.N.: Real-time testing of a fuzzy-logic-controller-based grid-connected photovoltaic inverter system. IEEE Trans. Ind. Appl. **51**(6), 4775–4784 (2015)
6. Castilla, M., Miret, J., Sosa, J.L., Matas, J.: Grid-fault control scheme for three-phase photovoltaic inverters with adjustable power quality characteristics. IEEE Trans. Power Electron. **25**, 2930–2940 (2010)
7. Wu, F.J., Sun, B., Duan, J.D., Zhao, K.: Online variable topology-type photovoltaic grid-connected inverter. IEEE Trans. Ind. Electron. **62**(8), 4814–4822 (2015)
8. Pabón Fernández, L.D., Diaz Rodriguez, J.L., Arevalo, E.A.: Multilevel power converter with variable frequency and low constant total harmonic distortion. In: IEEE 5th Colombian Workshop on Circuits and Systems (CWCAS), pp. 1–6 (2014)
9. Diaz Rodriguez, J.L., Pabon Fernandez, L.D., Pardo Garcia, A.: THD improvement of a PWM cascade multilevel power inverters using genetic algorithms as optimization method. WSEAS Trans. Power Syst. **10**, 46–54 (2015)
10. Nabae, A., Takahashi, I., Akagi, H.: A new neutral point clamped PWM inverter. IEEE Trans. Ins. Appl. **IA-17**(5), 518–523 (1981)
11. Pabón Fernández, L.D., Caicedo Peñaranda, E.A., Diaz Rodriguez, J.L.: Comparative analysis of 9 levels cascade multilevel converters with selective harmonic elimination. In: IEEE Workshop in Power Electronics and Power Quality Applications (PEPQA), Bogota, pp. 1–6 (2015)
12. Banaei, M.R., Khounjahan, H., Salary, E.: Single-source cascaded transformers multilevel inverter with reduced number of switches. Power Electron. IET **5**(9), 1748–1753 (2012)
13. Malinowski, M., Gopakumar, K., Rodriguez, J., Pérez, M.: A survey on cascaded multilevel inverters. IEEE Trans. Ind. Elect. **57**(7), 2197–2206 (2010)
14. Zhang, Y., Li, Y.W., Zargari, N.R., Cheng, Z.Y.: Improved selective harmonics elimination scheme with online harmonic compensation for high-power PWM converters. IEEE Trans. Power Electron. **30**(7), 3508–3517 (2015)

15. Yousefpoor, N., Fathi, S.H., Farokhnia, N., Abyaneh, H.A.: THD minimization applied directly on the line-to-line voltage of multilevel inverters. IEEE Trans. Ind. Elect. **59**(1), 373–380 (2012)
16. Nageswara Rao, G., Sangameswara Raju, P., Chandra Sekhar, K.: Harmonic elimination of cascaded H-bridge multilevel inverter based active power filter controlled by intelligent techniques. Int. J. Electr. Power Energy Syst. **61**, 56–63 (2014)
17. Shen, K.: Department of Electrical Engineering, Harbin Institute of Technology, Harbin, China. Zhao, D., Mei, J., Tolbert, L.M.: Elimination of harmonics in a modular multilevel converter using particle swarm optimization-based staircase modulation strategy. IEEE Trans. Ind. Electron. **61**(10), 5311–5322 (2014)
18. Adeyemo, I.A., Fakolujo, O.A., Adepoju, G.A.: Ant colony optimization approach to thd analysis in multilevel inverter with different levels. Int. J. Innovative Res. Sci. Eng. Technol. **4**(9) (2015)
19. Ozpineci, B., Tolbert, L.M., Chiasson, J.N.: Harmonic optimization of multilevel converters using genetic algorithms. IEEE Power Electron. Lett. **3**(3), 92–95 (2005)
20. Roberge, V., Tarbouchi, M., Okou, F.: Strategies to accelerate harmonic minimization in multilevel inverters using a parallel genetic algorithm on graphical processing unit. IEEE Trans. Power Electron. **29**(10), 5087–5090 (2014)
21. Diaz Rodriguez, J.L., Pabón Fernández, L.D., Caicedo, E.A.: Novel methodology for the calculation of transformers in power multilevel converters. Ing. Compet. **17**(1), 121–132 (2015)

Simulation Systems

Proposal for a Hybrid Expert System and an Optimization Model for the Routing Problem in the Courier Services

William Camilo Rodríguez-Vásquez[(⊠)],
Eduyn Ramiro López-Santana[(⊠)],
and Germán Andrés Méndez-Giraldo

Faculty of Engineering, Universidad Distrital Francisco José de Caldas,
Bogotá, Colombia
william.rodriguez.v@gmail.com,
{erlopezs,gmendez}@udistrital.edu.co

Abstract. Courier services consist generally in distributing packages or envelopes that are received daily for a set of customers geographically distributed through a fleet of vehicles. Thus, these services could be modeled as vehicle routing problem. The aim of this paper is to show an approach to solve this problem. We propose a three stage approached the first ones consist of scheduling, the second one is a clustering of customers, and the last one is a routing stage. Finally, we presented numerical results using a case study.

Keywords: Courier service · Clustering · Vehicle routing problem · Expert system

1 Introduction

Businesses in the courier service have grown in coverage and in operative complexity, although, in many of them, the traditional expertise of their workers is still used as the main input to execute the distribution operation, allowing the chance of human error to develop inconsistencies in the process, triggered, among other reasons, by employee turnover and the constant loss of the compounded knowledge and experience about the specific tasks involved in the process.

The courier service generally consists in distributing packages or envelopes that are managed daily to a set of customers geographically distributed through a fleet of vehicles. Thus, these services could be modeled as vehicle routing problem (VRP). Although to represent properly the service, many constraints present in the VRP components have to be addressed.

From these constraints is where different versions of the VRP arise [1], in the specific case of the courier service, these are some of the constraints that have been applied and others that can be applied: time windows is the most common constraint among customers, since appointments can be arranged before delivery and have a specific date and time to comply [2]; the capacity constraint, almost always is taken into account, it refers to the highest possible load capacity of the vehicles; time or

© Springer International Publishing AG 2016
J.C. Figueroa-García et al. (Eds.): WEA 2016, CCIS 657, pp. 141–152, 2016.
DOI: 10.1007/978-3-319-50880-1_13

distance constraint, in addition to the capacity constraint, each vehicle has a maximum traveling distance that can be reached, usually given in terms of distance or time [1]; multiple periods, when considering planning horizon set by a determined number of days in which clients have to be reached at least once. An extension of this constraints takes into consideration due dates of clients [3].

This paper proposes a methodology to solve the VRP in the courier services, considering time windows, multiple periods, capacity and distances as constraints.

The remainder of this paper is organized as follows. Section 2 presents a literature review of the VRP problems related to the courier service. Section 3 involves the formulation of the problem and the notation used, in Sect. 4 is the proposed solution, in Sect. 5 the differences of the proposal are discussed. The Sect. 6 shows the results of the proposal and finally the Sect. 7 concludes this work and state future research lines.

2 Literature Review

The VRP is one of the most researched combinatorial optimization problems [4]. According the history several variants of the VRP and their different solving methods have presented an exponential growth rate of 6% between 1956 and 2006 [5]. This growth seems to be steady according to more recent studies from 2009 to 2015 [6], concluding also that there is a trend in these researches towards VRP of including more real life characteristics.

2.1 VRP Solving Methods

To solve VRP a wide variety of methods have been proposed, being able to be clustered in exact methods, classic heuristics and metaheuristics [5], then a description of each of them is presented.

Exact methods: among the main exact methods used to solve the VRP are the Branch and Bound (B&B), Branch and Cut and Set-covering-based [1]. An example of a B&B can be found in [7], where B&B is used to solve a VRP with distance constraints. For the Branch and cut, an example of the application for the VRP with multiple periods can be found in [3]. An example of the Set-covering-based is the article [8].

Heuristics: the most used are the two-phase heuristics, among these there are three families of methods: the cluster-first route-second, the route-first cluster-second and the PEDAL algorithms [2]. In the first family, the classic example is the Sweep Algorithm [2], although, a new example of algorithms is the Adaptive Large Neighborhood Search framework (ALNS) in which five types of VRP can be solved. Shifting towards the second family, among the route-first cluster-second methods we have the Greedy Algorithm, in which examples can be found in [9] or [10].

Other heuristics, also very important, are the constructive heuristic, the classic example is the Clarke & Wright's Saving Algorithm [11]. This heuristic have been used even for VRP that with economic variables such as work shifts, variable costs and traffic jams [12]. Another, more recent example is presented in [13] using constructive heuristic as a step of the broader heuristic proposal.

Metaheuristics: these are used frequently in combinatorial optimization problems that are difficult to solve, that is why they have been widely applied to VRPs. Some of the most commonly used are: Tabu search (TS), developed from heuristic from local search while additionally including a solution evaluation, local searching tactics, termination criteria and elements such as tabus in a list and the tabu length [14]; Ant Colony Optimization (ACO), inspired in the feeding process of the ants, it is an algorithm of collective intelligence to solve particularly complex combinatorial optimization problems [15] and Genetic Algorithms (GA), defined as a technic of adaptive heuristic search that operates over a population of solutions, very different in comparison to most of the stochastic search methods that operate over only one solution [16].

2.2 Solving Methods Applied to Courier Services

Regarding all the recent researches about VRPs, studies or proposals related to these problems are uncommon, although, there are some proposals found in the literature.

Chang & Yen [17] proposes routing and scheduling strategies to help city couriers reduce operating costs and enhance service level. They formulated a multi-objective multiple TSP with several strict time windows and proposed a multi-objective scatter search framework that seeks to find the set of Pareto-optimal solutions to the problem. This model simultaneously minimizes the total traveled length and the unbalanced workload. They presented the study of a logistics corporation in Taiwan. Fikar & Hirsch [18] presented a solution procedure to a real life TSP problem for the Austrian Red Cross, a major home health care provider through a team of nurses. The main variable are the time windows of the nurses, which include traveling time and service times, both considered constant. Guiani et al. [19] describe anticipatory algorithms for the dynamic vehicle dispatching problem with pickups and deliveries, a problem that most local courier businesses deal with, seeking to minimize the expected inconveniences of the customers. Janssens et al. [20] shown the case of partition the distribution region into smaller micro-zones to be later assigned to a preferred vehicle in so-called tactical plan. Yan et al. [21] propose a planning and a real-time adjustment model to plan courier routes and schedules in urban areas to adjust planned routes in actual operations. The VRP includes demand and stochastic traveling times.

2.3 Comparison

Concerning to the literature review, this is the comparison of the referred publications about the VRP in the courier services and the proposal in this paper. In Table 1 can be shown that when applying the VRP in the courier service, the constraints that usually are taken into consideration are capacity and time windows, also one or two simultaneous constraints are used, while in the proposal of this article, other constraints are considered, such as distance or multiple time periods, therefore, the solution considers four restrictions are at the same time, implying a high level of complexity.

Table 1. Constraints of VRP used in courier services

Constraints	References					Our proposal
	[17]	[18]	[19]	[20]	[21]	
Capacity	x	x	x	x	x	x
Time windows	x	x				x
Distance						x
Pickup and delivery			x			
Multiperiod						x
Dynamic demand			x			
Stochastic demand					x	

3   Problem Statement

We consider a set of customers $V_c = \{1, 2, \ldots, N\}$ geographically distributed, in which each customer expects a product. The vehicles that visit the customers are identical $K = \{1, 2, \ldots, m\}$ and belong to a central hub $\{0\}$ that is considered to be the starting point and the end of all the vehicles. All customers must be visited once for each vehicle during the planning horizon of p days. The problem can be defined as a directed complete graph $G = \{V, A\}$ where $V = V_c \, U\{0\}$ is the set of vertices and $A = \{(i,j) : i, j \, \varepsilon \, V, i \neq j\}$ is the set of arcs. Each arc (i,j) has a non-negative associated value t_{ij} that represents the traveling time from i to j. The objective is to establish the set of routes to travel by the vehicles seeking to minimize the total length and to visit all customers.

The assumptions for the formulation of the analyzed problem are listed below: the visiting time is the same for all customers and all vehicles; The customers present a hard time window and have a due date to be visited; all vehicles are homogeneous and they have the same capacity; each vehicle has an availability limitation for the traveling time and service time; all vehicles start and finish in a central depot; all the traveling time are deterministic and satisfies the triangle inequality.

To solve the previously defined problem we proposed to decompose it in three stages, and then to solve them successively:

1. Scheduling: Defines the visit date of each vertex from the set Vc in the planning horizon of p days, considering the date, the due date to visit and the times t_{ij}, for all $(i,j) \in A$. An expert system is used, where its structure is set mainly from know-how, an inference engine that works as a rule interpreter and a subsystem that explains the expert system behavior when a solution is found [22].
2. Clustering: Cluster all the vertices of the set Vp according to the traveling time t_{ij}, that belongs to Ap, and assigns it to a k vehicle considering the capacity in its schedule $[n_k, p_k]$, its maximum load capacity Q and the time windows of the customers $[e_j, l_j]$.
3. Route design: It is an individual optimization process to establish the order in which each vehicle will visit all customers assigned during the clustering process, taking into account also the time windows of the customers and the available time of the vehicles.

Table 2 contains a summary of the sets, parameters and variables required in the formulation of the mathematical models of each one of the stages described above.

Table 2. Problem notation

Sets

V_c : Set of customers
V : Set of vertices
A : Set of arcs
P : Set of days in the planning horizon
V_p : Set of vertices to visit per day
A_p : Set of arcs that connect to the visiting vertices per day
V_{pk} : Set of vertices to visit per day for each k vehicle
A_{pk} : Set of arcs that connect to the visiting vertices per day for the k vehicle
K : Set of vehicles

Parameters

N : Number of customers
m : Number of vehicles
Tv : Visiting standard time
Q : Capacity
C : Vehicle cost per minute
$d_{j:}$ Demand of the j customer
e_j : Lower limit of the time window for the j customer
l_j : Upper limit of the time window for the j customer
n_k : Lower limit for the available time of the k vehicle
p_k : Upper limit for the available time of the k vehicle
R_k : Maximum time availability for the k vehicle
t_{ij} : Traveling time in minutes to the arcs $(i,j) \in A$
F_k : Fixed cost of the k vehicle
h_j : Date of the visit with the j customer
G_j : Due date to visit the j customer
D : Average visit capacity of the vehicles per hour
HD : Total available hours of all the vehicles

Binary Variables

z_{jp} : if j customer is visited on the p period
y_{jk} : If the j customer is visited by the k vehicle
x_{ij} : If the arc (i,j) is used for the optimal solution
y_k : If the vehicle k is used

Integer Variables

N_p : Amount of customers to visit on the p day

Continuous Variables

S_j : Moment in time in which the visit of the j customer starts
u_j : Accumulated load delivered up to reaching the j customer

---

4 Solution Proposal

In this section, the mathematical formulation for each stage is presented.

4.1   Scheduling

For all customers that require being visited during the planning horizon, the mathematical model is formulated as follows:

$$Min \frac{\sum_{p \in H} \sum_{\substack{i \in V \\ i \neq j}} \sum_{j \in V} t_{ij} z_{jp}}{N} \tag{1}$$

Subject to:

$$z_{jp} = f\left(h_j, G_j, t_{ij}, Q, m, HD, D\right) \quad \forall j \in V, p \in P \tag{2}$$

$$\sum_{p \in P} z_{jp} = 1 \quad \forall p \in H \tag{3}$$

$$\sum_{j \in V} z_{jp} \leq HD \cdot D \quad \forall p \in H \tag{4}$$

$$z_{jp} \in \{0, 1\} \quad \forall j \in V, p \in H \tag{5}$$

The objective function (1) seeks to minimize the average length between all customers to visit each day in the planning horizon, allowing to maximize the concentration in the visiting zones. Constraints (2) represents the relation between assigning a specific customer to a day depending on the appointments arranged with them, the due dates of the customers, the maximum load capacity of the vehicles, the amount of total vehicles available, the average visiting capacity of the vehicles by hour and the total available hours of the vehicles. In the scheduling stage, this relation is represented under a set of rules that belong to an expert system that include basic rules to comply with the constraints (an example is the date of the appointments arranged with customers) and priority rules (some examples are: prioritize customers that are closer to the due date, customers who do not have an appointment and are closer than one who does so they can be visited in the same day). Constraint (3) assures that each customer will have a determined visiting date in the planning horizon. Constraint (4) controls the maximum amount of deliveries that can be programmed to be visited according to the total load capacity. And finally, Constraint (5) defines the binary variable used.

4.2   Clustering

Performed each day in the planning horizon, the mathematical model is formulated as follows:

$$Min \frac{\sum_{k \in K} \sum_{i \in V_p} t_{ij} y_{jk}}{N_p} \tag{6}$$

Subject to:

$$e_j - n_k y_{jk} \geq 0 \quad \forall j \in V_p, k \in K \tag{7}$$

$$\sum_{j \in V_p} d_j y_{jk} \leq Q \quad \forall k \in K \tag{8}$$

$$y_{jk} \in \{0, 1\} \quad \forall j \in Vp \tag{9}$$

The objective function (6) seeks to minimize the average distance among all the customers to be visited by the k vehicle. The constraint (7) guarantees that customers with time windows are assigned to vehicles that start their shift before. Constraint (8) assures not to exceed the maximum load capacity of the vehicles. Constraint (9) defines the binary variable used.

4.3   Route Design

For each vehicle and each day in the planning horizon, the mathematical model is formulated as follows:

$$Min \sum_{i \in V} \sum_{\substack{j \in V \\ j \neq i}} t_{ij} C x_{ij} \tag{10}$$

Subject to:

$$\sum_{\substack{j \in V_k \\ j \neq i}} x_{ij} = 1 \quad \forall i, j \in V_k \tag{11}$$

$$\sum_{\substack{i \in V_k \\ i \neq j}} x_{ij} - \sum_{\substack{i \in V_k \\ i \neq j}} x_{ji} = 0 \quad \forall j \in V_k \tag{12}$$

$$(u_i + d_j - u_j) \leq M(1 - x_{ij}) \quad \forall i \in V_k, j \in V_k, i \neq j \tag{13}$$

$$(u_i + d_j - u_j) \geq -M(1 - x_{ij}) \quad \forall i \in V_k, j \in V_k, i \neq j \tag{14}$$

$$u_i \leq Q \quad \forall i \in V_k \tag{15}$$

$$s_i + t_{ij} + Tv - M(1 - x_{ij}) \leq s_j \quad \forall (i, j) \in A' \tag{16}$$

$$e_j \sum_{i \in V_k} x_{ji} \leq s_j \leq l_j \sum_{i \in V_k} x_{ji} \quad \forall j \in V_k \tag{17}$$

$$n_k \leq s_j \leq p_k \quad \forall j \in \{0, n+1\} \tag{18}$$

$$x_{ij} \in \{0, 1\} \quad \forall i, j \in V_k, i \neq j \tag{19}$$

$$u_j \geq 0 \quad \forall j \in V_k \tag{20}$$

The objective function (10) seeks to minimize the costs related to the visits, multiplying all the trips in each route by the cost per minute performed by a vehicle. Constraint (11) assures to visit each customer once. Constraint (12) allows keeping fluency between trips in a route (after visiting one customer, immediately starts doing another trip). Constraints (13) and (14) assign values to the accumulated load variables and prevent to form sub-routes. Constraint (15) guarantees that the capacity of the vehicles is not exceeded. Constraint (16) assures to comply with the time windows of the customers. Constraints (17) and (18) control that the routes traveled by the vehicles are between the available schedules. Constraint (19) defines the binary variable. And lastly constraint (20) guarantees that starting times and visits cannot have negative values.

5   Discussion

This section describes the proposed solving method for each stage defined in Sect. 4.

5.1   Scheduling

Regarding the courier service, and referring to the definition in this paper, scheduling is performed by the workers using mainly the know-how and expertise of the business to define the day in the planning horizon in which the visit of each customer has to be done, evaluating variables described in Sect. 4 in the scheduling stage, such as, the date of the appointments with customers, the due dates to visit customers, the maximum load of the vehicles, among others. This work experience requires to be represented in a model which allows complying with efficacy the scheduling and avoiding the chance of human error that is why we propose to synthesize this stage in an expert system. Well-designed systems replicate the cognitive process that experts use to solve particular problems [23]. Also, from the designed rules that came from workers experience, the expert system will use as a performance function, the objective function established in Eq. (1), that is the minimization of the average length between all customers to visit each day of the planning horizon.

5.2   Clustering

To reach a solution in this stage there are different methods that allow to group customers, in this case, this options used in [24] were tested to finally choose the most suitable one.

- *Centroid-Based*: heuristic algorithm: this heuristic is based in the geometrical centers of the clusters.
- *Sweep heuristic:* clustering based on polar coordinates. From an origin point an straight line is shown that starts rotating and creating a zone in which the customers must be assigned.
- *Proposed location model:* Some customers are previously selected from the pool of all the customers as possible locations of focusers. Around this focusers other nodes are assigned as terminals, and then, a cluster is created.

5.3   Route Design

Finally, after being able to allocate a set of customers every day in the planning horizon, as a result we can simplify the problem as a TSP with time windows, length constraints and schedule capacity.

To solve this problem a ACO metaheuristic model is proposed, because TSP with time windows is consider a NP-complete, or in other words, belong to the combinatorial optimization problems that are considered difficult to solve, but according with [25], ACO has had several successful implementations in a wide variety of combinatorial optimization problems. In these problems, generally ACO algorithms are linked with additional features, such as local optimizers against specific problems, that take ant solutions for local optimum [25]. Some recent examples of successful applications of the ACO metaheuristic for the TSP with time windows can be found in [26, 27]. Also, if we consider that ACO metaheuristic have also been used for the VRP with time windows, more proposals can be found in [15, 28, 29].

6   Results of Study Case

The proposal introduced by this paper was applied in a real scenario of a courier company in Bogotá-Colombia. The sample consisted on 3.522 documents in stock to be delivered in the north of the city of Bogota.

Table 3. Document attributes

Has a predefined delivery date in the planning horizon	Remaining days until the due date
Date of the appointment	Amount of previous visits
Results of the last visit	Latitude
Results of the last appointment call	Longitude

For the scheduling phase the proposed expert system requires three phases. The first identifies the documents with a predefined delivery time window and thus immediately sets a visiting day in the planning horizon. The second phase is a set of conditional rules that evaluate each document attributes and defines if they should be discarded or evaluated by the next phase. The last phase consists on a point system that evaluates some attributes in the documents to assign a score, which will allow to decide which documents should be visited and in the date of visitation in the planning horizon until reaching the limit of the maximum capacity of the vehicles. Table 3 shows some of the most important attributes considered in the expert system.

Table 4 shows an example of the execution of the three phases in the expert system for a 3-day planning horizon. It is important to consider that the objective of this expert system is to minimize the average length between documents to visit each day, considering the set of operative rules.

Table 4. Scheduling results in study case

	Amount documents	Average distance (km)
Sample after application of rules	1.586	8,0
Day 1	529	7,9
Day 2	529	8,1
Day 3	529	7,9

A centroid-based heuristic was applied to results for Day 1, that consist of two phases. In the first phase clusters are defined through the amount of seeds equal to the number of available vehicles, and then in phase 2 they get adjusted in the clusters. Some of the results are shown in Table 5.

Table 5. Clustering results

Cluster	Amount documents	Average distance (km)
1	27	3,5
2	23	4,3

Regarding to route design phase, with the defined clusters in the previous stage, an ACO was applied obtaining at the end the visiting order of each document and the total length of the whole route (Table 6).

Table 6. Optimal route

Cluster	Visit order	Total distance (km)	Average distance between documents (km)
1	1, 3, 2, 23, 15, 24, 16, 17, 26, 18, 25, 21, 12, 7, 10, 27, 9, 5, 8, 6, 11, 19, 22, 20, 14, 13, 4	37,9	1,4

7 Conclusions

In this paper we propose a solution for the VRP inspired in the courier services. In the problem formulation there were considered constraints regarding capacity, time windows, multi periods, due dates, distance constraint and schedule capacity. To solve the problem, we proposed to divide it in three stages. Scheduling phase, in which a visiting date is assigned for each customer in the planning horizon. Clustering phase, where customers are assigned to the most suitable zone and vehicle to be visited. And, the route design phase, that determines for each vehicle, the order in which each customer will be visited by each vehicle.

In addition, for each phase a solving method was established. In the scheduling phase an expert system will be designed, based on know-how and experience of the workers. For clustering phase, one of three clustering methodologies will be evaluated.

And, for the route design phase, after defining this stage as a TSP with time windows, distance constraints and schedule capacity, after proven effective, the ACO meta-heuristic will be used. Unlike other proposals applied to the VRP in the Courier service in which heuristics and metaheuristics are used separately, this article combines these two methods and an expert system in one solution, proving the possibility to solve a VRP with more constraints simultaneously, as real scenarios require.

This work generates possible future development lines, one of which is the validation of results with a large data set. In addition, we could be to explore methods of numerical ratings based on attributes subject to imprecision using fuzzy logic, among other techniques, to scheduling phase. Likewise, other optimization methods could be explored in order to improve the solution of clustering and route design phases.

Acknowledgements. The authors would like to thank the comments of the anonymous referees that significantly improved our paper and the anonymous courier services company that provide us the data input.

References

1. Farahani, R.Z., Rezapour, S., Kardar, L.: Logistics operations and management: concepts and models. Elsevier (2011). doi:10.1016/c2010-0-67008-8
2. Toth, P., Vigo, D.: The Vehicle Routing Problem. SIAM Monographs on Discrete Mathematics and Applications, vol. 9. SIAM, Philadelphia (2002). doi:10.1137/1. 9780898718515
3. Archetti, C., Jabali, O., Speranza, M.G.: Multi-period vehicle routing problem with due dates. Comput. Oper. Res. **61**, 122–134 (2015). doi:10.1016/j.cor.2015.03.014
4. Golden, B.L., Raghavan, S., Wasil, E.A.: The Vehicle Routing Problem: Latest Advances and New Challenges: Latest Advances and New Challenges. Springer, US (2008). doi:10. 1007/978-0-387-77778-8
5. Eksioglu, B., Vural, A.V., Reisman, A.: The vehicle routing problem: a taxonomic review. Comput. Ind. Eng. **57**, 1472–1483 (2009). doi:10.1016/j.cie.2009.05.009
6. Braekers, K., Ramaekers, K., Van Nieuwenhuyse, I.: The vehicle routing problem: state of the art classification and review. Comput. Ind. Eng. **99**, 300–313 (2016). doi:10.1016/j.cie. 2015.12.007
7. Almoustafa, S., Hanafi, S., Mladenović, N.: New exact method for large asymmetric distance-constrained vehicle routing problem. Eur. J. Oper. Res. **226**, 386–394 (2013). doi:10.1016/j.ejor.2012.11.040
8. Cacchiani, V., Hemmelmayr, V.C., Tricoire, F.: A set-covering based heuristic algorithm for the periodic vehicle routing problem. Discrete Appl. Math. **163**, 53–64 (2014). doi:10.1016/ j.dam.2012.08.032
9. Arroyave, M.R., Naranjo, V.V.: Development of a model of urban freight distribution with logistics platforms applied to the city. Ing. USBmed. **5**, 67–76 (2014). (in Spanish)
10. Sprenger, R., Mönch, L.: A methodology to solve large-scale cooperative transportation planning problems. Eur. J. Oper. Res. **223**, 626–636 (2012). doi:10.1016/j.ejor.2012.07.021
11. Clarke, G.U., Wright, J.W.: Scheduling of vehicles from a central depot to a number of delivery points. Oper. Res. **12**, 568–581 (1964). doi:10.1287/opre.12.4.568

12. Yepes Piqueras, V., Medina Folgado, J.R.: Economic optimization of transport networks VRPTW type. Rev. obras públicas Organo Prof los Ing caminos, canales y puertos, pp. 31–39 (2003). (in Spanish)

13. Lin, C.K.Y.: A vehicle routing problem with pickup and delivery time windows, and coordination of transportable resources. Comput. Oper. Res. **38**, 1596–1609 (2011). doi:10.1016/j.cor.2011.01.021

14. Jia, H., Li, Y., Dong, B., Ya, H.: An improved tabu search approach to vehicle routing problem. Procedia Soc. Behav. Sci. **96**, 1208–1217 (2013). doi:10.1016/j.sbspro.2013.08.138

15. Ding, Q., Hu, X., Sun, L., Wang, Y.: An improved ant colony optimization and its application to vehicle routing problem with time windows. Neurocomputing **98**, 101–107 (2012). doi:10.1016/j.neucom.2011.09.040

16. Pereira, F.B., Tavares, J.: Bio-inspired Algorithms for the Vehicle Routing Problem (2009). doi:10.1007/978-3-540-85152-3

17. Chang, T.-S., Yen, H.-M.: City-courier routing and scheduling problems. Eur. J. Oper. Res. **223**, 489–498 (2012). doi:10.1016/j.ejor.2012.06.007

18. Fikar, C., Hirsch, P.: A matheuristic for routing real-world home service transport systems facilitating walking. J. Clean. Prod. **105**, 300–310 (2015). doi:10.1016/j.jclepro.2014.07.013

19. Ghiani, G., Manni, E., Quaranta, A., Triki, C.: Anticipatory algorithms for same-day courier dispatching. Transp. Res. Part E Logist. Transp. Rev. **45**, 96–106 (2009). doi:10.1016/j.tre.2008.08.003

20. Janssens, J., Van den Bergh, J., Sörensen, K., Cattrysse, D.: Multi-objective microzone-based vehicle routing for courier companies: from tactical to operational planning. Eur. J. Oper. Res. **242**, 222–231 (2015). doi:10.1016/j.ejor.2014.09.026

21. Yan, S., Lin, J.-R., Lai, C.-W.: The planning and real-time adjustment of courier routing and scheduling under stochastic travel times and demands. Transp. Res. Part E Logist. Transp. Rev. **53**, 34–48 (2013). doi:10.1016/j.tre.2013.01.011

22. Badaró, S., Ibañez, L.J., Agüero, M.: Expert systems: fundamentals, methods and applications. Cienc. Tecnol. **1**, 349–363 (2013). (in Spanish)

23. Turban, E.: Decision Support and Expert Systems: Management Support Systems, 2nd edn. Prentice Hall PTR (1989)

24. Patiño-Chirva, J.A., Daza-Cruz, Y.X., López-Santana, E.R.: A hybrid mixed-integer optimization and clustering approach to selective collection services problem of domestic solid waste. Ingeniería **21**, 235–247 (2016)

25. Glover, F.W., Kochenberger, G.A.: Handbook of Metaheuristics (2003). doi:10.1007/b101874

26. Kara, I., Derya, T.: Formulations for Minimizing Tour Duration of the Traveling Salesman Problem with Time Windows. Procedia Econ. Financ. **26**, 1026–1034 (2015). doi:10.1016/S2212-5671(15)00926-0

27. López-Ibáñez, M., Blum, C.: Beam-ACO for the travelling salesman problem with time windows. Comput. Oper. Res. **37**, 1570–1583 (2010). doi:10.1016/j.cor.2009.11.015

28. Pureza, V., Morabito, R., Reimann, M.: Vehicle routing with multiple deliverymen: modeling and heuristic approaches for the VRPTW. Eur. J. Oper. Res. **218**, 636–647 (2012). doi:10.1016/j.ejor.2011.12.005

29. Yu, B., Yang, Z.Z., Yao, B.Z.: A hybrid algorithm for vehicle routing problem with time windows. Expert Syst. Appl. **38**, 435–441 (2011). doi:10.1016/j.eswa.2010.06.082

Use of Simulation in a Service Desk
of an Oilfield Services Company

Luisa Carabalí-Sánchez[1]([⊠]), Germán Andrés Méndez-Giraldo[1],
and Carlos Franco[2]

[1] Universidad Distrital Francisco José de Caldas, Bogotá, D.C., Colombia
lmcarabalis@correo.udistrital.edu.co,
gmendez@udistrital.edu.co
[2] Universidad del Rosario, Bogotá, D.C., Colombia
carlosa.franco@urosario.edu.co

Abstract. Service desks over the years have become an integral part of most businesses, whether telecommunications, industrial, banking, health, etc. That is why today the management of these companies face major challenges such as the proper planning of the agents, skills, processing times, breaks etc. For those major challenges, simulation is suitable for modeling the service desk.

This paper presents an application of simulation for the service desk of the oilfield services company in order to achieve better system performance and improve the customer service process. The name of the company will be anonymous due to security policies.

Keywords: Simulation · Service desk · Workforce · Process improvement

1 Introduction

In today's business environment, people and the companies they work for depend on complex technology. This is the result of a huge challenge: supporting the growing number of technology users when they need help. The service desk is the single point of contact (SPOC) within a company for managing customer incidents and service requests as well as resolving incidents by using various knowledge repositories, the service desk can handle service requests, license issues, change requests etc. [1].

The number of requests made to the service desks within companies is estimated to be larger because some of these factors [2]:

- The Internet-based applications and rising number of mobile devices.
- Questions and problems from infrastructure and computing practices.
- The installation and updating of security and compliance-related systems such as antivirus, firewall, and data protection systems.
- Upgrades to existing systems, operating systems, collaboration systems, and messaging systems.
- Problems with outdated equipment and legacy systems.
- Others including presentation tools, photo-editing tools, tax software, money-management systems.

J.C. Figueroa-García et al. (Eds.): WEA 2016, CCIS 657, pp. 153–164, 2016.
DOI: 10.1007/978-3-319-50880-1_14

The Bogotá Service Desk in its 10 years of operation, has grown and has become one of the four service desks of the anonymous Oilfield Service Company, leading world-wide; providing the first line IT supports more than 100,000 employees and contractors.

This service desk handles an approximate number of 2,500 daily interactions, and communicates with the user through four different media: web chats, calls, voicemails and emails. They are the first point of contact for users who have problems related to IT.

Due to the large number of users who are given support, forecasting methods and management of resources for solving the problems have been insufficient. Different situations such as loss of calls, service times and longer wait than desired, are presented likewise the complexity of each incident is different user depending, these features extend the customer service process, generating more expected interactions on queue and a point of high stress by analysts feeling overloaded with work. We see interesting and important opportunities not only with call arrivals patterns and handling times, but also overall call volumes, using techniques from risk analysis and experimental design along with simulation models to quantify system capacity and delivery risks [3].

By the above conditions in this paper, and because of the provisioning of IT services increasingly being based on the modularization of whole service processes, it offers certain potential for reducing costs and enhancing service quality at the same time [4]. We present the management decision to employ new techniques such as simulation that allows them to counter the problems and improve customer services, making a balance between the qualities of service provided.

The paper is organized amongst Sects. 2, 3, 4 and 5. A review and related works about simulation in call centers are presented in Sect. 2. We summarize a company overview in Sect. 3. Following next, descriptions of the system, data collections, model designs, and results are the bases of Sect. 4. In Sect. 5, we evaluated different alternatives based on the necessities of the company, the paper concludes with this section.

2 Literature Review and Related Work

Several studies in the field of process simulation have been proposed already. However, studies related with service desk simulations was difficult to find, but there are plenty of jobs related to call centers.

The distinction between the two is pretty fluid. As a matter of fact, just a simple search reveals equal numbers of people who do and don't believe there's a difference [5]. The difference between call centers and service desks are the mutual points [6]. If a call center is customer service oriented, the focus may be more toward improved responsiveness to customer inquiries. In a service desk setting, the main objective may be improving the overall performance of problem identification [7].

The approaches in [8] defines the value of simulation in call center design, planning, and management by examining key weaknesses and strengths of traditional approaches and industry trends. It discusses how call centers can maximize their investment in simulation. The authors of [9] shows how simulation can be of use to generate data that can be used to evaluate incoming call forecasting algorithms. The work in [10], introduce key notions and describe the decision problems commonly encountered in call center management also formulated some common decision problems and point to recently developed simulation-based solution techniques. The paper [11] describes the modeling of a skill-based routing call center using two distinct simulation-programming methods: the C language and the Arena software package.

3   Company Overview

The anonymous oilfield services company is the world's leading provider of technology for reservoir characterization, drilling, production, and processing to the oil and gas industry.

The Bogotá Service Desk, began operations in 2001, dedicated to providing IT support for the anonymous oilfield services company employees since its inception has grown significantly to become the unique single point of contact for the company. The area aims to be the central interface between enterprise applications and users, providing high-quality business services worldwide through a combination of proactive and reactive support. This objective promotes the best practices in the business processes of everyday life, and helps with business objectives, and quality of services amongst others.

The main objective of the service desk is to achieve customer satisfaction and offers a response team 14×7 dedicated to timely technical support. The service desk is given assistance in: hardware, software developed for the company, connectivity. Administrative services such as access to servers, creates accounts for different applications segments of the business, cellphones configurations, internet channel monitoring, remote management of routers and servers, etc.

3.1   Bogotá Service Desk Statistics

Interactions loaded throughout the year are variable and there is no uniformity of incoming interactions. Last year the average amount of incoming interactions was 34,136 emails, 9,768 calls, and web chats 3,459, and 32 voice messages.

Making a comparison with the amount of incoming interactions of 2015 and 2014 are among the range of variations given by the standard deviation. This is disturbing because the standard deviation of each type of interaction and high variability, was confirmed on arrival system interactions.

4   The Current System

4.1   Steps for the Simulation Study

The methodology followed to construct the simulation is proposed by Kelton & Law [12]. First, the problem was formulated and the plan to followed.

The aim of the situation model is to provide a model that will give support for management decision making, given that such decisions are taken under a high level of uncertainty.

The model aims to find solutions to questions such as:

- Is the number the analysts have suitable for the volume of incoming incidents?
- How can the system be sized to an unexpected volume of interactions?
- What changes can be made to improve system performance?

Performance measures used to evaluate the efficiency of different system configurations are:

- Number of users served.
- Number of analysts required.
- Percentage of analysts' occupation.
- Time to resolve.
- Interactions Queue.

The simulation develops a model dimensioning of resources that fits the reality of Bogotá Service Desk. As with most simulations, you have the freedom to relocate resources, reorganize activities or modify procedures, without the constraints of cost, time, and difficulty of implementation that would usually have to be tested in real conditions.

4.2   System Description

The Bogotá Service Desk acts as a single point of contact for the oilfield services company; records, and manages IT questions and/or problems.

Specific service desk responsibilities include:

- Record of incidents and response to problems.
- Management lifecycle of incidents and requests.
- Keep users informed about the status of services, incidents and requests.

The service desk works for 14 h a day, 7 days a week throughout the year. It has a staff of 51 analysts where 41 analysts are Level 1 (L1) and 10 analysts are Level 2 (L2). Analysts are cross-trained e.g. Have the ability to multitask in this case would resolve any incident regardless of category.

Analysts on level 1 and level 2 have different functions, level 1 are those that provide the most service desk support and level 2 provide support but have additional tasks to improve the overall objectives e.g. Tutoring for level 1 analysts, help with questions, problems they may have, etc.

There are 3 shifts of 8 h each. The first shift starts at 6 AM, the second shift at 9 AM and the third shift at 12 PM. Besides that, analysts have a break of 10 min in the morning and afternoon, 50 min for lunch.

There is a software package used called Apropos[1] to automatically distribute calls, mails, web chats and voice-mail, among the analysts; additionally the other software

---

[1] Apropos Interaction Management is the platform for managing interactions and analysts in the Service Desk.

package used is Remedy[2], where the tickets are generated to track the requirements incidents for the users.

Figure 1 shows the flowchart of the system modeled. It consists of a queue where interactions are routed to Bogotá or other service desk depending on working hours, hence pass Apropos which is the platform for managing interactions; being here a part escalates to the other service desk or the onsite support according to the requirement and the other party is to be processed by analysts. The interactions are passed through Remedy. It is the management platform where tickets are created and can be followed up to user requests.

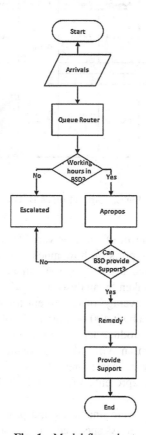

Fig. 1. Model flow chart

4.3   Data Collection

The data collection is drawn from information provided by the company, considering the random behavior of the events the tool used was Stat-fit, which is available in the

---

[2] Remedy is a Management Software that streamlines and automates the processes around IT service desk, asset management, and change management operations.

professional version of ProModel. It was used for testing goodness fit and the determination of the probability distributions.

The arrival rate represents the average arrival time between each entity entering the system, which in this case is an interaction.

After analysis and statistical adjustments, it is concluded that the time between arrivals is based on an exponential distribution. The Arrivals times are were classified by Day of the week and hour, Fig. 2 presents the results.

HOUR	Monday	Tuesday	Wednesday	Thursday	Friday	Saturday	Sunday
	Average	Average	Average	Average	Average	Average	Average
6-7.							
7-8.							
8-9.	Group 1	Group 2	Group 3	Group 4	Group 5		Group 15
9-10.						Group 13	
10-11.							
11-12.				Group 6			
12-13.				Group 7			Group 16
13-14.							
14-15.							
15-16.							
16-17.	Group 8	Group 9	Group 10	Group 11	Group 12	Group 14	
17-18.							Group 17
18-19							
19-20.							

	λ
Group1	2,53
Group2	3,00
Group3	2,97
Group4	2,94
Group5	3,47
Group6	1,23
Group7	0,68
Group8	0,26
Group9	0,24
Group10	0,29
Group11	0,29
Group12	0,31
Group13	2,61
Group14	1,47
Group15	9,29
Group16	4,78
Group17	2,45

Fig. 2. Arrival times BSD

The service times were the most difficult variable to collect due to the Bogotá Service Desk not having any reports on how much time an analyst spend solving an incident; all the statistics in the BSD are measurement by quantities. To solve this problem the total of incidents taken by analysts was divided by the amount of working net time, giving as a result an average of time spent for interaction.

The BSD monthly handles about 400 or more types of products. An initial analysis made showed that amount of product depends on the type to of the product; for this reason was decided to perform an ABC Model classification for the products where main products are in category A than represents 73.8% of all products, other fairly important in category B than represents 17.2% and the last ones in category C that represent the 9%.

For the analysts of level 2 were unable to find probability distributions as some cases not had enough information. As specified, initially analysts level 2 spent most of their time on other tasks such as mentoring than taking interactions, so for these analysts the times are average times. After this classification, the service times for the analyst level 1 and level 2 are shown in the Table 1.

4.4 Model Design

The entities for the system are the users, in this case, anonymous oilfield services company workers who communicate to the service desk for any problems related to IT.

Table 1. Service times Level 1 and Level 2 (Minutes).

PRODUCT	Lerel 1- SERVICE TIMES USER DISTRIBUTION	Levels 2 SERVICE TIMES AVERAGE TIME
LDAP- Directory Services	N(49.2, 18.6)	136,27
DSM- File Sharing	N(49.2, 18.6)	105,29
Teleworker- SecureGateway	N(49.2, 18.6)	136,27
PCS-Detected Is sue Resolution	$-932 + 981*(1./((1 /U(0.5,0.5))-1.))**(1./$ $,89.8)$	104,16
Windows 7	N(49.2, 18.6)	136,27
SDE-BitLocker	N(49.2, 18.6)	92,61
SCCM- Enterprise Image Management	$48.6-10.3*LN((1./U(0.5,0.5))-1.)$	105,29
Connected Backup	$49.8-10.6*LN((1./U(0.5,0.5))-1.)$	105,29
Enterprise Services- Not Listed	$48.8-8.52*LN((1./U(0.5,0 5))-1.)$	138,7
Exchange Email- Outlook	$-646 + 694*(1./((1./U(0.5,0.5))-1.))**(1./$ $66.8)$	105,29
Reader	$-810 + 859*(1./((1./U(0.5,0.5))-1.))**(1./$ $79.9)$	146,81
Internet Explorer	N(49.6,18.9)	116,27
SAP NAM Finance PC1	$-920 + 970*(1./((1./U(0.5,0.5))-1.))**(1./$ $93.7)$	160,24
PC Security Management- PCS	$47.2-10.2*LN((1./U(0.5,0.5))-1.)$	95,74
DSM-Print Queues	$-254 + ER(303,288)$	111,8
System Health Tool	$-2.02e + 003 + 2.06e + 003*(1./((1./U$ $(0.5,0.5))-1.))**(1./191)$	91,81
Exchange Email- Account Settings	$-616 + 666*(1./((1./U(0.5.0.5))-1.))**(1./$ $61.)$	102,39
Virus Qean-Up	N(47.6,16.1)	108,49
Quest	$-17.2 + W(4., 70.4)$	112,97
SDE- Desktop Encryption Services	$-765 + 814*(1./((1./U(0.5,0.5))-1.))**(1./$ $77.7)$	145,21
WinZip	$-164 + ER(214,146)$	90,14
Exchange Email-MailBox Management	$-1.2e + 003 + L(1.25e + 003,20.2)$	87,39
MDS Active Directory	$-764 + 813*(1./((1./U(0.5,0.5))-1.))**(1./$ $77.7)$	111,01
ToIP-Standard MACD	N(48.7,15.6)	93,27
Other Applications and Services- Not Li	$45.3-10.8*LN((1./U(0.5,0.5))-1.)$	136,27
Office	N(49.2,18.6)	136,27
DSM- Server DNS	N(49.2,18.6)	136,27

The locations in the model are:

- A router (1), which sends the entities to the Bogotá Service Desk or other Service Desk's (escalation) depending on the time.
- A queue (1), where the entities arrive and are sent to Apropos to be processed.
- One (1) location called BSD representing Apropos, where entities are processed, a percentage of these entities are escalated and the remaining are processed by the service desk analysts.
- To describe the analysts fifty-one (51) desks represented the level 1 and level 2 analysts.

The model represents one week of work for the system. For this reason, shifts are created to handle the simulation run time and the locations.

4.5   Processing

The entity (user) reaches the router SD's location that routes the interactions to BSD or other services desks depending on the opening hours of the office that is from 6 AM to 8 PM. After that pass to the location called BSD which processes about 26% of the incoming interactions passes to the analysts to be processed, and the other 74% is escalated to the next level of service outside the BSD. The 26% of interactions that remain in the system are processed by analysts depending on the type of product they belong after be processed the entity leave the system (Refer to Fig. 3).

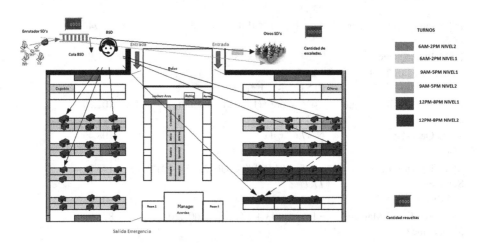

Fig. 3. Layout BSD simulation

4.6   System Output

For the verification, a detailed review of the model, and a statistical analysis was made. The validation was done using the Welch Method. As a result, the acceptance of the model gives results like the actual system.

After the model validation was performed, the simulation horizon runs 168 h, the equivalent of a week (Monday through Sunday).

The model showed that the average utilization of the service desk capacity is 95%. Which means that in a week, level 1's who bear the brunt of the operation, reach to solve about 50 interactions. These are roughly the 26% of the in-coming interactions, meaning that on average an analyst interacts with 190 incidents, can be a little more depending on whether or not they work weekends.

From the simulation, the number of incidents resolved by level 2 analysts equals just only 37% of the number of incidents resolved by analysts at level 1.

Other measurements found are the number of users served equaling 9,729. Escalated quantity incidents equals 7,377, which is expected to be 74% of users who initially arrive on the queue. The amount of created tickets is 2,519 which is expected to be 26% of users coming service desk and can provide them the service. The number of tickets (incidents) solved is 2,177 and waiting to be solved and out the system are 342.

5 Proposal for Improvement Based on the Simulation

Some of the problems that BSD Management want to attack using simulation is the unexpectedly large volume of interactions at the same time, and the effect on the analysts two scenarios will arise. For the first scenario the number of incoming interactions increase in 30% and for the second these interactions decreased 30%. The idea is to find a configuration that allows the BSD take action in case of emergency.

In addition to these alternatives, other alternatives will be created to improve the real system.

5.1 Increased Incoming Interactions by 30%

To achieve the assumption, the average of incoming interactions per day and hour are increased by 30%, finding new arrivals rates.

An alternative using backups analysts is the solution for this scenario, where a group of new analysts, in this case (12) are added to the operation in one shift which the BSD is not in operation, i.e. from 8 PM to 6 AM (Monday to Saturday) the sole purpose will be to process the incidents that are queued. Besides this, it is proposed that analysts level 2 work as an analyst level 1 and tutoring and mentoring tasks are distributed among the team leaders. Shifts and the number of analysts per shift remain the same from Monday to Sunday as in the current system.

In this alternative the averaged of utilization for the analysts is 97.7%, on the other hand, the time an incident delay in the system was reduced by approximately 8 min, from 48 min to 40 min with this alternative. Table 2 presents the differences between the real system and the alternative of 30% increase incoming incidents. (Refer Table 2).

Table 2. Differences between real vs 30% increase alternative.

	Real	Increase 30%	Difference
Number of users served	9500	11852	20%
Number of escalated incidents	8685	8537	2%
Number of tickets created	3253	3493	7%
Number of tickets solved	3347	3205	4%
Analyst needed	51	64	20%
Analyst utilization	/	97%	/
Service Time	49	40	23%
Incidents in queue	/	288	/

5.2 Decreased Incoming Interactions by 30%

As the previous scenario, the average of incoming interactions per day and hour are decreased by 30%, finding new arrivals rates.

The number of incidents in the queue is reduced to 45, the users entering to the system is approximately 6,678, (Refer Table 3).

Table 3. Differences between real vs 30% decrease alternative.

	Real	Decrease 30%	Difference
Number of users served	9500	6678	30%
Number of escalated incidents	8685	5124	41%
Number of tickets created	3253	1715	47%
Number of tickets solved	3347	1670	50%
Analyst needed	51	36	29%
Analyst utilization	/	95%	/
Service Time	49	46	6%
Incidents in queue	/	45	/

The ones escalated are approximately 5,124 and the incidents are solved 1,670. Obviously, this alternative allows a maximum capacity utilization of the service desk without overworked analysts by reducing the number of incidents. The number of analyst will be reduced too.

5.3 Improved Current System

To improve the current system, a simple proposal requires level 2 analysts work as a level 1 analyst, e.g. take incidents all the time and leave additional tasks such as mentoring and tutoring including the Team Leaders.

This proposal improves the system greatly. System utilization is only 90%. The average number of incidents resolved by the analyst is 47, and the average time spent on an incident system is 48 min. With this improvement, costs are reduced to only hire

Table 4. Differences between real vs improved system.

	Real	Improved	Difference
Number of users served	9500	9699	2%
Number of escalated incidents	8685	7395	15%
Number of tickets created	3253	2469	24%
Number of tickets solved	3347	2399	28%
Analyst needed	51	55	7%
Analyst utilization	/	90%	/
Service Time	49	48	2%
Incidents in queue	/	68	/

a small amount of analysts. In which finally, the most important resource (time) is well used; solving incidents quickly and effectively (Refer Table 4).

The results presented with the simulations made that the BSD Management decided to apply the improvement for the system, which level 1 analysts and level 2 analysts perform the same tasks; and with this applied change, data was collected to analyze the impact of the changes taken into the system.

A Mean Test is done to define if the application of the simulation have an effect in the real system.

The null hypothesis is rejected. The P-value = 0.039 is less than the significance level $\alpha = 0.05$. That means there are significant differences between the system before and after the change. Therefore, the change applied had an impact in the performance of the real system. The Mean test is valid for the global performance and according with the literature the validation is analyzed using the averages values.

6   Conclusions

This practical application of modeling has demonstrated the numerical advantages of using a simulation model to predict and improve service desk performance instead of using a queueing model as a representation of the real system. The queueing model can be a simplified representation of the system; due to the difficulty and complexity of the service desk operation, such as service times, amount of products handled is greater than 400, user availability, time zone, connectivity etc. A queueing model can never represent the system completely, as there are several uncontrollable variables.

While there are many papers on modelling of call centers and services desks, this paper explains the reason why simulation is being used to predict service desk performance. The main idea of this paper is on the system and data analysis, and solutions for the issues encountered developing the simulation model for such a complex system as the Bogotá Services Desk.

The proposed "what-if" scenario the number of incoming interactions increase in 30% showed that the alternative evaluated is useful. Although one requires more staff, the number of resolved incidents will increase by approximately 32% and inventory levels, i.e. incidents waiting to be solved is reduced by approximately 17%. For the second scenario where the interactions decreased 30%, the utilization is 95%, analysts are solving weekly an average of 46 incidents, the number of incidents on waiting was reduced from 342 to 45. The scenarios and alternatives evaluated with simulation indicated that the system was upgraded. The proposed distribution of resources increases the process utilization rates, times and numbers of users served. Additionally, each proposal involves a cost much lower than the current estimated.

Simulation allowed the company to have a better workforce planning, and within time, adjusts to future needs in a quantitative manner avoiding overloads or losses depending on the situation.

Acknowledgment. This work has been supported by the anonymous oilfield services company. The authors would like to thank the management from the service desk to give us the change to do this work. We have learned about the call center industry, management, and data analysis, which has contributed to our ability to model and analyze these systems.

References

1. Office of Government Commerce. http://www.inf.unideb.hu
2. Knapp, D.: A Guide to Customer Service Skills for the Service Desk Professional. Cenage Learning, Boston (2015)
3. Mehrova, V., Fama, J.: Call center simulation modeling: methods, challenges, and opportunities. In: Proceedings of the 35th Conference on Winter Simulation: Driving Innovation, Winter Simulation Conference, pp. 136–143 (2003)
4. Bohmann, T., Junginger, M., Krcmar, H.: Modular service architectures: a concept and method for engineering IT services. In: Proceedings of the 36th Annual Hawaii International Conference on System Sciences, pp. 74–83 (2003)
5. Bmc Software. http://www.bmc.com/blogs/help-desk-vs-service-desk-whats-difference/
6. Day, C.: Call Center Operations: Profiting from Teleservices. McGraw-Hill, United States (2000)
7. Bartsch, C., Mevius, M., Oberweis, A.: Simulation environment for IT service support processes: supporting service providers in estimating service levels for incident management. In: Information, Process, and Knowledge Management in Second International Conference, pp. 23–31 (2010)
8. Bapat, V., Pruitte, E.B.: Using simulation in call centers. In: Simulation Conference Proceedings, pp. 1395–1399 (1998)
9. Steinmann, G., de Freitas Filho, P.J.: Using simulation to evaluate call forecasting algorithms for inbound call center. In: Proceedings of the 2013 Winter Simulation Conference, pp. 1132–1139 (2013)
10. Avramidis, A.N., L'Ecuyer, P.: Modeling and simulation of call centers. In: Proceedings of the Winter Simulation Conference, pp. 144–152 (2005)
11. Wallace, R.B., Saltzman, R.M.: Comparing skill-based routing call center simulations using C programming and arena models. In: Proceedings of the 37th Conference on Winter Simulation, pp. 2636–2644 (2005)
12. Kelton, D.W., Law, A.M.: Simulation Modeling and Analysis. McGraw-Hill, New York (2000)

Effects of Using Multimodal Transport over the Logistics Performance of the Food Chain of Uchuva

Javier Arturo Orjuela-Castro[✉], David Andrés Sepulveda-Garcia,
and Ivan Danilo Ospina-Contreras

Universidad Distrital Francisco José de Caldas, Bogotá, Colombia
jorjuela@udistrital.edu.co, dasepgarcia2916@gmail.com,
ivano.ospina@gmail.com

Abstract. One of the most exported fruit from Colombia to Europe has been Uchuva, given its exotic character, taste and nutritional content [1]. Due to the importance of this product for Colombian exports of fruits and the latest trends in transport, this research studies the impact of using multimodal transport over the logistics performance food supply of Uchuva using the system dynamics approach. The model was built in Ithink, and it provides a configuration of the Colombian fruit supply chain, considering aspects such perishability of the fruit, logistics and environment. The indicators studied are: transportation costs, total time of transport, losses of food due transport and inventory, and CO_2 emissions caused by the transport mode.

Keywords: Multimodal transport · Fruit perishable food supply chain · Uchuva · Dynamic system model

1 Introduction

Multimodal transport arises from the pressure of world economic development in which the need to place products in foreign markets through an integrated transport system that is coordinated, effective, inexpensive, viable and environmentally sustainable is required [2]. Using containers for transporting has favored intermodal transport systems in the recent years. Authors who have addressed the definition of multimodal transport have not achieved uniformity in the definition. There is one stream defining multimodal transport as intermodal, while another stream defines it as a type of intermodal. However, for purposes of this research we have used the concept described by [3], which states that multimodal transport is the movement of products through the sequence of at least two different modes of transport, in a containing unit that can be a box, container or trailer. The use of multimodal transport systems is assumed to reduce costs, increase system efficiency and service level through the use of sustainable modes of transport, while generating logistical benefits in terms of the reducing widespread distribution of costs [4].

The reduced useful life time of perishable fruits has become the main problem for the overall planning of fruit transport networks, making it necessary to take into consideration conservation mechanisms, product quality, transportation times, packaging and

© Springer International Publishing AG 2016
J.C. Figueroa-García et al. (Eds.): WEA 2016, CCIS 657, pp. 165–177, 2016.
DOI: 10.1007/978-3-319-50880-1_15

operations for loading and unloading it. For this purpose, multimodality is an option that allows competitiveness due to reduced transit times in long distances [5], helping to solve the problems of dispersion and conservation [6].

The application of system dynamics for the study of multimodal transport systems has been limited. Aschauer [7] determines the interdependencies between logistics strategy and movements of the transport networks. Pérez [8] evaluates the efficiency and effectiveness of logistics for the connection between all parties involved in an intermodal system. Amro [9] provides the integration of transport and infrastructure variables, in the case of electric type transport, the author proposes a hybrid model using system dynamics and Petri nets.

Another model was developed by Arbués et al. [10] in which they determine the flow of vehicles carrying consumer goods by road and they also establish the variables related to infrastructure that are positively affecting current operations of transport. Among the few applications of system dynamics in food transportation, the work of Orjuela et al. [11] is highlighted because they present a model that studies the dynamic behavior between the food supply chain and the requirements of transport infrastructure and food security in Bogota-Colombia. This research examines the impact of changes in modes of transport in intermodal logistics over performance measures of the agro industrial chain of Uchuva. The indicators evaluated were: (i) overall costs of the transport system, (ii) total time of transport, (iii) loss of fruit quality by travel time and, (iv) CO_2 emissions generated by transportation mode. The following section presents the model through causal loop diagrams and the Forrester model, then we present the results and analysis of the study. Conclusions of the research process and future work are finally presented.

2   Methodology

The methodology implemented to the model contemplates the use of information primary and secondary.

For primary information was applied several surveys along the supply chain, to the most important echelons On the Table 1 the number of survey by echelon are related. On the other hand, secondary information was collected with governmental and others various related sources multimodal transport work.

Table 1. Primary Information.

	Hypermarkets	Retailers	Wholesalers	Agroindustry	Carriers
Inquest	2	79	9	1	16

3   System Dynamics Model

3.1   Problem Description

The latest trends research in logistics transportation networks focus towards effective integrated transportation modes that are coordinated, at a low cost, viable and environmentally sustainable. Intermodal systems are evaluated in order to discourage overuse of land transport, meeting delivery times generating lower costs and being environmentally friendly [12]. Colombian fruit chain stands out from other food chains for its dynamism and potential, excelling in areas such as employment generation and international trade [13]. Perishability feature in these types of goods poses an additional planning transportation problematic. Research regarding intermodal transport systems of perishable goods is emerging, however studies show that using appropriate units of transport and making the correct choice of transportation modes, companies can take advantage of the multi-modality for food transport such: (i) economies of scale, (ii) cost reduction [3], (iii) transportation times [14] and, (iv) environmental pollution [15].

The dynamic problem in transporting perishable goods involves the study of the relationship between emissions, costs, transport times and quality loss. The causal diagram showing this behavior is presented in Fig. 1.

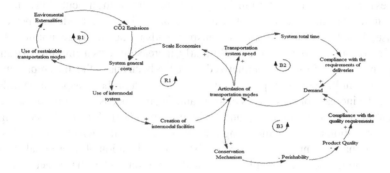

Fig. 1. Causal loop diagram for the problem of multimodal transport of Uchuva.

This causal loop diagram depicts four feedback loops, one reinforcing and three balancing. Each of the feedback loops is used for analysing a measure of logistics performance, as we describe below in more detail. This first balancing loop B1 (See Fig. 2) explains the relationship between the use of sustainable modes of transport and environmental pollution expressed in CO_2 emissions. Sustainable transport has less negative environmental externalities. Externalities in terms of increments of CO_2 emissions, which in turn represent greater overall system costs, given that this model includes a penalty for tons of CO_2 emitted to the environment. However, rising logistics cost urges to use more sustainable modes of transport modes.

Including CO_2 emissions and greenhouse gases has taken relevance in the latest research about multimodal transportation, due to global warming. It's important to set indicators to determine contamination levels and compare possible combinations of transport modes in order to choose the most sustainable alternative [16]. A modal shift from road transport to maritime and rail transport can reduce emissions of greenhouse gases and social impacts [17]. On the other hand, global supply chains require cost optimization of supply, production and distribution, including minimization of negative impacts in the environment, which must be considered because of their contribution to sustainable development, allowing build competitive advantage [18].

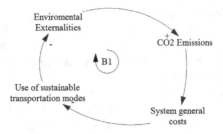

Fig. 2. Balancing loop for CO_2 emissions.

The reinforcing loop shown in Fig. 3 corresponds to the overall costs of the system. This costs are associated with the use of intermodal systems, the articulation of modes of transport and creation of terminals for this purpose. The use of intermodal systems increases the creation of such terminals, allowing to increase the articulation of transport modes, translated into the speed at which exchanges in every mode are performed. Likewise, the articulation of modes of transport leads to increasing economies of scale and lower overall transportation costs. Similarly, increasing costs in intermodal transport systems discourages its use. Containerized cargo has been one of the most representative elements for multimodal transport, creating a revolution in the transportation industry, allowing the increase of economies of scale and driving speeds to be improved, besides representing a reduction in labour and packaging costs [19]. A factor influencing cost is the combination of routes, including aspects of staff and its own characteristics [20]. On the other hand, it must be included the problem of location of intermodal terminals in order to minimize transportation costs and operation, given that it determines the routes in the transport network [21].

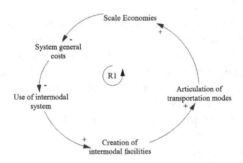

Fig. 3. Reinforcing loop for the overall costs of the system.

The balancing loop shown in Fig. 4 presents the total time of the transport system. This indicator of logistics performance is highly important given the characteristics of perishability of the fruit. Articulating efficiently the modes of transports allows to increase the speed of the transport system, resulting in less total time. The increased time reduces delivery performance, however, when compliance increases so does the demand, which leads to a reduction of the efficiency of transport modes due to the complexity of the system.

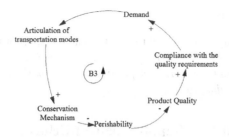

Fig. 4. Balancing loop for the total time of the transport system.

In their work, [22] established the importance of two significant factors in the efficiency of food products: (i) the transport speed, and (ii) quality preservation, which are directly related to the transportation time and the system response. [23] analyzed possible food damage due to transportation times and frequent stops made to serve consumers.

Given the importance of quality for export of Uchuva, this performance measure in assessing the logistics chain performance it is included. It is related to the articulation of transport modes, which in turn relates implicitly with transport time, a determinant of the final product quality. In this balancing loop (See Fig. 5), the efficient coordination of transport modes can be used to allow more product conservation mechanisms, reducing their perishability. When the perishability increases the quality decreases. When quality increases so does compliance in terms of quality requirements, which in turn increases the demand and decreases efficient articulation of modes, by the increasing the system complexity.

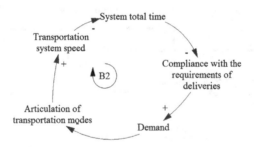

Fig. 5. Balancing loop for losses fruit quality.

Ilicali et al. [24] studied the importance of designing mechanisms for the preservation of food products, including models predicting freezing times for Papayas. On the other hand, [25] claim that food preservation in their intrinsic and extrinsic properties is highly important to maintain the highest quality, derived from transport and packaging in the life cycle of food. In addition to the distribution of food products, as Akkerman et al. [26] state, quality, sustainability and food security, define the strategic level of the network design, while network planning is taken into account at the tactical level and planning food transportation is boarded at the operational level.

3.2 Dynamic Hypothesis

The hypothesis of the dynamic model for multimodal transport of Uchuva in Colombia is: "*the use of multimodal transport systems improves logistics indicators of time and cost while allowing to maintain product quality and lower pollution levels which reduce the environmental sustainability of the system*".

4 Forrester Model for Supply Chain of Uchuva

4.1 General Model for the Supply Chain

The Forrester diagram for this model is analogous to the one presented by [27, 28], in which we based our work. We added the corresponding exports of Uchuva, which is framed within a black box in the following figure.

In Fig. 6, one can see the supply chain for Uchuva consisting of the links in the chain from the farmer or agribusiness to the wholesaler, retailer, exporter and multimodal transportations mode used for exporting. Relations between the links in the chain are presented and material flows are represented by the blue lines while information flows are represented by the red lines.

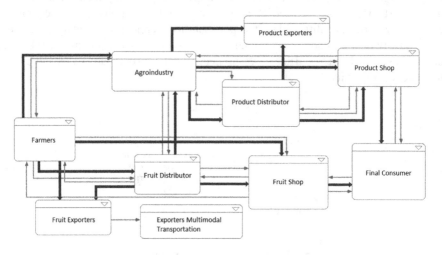

Fig. 6. Forrrester diagram for the agroindustrial supply chain of Uchuva (Color figure online)

4.2 Model Structure

From the initial model formulated by [27], we kept the structure proposed by the authors and transport indicators, average inventory, level of missing goods, fruit losses and satisfaction of demand are also kept. However, for this work several structures were added, in order to assess the impact of multimodal transport logistics over performance indicators affected by the use of multimodal transport systems, which are shown in Table 2.

Table 2. Performance measures for the model

Indicator	Performance measure	Units
Pollution generated by the multimodal transport	Contamination level from the usage of transport modes.	Ton
Transit time	Time spent from the exit of one mode of transport (source) to the arrival of transport mode 2 (the destination)	Day
Costs associated with the transport operation	Multimodal transport costs including operating costs in transit and intermodal terminals	USD
Transported fruit quality	Losses due to transport time	Ton

Multimodal Transport. One of the fundamental structures of the model corresponds to the multimodal transport. This can be seen in Fig. 7:

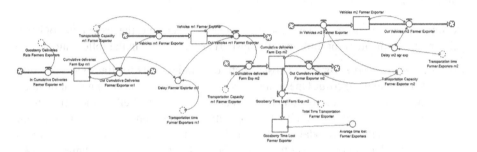

Fig. 7. Structure of multimodal transport

The structure starts with the delivery rate of fruit between one link and another. This is determined by the commands generated relative to the product inventory and the level of accumulated missing. This delivery rate is related to the capacity of the first mode of transport involved. It refers to the desired volume capacity to transport, without necessary taking the total capacity of the transport mode. The stock of accumulated delivery is fed by the delivery rate and decreases by the accumulated volume divided into the capacity of the first mode of transport (m1). Performing this operation ensures that the output is dimensionless in terms of load units of transport (m1). The outflow of the stock is modelled with a conditional logic that does not allow the volume to flow out (m1) before it reaches the defined volume capacity. Structure (1) is used for deliveries accumulation (m1) of the farmer and is written in the language of modelling software Ithink:

$$Out\ Cumulative\ Deliveries\ Farmer\ Exporters\ m1\ =$$
$$IF(Cumulative\_deliveries\_Farm\_Exp\_m1 < Transportation\_Capacity\_m1\_Farmer\_Exporter) \quad (1)$$
$$THEN(0)ELSE(ROUND(Cumulative\_deliveries\_Farm\_Exp\_m1))$$

This conditional evaluates the accumulated deliveries flowing out from the stock of load units which is not less than the set capacity of transport. When this capability is matched or exceeded, it takes the stock of deliveries and divided it into the set capacity for the number of cargo units. Loading units crossing the set capacity are accumulated in the stock of load units (m1). These units flow out of this level at a rate shown in structure (2) and with a delay as shown in structure (3).

$$
\begin{aligned}
& Out\ vehicles\ m1\ Farmers\ Exporters\ = \\
& DELAY\ (Vehicles\_m1\_Farmer\_Exporter,\ Delay\_Farmer\_Exporter\_m1)
\end{aligned}
\tag{2}
$$

$$
\begin{aligned}
Delay\ Farmers\ Exporters\ m1\ =\ & Cumulative\_deliveries\_Farm\_Exp\_m1 \\
& *\ Transportation\_time\_Farmer\_Exporters\_m1
\end{aligned}
\tag{3}
$$

Similar to the accumulator (m1), a stock that accumulates cargo transportation from mode one to fulfil the required mode 2 (m2) capacity is placed. These are passed directly to the stock of number of vehicles (m2) and flows out similarly with a delay analogously to the outflow of the units in mode one. The structure depicted in Fig. 7 was set up to set the number of transport units required considering scheduled deliveries and capabilities of transport modes to use.

Performance Indicators. The structures used to determine the extent of logistics performance indicators for multimodal transport are presented in the following part.

(a) *General transport costs:* The cost structure includes costs for transport operation and environmental costs. Operating costs are obtained by multiplying the unit value by the amount of transport units, which are a result of modelling the structure of multimodal transport. Given that the operation is intermodal, it is calculated from the origin to the intermodal terminal and from the terminal to its destination, these costs are added to the emission costs, so the total transport cost is obtained via (4).

$$
\begin{aligned}
Total\ Transportation\ & Costs\ Farmers\ Exporters\ = \\
Operational\_ & Transportation\_Cost\_Farmers\_Exporters\_m2 \\
& +\ Enviromental\_Transportation\_Costs\_Farmers\_Exporters \\
& +\ Operational\_Transportation\_Cost\_Farmers\_Exporters\_m1
\end{aligned}
\tag{4}
$$

(b) *Pollution from transport usage:* The structure to determine the levels of CO_2 emissions is calculated from the amount of cargo units derived from the structure of multimodal transport. In this case, we multiply the units of cargo by the unit quantity of emissions, expressed in tons per kilometre, as well as for tons to transport and kilometres on average still to go, structure (5).

$$
\begin{aligned}
Transportation\ Emissions\ & Farmers\ Exporters\ m1\ = \\
& Unit\_Emissions\_Farmers\_Exporters\_m1 \\
& *\ Distance\_between\_Farmers\_and\_Intermodal\_Hub \\
& *\ Out\_Cumulative\_Deliveries\_Farmer\_Exporter\_m1
\end{aligned}
\tag{5}
$$

(c) *Transport time between links:* The time between links is determined by the delay between the links established by mode 1 and mode 2, in the structure of certain multimodal transportation. In this case, since the carriage is performed from the farmer to the export destination, we include the time of post-harvest operations as product classification, washing, packaging, etc.

$$Total\ Time\ Transportation\ Farmers\ Exporters =$$
$$Postharvest\_Time + Delay\_Farmer\_Exporter\_m1 \qquad (6)$$
$$+ Delay\_m2\_agr\_exp$$

(d) *Losses caused by transport time:* Product quality is lost by increments in transport time, due to the perishability of the fruit, so that we have included a structure to determine the amount of losses from the total operating time of transport. The level of losses changes at a rate that behaves according to the total time of transport, this in turn will set the average losses and stablishes indicators for the related carrying quantity and the total time of the transport system. The structure for the rate of loss is given by (7):

$$Fruit\ Time\ Lost\ Farmers\ Exporters =$$
$$IF(Total\_Time\_Transportation\_Farmer\_Exporter < 25) \qquad (7)$$
$$THEN(0)ELSE(Cumulative\_deliveries\_Farm\_Exp\_m2)$$

5 Experimentation and Results

5.1 Experimental Design

The experimental design of this study follows the steps given by [29], which takes 5 simulations for each multimodal scenario, using in each simulation a different seed value, which in this case are 1, 2, 3, 4 and 5. The simulation time is 10 years, 3,650 days, and we evaluate the effect of the multi modal transport in the long term using a DT = 0.25. The results presented in Table 2 correspond to the average daily data.

In order to establish the incidence of multimodal transportation in the performance measures we established three scenarios to be simulated: Scenario 1. Exports are performed the way it is currently done. Uchuva fruit is taken terrestrially to the airport and then by plane it's exported to Europe. Scenario 2. Exports are performed by terrestrial mode to the ports of the Colombian coasts and then from there maritime transport is used until Europe. Scenario 3. Exports are performed using railways to the country's ports, and from there maritime transport is used until Europe.

5.2 Results

After performing the analysis of each of the performance indicators in all three scenarios, it can be seen that for scenario 3, two out of the four indicators generated positive results. The use of intermodal railway and plane transport systems can leverage the efficiency of the two modes due to economies of scale and low environmental pollution presented the usage of railways. In addition, results of the scenarios in which air transport mode is used, exhibit a significant reduction in transport times what is perceived in terms of reduction of quality losses. From the results (See Table 3), it has been observed that the use of high capacity modes of transport can reduce costs by achieving economies of scale, in addition it helps reducing emissions to the environment, as reflected in scenario 3.

Table 3. Simulation results for all of the scenarios for Uchuva

Performance indicators (Farmer Exporter (F.E), Distributor Exporter (D.E.))									
Scenario	CO₂ emission (Ton)		Costs (USD)		Scenario	Time (Day)		Quality (Ton)	
	F.E.	D.E.	F.E.	D.E.		F.E.	D.E.	F.E.	D.E.
3	0,196	0,057	1.090	365	1	2,959	1,171	0	0

The use of modes of transport with higher speed produces a significant reduction in transport times, a fact that directly affects the quality indicator of fruit. However, it is important to find the balance between the proposed indicators, according to the perspective of logistics planners, in order to meet customer needs obtaining profitability. In Fig. 8, we see that the model is rapidly approaching a fulfilment of 90% of demand. This is a very important tool to forecast sustained growth in demand in the domestic market and even higher in the international market (Fig. 9).

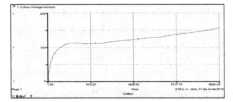

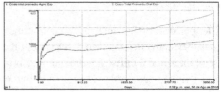

Fig. 8. Average Inventory along the supply chain.

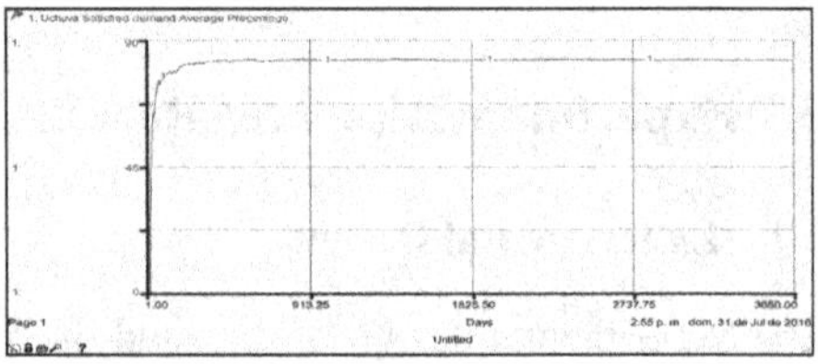

Fig. 9. Compliance with the end-user demand of Uchuva.

Given that scenario 3 presents satisfactory results for two of the four indicators, this scenario is the most desirable, and Figs. 10, 11, 12 and 13 show the proposed indicators under this scenario. Figure 10 exhibits the behavior of CO₂ emission during the 10 years of simulation for scenario 3. One can perceive an increased level of emissions in the exports of the farmer, supported in the path that must be carried out and the location from the producers to the export ports. Figure 11 exhibits the behavior of the transportation costs in scenario 3. A significant reduction is observed regarding to other scenarios

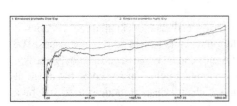

Fig. 10. CO₂ emissions for Uchuva export for the farmer and the distributor.

Fig. 11. Total cost of transportation Uchuva export for scenario 3, including export of the farmer and the distributor.

and there is a slight increase in exports' costs of the farmers, which is based on the journeys made and the allocation of the fruit from the two links involved.

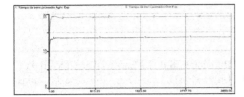 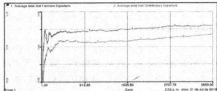

Fig. 12. Total transport time for Uchuva export under scenario 3 for the farmer and the distributor.

Fig. 13. Losses caused by the total time of transport for Uchuva export for scenario 3 for the farmer and distributor.

Figure 12 exhibits the behavior of the average transport time for the export of Uchuva in scenario 3. It can be seen a quite similar behavior, although with a small increase of the farmer, which is explained by the location. Figure 13 exhibits the losses caused by transportation time. Given the life cycle of Uchuva, we used 25 days to assess the amount of losses from this time compared to the total time of transport.

5.3   Experimental Design Validation of Simulation

Tests for validation of system behavior were made and a way to verify the consistency of the system is to test it under extreme conditions [30]. The first condition for validation of the model was to eliminate the supply of Uchuva along the chain. For Uchuva, it was achieved, generating a yield per hectare of zero. Under the parameters described above, inventory levels and transportation sectors of the chain and the response variables of quality, quantity, cost and pollution were zero.

6   Conclusions

We have developed a system dynamics model that determines the impact of intermodal transportation systems over the logistics performance in the supply chain of Uchuva, observing the behavior of variables such CO_2 emissions, cost, time and quality. The structure and modelling used in this project exceeds the previously developed given that we include multimodal transport through its own structure and impacts of pollution. Two of the three indicators of logistics performance improved when using multimodal transport. Scenario 3 exhibits a reduction in logistics costs and environmental emissions. Scenario 1 maintains efficient performance indicators; however, it still maintains high levels of carbon dioxide emissions. Scenario 2 exhibits low contamination levels but high logistics costs. Allowing us to conclude that scenario 3, which includes rail and maritime system shows a reduction of costs and CO_2 emissions indicating it as the optimal scenario.

Through this work, we have contributed to the analysis of the problem of environmental sustainability in the transport of food supply chain which is a current concern in logistics. The inclusion of the feedback loop for CO_2 emissions and the general costs of the system allows to assess the reduction of pollution transport in the supply chain of Uchuva and contributes to its sustainability.

References

1. Orjuela Castro, J.A., Calderón, M.E., Buitrago Hernández, S.P.: La Cadena Agroindustrial de Frutas, Uchuva y Tomate de Arbol. Ed., p. 191. Universidad Distrital Francisco José de Caldas (2006)
2. Crainic, T., Kim, K.: Intermodal transportation. In: Handbook in OR & MS. Elsevier (2007)
3. SteadieSeifi, M., Nuijten, W., Woensel, V., Raoufi, R.: Multimodal freight transportation planning: a literature review. Eur. J. Oper. Res. **223**(1), 1–15 (2013)
4. Ambrosino, D., Sciomachen, A.: Hub locations in urban multimodal networks. Eur. Transp. **51**, 1–14 (2012)
5. Caris, A., Macharis, C., Janssens, G.: Decision support in intermodal transport: a new research agenda. Comput. Ind. **64**(2), 105–122 (2013)
6. Malorgio, G., Felice, A.: Trade and logistics: the fruit and vegetables industry. In: Mediterra 2014, pp. 149–171 (2014)
7. Aschauer, G.: A systemic model for the interpendencies between logistics strategy and transportation movements. University of Applied Sciences (2006)
8. Pérez-Lespier, L.: Examining the efficiency of multimodal transportation systems: a systems dynamics approach. Ed. Missouri University of Science and Technology (2013)
9. Farid, A.: A hybrid dynamic system model for multimodal transportation electrification. IEEE Trans. Control Syst. Technol. **99** (2016)
10. Arbués, P., Baños, J.: A dynamic approach to road freight flows modeling in Spain. Transportation **43**(3), 549–564 (2016)
11. Orjuela Castro, J.A., Herrera Ramirez, M.M., Casilimas G, W.: Impact analysis of transport capacity and food safety in Bogota. In: 2015 Workshop on Engineering Applications (2015)
12. Crainic, T.: Service design models for rail intermodal transportation. In: CIRRELT-2007-04 (2007)
13. Orjuela, J., Castañeda, I., Canal, J., Rivera, J.: La logística en la cadena de frutas. Frutas y Hortalizas **39**, 10–15 (2015)
14. Ahumada, O., Villalobos, J.R.: A tactical model for planning the production and distribution of fresh produce. Ann. Oper. Res. **190**, 339–358 (2009)
15. Pérez-Mesa, J.C., Galdeano-Gómez, E., Salinas, J.: Logistics network and externalities for short sea transport: an analysis of horticultural exports from southeast Spain. Transp. Policy **24**, 188–198 (2012)
16. Jiang, B., Li, J., Mao, X.: Container ports multimodal transport in china from the view of low carbon. Asian J. Shipping Logistics **28**(3), 321–344 (2012)
17. Inghels, D., Dullaert, W., Vigo, D.: A service network design model for multimodal municipal solid waste transport. Eur. J. Oper. Res. **254**(1), 68–79 (2016)
18. Liotta, G., Stecca, G., Kaihara, T.: Optimization of freight flows and sourcing in sustainable production and transportation networks. Int. J. Prod. Econ. **164**, 351–365 (2014)
19. Rajkovic, R., Zrnic, N., Kirin, S., Dragovic, B.: A review of multi-objective optimization of container flow using sea and land legs together. FME Trans. **44**, 204–211 (2016)
20. Knapen, L., Hartman, I., Schulz, D., Bellemans, T., Janssens, D., Wets, G.: Determining structural route components from GPS traces. Transp. Res. Part B **90**, 156–171 (2016)

21. Lin, C.-C., Chiang, Y.-I., Lin, S.-W.: Efficient model and heuristic for the intermodal terminal location. Comput. Oper. Res. **51**, 41–51 (2014)
22. Ostrouh, A., Kuftinova, N.: Automation of planning and management of the transportation of production for food- processing industry enterprises. Autom. Control Comput. Sci. **46**, 57–67 (2011)
23. Hsu, C.-I., Hung, S.-F., Li, H.-C.: Vehicle routing problem with time-windows for perishable food delivery. J. Food Eng. **80**(2), 465–475 (2007)
24. Ilicali, C., Icier, F.: Freezing time prediction for partially dried papaya puree with infinite cylinder geometry. J. Food Eng. **100**(4), 696–704 (2010)
25. Dunno, K., Cooksey, K., Gerard, P., Thomas, R., Whiteside, W.: The effects of transportation hazards on shelf life of packaged potato chips. Food Packag. Shelfe Life **8**, 9–13 (2016)
26. Akkerman, R., Farahami, P., Grunow, M.: Quality, safety and sustainability in food distribution: a review of quantitative operations management approaches and challenges. OR Spectrum **32**(4), 863–904 (2010)
27. Orjuela, J., Caicedo, A., Ruiz, A.: Simulación de Mecanismos de Integración Externa en la Cadena Agroindustrial de Mora de Bogotá-Cundinamarca. Una Evaluación del Desempeño Logístico. XIII Congreso Latinoamericano de Dinamica de Sistemas, Cartagena (2015)
28. Caicedo, A.L., Ruiz, A.F., J. Orjuela A. C, Efecto de los Mecanismos de Integración Externa en el Desempeño Logístico de la Cadena de Frutas. Ed., p. 172. Universidad Distrital francisco José de Caldas (2015)
29. Yasarcan, H.: Information sharing in supply chains: a system approach. In: 29th International Conference of the System Dynamics Society, Washington, DC (2011)
30. Steerman, J.: Business Dynamics: System Thinking and Modeling for a Complex World. Irwin/McGraw-Hill, Boston (2000)

A Simulation Model to Improve Customer Service in an Information Security Company

Germán Andrés Méndez-Giraldo, Néstor David Rodriguez-Garzón[✉],
and Pablo Cesar Aranda-Rivera

Universidad Distrital Francisco José de Caldas, Bogotá, D.C., Colombia
gmendez@udistrital.edu.co, nrodriguez@easysol.net,
pabloarandaprod@hotmail.com

Abstract. Given the current nature of electronic fraud prevention, there is a demand for high-quality and prompt customer service. These organizations must design well thought out strategies for improving customer service, especially with regard to reducing attention times, as any delays can lead to a higher level of fraud losses. With this in mind, organizations must develop a Shift- allocation proposal based on multiple criteria. The criteria must be validated through simulation techniques that permit optimizing two performance metrics: waiting times and costs.

Keywords: Shift allocation · Discrete-event simulation · Information security services

1 Introduction

For companies that provide services through digital channels, the risk of online attack is an always-present threat, especially for online payment platforms. Nowadays, electronic banking and other online services are steadily growing around the world. So too is the threat of losing money or sensitive customer information to a cyberattack. Information security consists of securing online information resources (data and/or software). The information contained in these spaces must be available only to certified personnel and legitimate users, and within the limits defined by the company [1].

Information security covers different business processes, including those that allow organizations to control online transactions in real time and detect signs of abnormal behavior. Also, any security systems implemented must be able to trigger swift alerts in order to avoid data or identity theft, financial losses, and DDoS incidents. Events that are not efficiently dealt with may generate loss of user loyalty and customer business [2].

A leading information-security company has published its most recent study for Latin America. In this study, the company shows the numbers of online incidents recorded in 2014. Table 1 presents the ranking of Latin-American countries according to registered attacks in a global context [3].

© Springer International Publishing AG 2016
J.C. Figueroa-García et al. (Eds.): WEA 2016, CCIS 657, pp. 178–187, 2016.
DOI: 10.1007/978-3-319-50880-1_16

Table 1. Latin-American electronic attack statistics

World ranking	Country	% of users targeted by malware	No. of incidents
38	Brazil	32.0	22.122.995
63	Peru	28.7	4.537.175
64	Panama	28.5	929.976
74	Mexico	27.0	17.514.481
80	Honduras	26.5	458.438
90	El Salvador	25.4	439.970
92	Nicaragua	24.9	310.517
95	Ecuador	24.6	3.157.211
97	Colombia	24.4	4.991.622
98	Chile	24.2	1.813.276
99	Guatemala	24.2	822.242
112	Dominican Republic	22.8	435.710
125	Costa Rica	21.6	588.932
132	Argentina	21.2	1.375.126
148	Uruguay	19.6	175.873
165	Paraguay	17.9	238189
232	Cuba	7.9	30586

In 2014 there were nearly 60 million incidents related to electronic fraud in Latin America. Attackers were not limited to any one specific attack. They employed many different attack methods, such as USB devices, which is the top vector for offline attacks.

The total number of incidents in both categories (online and offline) surpassed 200 million fraud attempts. And this is only in Latin America.

Brazil and Peru occupy the top two places for the highest percentage of users targeted· by some kind of attack. The most vulnerable countries in terms of offline attacks are Mexico, Colombia and Ecuador. This is no coincidence, since the criminals launching the highest number of attacks are based in these countries [3]. Mitigating risk through strategies focused on detecting and preventing fraud in all channels, devices and clouds must be the priority for all financial institutions interested in the security of their customers.

2 Literature Review

Measuring customer satisfaction is directly related to the quality of the services provided. The level of satisfaction should be interpreted from a general judgment of the customer, resulting from the comparison of services delivered against prior expectations. Polls conducted by companies not only provide insight into the user opinions, but also allow them to identify key aspects of client loyalty and perceived value.

According to Jian Jun & Yang, attention, reliability, product portfolio, ease of use, and security are the crucial aspects of quality electronic services, and impact both perceived value and customer loyalty [4].

In a highly-volatile environment with increasingly more demanding clients, companies face the difficult task of creating true customer service value. In today's world, simply offering a good product or service is not enough. A comprehensive value-creation model goes beyond basic staff/client interaction and analyzes the complexities of user relationships, communications and knowledge building [5].

Adequately managing complaints not only transforms a user's experience, but also improves customer loyalty and financial performance [6]. This effect is known as the Recovery Paradox. It is the result of swiftly recovering an affected service. This also increases sales and client satisfaction levels. However, if clients receive insufficient service, for instance, their needs are not met in a timely or appropriate fashion, then customer loyalty and trust is eroded. This can escalate to reputation damage and client loss [7, 8].

Wait times and customer attention are key factors in achieving a high level of satisfaction. Customers are extremely sensitive when it comes to incidents that may jeopardize information security and transaction integrity.

Usually, a company learns about incidents through their customer service desks or call centers. In the context of information security, these departments are in charge of detecting monitoring and managing round-the-clock security-related incidents, networks, end-user devices and any internal system components [9]. Their operational success is defined by different factors, such as staff members and work culture, but more importantly, staff engagement, commitment and process management [10].

These factors must be defined in accordance with the objectives of the call center. This includes the specific responsibilities of each employee, the customer environment, attention and productivity metrics, and/or staff management.

In this way, constant monitoring of security systems, technology, processes and staff is vital to keep transactions safe, even in view of the constantly-evolving cyber threats. Improving processes to make security systems adaptable to a challenging reality allows companies to minimize possible risks to their infrastructure and deliver greater value. All of these factors must be considered when attempting to implement a new customer service methodology.

SOCs (Security Operations Centers) face the challenge of implementing an operational infrastructure that is both strong and flexible, and that allows them to work in an increasingly-dynamic environment. The ever-growing number of online transactions and the great diversity of digital threats are key factors driving the rapid evolution of this environment. In the world of information security, every second matters when detecting and mitigating attacks. With this in mind, the best scenario for a SOC is having an appropriate number of well-trained staff members who can handle incidents effectively.

But how do you determine the number of staff members required for full coverage? So far, the research on simulation models has proven useful in the transportation, health and energy industries, but not so much in the context of information security. Given the crucial role of assigning staff, the purpose of this document is to show the promise of a flexible simulation model applied for analyzing different variables of the SOC environment. This can possibly yield significant operational and financial benefits related to staff management and incident processing.

3 Modeling Methodology

To solve customer service problems, it is necessary to start from a Row Model of Special Waiting. First, it is crucial to analyze the customer service process in order to consider all employed techniques.

As Passmore & Zhan have put it, their model has a sequence of stages that determine the needs of call center staff in order to maintain quality and efficiency. The procedure examines the volume of calls (load) and correlates to specific efficacy indicators that help answer questions such as: How much load can a server handle during the planning stages? How many servers does it take to get the job done? And what time intervals should you program into your servers in order to reduce operating costs? [11]. The type of planning the authors propose features three fundamental aspects intended to help solve a step-based customer service model (see Fig. 1):

Demand Analysis: Main incidents should be assessed and detailed according to a Pareto Analysis. This type of analysis prioritizes the main flaws in high-priority clients (e.g. public institutions, utility providers, national security entities, etc.).

Service Analysis: It is not enough just knowing the events, it is also necessary to know how server types and service hours. Also, it is important to know whether the operators are human or not in order to determine Attention Times or any related issues.

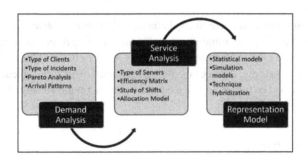

Fig. 1. Proposed methodology

Finally, the tools required for this type of modeling must be analyzed. In general terms, simulation can be seen as a fitting tool for these situations. However, simulation can be used in isolation or in hybrid modes (with other operation research tools).

For example, Khan has developed several multi-purpose programming models for allocating resources in data centers. These models consider different functions, including the service times evaluated in the Makespan. However, these do not include the human factor [12, 13].

In the case of hybrid modes, some proposals have been presented for implementing the newspaper seller model solving staff assignment, which employs simulation techniques in order to optimize costs [14]. Based on the simulation model, the new incident management could improve the current service. The new process can prioritize incident severity and assign staff accordingly (the right man for the right job) [15].

The simulation considers different parameters, including incident weighting, staff, resolution times, etc. For instance, the times for executing different incident-management processes were defined in accordance with the recommendations made in previously-defined management model and escalation levels [16].

4   Simulation Model

Easy Solutions is a leading security vendor focused on the comprehensive detection and prevention of electronic fraud across all devices, channels and clouds. Their products range from anti-phishing and secure browsing to multifactor authentication and transaction anomaly detection.

The simulation model presented is based on Easy Solutions' Fraud Intelligence service.

We propose a simulation model that helps to understand, analyze and improve the SOC (Security Operation Center) processes. The model should respond to variable operations and focus on the company's strategy for detecting and preventing electronic fraud.

The objective is to develop a tool that supports the decision-making process and that is focused on variables such as the number of users per work shift, agent profiles, and no-activity times.

This proposal takes into account the behavior of phishing, pharming, and malware attacks, while attempting to maintain Easy Solutions' leading threat takedown time (4 h).

The tool we have selected for the simulation is AnyLogic 7.0. This tool allows us to combine dynamic systems, discreet events, continuous events and agents on a single simulation platform. The tool is Java-based and features a wide variety of functions that facilitate model designing.

4.1   Demand Analysis

The Security Operation Center, or SOC, is the Easy Solutions department in charge of monitoring incidents and providing an appropriate response. The types of fraud attacks that they cover are: (1) Phishing Sites (2) Rogue Mobile Apps (3) Compromised Bank Cards (4) Similar Domains (5) Redirection to Phishing Sites (6) Copyright Infringement (7) Data-Capturing URLs (8) Unauthorized Use of Trademark (9) and others.

The SOC continuously receives alerts from multiple sources: Detect Brand Monitoring (DBM), Suspicious Email Reports (ABUSEBOX), Weblogs, DMARC Compass(R), DSB, and DMS among others. The incidents reported by these resources are classified as Proactive or Reactive. Proactive occurs when Easy Solutions agents find fraudulent URLs in reporting platforms or databases. When fraudulent material is found, the agents provide an agile and appropriate solution before clients or their customers are affected; Reactive: Whenever a client reports an incident via the Easy Solutions support channels.

4.2 Service Analysis

The SOC is comprised of two teams of service agents defined as LATAM (Latin America) and NON LATAM (rest of the world). SOC staff is currently made up of 10 to 14 service agents with varying schedules (three shifts, Monday through Sunday).

SOC staff is qualified in different information security abilities, including networks, applications and reverse engineering. Also, there are directors that ensure that the information is always presented in a clear an efficient manner. SOC roles include: Security analyst, Security specialist, Threat investigator, and Area director. The electronic-fraud detection process has four main stages (see Fig. 2):

Ticket Creation: Before creating a ticket, the following validations must take place. (A) The attack is currently active. (B) There is no other ticket with the same URL. Although the ticket creation process employs a script that verifies that there are no duplicated URLs in open cases, currently it is not able to detect subtle differences, such as the domain's previous "www". (C) Ticket-management exceptions should be verified as well (varies according to each client).

Ticket Acceptance: After the ticket is created, the following step is accepting it. With this action, the client receives a notification that the ticket has been assigned to an agent (it is critical to accept the ticket as soon as it is created). If the case was created by the client, it is necessary to validate if the attack is currently active.

Management Records: After a ticket has been created and accepted, the case must be tracked. If a particular ticket requires takedown services, then the agents initiate the corresponding procedure and inform the client a plan is currently active. Service agents will create records of any actions taken in order to keep evidence of their work. In case that the ticket does not require takedown services, it must be met with a corresponding solution. Also, if new events arise, all information must be added to ticket records so clients are always aware of their case's progress.

Ticket Closure: After the attack has been identified and deactivated, or a solution it has been provided, agents close the ticket. For this, they select the option Close Ticket in the top menu of their interface and proceed to fill the closure form.

4.3 Simulation Model

For analyzing input data, we worked with Arrival Times (Proactive and Reactive services). Once the data was filtered, and using a Promodel Stat Fit, we conducted independence, goodness and fitting tests (see Fig. 3).

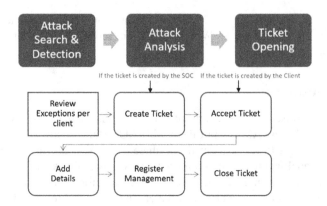

Fig. 2. Service process

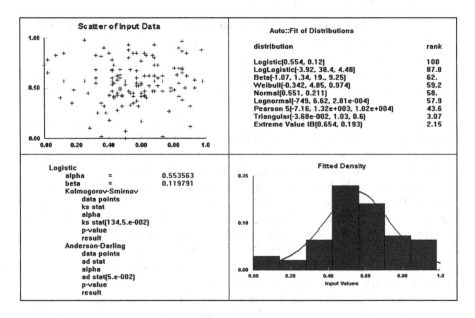

Fig. 3. Data analysis

For analyzing service times, we use the initial database and define a set of data called Summary. The purpose of this is to obtain a guidance summary of the way attacks are distributed (by region or source). Attacks are then grouped in different categories: LATAM Proactive, Non-LATAM Proactive, Non-Proactive LATAM and Non-Proactive Non-LATAM.

Attention time is the time it takes for an agent to accept a ticket and initiate its management (the time is registered in minutes). The same statistical behavior has been found among several types of attacks. In this way, we have resorted to grouping attacks by type in order to obtain the probability functions adaptable to the simulation model.

For analyzing attention times, we took the initial database and obtained the probability function for each attack according to their source (Proactive and Non-Proactive) and origin region (LATAM and Non-LATAM).

As we previously described, there are two types of information sources that feed the agents' work: Proactive and Non-Proactive incidents. Using a specific functions, both sources are incorporated alongside their corresponding characterization and probability distributions. Once the sources have been defined, the regions are next (LATAM and Non-LATAM). In Fig. 4, we present the process for AnyLogic software.

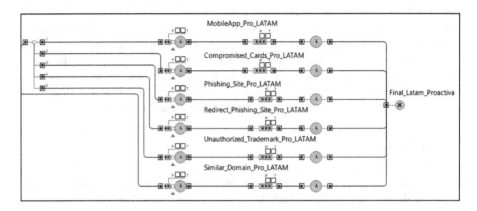

Fig. 4. AnyLogic simulation model

In order to implement the model, several boards were designed based on system operation parameters, probability functions for event arrivals, request attention, and system behavior output/control variables.

Finally, a panel display system operation and facilitates the alteration of variables and parameters in order to evaluate system behavior in different scenarios. Two visualization panels were created for both regions LATAM and Non-LATAM (see Fig. 5).

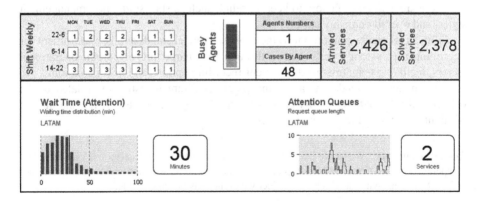

Fig. 5. AnyLogic simulation model – general visualization panel

4.4 Scenarios

We proposed five scenarios that allowed us to evaluate the most important output variables of the model. We concluded that there is a higher workload in Non-LATAM regions, which is an indicator that this group of clients requires more dedicated SOC attention and resources.

The most favorable scenario represents an increase of 50% in cases received by the SOC, which in turn reveals the need for more staff members per shift in order to maintain optimal staffing levels. In this way, there would be 3–4 agents per shift (Monday through Friday) with one more agent on the weekends.

In terms of scenario variables, we noticed that the modification of parameters, number of agents or number of cases has a direct impact on three highly-important output variables: attention time, case queueing and resolution time. Identifying these key parameters facilitates SOC managers to schedule agents and allocate resources more effectively. This helps to preemptively counteract future incidents that may cause friction with clients, such as downtimes, delays, extra third-party costs, etc.

5 Conclusions

Small variations in the number of agents per shift can have serious consequences on key aspects of the service provided, such as attention times, case queueing and average resolution times. These variations not only affect the service, but also agent performance, due to their increased workload volume. If such scenario goes on unchecked, his eventually erode agent motivation and lead to staff turnover.

Analysis of the current shift scheduling reveals that there is an appropriate number of staff members to efficiently and correctly cover any service requirements. Nevertheless, we must note that any increase in call volume would destabilize the current workload and a similar analysis would be necessary.

It is also important to consider that the quality of SOC services is directly related to adequate shift management and workload volume.

There are also other factors to keep in mind, such as staff suitability, management styles, and overall company culture.

From an efficiency point of view, the proposed model stands as a key instrument for improving the system's performance through the sharpening of certain operational factors, including team organization, event-recording options and ticket creation.

This model is intended as a starting point for future investigation related to the behavior of information security centers in terms of operations, efficiency and quality of client services and response processes.

Acknowledgments. We would like to thank SOC Director Fernando Cuervo and Vice President of Operations Julian Arguelles for their help with sharing their information management processes at Easy Solutions, without which this project would not have been possible.

References

1. Fernandez, J., Alonso, E.: Seguridad en informática. Aprocal Web (2003). http://www.aprocal.org.mx/
2. CESG: Good Practice Guide Transaction. National technical authority on information assurance. Guide No. 53 (2013)
3. Kasperski Lab.: 2014 desde la perspectiva viral en cifras en América Latina: predicciones para 2015. Kaspersky Web. http://latam.kaspersky.com/sobre-kaspersky/centro-de-prensa/blog-de-kaspersky/2014/analisis2014pronosticos2015LatAm
4. Jiang, L., Jun, M., Yang, Z.: Customer-perceived value and loyalty: how do key service quality dimensions matter in the context of B2C e-commerce. Serv. Bus. 10(2), 301–317 (2015)
5. Grönroos, C., Voima, P.: Critical service logic: making sense of value creation and co-creation. J. Acad. Mark. Sci. 41(2), 133–150 (2013)
6. Hansen, T., Wilke, R., Zaichkowsky, L.: How retailers handle complaint management. J. Consum. Satisfaction Dissatisfaction Complaining Behav. 22, 1–23 (2009)
7. Chan, H.C., Ngai, E.W.: What makes customers discontent with service providers? An empirical analysis of complaint handling in information and communication technology services. J. Bus. Ethics 91(1), 73–110 (2010)
8. Hanif, A., Khalid, W.: Customer service-a tool to improve Quality of Experience (QoE). In: 2012 IEEE Conference on Technology and Society in Asia (T&SA), pp 1–6 (2012)
9. Jäntti, M., Kalliokoski, J.: Identifying knowledge management challenges in a service desk: a case study. In: Second International Conference on Information, Process, and Knowledge Management, eKNOW 2010, pp 1–6 (2010)
10. Leonard, A., Strydom, I.: A conceptual framework for managing service desks: a South African perspective. In: 2011 Proceedings of PICMET 2011: Technology Management in the Energy Smart World (PICMET), pp 1–6 (2011)
11. Passmore, C.M., Zhan, J.: Determining appropriate staffing adjustments in a call center staff group. In: 2013 International Conference on Social Computing (SocialCom), pp 1–6 (2013)
12. Khan, S., Min-Allah, N.: A goal programming based energy efficient resource allocation in data centers. J. Supercomput. 61(3), 502–519 (2012)
13. Khan, S.: A multi-objective programming approach for resource allocation in data centers. In: International Conference on Parallel and Distributed Processing Techniques and Applications (PDPTA), pp 1–6 (2009)
14. Liao, S., Van Delft, C., Koole, G., Dallery, Y., Jouin, O.: Call center capacity allocation with random workload. In: International Conference on Computers & Industrial Engineering, CIE 2009, pp 1–6 (2009)
15. Punyateera, J., Leelasantitham, A., Kiattitsin, S., Muttitanon, W.: Study of service desk for NEdNet using incident management (service operation) of ITIL V.3. In: 2014 Asia-Pacific Signal and Information Processing Association Annual Summit and Conference (APSIPA), pp 1–6 (2014)
16. Andrade, R., Fuertes, W.: Diseño y dimensionamiento de un equipo de respuesta ante incidentes de seguridad informática (CSIRT). Repositorio Institucional de la Universidad de las Fuerzas Armadas ESPE (2013)

Multi-agent Approach for Solving the Dynamic Home Health Care Routing Problem

Eduyn Ramiro López-Santana, Julián Alberto Espejo-Díaz[✉],
and Germán Andrés Méndez-Giraldo

Faculty of Engineering,
Universidad Distrital Francisco José de Caldas, Bogotá, Colombia
{erlopezs, gmendez}@udistrital.edu.co,
jaespejod@correo.udistrital.edu.co

Abstract. This paper presents the design, conceptualization and implementation of a multi-agent system which solves dynamically the caregivers' routing problem accepting new requests when the system is already running. To do so we propose a multi-agent approach that allows to simulate a home health care system using a mixed integer programming model to better make the routing schemes of the caregivers. The approach was implemented in the Jade middleware, was tested in multiple scenarios changing the numbers of caregivers, the length and the numbers periods of simulation and finally numerical results for the simulations are presented.

Keywords: Dynamic routing · Home health care · Multi-agent systems · Simulation · JADE

1 Introduction

Home health care (HHC) represents an alternative to the traditional hospitalization which consists in delivering medical, paramedical and social services to patients at their homes rather than in a hospital [1, 2]. This way of providing health services reduces costs in health structures and allows better living conditions for many patients [3]. The home health providers are facing difficult conditions such as the increasing and ageing of population as well as shortages in financial resources [4]. In order to deal with the previous conditions, HHC providers must develop methods or techniques which allow to optimize their operations and also make better decisions. One of the most important decision in planning HHC services is the routing of caregivers, which means to decide in which sequence each caregiver will visit patients assigned to him/her [5].

HHC routing problem can be classified as static or dynamic. The static version of the problem is presented when the input data are given in advance and do not depend on time. In the dynamic version of the problem there are some information that depends on time, e.g. a new request may appear while the system is already running and the routing has to be done again to better serve the new request [6]. This paper addresses the dynamic version of the problem using a multi-agent approach which allows to handle new requests. A mixed integer program is used in the approach in order to make the routing of the caregivers.

© Springer International Publishing AG 2016
J.C. Figueroa-García et al. (Eds.): WEA 2016, CCIS 657, pp. 188–200, 2016.
DOI: 10.1007/978-3-319-50880-1_17

The paper is organized as follows. Section 2 presents a brief literature review on multi-agent applications and HHC routing problem. Section 3 state the dynamic HHC problem. The design of the multi agent approach detailing agents' activities, interactions and communication processes is presented in Sect. 4. Section 5 presents the mathematical model for the problem that is used in the multi-agent approach. Section 6 describes the implementation of the approach in the Jade-Java middleware, Sect. 7 presents computational results of the HHC simulations and finally Sect. 8 shows some conclusions and suggestions for future research.

2 Literature Review

There have been several research studies aimed at built multi-agent applications in many fields. Multi-agent systems are comprised of individual agents characterized by their autonomy, intelligence, distribution and collaboration [7]. Therefore, the multi-agent paradigm results promising for approaching different problems and there is much interest in developing agent based models for many application problem domains [8]. Job shop scheduling [7], dynamic vehicle routing problem [6], energy management [9], maintenance systems [10], manufacturing [11], course scheduling [12], exam scheduling [13], stock transactions [14] and supply chain planning [15] are some problems which were tackled using multi-agent systems. A review of different models and applications for multi-agents system is presented in [16].

On the other hand, HHC routing problem can be viewed as a combination of staff rostering problem and vehicle routing problem (VRP) [17]. Kergosien, Lenté & Billaut [18] formulated the problem as an extension of the traveling salesman problem (TSP). A literature review about scheduling and/or routing problems as a VRP or TSP in the HHC context is presented in [5]. There are several objectives in the problem such as minimization of the travel and/or waiting times [19], minimization of operational costs [3] or minimization of the travelled distances [2]. Among the constraints of the problem, patients' time windows [20], caregivers' skills [20], caregivers' working time are by far the most common constraints in the literature. Several solutions methods has been used to tackle the problem. Mixed integer programming [21], branch and bound [22] and column generation [23] are the common exact methods in the literature. Among approximate methods there are tabu search [24], simulated annealing [25] and local search algorithms [26].

In this work we present a multi-agent approach for solving dynamically the care-givers' routing problem. The multi-agent approach uses a multi-objective mixed integer model to make the routing which is updated by the agents when new requests appears. The mathematical model aims to minimize the travelled time as well as the delay in the arrival time at the patients' locations, considering, patients' priority in their attention, caregivers' skills, working time and finally departure and arrival locations.

3 Description of the Dynamic Caregiver Routing Problem

The routing of caregivers is a complex activity mostly made manually in which multiple optimization criteria have to be taken into consideration [21]. Our objective is dynamically allocate and route caregivers to patients by reducing transportations time and reducing the caregivers delay in arriving to patients' locations. The previous objectives have to be pursued while respecting several constraints such as caregivers' skills, caregivers' working time and patients' required qualifications. It is worth noting that the dynamic component of the problem lies in dealing with new patients joining in the system, therefore multiple routing schemes have to be done in the same planning horizon to better serve the new requests.

We consider a set of patients who need home visitations. Each visitation or service is characterized by a required skill and duration. We also consider the priority in the service in order to visit as soon as possible patients with critical clinical situations. The priority takes values from 1 (urgent visitation) to 5 (least urgent visitation) and their attention times are established by the TRIAGE times. It is important to mention that the TRIAGE concept establish the response times in medical emergencies according to the patients' priority, for instance, if a patient has a priority level of 3 it is recommended to serve him/her within a time of 60 min based on the response time of the third level of the TRIAGE [27]. The objective is to send caregivers to patients' locations taking into account the TRIAGE response times as possible while minimizing the transportation times of the caregivers. Furthermore, the caregivers start and end their routes at their homes, have a maximum working time and are characterized by a qualification which take values from 1 (usual cares) to 5 (specialized cares). The visitation is only performed if the resource qualification is higher or equal than the patient need.

In addition to the previous statements another considerations to the problem were made. If in a planning horizon a patient requires two or more visitations it will be created a new node for each new request, travel times are deterministic, the caregivers work in the same geographical area and can operate in all the patients' territory, the service starts as soon as a caregiver arrives to the patient location and the travel times from a location to another are the same no matter the direction.

4 Multi-agent Approach

Multi-agent systems consist of individual, autonomous and interacting agents [8]. Developing a multi-agent system for solving dynamic HHC routing problem comprise the automatization of the routing problem allowing new requests when the system is already running. We strongly believe that the agent orientation is an appropriate paradigm for dynamic routing of health care staff. The challenge here is to define the entities, their interactions and communication protocols. First of all, we have to describe each entity and establish their interactions. A brief description of each agent is presented and a case use diagram is presented in Fig. 1 showing the process of the HHC problem and it is complemented with a case use template presented in Table 1.

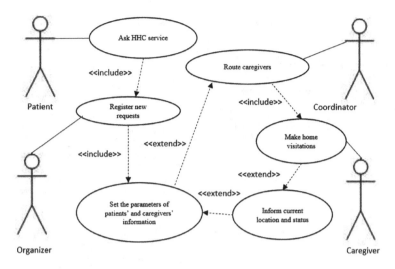

Fig. 1. Use case diagram for the dynamic HHC routing problem.

Table 1. Use case template for the dynamic HHC routing problem.

Actors	Patient, organizer, coordinator and caregiver
Objective	Provide the HHC service by routing caregivers to patients' locations
Description	Patients ask for HHC service, their requests are registered and parameterized in order to make the routing of the caregivers which will serve them
Preconditions	It must exist at least one request for HHC services
Alternative flows	If there is not a patient request the routing is not made
Post conditions	After a home visitation is made there have to be a notification

- Patient: communicate with the HHC provider and describe his/her symptoms and current location.
- Organizer: register the patients' requests and the caregivers' locations and status, parameterizes the previous information and send these parameters to the coordinator.
- Coordinator: Receives the parameters of the system, make the caregivers routing schemes using a mathematical model and finally send the routes to the caregivers.
- Caregiver: Receives the routes, make the home visitations and inform their location and status to the organizer.

The next step is to detail the functionality of each agent by describing their tasks as an activities sequence. The process consists in a set of patients asking for HHC services, the requests are registered and parameterized by the organizer agent, after that the organizer agent send the parameterization to the coordinator agent who is responsible of making the caregivers routing using a HHC mathematical model

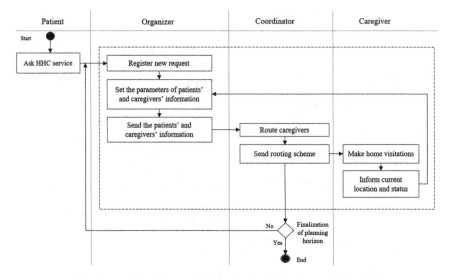

Fig. 2. Activity diagram for the dynamic HHC routing problem

generating the routing scheme, that scheme is distributed to each caregiver who will perform the home visitations satisfying the patients' needs. The previous process is shown is the Fig. 2 as an activity diagram.

Finally, the process of communication between agents consists in sending and receiving messages as seen in the message sequence diagram of Fig. 3. It is worth to note that the coordinator agent receives information from the organizer and that information is the input for the mathematical model presented in the next section.

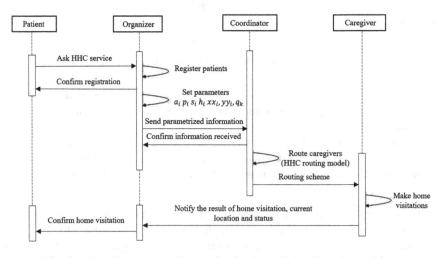

Fig. 3. Message sequence diagram for the dynamic HHC routing problem

5   Mathematical Formulation of the HHC Routing Problem

In this section is presented the mathematical model which is used as a problem solver by the coordinator agent in order to better make the routing schemes satisfying all the conditions presented in the description of the problem.

We consider a HHC system, in which a set of patients $P = \{1, 2 \ldots, N\}$ geographically distributed over a region are meant to be visited and served at their homes. To do so the HHC provider has a set of caregivers $K = \{1, 2, \ldots, m\}$ who are heterogeneous with respect to their skills. Thus, the problem can be defined in a non-directed graph $G = (V, A)$ with a set of nodes $V = KI \cup P \cup KF$, where KI are the caregivers start locations, P the patients' homes and KF are fictitious nodes which represents the destiny of caregivers where $KI = KF$. The set of arcs is defined by $A = \{(i, j) : i, j \in V, i \neq j\}$ and each arc (i, j) has associated a non-negative value t_{ij} which represents the travel time between nodes i and j. Each patient $i \in P$ presents a medical condition who requires a minimum level of skill h_i for their attention being 1 the lowest level. The priority in the attention is determined by p_i being 1 the highest priority which makes the patient being served as soon as possible. The duration of the home visitation is determined by s_i and it has to start after the notification of the need a_i. On the other hand, each caregiver k starts and ends every route in their homes (multi-depot) and have a maximum amount of working time in which l_k represents the start and u_k the end of the workday. Additionally, each caregiver is classified based on their medical skill q_k being 1 the lowest caregiver qualification. The previous parameter is matched with the skill required for the patient to perform the visitation, it means the visitation takes place only if the caregiver qualification q_k is higher or equal to the qualification h_i needed by the patient.

In order to serve the patient as soon as possible based on their priority is minimized the patient service promise Z_i. To do so we take into account the TRIAGE concept and times mentioned before. Figure 4 shows the quadratic function of the TRIAGE which was obtained using the times and levels presented in [28]. The coefficients of the quadratic function will be used in the mathematical model constructing the lower bound of Z_i, where $\gamma = 16.071$, $\delta = -37.929$ and $\varepsilon = 24$ as seen in Fig. 4. Finally, in the mathematical model the auxiliary sets $V1 = KI + P$, $V2 = P + KF$, high value M and the constant G which represents the size of set P plus size of set KI were used.

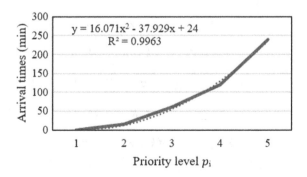

Fig. 4. Quadratic function of TRIAGE

We propose two objective functions which are the minimization of the travel times of the caregivers (2) and the minimization of the service promise to the patients (3). It was done using a weighed sum to establish the importance of each objective function according to coefficients α and β (1).

$$\min \alpha FO_1 + \beta FO_2 \tag{1}$$

$$FO_1 = \sum_{i \in V} \sum_{j \in V} \sum_{k \in K} X_{ijk} t_{ij} \tag{2}$$

$$FO_2 = \sum_{i \in P} Z_i / |P| \tag{3}$$

subject to,

$$\sum_{k \in K} \sum_{i \in V1} X_{ijk} = 1 \qquad \forall j \in P \tag{4}$$

$$\sum_{j \in V1} X_{jek} = \sum_{j \in V2} X_{ejk} \qquad \forall k \in K, e \in P \tag{5}$$

$$\sum_{j \in V2} X_{ijk|i=k} = 1 \qquad \forall k \in K, i \in KI \tag{6}$$

$$\sum_{i \in KI} \sum_{j \in V2} X_{ijk} = 0 \qquad \forall k \in K \tag{7}$$

$$\sum_{i \in V1} X_{ik+Gk} = 1 \qquad \forall k \in K \tag{8}$$

$$\sum_{i \in V1} \sum_{j \in KF|j \neq k + G} X_{ijk} = 0 \qquad \forall k \in K \tag{9}$$

$$Y_{ik} + t_{ij} + s_i - M(1 - X_{ijk}) \leq Y_{jk} \qquad \forall k \in K, (i,j) \in P \tag{10}$$

$$Y_{ik} + t_{ij} - M(1 - X_{ijk}) \leq Y_{jk} \qquad \forall k \in K, i \in KI, j \in V2 \tag{11}$$

$$Y_{ik} + t_{ij} - M(1 - X_{ijk}) \leq Y_{jk} \qquad \forall k \in K, i \in V1, j \in KF \tag{12}$$

$$Y_{ik} \geq a_i \qquad \forall k \in K, i \in P \tag{13}$$

$$\gamma p_i^2 - \delta p_i + \varepsilon + a_i \leq Z_i \qquad \forall i \in P \tag{14}$$

$$Y_{ik} \leq Z_i \qquad \forall k \in K, i \in P \tag{15}$$

$$h_j - M(1 - X_{ijk}) \leq q_k \qquad \forall k \in K, i \in V1, j \in P \tag{16}$$

$$Y_{ik} \geq l_i \qquad k \in K, i \in KI \tag{17}$$

$$Y_{jk} \leq u_j \qquad \forall k \in K, j \in KF \tag{18}$$

$$X_{ijk} \in \{0,1\} \qquad \forall (i,j) \in V | i \neq j, k \in K \tag{19}$$

$$Y_{ik} \geq 0 \qquad \forall i \in V, k \in K \tag{20}$$

$$Z_i \geq 0 \qquad \forall i \in P \tag{21}$$

Constraint (4) forces that all patients are served exactly once. The flow constraints for each node are presented in (5). Constraints (6), (7), (8) and (9) ensures each caregiver starts and ends every route in his/her home. Arrival time at patients' locations are calculated in (10). Caregivers' departure and return times to their homes are calculated in (11) and (12). Constraint (13) ensure the visitations are not performed before the patient's moment of request. In (14) it is calculated the minimum value of service promise for each patient considering their priority. Constraint (15) links the patients' service promise to the arrival time at patients' locations. The observation of caregiver's skill is presented in (16). The working day of caregivers is limited by constraints (17) and (18). Constraint (19) sets the domains of the decision variables X_{ijk} and finally (20) and (21) are nonnegative variable conditions for arrival times and promise service. The previous mathematical model of the HHC routing problem is presented in detail in [29].

6 Implementation

The multi-agent approach was implemented using JADE (Java Agent DEvelopment Framework), a software framework proposed by [30]. JADE is a structured open-source platform which make easier to make implementation of multi-agent systems in according with the FIPA specifications. JADE include both the libraries (i.e. java classes) required to develop the agents' architecture and the runtime environment to allow several agents to execute concurrently. Figure 5 presents an agents tree which shows the equivalent of each agent in the multi-agent implementation and then is described each agent in the implementation.

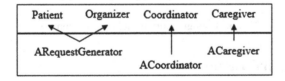

Fig. 5. Agents' tree diagram of the proposal approach

- ARequestGenerator: an agent which reads or generates new orders and sends them to the ACoordinator. To do so the agent counts on several behaviors which allows him to block the generations a specific time based on the patients' arrival distribution in the system. The agent generates the arrival time of the patient request a_i, the duration of the visitation s_i, the skill required by the patient h_i, the travel times between the patient and the another active patients and resources in the system t_{ij}

and the patients' priority p_i. Additionally, the agent manages the current location and status of the caregivers. To send the previous information the agent writes the information in a plain text file and uses an ACL inform message in which notify the coordinator agent to read the parameters in the text file.

- ACoordinator: an agent which receives the ARequestGenerator information of the system, solve the problem using the mathematical model and send an ACL inform message to each caregiver in the solution with the routs in order to them perform the visitations.

- ACaregiver: an agent which receives the routing scheme from the ACoordinator agent. The agent makes the home visitations and inform to the ARequestGenerator agent his location which is the last patient on his/her route and also informs the moment in which the agent will be available for receiving new routing schemes. When the agent performs a visitation it sends an inform-done message to the organizer agent.

Finally, it is worth noting that the multi-agent approach splits the planning horizon into several periods in which a certain number of requests are received and served as seen in Fig. 6.

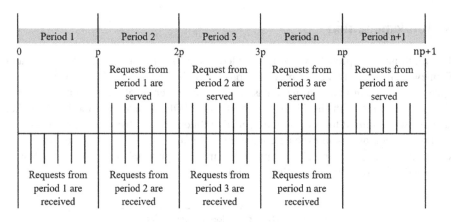

Fig. 6. Configuration of multi-agent approach

7   Computational Results

In order to test the multi-agent approach, it is simulated a HHC system which aims to serve 40 patients in a planning horizon of 600 min with a requests inter arrival time of 15 min. The first scenario is set up with 5 periods of 120 min each one serving 8 patients per period and 4 caregivers. In the second scenario the configuration is the same as first scenario modifying the number of caregivers from 4 to 2. The third scenario is set up with 8 periods of 75 min each one serving 5 patients per period and 4 caregivers. Finally, in the fourth scenario the configuration is the same as third scenario modifying the number of caregivers from 4 to 2. The additional parameters of the

Table 2. Results for simulation scenarios

Scenario	α	β	FO	FO_1	FO_2	Average waiting time (mins)
1	0.8	0.2	3264.473	3113.0488	3870.17	79.417
	0.6	0.4	3395.076	3103.4933	3832.45	78.24
	0.4	0.6	3471.326	3008.9525	3779.575	70.005
	0.2	0.8	3552.874	3185.96	3644.6025	69.555
2	0.8	0.2	3344.2949	3209.6913	3882.7095	80.771
	0.6	0.4	3478.901	3209.6917	3882.715	77.954
	0.4	0.6	3528.116	3099.23	3814.04	73.737
	0.2	0.8	3654.445	3179.705	3773.13	69.812
3	0.8	0.2	3863.085	3449.9825	5515.495	37.519
	0.6	0.4	4276.188	3449.98	5515.5	37.343
	0.4	0.6	4688.701	3470.7025	5500.7	36.293
	0.2	0.8	5110.72	3520.125	5508.3688	36.77
4	0.8	0.2	4931.097	4529.1725	6538.795	44.304
	0.6	0.4	4969.092	4529.1717	5628.9725	44.311
	0.4	0.6	5183.065	4559.4675	5598.7967	49.924
	0.2	0.8	5384.9932	4681.381	5560.8963	40.276

system that were used in the simulation were generated randomly being the same for all simulation scenarios. Table 2 presents the results for different α and β values for all scenarios. As a performance measures it was used the cumulative values for the objective functions as well as the average waiting time of the patients for the service.

The numerical results indicate that using a higher value of β which is related to the minimization of service promise the overall objective function for the system increases and also the average waiting time for the patients decrease. The number of caregivers also have an impact in the average waiting time which is observed in the second and fourth scenarios where the average waiting times are lower than the first and third scenarios where the number of caregivers was the double.

8   Conclusions

This paper proposes a multi-agent approach which can be used to simulate the dynamic HHC routing problem. The approach uses a mixed integer programming (MIP) model to better route the caregivers in order to better serve the patients' needs. The implementation of the approach is being built in the Jade middleware.

The coordinator agent solves the optimization problem based on the objectives and constraints of the HHC system in order to minimize the travelled time and the patients' service promise. The MIP model taking into account the skills of health operators and priorities in patient care and balance the travelled time and the patients' service promise. This model is solved to optimally using a commercial optimization solver and it works well for small problems up to 15 patients but for biggest problems we will need to propose heuristics and/or metaheuristics to speed up the computational time. The jade middleware provides the runtime environment which allows several agents to execute at the same time and also allows the interaction of the agents.

Future work should focus on the extension of the problem to a stochastic setting, in which unexpected failures occur on the routes and the operators are rescheduled. Also, for larger instances and real-world problems, a metaheuristic solution can be developed to solve, within a reasonable execution time.

Acknowledgements. We thank Fair Isaac Corporation (FICO) for providing us with Xpress-MP licenses under the Academic Partner Program subscribed with Universidad Distrital Francisco Jose de Caldas (Colombia), and thank Centro de Investigaciones y Desarrollo Científico at Universidad Distrital (Colombia) by supporting partially under Grant No. 2-602-468-14. Last, but not least, the authors would like to thank the comments of the anonymous referees that significantly improved our paper.

References

1. Benzarti, E., Sahin, E., Dallery, Y.: A literature review on operations management based models developed for home health care services, Paris, France (2010)
2. Yalcindag, S., Matta, A., Sahin, E.: Operator assignment and routing problems in home health care services. In: 2012 IEEE International Conference on Automation Science and Engineering (CASE), pp. 329–334 (2012)
3. Triki, N., Garaix, T., Xie, X.: A two-phase approach for periodic home health care planning. In: 2014 IEEE International Conference on Automation Science and Engineering (CASE), pp. 518–523. IEEE (2014)
4. Gutiérrez, E.V., Galvis, O.D., López, D.A., Mock-Kow, J.S., Zapata, I., Vidal, C.J.: Gestión logística en la prestación de servicios de hospitalización domiciliaria en el Valle del Cauca: caracterización y diagnóstico. Estudios Gerenciales **30**, 441–450 (2014)
5. Yalcindag, S., Matta, A., Sahin, E.: Human resource scheduling and routing problems in home health care context: a literature review. In: 37th Conference on Operational Research Applied to Health Services (ORAHS), Cardiff, pp. 1–34 (2012)
6. Barbucha, D., Jedrzejowicz, P.: Multi-agent platform for solving the dynamic vehicle routing problem. In: 11th International IEEE Conference on Intelligent Transportation Systems, ITSC 2008, pp. 517–522 (2008)
7. Yu-xian, Z., Lei, L., Hong, W., Yan-yan, Z., Xu, G., Meng, C.: Approach to the distributed job shop scheduling based on multi-agent. In: 2008 IEEE International Conference on Automation and Logistics, pp. 2031–2034 (2008)
8. Macal, C.M., North, M.J.: Introductory tutorial: agent-based modeling and simulation, pp. 1451–1464 (2011)
9. Abras, S., Kieny, C., Ploix, S., Wurtz, F.: MAS architecture for energy management: developing smart networks with JADE platform. In: 2013 IEEE International Conference on Smart Instrumentation, Measurement and Applications, ICSIMA 2013, pp. 26–27 (2013)
10. Fasanotti, L.: A distributed intelligent maintenance system based on artificial immune approach and multi-agent systems. In: Proceedings - 2014 12th IEEE International Conference on Industrial Informatics, INDIN 2014, pp. 783–786 (2014)

11. Xu, M.: Production scheduling of agile manufacturing based on multi-agents. In: 2nd International Symposium on Knowledge Acquisition and Modeling, KAM 2009, vol. 2, pp. 323–325 (2009)
12. Weili, D., Songmengqiu: Multi agents based for humanistic intelligent class scheduling system. In: Proceedings - 3rd International Symposium on Information Science and Engineering, ISISE 2010, pp. 476–480 (2011)
13. Wahaishi, A.M., Aburukba, R.O.: An agent-based personal assistant for exam scheduling. In: Computer and Information Technology (WCCIT) (2013)
14. Garcés, A.E., Moreno, J., Múnera, S.: Modelo de simulación de una subasta de doble punta mediante el paradigma multi-agente. Revista Avances en Sistemas e Informática 6, 197–206 (2009)
15. De Santa-Eulalia, L.A., D'Amours, S., Frayret, J.M.: Modeling agent-based simulations for supply chain planning: the FAMASS methodological framework. In: Conference Proceedings - IEEE International Conference on Systems, Man and Cybernetics, pp. 1710–1718 (2010)
16. Zhang, Y., Wu, Q., Tang, X., Ma, Z.: Progresses for multi-agents system models. In: The 2nd International Conference on Computer and Automation Engineering, ICCAE 2010, vol. 3, pp. 44–48 (2010)
17. Yuan, Z., Fügenschuh, A.: Home health care scheduling: a case study. In: Applied Mathematics and Optimization Series, pp. 1–18 (2015)
18. Kergosien, Y., Lenté, C., Billaut, J.: Home health care problem an extended multiple Traveling Salesman Problem. In: Multidisciplinary International Conference on Scheduling: Theory and Applications (MISTA 2009), pp. 1–8 (2009)
19. Redjem, R., Marcon, E.: Operations management in the home care services: a heuristic for the caregivers' routing problem. Flexible Serv. Manufact. J. 28, 280–303 (2016)
20. Torres-Ramos, A., Alfonso-Lizarazo, E., Reyes-Rubiano, L., Quintero-Araújo, C.: Mathematical model for the home health care routing and scheduling problem with multiple treatments and time windows. In: Proceedings of the 1st International Conference on Mathematical Methods & Computational Techniques in Science & Engineering (MMCTSE 2014), pp. 140–145 (2014)
21. En-nahli, L., Allaoui, H., Nouaouri, I.: A multi-objective modelling to human resource assignment and routing problem for home health care services. IFAC-PapersOnLine 48, 698–703 (2015)
22. Bard, J.F., Shao, Y., Qi, X., Jarrah, A.I.: The traveling therapist scheduling problem. IIE Trans. 46, 683–706 (2014)
23. Yuan, B., Liu, R., Jiang, Z.: Home health care crew scheduling and routing problem with stochastic service times. In: 2014 IEEE International Conference on Automation Science and Engineering (CASE), pp. 564–569 (2014)
24. Misir, M., Verbeeck, K., De Causmaecker, P., Berghe, G.V.: Hyper-heuristics with a dynamic heuristic set for the home care scheduling problem. In: IEEE Congress on Evolutionary Computation, pp. 1–8. IEEE (2010)
25. Hiermann, G., Prandtstetter, M., Rendl, A., Puchinger, J., Raidl, G.R.: Metaheuristics for solving a multimodal home-healthcare scheduling problem. Central Eur. J. Oper. Res. 23, 89–113 (2015)
26. Steeg, J., Schröder, M.: A hybrid approach to solve the periodic home health care problem. In: Operations Research Proceedings 2007 Selected Papers of the Annual International Conference of the German Operations Research Society (GOR), 5–7 September 2007, pp. 297–302, Saarbrücken (2008)
27. Soler, W., Muñoz, M.G., Bragulat, E., Alvarez, A.: Triage: a key tool in emergency care. Anales del sistema sanitario de Navarra 33(Suppl. 1), 55–68 (2010)

28. García, M.M.: Estudio Del Triaje En Un Servicio De Urgencias Hospitalario. Revista Enfermería CyL. **5**, 42–49 (2013)
29. López-Santana, E., Espejo-Díaz, J., Méndez-Giraldo, G.: Modelo de programación entera mixta para programación y ruteo en cuidado a la salud domiciliaria considerando la promesa de servicio. In: III Congreso Internacional de Industria y Organizaciones – Gestión de Cadenas de Abastecimiento en un Mundo Cambiante (in press, 2016). Accepted
30. Bellifemine, F., Caire, G., Greenwood, D.: Developing Multi-Agent Systems with JADE. Willey series in Agent Technology. Wiley, New York (2007)

A Dynamic Model of Logistic Management for Obtaining Activated Carbon

Germán Andrés Méndez-Giraldo$^{(\boxtimes)}$, Julio Estevez$^{(\boxtimes)}$, Cristhian Pinto-Anaya$^{(\boxtimes)}$, and Jorge Ruiz-Vaca$^{(\boxtimes)}$

Universidad Distrital Francisco José de Caldas, Bogotá D.C., Colombia
gmendez@udistrital.edu.co,
{cestevezj,cdpintoa,jeruizv}@correo.udistrital.edu.co

Abstract. Activated carbon has multiple uses both to meet industrial needs as domestic. This grow in the demand has allowed Colombian industry to look for organic sources for obtaining it. Tecsol has advanced more than 20 years of research on this field. Today, they want to turn their pilot plant used in research projects to turn it into an industrial plant. This requires ensuring the supply of organic material such as using ovens at maximum capacity. As this is a new system, it should estimate the sales potential and then determine the best logistics parameters. The developed model uses continuous simulation based on the Forrester model. The industrial dynamical model determines a trade-off between different manufacturing resources and its impact on financial results. Its implementation in IThink can respond to many different questions about the main logistic components changing over time.

Keywords: Activated carbon · Logistic model · System dynamics

1 Introduction

The business management has changed radically in recent decades; nowadays, organizations have faced new paradigms in economic, social and market areas [1]. As a result of these changes, it is necessary to make decisions in order to efficiently use resources in the production system, the customer satisfaction is the most important choice, but also the most difficult to keep. Increasing of customer demand, the manufacturing requirements increases too, it is necessary to find an equilibrium of resources with performance such as increased inventory, eliminating idle time but increase scrap or cost of stock maintenance. Alternatively, it is possible to reduce spaces, that minimizes movements of goods and areas of stocking, but reduces production level too, among others considerations [2]. All this, can be solved with the use of optimization techniques in order to reduce costs independently for each component. The main problem is that local optima do not guarantee the global optimum. Thus, how is it possible to find a solution in order to satisfy variability of demand, the rational use of available resources and to observe restrictions of the productive system? Managers need to adopt new ways of proceeding based on suitable models, some of them of mathematical type, especially

© Springer International Publishing AG 2016
J.C. Figueroa-García et al. (Eds.): WEA 2016, CCIS 657, pp. 201–211, 2016.
DOI: 10.1007/978-3-319-50880-1_18

those based on the simulation [3], however, these "complex tools" can become an obstacle for its use.

Industries TECSOL has been developing research projects for more than 20 years. These studies ranging from laboratory tests, scale trials and the production in pilot plant of activated carbon (AC). Nowadays, this enterprise, with the support of Colciencias is working in the convert of AC pilot plant to carry it an industrial plant. To achieve this, it is necessary to design a continuous production line to satisfy with quality and quantity parameters according to market requirements, but above all that meets the constraints of chemical process. This production line is continuous, and it must ensure, among other things, adequate supply of materials and production levels, that meet the needs of demand by adjusting the capacity of the facilities.

This paper shows a dynamic model, easy to use and that answers many logistic environment questions. It lets you to determine the best policies to adopt in the management production system of AC from organic material, particularly in the case of *cuesco*. This paper begins with the theoretical structure aspects, such as obtaining activated carbon from *cuesco*, the main aspects of the logistics and dynamics of systems used to build the dynamic model of logistic. Subsequently, the proposed model explains each of the sectors that shape it. Finally, stages of verification and design of policies determine the main resources needed in Tecsol's production process.

2   Literature Review and Related Work

The AC is a porous solid material used as adsorbent for removal of impurities, odors and colors, both gaseous as liquid. The adsorbent property of AC is due to its high specific surface, about several hundred square meters per gram, and their functional groups of oxygen. All these in an intricate network of pores ranging in size from 5 Å for micro-pore, 5–50 Å for meso-pore and greater than 55 Å for macro-pore. The pore size determines the application to be given to AC, and it must be commensurate with the size of the molecule that is intended to remove [4].

Besides, Colombia is one of the most important producers of palm oil, in which process, for each produced palm oil unit is generated twice the quantity of cuesco residue [5]. The physico-chemical characteristics and abundance of cuesco palm in Colombia have motivated Tecsol to study it as a raw material for the production of AC, beginning with identification of the rotary oven technology with physical activation by water vapor and CO_2, as the most suitable for this process.

These technical specifications have been obtained in the phase of R&D and forms a new knowledge of the company; they are not specified in the work, as they are confidential; but are taken into account in the development of models, especially in the simulation. Below, there are some considerations logistical aspects and features of the dynamics of systems are shown to finally show some experiences in this section by integrating these two aspects.

The logistic operation of a production system, begins with the forecast in order to meet customer demand. After that, it requires the development and implementation of plans and production schedules, detailing how to use resources to convert raw materials into finished products. These resources also include employees, machines, tools and materials used, include services, information and procedures, among others. In the case of the production of activated carbon the production system is of type known as Flow Shop, where all jobs have the same route although not identical, and visit each machine only once [6, 7]. Production machinery is configured to perform sequential operations organized in a production line that is designed for a particular product [8, 9] (or group of similar products) [10, 11].

The equipment's design have similar production rates at each stage. In high-volume environments, this type of production systems are very efficient and typically has little flow times [12]. Due to the high volume requirements of such systems, it can justify the presence of special processing equipment and production systems as a strategy entirely dedicated to the production. The processing is fully adapted to the product. The production process is generally integrated, it uses mechanization and automation to achieve standardization and to reduce costs [13, 14].

These production systems are type push, the orders are released on the first stage of production and they push the work in progress to the next station and so on, until the product reaches the last station. The management system should begin with a forecast of demand, including safety stocks and lead times, after that, it is necessary to estimate requirements of resources for each station. The production program is based on the MRP (Material Requirements Planning), to schedule each operation of the production route based on its material structure. In push system, the inventory policy is one of the main success factors.

The goal for inventory policy depends of its category, there are six types of items, mainly: Raw materials, work in process, finished product, material on transit between facilities, maintenance parts and miscellaneous type; for this research there were only considered the first four types. The most important objective in the inventory policy is seek to achieve a balance between too little inventory (with possible shortages of raw materials) and too much inventory (with investment and associated storage costs) [15]. Operations managers must take two basic decisions about the inventory system: ¿When should you order; and how much should you be ordered?

The best inventory policy for a continuous flow system is the continuous review. Under this policy, the inventory level is continuously monitored and the quantity ordered is always the same and equal to difference between the inventory level desired and the level of inventory on hand. These orders are placed, as long as the inventory level has fallen to level less than, or equal to the reorder level (regardless of the length of time) [16].

The philosophy of dynamical systems (DS) of an organization arises from its structure; this includes not only the physical aspects of the production process, but is also related to more important issues, such as policies, traditions and culture. All this affects the decision-making processes. Other features are present in the flow of information, such as amplification, delay and feedback loops. In the same way that complex systems engineering does, DS responds to nonlinear effects such as the case of industrial management, where the complexity of the system depends on the components and processes and responses are not based on a cause-effect relationship [17].

Industrial dynamics (ID) is the origin of the DS and its structure, math and development therefore are the same. For example, DI studies the characteristics of feedback of information on industrial activity and the use of models for planning in the organization seeking to improve and establish business policies, [18, 19]. The functional areas of management that can be studied by industrial dynamics are marketing, production, accounting, research and development and capital investment. The representation of the model is based on the feedback information, knowledge of decision-making processes, the experimental approach of complex systems and the use of digital computers as a means to simulate real mathematical models as in the dynamic systems.

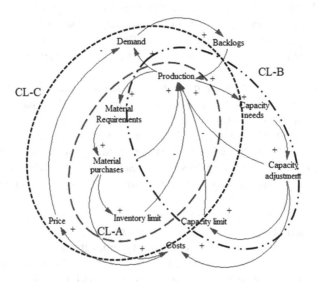

Fig. 1. Causal loop cycle logistic model

This causal diagram (Fig. 1) defines three feedback loops, the first two denoted by CL-A and CL-B; these work with two major manufacturing resources for the chemical industry, materials and equipment's capacity. It describes if orders increase, the resource requirements too; thus, it is necessary to adjust or by purchasing (material) or by more machines or new shifts (capabilities). However, these actions have restrictions: economic resources, physical spaces or both, as they are in the case of Tecsol. This causes the system not to explode it, and conversely it seeks a balance. The third feedback loop studies the economic flow: If resources are increased to meet the demand, costs increases and causes an increase in prices, this makes the product unattractive for customers and discourages its demand or at least that order decrease for the company.

Other studies show the benefits of the system dynamics; one of them shows the integration between DS with discrete simulation to represent logistics systems; particularly, to model inventory levels in the supply chain [20]. Other study analyzes lead-times of probabilistic type [21], another one shows integrating between inventories levels with work force requirements modeling using Industrial Dynamics techniques [22]. In the literature, there are many other contributions of these techniques that help logistics management.

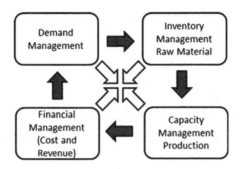

Fig. 2. Diagram of integrated logistics model

3 Proposed Model

The proposed model can help to resolve multiple logistic questions, for production of activated carbon in Tecsol. It was developed with the simulation software IThink 9.02. The model consists of four parts (see Fig. 2), so each sector is interconnected sequentially (dark arrows which represent the administrative process). For example, firstly it must estimate demand and after that, is essential to do other management activities such as revising resources needed (materials and capacities); finally, it is necessary to control financial aspects such as costs caused and profits generated.

However, in this diagram also, it stands out the dynamic component, since each sector affects others (clear arrows). For example, if there is not enough capacity, the demand satisfaction decreases and affects its financial goals. When profits reduces, it is not possible to get others resources like materials, capacity, mainly, all that creates a negative reinforcing loop known as vicious circle. Figure 3 shows a part of the general model. In the first sector has been modeled the demand management. It calculates the demand for activated carbon with a linear regression model and uses data of import of this material. However, this value must be affected by two parameters: the coverage percent and monthly seasonal coefficient. In the first case, it estimates an import substitution and therefore is calculated between 1 to 5% of these forecasts, for next three years. The monthly seasonal coefficient is represented with a random variable that it is based on the historical data of import.

The second sector is cuesco's inventories management; it uses a periodic review policy, where it is necessary to set up two parameters: level of review and order quantity. Additionally there are three constraints: Storage capacity, lead-time and replenishment batch sizes. It is necessary to estimate the grossing requirements of cuesco, since only a percentage of this will become activated carbon. Constraints are modeled as parameters to create scenarios. These options help managers to make decisions according with their needs. Currently, Tecsol has a storage capacity of 10 t of cuesco. Its supplier can sell in lots of one t and takes 5 days for delivery.

In the case of calculating, the order quantity (Q) is modeled according to the following equation:

$$(Leadtime + 1) * Milling\_capacity\_per\_hour * Shifts * 8 \qquad (1)$$

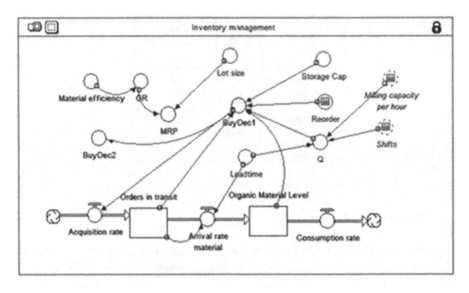

Fig. 3. Layout of logistic model in Ithink

In this case it must be ordered material depending on: the milling capacity, replenishment time, security stock. The user can modify parameters such as capacity and number of shifts (each of eight hours).

The third sector is undoubtedly the most complex; Fig. 4 represents the manufacturing system through the production process. This process consists on the following activities: material preparation (adequacy), milling, carbonization, activation, dosing and packaging. The last two are not included in the dynamic model due to the fact that the process is continuous; and while processes of milling, carbonization and activation are automatically; parallel, processes of dosing and packaging are manually done.

Fig. 4. Process flowchart

The fourth sector refers to financial management, which includes costs, prices and everything related to cost accounting. Many components of this sector are parameters but all of them are exclusive domain of the company Tecsol. These are aggregate costs of labor, materials and overhead. Additionally, there are costs of handled inventory management such as inventory costs and ordering costs. These allow analyzing policies given in the sector 2. The only parameter included in the user interface is the sales price; which upper and lower limit has been studied based on the cost structure and the value assigned by the competition.

This model then simulates the dynamic behavior of the industry. For example, to increase demand coverage, it needs to buy more *cuesco* and to adjust capacities of workstations (manuals and automatics). These relationships are non-linear character because the production process is of chemical transformation. At some level of these resources, a bottleneck occurs and it is not always the same. This bottleneck is solved but later creates another bottleneck cyclically. This cannot be indefinitely because some resources cannot increase in the short term or because profits are lower. The proposed model shows impacts of different levels of resources and its results in terms of logistics performance measures and their economic impact.

4   Experimentation and Results

The goals of this research were to make a logistic model to answer the following questions: what is the best level of capacity for each workstation? In addition, what is the best inventory policy? Firstly, it proceeded to validate the proposed model with extreme points to find mathematical or logical errors. After that, it made a design of experiment (DOE) with 5 factors and 18 levels. For experimentation there were used the following parameters: milling capacity per hour, shifts, carbonized capacity, activation capacity and price.

Table 1. Experimental setting

Factor	No. of levels	Unit	Levels
Milling per Hour	4	(k/h)	50
			100
			150
			200
Shifts	3	(n. a.)	1
			2
			3
Carbonizati on capacity	4	(k/h)	50
			100
			150
			200
Activation capacity	3	(k/h)	50
			75
			100
Price	4	COP $	4500
			5500
			6500
			7500

The possible values are shown in Table 1. These values were set in the pre-feasibility studies. The complete experiment consists of 576 cases ($4 \times 3 \times 4 \times 3 \times 4$), in order to determine the best operation parameters. For this reason was necessary evaluate each case with three different performance measurement, see Table 2.

Table 2. Experimental design used

Performance measure	Expression
Average efficiency	Average(Demand of AC/Delivery AC)
Marginal contribution	Average((Total Profit – Total Cost)/ Total Sales)
Total profits (millions)	Sum(Total Sales – Total Cost)

To facilitate the handling of experimentation has been built a user interface in the simulation software where a graph is displayed with the effectiveness index and the marginal contribution. Additionally, a numerical indicator displays the final value of these two measures and the average total profit in millions. Finally, a table appears with the most important values for process controlling; see Fig. 5.

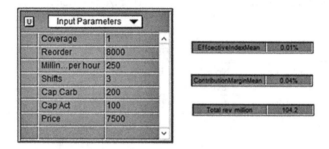

Fig. 5. User's interface

When the different experiments are ran, the best results were upper limits of parameters, while in some cases these values were not the best for average efficiency and profits average (in most cases). To the first ten experiments (ordered from highest to lowest values) the performance measure contribution were lower. In Table 3 appear the top five scenarios for average efficiency (total profits) and marginal contribution. The difference between total profits and the marginal contribution is that to achieve first measure is necessary working the total production time, but this generates an idle time which is valued in the second measure, which is why for the first case is always better to work three shifts while for the second, is better a single one. In Table 3 showing that, most answers are given at a price of 7500 because it is better, a high price than a low one. However, price setting depends on exchange rates and competitors price. Then, it is important to understand the behavior system when price takes different levels, specially, in the case of total profits (see Table 4).

Table 3. Analysis of parameters for different prices

Experiment rank	Price	Total profit	Milling	Shifts	Cap-Carb	Cap-Act
1	7500	1460.3	200	3	200	75
7	6500	1239.3	200	3	200	100
16	5500	1020.4	200	3	200	100
50	4500	801	200	3	200	100

To improve the model's solution and in order to answer the question about the inventory policy; there are incorporated into an scenario analysis, an additional parameter that is reorder point and capacity of milling is modified to expand because, as evidenced, this workstation is the bottleneck of production system.

Another 30 scenarios were presented to evaluate the best inventory policy, this was when it had a reorder point of 8000 kilos, and a quantity to buy (Q) equal to 36 t. This policy allowed a milling capacity of 250 kilos per hour and a workload for ovens of carbonization and activation of 200 and 100 kilos per hour respectively. The best price of COP $7500 generates an index of average efficiency of 10% which is the maximum value, and contribution rate marginal 0.64 with a profit of 1812.6 (millions for first year).

Cuesco's gross requirements (GR) showed some variation according to AC demand. With the use of MRP, these values are adjusting to the lot size, which in this case is 1 ton. Both the order quantity as the reorder point has not changed over time. Finally, the dynamic logistic model allowed it to control the different cost components. For example, in Fig. 6, the values represent costs of labor, materials, cost of goods in process, total costs and the value of sales for first month of simulation. The model, in general, provides much more information useful for decision-making process. The manager could analyzing each policy or scenario, based on cost information to choose the best option.

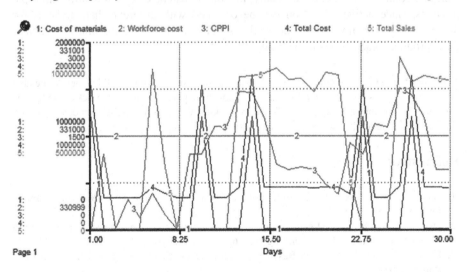

Fig. 6. Cost analysis

5   Conclusions

Simulation can anticipates the future to predict what may happen in a new production plant. This is necessary to find the best operational values to establish policies of manufacturing according with market needs and the company's capacity. For example, in Tecsol is not always better to work at complete capacity, since material availability can limit milling process rate and subsequently, production at ovens.

Parameters of milling, carbonization and activation process capacities were obtained of earlier researches made by Tecsol and in this model only were used as levels ranges in the design of experiments. Efficiencies of these work centers are modeled as random variables and let to find the best equilibrium between processing amount and efficiency on total system. A higher level of production, increase costs and revenues but the utility is not always better in those scenarios higher production. This is because it requires more material inventory and more use of workstations that sometimes raise the idle capacity.

In general, this dynamic logistic model facilitates the work planning of different resources in obtaining activated carbon for the Tecsol. It can anticipate the variation over time, identifying bottlenecks and enabling analyze the impact of parameters values assigned. In this way, they can get a greater efficiency, rationality of resources through improving marginal contribution rates, and to get the most profit possible.

6   Future Work

This dynamic model can be extended and improved so that it can helps production scheduling. This is important in order to synchronize the quantities to be processed in each season of the process and to reduce inventories in process and improve the average marginal contribution rate. Additionally, this model can be extended to allow multiple products, since activated carbon can be obtained with different characteristics for different usage; this involves residence times and particular operation times for each of these product presentations in each step of process.

Acknowledgement. We appreciate Colciencias support for allowing small business to be able to develop projects to convert pilot plants in industrial plants, besides, we acknowledge the company Tecsol that allowed the SES group working this type of logistic models based on simulation, and finally, thanks to CIDC for its support to group in this research.

References

1. Gunasekaran, A., Ngai, E.: The future of operations management: an outlook and analysis. Int. J. Prod. Econ. **135**, 687–701 (2011)
2. Oko, A., Singh Kang, P.: Lean six sigma approach to improve the admissions process for a Nigerian HE Institute. Int. J. Sci. Eng. Res. **6**, 368–378 (2016)
3. Paolucci, M., Sacile, R.: Agent-Based Manufacturing and Control Systems. CRC Press, Boca Raton (2005)

4. Centro de Desarrollo Industrial TECSOL: Identificación de alternativas para producción de carbón activado a partir de carbón del Cerrejón y su análisis de mercado nacional e internacional. Bogotá (2013)
5. Gómez, A., Klose, W., Rincón, S.: Pirolisis de biomasa. Kassel Univ. Press, Kassel (2008)
6. Framinan, J., Leisten, R., Ruiz, R.: Manufacturing Scheduling Systems. Springer, London (2014)
7. Singh, N., Rajamani, D.: Cellular Manufacturing Systems. Chapman & Hall, London (1996)
8. Çelikbilek, C., Süer, G.: Joint optimization model for manufacturing scheduling and transportation mode selection. In: Asian Conference of Management Science and Applications (2013)
9. Cable, A., Melone, P.: Method for improving the utilization of manufacturing machines. Manufacturing processes, US20150142548 A1 (2015)
10. Bagchi, T.: Multiobjective Scheduling by Genetic Algorithms. Kluwer Academic Publishers, Boston (1999)
11. Chase, R., Aquilano, N., Jacobs, F.: Operations Management for Competitive Advantage. McGraw-Hill, Boston (2004)
12. Askin, R., Goldberg, J.: Design and Analysis of Lean Production Systems. Wiley, New York (2002)
13. Chaudhari, S., Yawale, V., Dalu, R.: Low cost approach to manufacturing problem solving. Int. J. Mater. Sci. Eng. (2014)
14. Buffa, E., Sarin, R.: Administración de la producción y de las operaciones. Ed. Limusa, Mexico (1992)
15. Ross, D.: Procurement and Supplier Management. Distribution Planning and Control. Springer Science, Business Media, New York (2015)
16. Elsayed, E., Boucher, T.: Analysis and Control of Production Systems. Prentice-Hall, Englewood Cliffs (1994)
17. Forrester, F.: Principles of Systems. Wright-Allen Press, Cambridge (1968)
18. Forrester, F.: Industrial Dynamics. M.I.T. Press, Cambridge (1961)
19. Sterman, J.: Business Dynamics. McGraw-Hill, Boston (2000)
20. Umeda, S.: Supply-chain simulation integrated discrete-event modeling with system-dynamics modeling. In: Olhager, J., Persson, F. (eds.) Advances in Production Management Systems, vol. 246, pp. 329–336. Springer, New York (2007)
21. Kulkarni, V., Yan, K.: Production-inventory systems in stochastic environment and stochastic lead times. Queueing Syst. **70**, 207–231 (2011)
22. Ng, T., Sy, C.: A resilience optimization approach for workforce-inventory control dynamics under uncertainty. J. Sched. **17**, 427–444 (2013)

A Knowledge-Based Expert System for Scheduling in Services Systems

Eduyn Ramiro López-Santana[✉] and Germán Andrés Méndez-Giraldo

Faculty of Engineering, Universidad Distrital Francisco José de Caldas, Bogotá, Colombia
{erlopezs,gmendez}@udistrital.edu.co

Abstract. This paper studies a knowledge-based expert systems for the scheduling problem in service systems. We establish some differences between manufacturing and services systems in order to identify the aspects that influence in the scheduling process. We review the main techniques to solve the scheduling problem related with classical methods, metaheuristics, artificial intelligence and knowledge-based expert systems approaches. Finally, we propose a structure of knowledge-based systems in order to solve the scheduling problem in services systems. We apply our approach in a health service system in order to show the setting and the results of our knowledge-based expert system.

Keywords: Knowledge-based system · Expert system · Scheduling · Service system

1 Introduction

In many real-world systems exists a decision-making process related with the allocation of resources to perform a set of tasks in a specific planning horizon subject several operational constraints such capacity or unavailability of resources, due dates, priorities, cancelations, among others in order to optimize one or more objectives. This process is named scheduling and has applications in computer science, logistic, distribution, production, workforce, maintenance, healthcare, among others [1–3].

A typical classification of the scheduling problems is theirs the application fields such manufacturing and service systems [2]. A generic manufacturing system consists of a set of machines and jobs that are interacting to produce a good in which the material flows thorough the machines that transform it in end item. In the literature, there are different applications of scheduling in manufacturing environments for example flow shop, job shop and open shop problems and variants or combinations of these that are described in detail by [2–5].

Service systems consist of activities that are offered using human or mechanical power in order to satisfy people's needs or wishes [2], also consist of a set of interacting resources provided by the customer and the provider [6]. The scheduling problems are more difficult to classify in services as the manufacturing environments. In [3, 7–9] different applications of scheduling in services are presented as reservation problems, timetabling allocations, routing problems, maintenance, workforce problem, among others.

© Springer International Publishing AG 2016
J.C. Figueroa-García et al. (Eds.): WEA 2016, CCIS 657, pp. 212–224, 2016.
DOI: 10.1007/978-3-319-50880-1_19

In the field of knowledge-based expert systems there are several applications in scheduling problems. The terms expert system (ES) and knowledge-based expert systems (KBES) can therefore be used interchangeably. Kusiak and Chen [10] discussed applications of ES in manufacturing planning and scheduling. They describe some expert systems applied in several manufacturing environments applying rules and frames. Johnson et al. [11] present an expert system to scheduling in job shop problems. They developed an ES that produce a specific schedule for the problem according to a procedure mathematically proven to provide a satisfactory and often optimal solution, given the criteria for the problem. The authors used a simulation model to test the effectiveness of a selected technique with respect to the chosen performance measure. Kusiak [12] presents a knowledge-based systems (KBS) to scheduling in automated manufacturing system. His KBS contains a heuristic algorithm that selected and execute the best algorithm of a set of scheduling problems. Mendez et al. [13] present an ES to scheduling in job shop problems. Their approach select the best algorithm to solve the scheduling problem according with the features of the specific problem. Chen [14] states a self-adaptive agent-based fuzzy-neural system to solve a scheduling problem in a wafer fabrication factory. Their results improve the performance of scheduling jobs in the simulated wafer fabrication factory, especially with respect to the average cycle time and cycle time standard deviation.

When examining the literature, one should notice the lack of application of KBES in scheduling problems in service systems. Indeed, most of the papers deal with manufacturing environments. The objective of this paper consists to identify the aspects that lead how to modeling a KBES to the scheduling problem in service systems.

The remainder of this paper is organized as follows. Section 2 reviews services systems and the main features of the scheduling problem and its solution techniques. Section 3 introduce the KBESs and define its components. Section 4 states our KBES approach to solve the scheduling problem in service systems. Section 5 presents an example of application in a health service system. Finally, Sect. 6 concludes this work and provides possible research directions.

2   Scheduling Problem in Service Systems

In this section, we describe the service systems and scheduling problems. First, we introduce the service systems and state the differences between manufacturing and service systems. Then, we present the scheduling problems and a review of the solution techniques.

2.1   Service Systems

Service can be defined as the application of competences for the benefit of another [15] and a solution and a customer's experience that satisfy her or his wishes [16]. Service systems is as a set of activities performed by resources (machines and people) to meet the needs or desires of people through the transformation of the initial state of any of the customer's resources [2]. Also, service systems consist of service providers and service customers working together to coproduce value in complex value networks where providers and customers might be individuals, firms, government agencies, or any organization of people and technologies [17].

Service systems are becoming a strategic area of scientific research from multidisciplinary approaches. An academic community has emerged such as Service Science or Service Science Management and Engineering [17, 18]. Likewise, the service systems are in many aspects different from manufacturing systems as is described in [2, 6, 15]. Table 1 summarizes the main differences between manufacturing and service systems. In addition, for both systems, the demand is difficult to forecast, it is subject to variability and dynamic conditions that involves rescheduling, adjustments and synchronization of several resources complete a service.

Table 1. Differences between manufacturing and service systems.

Features	Manufacturing systems	Services systems
Goods	Physical products, durable	Intangible, perishable
Inventory of goods	Allowed	No allowed
Demand	The demand could be postponed	The demand cannot be postponed
Contact with customers	Generally is during the sale process	Generally is during the service generation
Time response to demand	Lead Time	Customer tolerance, patience function
Location (Place)	Not necessarily close to the customer	Several: ranging from in situ to remote
Quality measurement	There are objective characteristics of the products	May be subjective and difficult
Consumption and production time	Are not given simultaneously	Are given simultaneously
Capacity lacks	Generate inventory or delays	Generate queues or dropouts
Resources	The resource are machines that operates automatized or by a human resource	The use of machines the for service is often less important than the employment of people
Ownership	The ownership of a product is transferred to the customer	The ownership of a product is not transferred to the customer

On the other hand, it is very common to be dependent on the expertise and knowledge of people in the service systems. Firms often delegate the planning and scheduling of activities (decision-making) for highly complex systems to experienced staff; trusting their intuition and knowledge. However, when there is too much information and relationships that make the understanding of the system a complex task, they find themselves limited. Moreover, it often takes a long time to generate (usually manually) a feasible schedule and work-plan. It is therefore necessary that the services system use, in an orderly and systematic way, the individual knowledge of experienced staff to solve collectively the scheduling problem.

2.2   Scheduling Problem

The general scheduling problem consists in finding the best sequence to perform a number of jobs in a number of machines (or resources) in order to optimize a one or more objective functions [3]. This problem is typically NP-hard and thus is difficult to find an optimal solution since the computation time increases exponentially with the problem size [3].

The scheduling problems can be classified in deterministic and stochastic problems. In the deterministic case the information about processing times, release date, due dates, capacity, among others has a constant value while in stochastic case the information has a stochastic variability [3]. Another classification consists in static and dynamic scheduling [9]. If the jobs arrive simultaneously and all resources and all information are available at beginning of planning horizon, then the scheduling problem is said to be static. If jobs arrive intermittently and the resources are subject to several kinds of perturbations, the problem is dynamic. The complexity to solve the scheduling problem increases from deterministic to stochastic and increases from static to dynamic environments [1, 3]. In summary, Table 2 presents some techniques to solve the static and dynamics scheduling problems. Many of real-world scheduling problems in service systems are categorized in stochastic and dynamic environments [4, 9] thus it is hard to solve since the complex nature of services.

Table 2. Features of solution techniques to static and dynamics scheduling problems

	Static	Dynamic
Deterministic	Relatively easy to solve with: - Mathematical programming - Heuristics	Medium difficulty to solve with: - Mathematical programming - Heuristics and metaheuristics - Simulation - Hybrid systems
Stochastic	Medium difficulty to solve with: - Stochastic programming - Heuristics and metaheuristics - Simulation - Hybrid systems	Hard to solve with: - Heuristics and metaheuristics - Simulation - Artificial intelligence - Hybrid systems

The scheduling problems has been immensely studied in the literature. From classical approaches, the mathematical programming has many applications, for instance integer programming and mixed integer programming in order to minimize the makespan can be model as Traveling Salesman Problem formulation or the Allocation Problem formulation. The difficult of them is the high-required time to found an optimal solution because the scale of problem increase as the number of jobs (n) and machines (m) increase in the order of $(n!)^m$. Table 3 summarizes some approaches in the literature to solve scheduling problems.

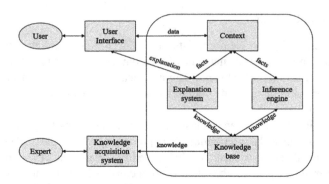

Fig. 1. Architecture of a KBES (modified of [33])

Table 3. Summary of approaches to scheduling problems

Approach	Techniques
Mathematical programming	Mixed Integer programming [3], Dynamic programming [19] Dispatching rules [5, 20]
Metaheuristics	Simulated Annealing, Tabu Search [20–22], Genetic Algorithms [23], Swarm optimization [24, 25]
Artificial Intelligence (AI)	Cellular automata [26, 27], Multi agent systems [28], Collective intelligence [24, 29], Cooperative systems [30], Expert systems [13, 31]

From AI and intelligent systems approaches, the applications is scarcer than classical methods, heuristics and metaheuristics. This perspective consists in embedding the computational intelligence methods (heuristics, metaheuristics and bio-inspired methods) to solve approximately each new problem on-line. Then, it responses to the dynamics environment of scheduling problems.

For this review, we can identify that the techniques addressed in the literature are scarce in the use of AI methods for solve scheduling problems related with service systems. Thus, we study and propose a KBES to solve the scheduling problems in a service environment.

3   Knowledge-Based Expert Systems (KBES) in Scheduling

The KBES is specialized in a specific field and aim to solve problems through reasoning methods that emulate the performance of a human expert [13, 32]. A KBES is a computer program that reasons and uses a knowledge base to solve complex problems in a particular domain [33, 34]. Figure 1 presents the architecture of a KBES. The major components of a KBES are a knowledge base and an inference engine consisting in one or more inference mechanism. The knowledge base is a collection of knowledge required for problem solving and the inference engine checks the available facts, selects the appropriate knowledge source for the knowledge base, matches the facts with the knowledge and generates additional facts [33].

The KBES operate the following way [33]. When a KBES starts the process of inference, it is required a context or working memory that represents the set of established facts. The explanation system simulates the process of an expert answers the questions: *How* a decision is arrived at? and *Why* a data us need? Since the knowledge base has to be continuously update and/or appended depending on the growth of knowledge in the domain, an interface between expert and KBES is necessary. The knowledge acquisition system executes this interface, and is not an on-line component, it can be implemented in many ways. In addition, another interface is necessary between the user and the KBES. The User interface allows the user interacts with the KBES giving data, defining facts and monitoring the status of the problem solving.

The knowledge base is the component where all knowledge provided by experts is stored in an orderly and structured way under a set of relationships, such as rules or probability distributions, facts and heuristics that represent the thinking of the expert. The major of KBES use rules the basis of its operation, but can also be used representation schemes such as semantic networks, frames, among others. The knowledge base is independent of the mechanisms of inference and search methods. It is necessary to differentiate between data and knowledge, since knowledge refers to the set of relationships between a set of objects, and are permanent, while data are facts of a given situation and are variable, so they are destroyed after use.

The inference engine performs two main tasks [35]. The first one, it examines the facts and rules, and if possible, add new facts. The second one, it choose the order in which inferences are made. Notably, the findings obtained by the inference engine, are made based on deterministic or stochastic information data and can be simple or compound.

There is a little use of KBES in the literature of scheduling problems and mainly in manufacturing environments. The KBES provide flexible means to solve a variety of problems that often cannot be solved by traditional methods. The KBES is a tendency of Artificial Intelligence related to the design and implementation of programs that are able to emulate or expand the human skills, such as problem solving, visual perception and understanding of language cognitive skills. These features allow the KBES are an alternative to solve the scheduling problems [12, 13, 31].

Mendez et al. [13] present an ES for scheduling in manufacturing systems. The authors state the advantages of using an ES in terms of availability in contrast to the human; the ES has all the expertise inside, never tires or dies. Depending on the software and hardware, an ES can respond faster. On the other hand, even the best experts can make mistakes or they can forget an important point, once an ES is programmed to request and use certain inputs, it is not prone to be forgetful. The ES also have disadvantages as suggested [13] regarding the scope of the problem has to be defined in closed way to make the task of building the knowledge base is feasible.

4   KBES Approach to Scheduling in Service Systems

Figure 2 presents the proposed general framework to solve the scheduling problem in service systems according with [36]. This framework has two inputs, a service system

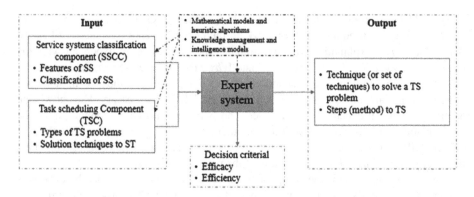

Fig. 2. General framework of a KBES to scheduling in service systems

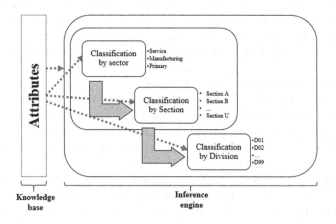

Fig. 3. A KBES to classify service systems

classification component and the task scheduling component (SSCC). The ES takes these inputs and selects the technique (or set of techniques) to solve a scheduling problem and/or the Steps (method) to solve this problem.

Figure 3 presents the SSCC proposed by [37]. The KBES consists in a classification system for the International Standard Industrial Classification (ISIC) system in the Colombian context, also to classify according to economy sector as Services, Manufacturing and Primary proposed by the authors for the section level and division level. Additionally it is taken as instances for database-level Group, i.e. in total has 249 instances for the selection of rules. In Fig. 3, the knowledge base consists in a set of 12 attributes: Coproduction, Dependence, Accumulation, Technology, Property, Simultaneity, Flexibility, Nature, Durability, Place, Scheduled and Standardization. The data was collected using interview with an expert and secondary information sources. The inference engine was made with an algorithm to generate tree C4.5 using the entropy information measure. The attributes were modeled using a knowledge acquisition model based in a non-linear optimization and an adaptive neuro-fuzzy inference system (ANFIS) approach (for details see [38]). The set of characteristics are defined in Table 4.

Table 4. List of characteristics (R_a)

r	Characteristic	r	Characteristic	r	Characteristic
1	Presence	12	Initial waiting time	22	Personalization
2	Behavior	13	Space	23	Appearance
3	Continuity	14	Cost of storage	24	Complementary products
4	Abandonment	15	Using machines/ equipment	25	Knowledge
5	Operation	16	Using people	26	Consumption
6	Autonomy	17	Interaction	27	Place
7	Influence	18	Beneficiary	28	Displacement
8	Storage	19	Permission	29	Activity program
9	Storage time	20	Commercializati on	30	Resource Scheduling
10	Anticipation	21	Virtual	31	Standardization
11	Wait time				

Figure 4 shows the TSC. This KBES consists in a classification system for according with the scheduling problems in services systems proposed by [9]. In addition, we select the solution technique according with the review about classical, bio-inspired and complex systems engineering approaches. Finally, the KBES determines the input parameters and outputs for a specific problem according with a performance measure (or measures).

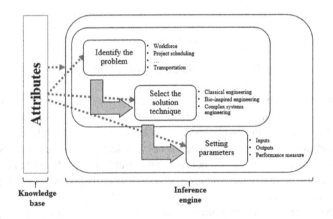

Fig. 4. A KBES to classify scheduling problems in service systems

5   Application of a Home Health Care Service System

In this section we show the application of our KBES in a specific heath service system known as Home Health Care (HHC). The HHC is an alternative way to the traditional hospitalization which consists in delivering medical, paramedical and social services to patients at their homes rather than in a hospital [39, 40].

We apply our KBES to a sample of five workers in a HHC system. The first KBES was applied according with [38], we define the subset of characteristics R_a for each attribute a, the number of MFs (m_r). The type of MFs (μ_r) correspond to triangular (trimf), general bell (gbelmf) or trapezoidal (trapmf).

Figure 5 presents the results of SSCC for a sample of 5 organizations. In addition, we present the reference value of model developed in [37, 38] and the average of the sample. In the sample, there is a consensus for all attributes except dependence, place and flexibility which as a small deviation 0.81, 1.10 and 0.64 respectively. Respect to reference value, attributes as nature, durability, coproduction, property and simultaneity are too closed. In addition, place and scheduled attributes have a small deviation. However, the rest of attributes have big differences respect to reference value. With these results we need to update the knowledge base in order to our KBES learn with these new information. The classification obtained is as service, section Q, and division 86.

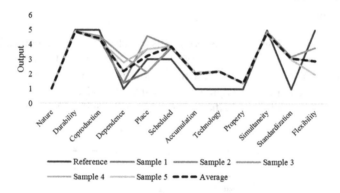

Fig. 5. Results of SSCC applied of HHC system

One of the most important decision in planning home health care services is the routing of caregivers, which means to decide in which sequence each caregiver will visit patients assigned to him/her [41]. There have been several research studies aimed at solve HHC routing problem, for instance in [42] was designed a support decision system for routing health operators using a heuristic procedure. The problem can be viewed as a combination of staff rostering problem and vehicle routing problem (VRP) [43]. Then, the problem is classified as workforce and routing problem.

Respect to solution techniques, there are applications of Mixed integer programming, branch and bound, dynamic programming, column generation and set partitioning problem, as is stated in [44] as common exact methods in the literature. On the other hand multi-agent systems has also been used for solving allocation and scheduling processes as seen in [45].

According with [44], we take into account constraints as time windows of the patients, caregivers skills, caregivers working time, precedence (a prior visit of another staff member) and multiple depots. For the HHC problem is selected a multi-agent approach for solving dynamically the caregivers' routing problem. The multi-agent approach uses a multi-objective mixed integer model to make the routing which is updated by the agents when a new request appears presented in [44]. The mathematical model aims to minimize the time travelled as well as the delay in the arrival time at the patients' locations, taking into account caregivers' skills, patients' priority in their attention, caregivers' working time and caregivers' departure and arrival locations.

6   Conclusions

This paper reviews the scheduling problems in service systems and presents a structure of a general KBES to solve this problem. We find that the KBES approaches is scarce in the literature about scheduling in service systems. We identify some differences between manufacturing and service systems and also some features of service systems and the solution techniques in order to build a KBES.

The proposed general KBES was supported in two sub-KBES. The first one is a service systems classification component (SSCC) applied to ISIC system. The proposed scheme takes into account the variables associated with customers, the system and the characteristics of the outputs in order to determine this information under the industry, section and division to which it belongs. On the other hand, the rules system is systematic and hierarchical because it must first determine the sector to which it belongs economic activity, with this result and other attributes to determine the section, and finally with these two additional results determine the division. This result is useful for companies to determine their classification and for entities that consolidate information for statistical purposes. The second one is a task scheduling component (TSC) that allows identifying the scheduling problem (or problems). After, it selects the best solution technique (or techniques) and setting the input data, parameters, outputs and performance measure in order to solve the problem.

In the application of our KBES to HHC system is presented the setting of the input parameter in order to classify the service system and it is proposed a scheduling technique selection in order to solve the problem according with the classical method in the literature reviews. As result, we selected a multi-agent approach for solving dynamically the caregivers' routing problem, this approach uses a mixed integer programming model to route the caregivers in order to serve the patients' needs. The implementation of the approach will be built in the JADE-java middleware.

This work generates possible future development lines, one of which is the validation of results with a set of real companies and improving the database of information. Another possible improvement is to explore methods of numerical ratings based on attributes subject to imprecision using fuzzy logic, among other techniques.

Acknowledgements. The first author would like to thank the Universidad Distrital Francisco Jose de Caldas for their assistance in providing a research scholarship for his Ph.D. thesis. Last, but not least, the authors would like to thank the comments of the anonymous referees that significantly improved our paper.

References

1. Conway, R.W., Maxwell, W.L., Miller, L.W.: Theory of Scheduling. Addison Wesley, Reading (1967)
2. Pinedo, M.L.: Planning and Scheduling in Manufacturing and Services. Springer, New York (2009)
3. Pinedo, M.L.: Scheduling: Theory, Algorithms, and Systems. Springer, New York (2012)
4. Ouelhadj, D., Petrovic, S.: A survey of dynamic scheduling in manufacturing systems. J. Sched. **12**, 417–431 (2009)
5. Méndez-Giraldo, G.: Programación de tareas-Scheduling. Universidad Distrital Francisco José de Caldas, Bogotá (2011)
6. Böttcher, M., Fähnrich, K.-P.: Service systems modeling: concepts, formalized meta-model and technical concretion. In: Demirkan, H., Spohrer, J.C., Krishna, V. (eds.) The Science of Service Systems, pp. 131–149. Springer, US (2011)
7. Wang, Z., Xing, W., Chen, B.: On-line service scheduling. J. Sched. **12**, 31–43 (2009)
8. Huang, K.-C., Huang, T.-C., Tsai, M.-J., Chang, H.-Y.: Moldable job scheduling for HPC as a service. In: Park, J.J., Stojmenovic, I., Choi, M., Xhafa, F. (eds.) Future Information Technology. LNCS, vol. 276, pp. 43–48. Springer, Heidelberg (2014)
9. Pinedo, M., Zacharias, C., Zhu, N.: Scheduling in the service industries: An overview. J. Syst. Sci. Syst. Eng. **24**, 1–48 (2015)
10. Kusiak, A., Chen, M.: Expert systems for planning and scheduling manufacturing systems. Eur. J. Oper. Res. **34**, 113–130 (1988)
11. Johnson Jr., L.M., Dileepan, P., Sen, T.: Knowledge based scheduling systems: a framework. J. Intell. Manuf. **1**, 117–123 (1990)
12. Kusiak, A.: KBSS: A knowledge-based system for scheduling in automated manufacturing. Math. Comput. Model. **13**, 37–55 (1990)
13. Méndez-Giraldo, G., Álvarez, L., Caicedo, C., Malaver, M.: Expert system for scheduling production-research and development of a prototype (in Spanish). Universidad Distrital Francisco José de Caldas, Colombia (2013)
14. Chen, T.: A self-adaptive agent-based fuzzy-neural scheduling system for a wafer fabrication factory. Expert Syst. Appl. **38**, 7158–7168 (2011)
15. Vargo, S.L., Lusch, R.F.: Service-dominant logic: continuing the evolution. J. Acad. Mark. Sci. **36**, 1–10 (2008)
16. Spohrer, J.C., Demirkan, H., Krishna, V.: Service and science. In: Demirkan, H., Spohrer, J.C., Krishna, V. (eds.) The Science of Service Systems, pp. 325–358. Springer, New York (2011)
17. Spohrer, J., Maglio, P.P., Bailey, J., Gruhl, D.: Steps toward a science of service systems. Computer **40**, 71–77 (2007)
18. Demirkan, H., Spohrer, J.C., Krishna, V.: Introduction of the science of service systems. In: Demirkan, H., Spohrer, J.C., Krishna, V. (eds.) The Science of Service Systems, pp. 1–11. Springer, Boston (2011)
19. Huynh Tuong, N., Soukhal, A., Billaut, J.-C.: A new dynamic programming formulation for scheduling independent tasks with common due date on parallel machines. Eur. J. Oper. Res. **202**, 646–653 (2010)
20. Laha, D.: Heuristics and Metaheuristics for Solving Scheduling Problems. Handbook of Computational Intelligence in Manufacturing and Production Management, pp. 1–18 (2007)
21. Sadegheih, A.: Scheduling problem using genetic algorithm, simulated annealing and the effects of parameter values on GA performance. Appl. Math. Model. **30**, 147–154 (2006)
22. Werner, F.: Genetic algorithms for shop scheduling problems: a survey. Preprint 11, 31 (2011)

23. Omara, F.A., Arafa, M.M.: Genetic algorithms for task scheduling problem. J. Parallel Distrib. Comput. **70**, 13–22 (2010)
24. Madureira, A., Pereira, I., Pereira, P., Abraham, A.: Negotiation mechanism for self-organized scheduling system with collective intelligence. Neurocomputing **132**, 97–110 (2014)
25. Madureira, A., Cunha, B., Pereira, I.: Cooperation mechanism for distributed resource scheduling through artificial bee colony based self-organized scheduling system. In: Proceedings of the 2014 IEEE Congress on Evolutionary Computation, CEC 2014, pp. 565–572 (2014)
26. Witkowski, T., Antczak, A., Antczak, P., Elzway, S.: Some results on evolving cellular automata applied to the production scheduling problem. In: Cellular Automata - Simplicity Behind Complexity, pp. 377–398 (2011)
27. Abdolzadeh, M., Rashidi, H.: Solving job shop scheduling problem using cellular learning automata. In: Third UKSim European Symposium on Computer Modeling and Simulation. pp. 49–54. IEEE (2009)
28. Hsieh, F.-S., Lin, J.-B.: Scheduling patients in hospitals based on multi-agent systems. In: Ali, M., Pan, J.-S., Chen, S.-M., Horng, M.-F. (eds.) IEA/AIE 2014. LNCS (LNAI), vol. 8481, pp. 32–42. Springer International Publishing, Cham (2014). doi:10.1007/978-3-319-07455-9_4
29. Madureira, A., Pereira, I., Sousa, N.: Collective intelligence on dynamic manufacturing scheduling optimization. In: 2010 IEEE Fifth International Conference on Bio-Inspired Computing: Theories and Applications (BIC-TA). pp. 1693–1697 (2010)
30. Méndez-Giraldo, G.: Assisted Cooperative Systems for Production Scheduling in the Colombian Manufacturing Industry (in spanish). Universidad Distrital Francisco José de Caldas, Centro de Investigaciones y Desarrollo Científico, Bogotá, Colombia (2001)
31. Metaxiotis, K.S., Askounis, D., Psarras, J.: Expert systems in production planning and scheduling: a state-of-the-art survey. J. Intell. Manuf. **13**, 253–260 (2002)
32. Díez, R.P., Gómez, A.G., Martínez, N. de A.: Introduction to artificial intelligence expert systems, artificial neural networks and evolutionary computation (in spanish). Universidad de Oviedo (2001)
33. Krishnamoorthy, C.S., Rajeev, S.: Artificial intelligence and expert systems for engineers. CRC Press, Boca Raton (1996)
34. Kusiak, A.: Intelligent manufacturing systems. Prentice Hall International, London (1990)
35. Harmon, P., King, D.: Expert systems: applications of artificial intelligence in business (in spanish). Ediciones Díaz de Santos (1988)
36. Lopez-Santana, E.R., Castro, S.J.B., Giraldo, G.A.M.: Methodologic model to scheduling on service systems: a software engineering approach (in spanish). Redes de Ingeniería **7**, 55–66 (2016)
37. López-Santana, E.R., Méndez-Giraldo, G.: Proposal for a rule-based classification system for service systems (in spanish). In: Proceedings of Fifth International Conference on Computing Mexico-Colombia and XV Academic Conference on Artificial Intelligence, pp. 1–8, Cartagena (2015)
38. López-Santana, E.R., Méndez-Giraldo, G.A.: A Non-linear Optimization Model and ANFIS-Based Approach to Knowledge Acquisition to Classify Service Systems. In: Huang, D.-S., Han, K., Hussain, A. (eds.) ICIC 2016. LNCS (LNAI), vol. 9773, pp. 789–801. Springer International Publishing, Cham (2016). doi:10.1007/978-3-319-42297-8_73
39. Benzarti, E., Sahin, E., Dallery, Y.: A literature review on operations management based models developed for home health care services, Paris, France (2010)
40. Yalcindag, S., Matta, A., Sahin, E.: Operator assignment and routing problems in home health care services. In: 2012 IEEE International Conference on Automation Science and Engineering (CASE), pp. 329–334 (2012)

41. Yalcindag, S., Matta, A., Sahin, E.: Human resource scheduling and routing problems in home health care context: a literature review. In: 37th Conference on Operational Research Applied to Health Services (ORAHS), pp. 1–34. At Cardiff (2012)

42. Begur, S.., Miller, D.M., Weaber, J..: An integrated spatial decision support system for scheduling and routing home health care nurses. Institute of Operations Research and Management Science, pp. 35–48 (1997)

43. Yuan, Z., Fügenschuh, A.: Home health care scheduling: a case study. In: Applied Mathematics and Optimization Series, pp. 1–18 (2015)

44. López-Santana, E.R., Espejo-Díaz, J., Méndez-Giraldo, G.: Mixed integer programming model for scheduling and routing in the home health care considering service promise (in spanish). In: III Congreso Internacional de Industria y Organizaciones – "Gestión de Cadenas de Abastecimiento en un Mundo Cambiante", pp. 1–8, Cali, Colombia (2016)

45. Wahaishi, A.M., Aburukba, R.O.: An agent-based personal assistant for exam scheduling. In: Computer and Information Technology (WCCIT) (2013)

Simulation of the Coffee Berry Borer Expansion in Colombian Crops Using a Model of Multiple Swarms

Nychol Bazurto, Helbert Espitia[(✉)], and Carlos Martínez

Universidad Distrital Francisco José de Caldas, Bogotá, Colombia
{nbazurtog,heespitiac,caralmartinez}@correo.udistrital.edu.co

Abstract. In this paper a simulation of a basic model of multiple swarms of particles is presented, illustrating the behavior of the coffee berry borer infestation in Colombian coffee crops generating information. In regard of this problem it is used engineering techniques, which aims to promote impact of the level at which the pest harms the national economy. The results show an adequate performance of the model and simulation proposed.

Keywords: Coffee berry borer · Multiple swarms · Simulation

1 Introduction

The Colombian economy has key products in the export area, such as coal, petroleum and petroleum products, ferronickel and coffee. The latter has symbolized from January to August 2014, 1'512.632 about thousands of dollars [1] and also had the most dynamic agricultural GDP, with a 20.7% variation in the first half of 2014 [2,3]. Therefore, it is a product whose production should be optimal. However, coffee production is affected by various pests: rust, drill, leafminers, and others, which cause damage in different ways [4]. Among the threats that affect this product, the coffee borer is the most important. An insect that pierces the fruit and reproduces inside it. Also, it has the ability to move aerially [5–7], affecting up to 90% of national coffee production in past years, generating a high social impact [8].

Because of this, the different institutions involved in the coffee growing area developed techniques and studies to promote the reduction of insect damage [9], however, in this area the models used to describe the movement of the insect are limited, rather that, focus on population growth and factors affecting its dynamics as competition between species but not in determining the risk of proliferation given by selected characteristics [10,11].

Taking these circumstances, we propose a simulation based on particle swarm [12], model previously developed [13] and own studies using other techniques [14], where the levels of pest infestation were confirmed.

© Springer International Publishing AG 2016
J.C. Figueroa-García et al. (Eds.): WEA 2016, CCIS 657, pp. 225–232, 2016.
DOI: 10.1007/978-3-319-50880-1_20

2   Coffee Berry Borer and Particles Swarm

There are certain models related to PSO that simulate the dynamics of different groups and families, such as, the work of (Zhenzhou) [15] where the search of an optimal through families of particle swarms is implemented using a technique known as FPSO (Family Particle Swarm Optimization), which makes emphasis on the development of trees with these families for organizing swarms of these groups. Moreover, in the work made by (Braton) [16], it can identify an approach to the generalization of a swarms algorithm applying the technique of PSO particles mentioned above, aiming to use all improvements achieved by researches. However, the approach of previous works belongs to a heuristic optimization algorithm; here lies the difference with the proposed work, given that what is involved is not an optimization algorithm but legitimate pursuit of simulating multiple swarms particles (on a swarm model, not a optimization technique), focusing on the behavior swarm itself.

Moreover, between related studies with the modeling of the coffee borer, there is a work based on the coffee agroecosystem as second part of a general work about the coffee, in which a model to the growth and development of coffee is proposed [9], given some dynamics of the coffee berry borer, focusing on biological aspects like insect intrinsic mortality, intra-species competition, mortality by rain, effects of control traps on this pest, as well as the effect of climate in its growth. This study, however, does not focus on the dynamics of pest spreading, denoting the limited existence of models in this aspect.

However, the present authors made proposals of fuzzy and ANFIS models to simulate expansion of coffee borer in Colombian coffee plantations [14], where relevant variables were considered, such as temperature, altitude, harvesting quality and culture age, identifying the importance of climate like determinant factor in the expansion of the coffee borer. In this work, it was possible to replicate the behavior of data from the document Cenicafé Integrated Management of the coffee borer (MIB), taking into account the climatic cycles periods. The development of the proposed model could be able to identify the changes brought in pest behavior with respect to the variations of each period.

3   Swarm Intelligence and Particles Swarm

Nature has been for centuries a source of inspiration for humanity, because of the perfection of its various mechanisms, which seems to combine without being prepared for it.

Within the existing particular behaviors, some insects, birds and marine animals, easily showing patterns in their motion, common activities for their survival as protection against predators, find food, energy saving swimming or flying together [17]. These behaviors are possible due to global messages of individuals, such as the use of dances (in the case of bees), pheromone (ants) or simply by altering their environment [18]), as would be with the coffee borer case, where one perforated fruit is a message for female to discard that food source [19].

This collective or swarm intelligence has been described by various authors, however, mostly of them keeping repulsion, alignment and attraction characteristics (or a couple of them). Among the particles swarm models each individual is considered as a particle with certain characteristics: direction and speed.

In 1995 [12], the author throws a statistical physics approach to establish a quantitative understanding of the behavior of swarms in the presence of a disturbance (natural consequences of various factors), thus introducing the SPPs (Self Propelled Particles) moving with a fixed speed v_0 absolute and relative to the average direction of its neighbor by a distance R, described by Eqs. (1) and (2).

$$\boldsymbol{v}_i[n+1] = v_0 \frac{\langle \boldsymbol{v}_j[n] \rangle_R}{|\langle \boldsymbol{v}_j[n] \rangle_R|} + \text{disturbance} \tag{1}$$

$$\boldsymbol{x}_i[n+1] = \boldsymbol{x}_i[n] + \boldsymbol{v}[n+1] \tag{2}$$

In 2005 [13], they released a Self-Propelled Particles with Soft-Core Interactions model was taken as the basis for the present work (see Eqs. 3 and 4).

$$\frac{\partial \boldsymbol{x}_i}{\partial t} = \boldsymbol{v}_i, \tag{3}$$

$$m\frac{\partial \boldsymbol{v}_i}{\partial t} = (\alpha - \beta|\boldsymbol{v}_i|^2)\boldsymbol{v}_i - \boldsymbol{\nabla}_i U(\boldsymbol{x}_i) \tag{4}$$

where:

$$U(\boldsymbol{x}_i) = \sum_{j \neq i} [C_r e^{-|\boldsymbol{x}_i - \boldsymbol{x}_j|/l_r} - C_a e^{-|\boldsymbol{x}_i - \boldsymbol{x}_j|/l_a}] \tag{5}$$

This model allows the simulation of a swarm where the above equations for each individual (population N) are calculated with respect to its neighbors, allowing convergence to a minimum, preserving a pattern, thresholds affected by repulsion and attraction.

4   Particle Swarm Simulation Proposal

As mentioned above the complete model is based on [13]. This model initially provides a swarm where the particles are dispersed in a given region which by means of the formulas 4 and 5, are affected by distances regulated neighboring each other in direction and speed.

On the other hand, the coffee berry borer is not a pest that is characterized by focusing on one point, in fact, their impact on the coffee is due to its ability to spread and proliferate. Hence, this model can add an interaction such that more swarms are generated, tending to a minimum. The simulation model proposed is represented in the flowchart of Fig. 1.

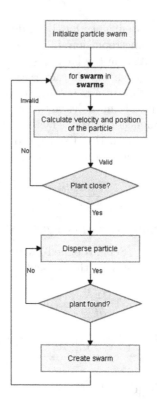

Fig. 1. Simulation algorithm diagram.

In first place, to calculate the position x and velocity v, differential equations are converted to discrete time so that we have:

$$x_{i,e}[n+1] = x_{i,e}[n] + v_{i,e}[n]\Delta t \tag{6}$$

$$v_{i,e}[n+1] = v_{i,e}[n] + \left[(\alpha - \beta v_{i,e}^2[n])\, v_{i,e}[n] \right. \tag{7}$$

$$\left. - \nabla U_{int}(x_{i,e}[n]) - \nabla U_{caf}(x_{i,e}[n])\right]\frac{\Delta t}{m_{i,e}}$$

where $e = 1, ..., N_g$ corresponds to the index for each swarm, $i = 1, 2, ..., N_e$ the index for each individual, N_e total number of individuals in the swarm e, N_g total number of swarms, Δt the simulation time increment, and n variable associated with discrete time.

Additionally, the potential interaction has the form:

$$U_{int}(x_{i,e}) = \sum_{\substack{j \neq i}}^{N_e} \left(C_r e^{-|x_{i,e}[n] - x_{j,e}[n]|/l_r} - C_a e^{-|x_{i,e}[n] - x_{j,e}[n]|/l_a}\right) \tag{8}$$

therefore, the interaction force calculated as $\boldsymbol{F}_{int} = -\nabla U_{int}$ is:

$$\boldsymbol{F}_{int}(\boldsymbol{x}_{i,e}) = -\sum_{j\neq i}^{N_e}\left(\frac{C_r}{l_r}e^{-|\boldsymbol{x}_{i,e}[n]-\boldsymbol{x}_{j,e}[n]|/l_r} - \frac{C_a}{l_a}e^{-|\boldsymbol{x}_{i,e}[n]-\boldsymbol{x}_{j,e}[n]|/l_a}\right) \qquad (9)$$

Coffee plantation information is represented by the potential U_{caf} which is constructed so that maximum and minimum values uniformly distributed in the plantation are taken. Minimum values represent the coffee plant, while maximum represent grooves that separate them. For the case under consideration this potential has the form:

$$U_{caf}(\boldsymbol{x}) = b_1 \cos(c_1 x_1)^2 + b_2 \sin(c_2 x_2)^2 \qquad (10)$$

where, c_1, c_2, b_1 and b_2, are constants which allow to have a proper sizing of the coffee plantation.

Secondly, in order to establish when the swarm had infected a coffee plant, a proximity metric swarm is defined by the plant in the form:

$$\Delta_e = \min_{p=1,\dots,N_p} |\boldsymbol{X}_e - \boldsymbol{x}_p| \qquad (11)$$

where $p = 1,\dots, N_p$ corresponds to the index for each of the coffee plants, associated with the minimum values of U_{caf}, located at $\boldsymbol{x}_p$. Additionally $\boldsymbol{X}_e$ corresponds to the average position of a swarm e which can be calculated as:

$$\boldsymbol{X}_e = \frac{1}{N_e}\sum_{i=1}^{N_e}(\boldsymbol{x}_{i,e}) \qquad (12)$$

The value of Δ_e can set the time when the swarm infests a plant by the following expression:

$$\begin{cases} \text{Infested,} & \text{if; } \Delta_e \leq \gamma; \\ \text{Uninfested,} & \text{if; } \Delta_e > \gamma. \end{cases} \qquad (13)$$

in this equation γ corresponds to a radius or distance for which it is considered that the swarm is nearby. From a practical standpoint this parameter is associated with particular dimensions of the plant foliage.

After a swarm infests a plant proceeds to make the dispersion process of the swarm e, for which the potential associated with the plantation is canceled U_{caf}. This process is performed until a particle manages to find another plant to which it has the following condition:

$$\begin{cases} \text{Plant found,} & \text{if; } \Delta_i \leq \eta; \\ \text{Plant not found,} & \text{if; } \Delta_i > \eta. \end{cases} \qquad (14)$$

as discussed earlier, this same condition is used to modify the potential U_{caf} form:

$$U_{caf} = \begin{cases} 0, & \text{if; } \Delta_i \leq \eta; \\ b_1 \cos(c_1 x_1)^2 + b_2 \sin(c_2 x_2)^2, & \text{if; } \Delta_i > \eta. \end{cases} \qquad (15)$$

in this case, Δ_i corresponds to the distance of a particle to another minimum value (associated with the swarm e). Moreover, η corresponds the distance for which it is considered that the particle is near a plant. The expression that calculates Δ_i is:

$$\Delta_i = \min_{\substack{p=1,\dots,N_p \\ e \neq p}} |x_{i,e} - x_p| \tag{16}$$

Finally, after the plant is found a new swarm is created, then:

$$e = \begin{cases} e+1, & \text{if; Plant found;} \\ e, & \text{if; Plant not found.} \end{cases} \tag{17}$$

This new swarm is created progressively along iterations, considering a vector of random numbers (uniform distribution) δ which has a maximum dispersion $|\delta|$, which is associated with the size of the plant. The position of the new individual is established considering the individual infecting the coffee and the vector δ, then:

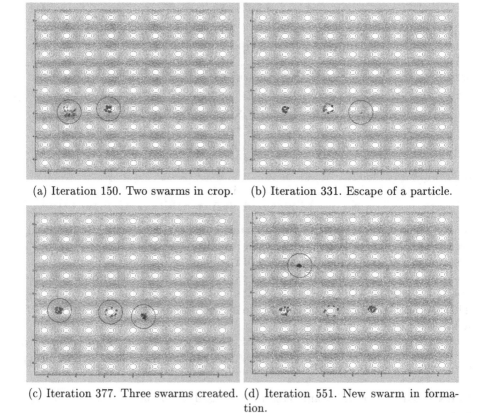

(a) Iteration 150. Two swarms in crop.   (b) Iteration 331. Escape of a particle.

(c) Iteration 377. Three swarms created. (d) Iteration 551. New swarm in formation.

Fig. 2. Multiple particle swarm simulation. (Color figure online)

$$x_{j,g} = x_{i,g} + \delta_i \tag{18}$$

where j represents the new individual of the new swarm g. It is important to note that the particle to find a new plant no longer belongs to swarm e to be on the new swarm g.

5 Results

The surface used is shaped like a bucket of eggs, with peaks and valleys, each represents a minimum valley or peak ground and each land space between them.

Figure 2 shows the resulting simulation algorithm, where initially a swarm is generated, then it is at a minimum (a plant) and a particle moves away to find another plant and in turn creates a new swarm. Each swarm will continue the production of more particles generating more population, so infesting coffee cultivation.

This also makes constant verification that prevents two or more swarms to gather in the same minimum (it is ideal, because if a particle escaped reaches a plant that is already infested, will fly to another).

Initially, a swarm that tends to settle in a minimum is generated. The region has a shape where minimum be considered plants (green concentric circles) and peak areas are considered the space amongst plants. When the swarm has established a particle leak to find a new plant, a new swarm is generated, this process is iteratively performed. Moreover, to detect if the particle must move away, the simulation needs to calculate constantly the particle speed and distance in respect their neighbors.

6 Conclusions

The proposed algorithm works and performs simulations according to the behavior of the coffee berry borer, preserving the characteristics of swarm (attraction and repulsion) in each swarm created. In future work, function and features that modify the intensity of the infestation will be included.

In future work, it is expected to include mathematical formulation regarding the variables identified in previous studies on the behavior of the coffee berry borer. Also it is expected to perform a statistical analysis of simulations for different scenarios.

References

1. DANE: Colombia exportaciones de café, carbón petróleo y sus derivados, ferroníquel y no tradicionales según valores y kilos netos. Información estadística, DANE, Bogotá (2014)
2. DANE: Cuentas Trimestrales - Colombia Producto Interno Bruto (PIB) Segundo Trimestre de 2014. Boletín técnico DANE, Bogotá, p. 23 (2014)

3. Federación Nacional de Cafeteros de Colombia: Producción de café de Colombia superó los 11 millones de sacos en últimos 12 meses, Septiembre 2014
4. Federación Nacional de Cafeteros, Centro Nacional de Investigaciones de Café: Manejo de otras plagas del café. Cartilla no. 15 (2005)
5. Federación Nacional de Cafeteros, Centro Nacional de Investigaciones de Café: Manejo integrado de la broca. Cartilla no. 14 (2004)
6. Benavides, P.: Vuelos de la broca del café durante la cosecha principal. Brocarta (45) (2011)
7. Bustillo, A.: Una revisión sobre la broca del café, Hypothenemus hampei (Coleoptera: Curculionidae: Scolytinae), en Colombia. Revista Colombiana de Entomología 32(2), 101–116 (2006)
8. Ramírez, R.: La broca del café en Líbano: impacto socioproductivo y cultural en los años 90. Revista de Estudios Sociales (32), 158–171 (2009)
9. Matheus, H., Gaviria, M., Jurado, O.: Avances en el manejo integrado de la broca del café Hypothenemus hampei Ferr., en Colombia. Instituto Colombiano Agropecuario, Colombia (2004)
10. Rodríguez, D., Cure, J., Gutiérrez, A., Cotes, J., Cantor, F.: A coffee agroecosystem model: I. Growth and development of the coffee plant. Ecol. Model. 222(19), 3626–3639 (2011)
11. Rodríguez, D., Cure, J., Gutiérrez, A., Cotes, J., Cantor, F.: A coffee agroecosystem model: II. Dynamics of coffee berry borer. Ecol. Model. 248(19), 203–214 (2013)
12. Vicsek, T., Czirók, A., Ben-Jacob, E., Cohen, I., Shochet, O.: Novel type of phase transition in a system of self-driven particles. Phys. Rev. Lett. 75(6), 1226–1229 (1995)
13. D'Orsogna, M., Chuang, Y., Bertozzi, A., Chayes, L.: Self-propelled particles with soft-core interactions: patterns, stability, and collapse. Phys. Rev. Lett. 96(10), 104302 (2006)
14. Bazurto, N., Martínez, C., Espitia, H.: Fuzzy model proposal for the coffee berry borer expansion at Colombian coffee fields. Adv. Intell. Syst. Comput. 232, 247–252 (2013)
15. An, Z., Shi, X., Zhang, J., Li, B.: A family particle swarm optimization based on the family tree. In: IEEE International Conference on Image Analysis and Signal Processing, pp. 46–51 (2011)
16. Bratton, D., Kennedy, J.: Defining a standard for particle swarm optimization. In: IEEE Swarm Intelligence Symposium (SIS) (2007)
17. Cañizo, J., Carrillo, J., Rosado, J.: Collective behavior of animals: swarming and complex patterns. ARBOR Ciencia, Pensamiento y Cultura CLXXXVI (746), 1035–1049 (2010)
18. Muñoz, J.: Inteligencia computacional inspirada en la vida. SPICUM - Universidad de Málaga (2010)
19. Muñoz, M.: Inteligencia de enjambres: sociedades para la solución de problemas (una revisión). Ingeniería e Investigación 28(2), 119–130 (2008)

Fuzzy Sets and Systems

Comparison Between Interval Type-2 and Three Valued Algebra Fuzzy Logic Controllers

Erika Vanegas-Moreno[✉], Carlos-Andrés Cholo, and Jairo Soriano-Mendez

Faculty of Engineering, Universidad Distrital Francisco José de Caldas,
Bogotá, Colombia
{ejvanegasm,cacholoa}@correo.udistrital.edu.co,
jairosoriano@udistrital.edu.co

Abstract. The following article shows the implementation of fuzzy logic controllers Type-1 and Interval Type-2, designed firstly for a diesel motor and implemented on a nonlinear second order system. Additionally, another way of implementing the Type-2 fuzzy logic controllers, is shown, using Kleene algebra, due to its benefits during the implementation of a simple function. Likewise, a variation is performed where a type reduction is applied to an algebraic expression. Finally, it is desired to observe the behavior of the controllers given the uncertainty sources.

Keywords: Type-1 FLC · IT2 FLC · Kleene algebra · Limit cycles · Type reduction · Simple function

1 Introduction

Fuzzy logic controllers allow through knowledge of one or several experts, generate a knowledge base that will provide the system the capacity of making decisions on what actions to take in certain cases. Fuzzy logic has the characteristic of being able to acquire values in the $[0, 1]$ interval, a value which is then associated with a linguistic label, word or adjective (Hernandez *et al.*) [2]. In this manner, membership functions are defined for each fuzzy set, indicating the degree to which the represented concept is included by the label, this type of sets are known as Type-1. The interval Type-2 fuzzy logic controllers (FLC) can address the linguistic uncertainty as well as the numeric uncertainty, given the present uncertainty present in measurements. These have an advantage compared to controllers such as PID and Type-1 FLCs that they present a smaller number of rules and respond in a better way before perturbations present in the system.

Limit cycles are closed and isolated trajectories, where the contiguous trajectories tend to take the same path of the closed orbit. In the time domain the existence of limit cycles is generated by a continuous oscillation and presents the same amplitude in steady state (Strogatz) [9].

J.C. Figueroa-García et al. (Eds.): WEA 2016, CCIS 657, pp. 235–246, 2016.
DOI: 10.1007/978-3-319-50880-1_21

2 Design Stage

From the proposed design (Lynch *et al.*) [4], in which implemented Type-1 and Type-2 FLCs are applied on a velocity control system for a diesel motor, the inputs of the control system are defined as the difference between the reference velocity and the current velocity of the system (e) and the change rate of the error (δ). The system presents an inherent feature of uncertainty due to the influence of its operating environment such as electromagnetic noise, vibrations and interference of radiofrequency; thus this system is useful to evaluate the behavior of the FLC, taking as reference the obtained results with the proposed designs in (Lynch *et al.*) [4] and comparing the performance of the controllers proposed from the three valued algebra.

Since there is not a mathematical model that describes the system to be controlled, the decision of using a nonlinear system was made to perform the simulation process. The second order system chosen is the inverted pendulum, because it is a classical scheme in control theory, it has an unstable and non-linear characteristic, apart from having multiple stationary states, therefore the objective of the control system is to take the system from an unstable state to a stable one. The system is described by the following differential equation:

$$\frac{d^2\theta}{dt^2} = 4\sin\theta - 0.4\frac{d\theta}{dt} + u \tag{1}$$

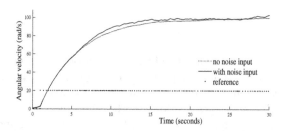

Fig. 1. Open loop output of inverted pendulum

2.1 Input and Output Sets

To solve the proposed problem, a classical control scheme is proposed, where the reference is sampling and it is compared to the current value of the model, therefore obtaining the error signal and its variation. Initially in (Lynch *et al.*) [4] it is proposed that the input sets are trapezoidal, nevertheless it is decided to use a function that can be describe by means of a mathematical formula, therefore selecting a sigmoidal type described in Eq. 2 for ease the simulation execution, as is shown in the progressive growth of Fig. 2(a). Due to the set of

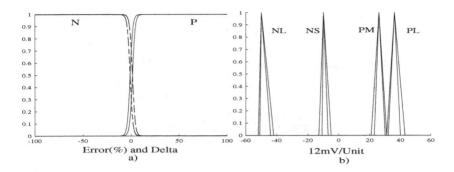

Fig. 2. (a) Type-2 fuzzy sets for input, (b) Type-2 fuzzy sets for output

inputs found in term of the error and its variation, the membership interval is between −100 and 100, since it is expressed in percentage terms.

$$P(t) = \frac{1}{1 + e^{\pm t}} \tag{2}$$

The output sets are represented by: Large Negative (NL), Small Negative (NS), Medium Positive (PM) and Large Positive (PL) shown in Fig. 2(b). Its membership interval is between −60 and 60, as it was possible to incorporate the linguistic and numeric uncertainty of the problem according to experts in (Lynch *et al.*) [4].

2.2 Rule Base

- If the error is negative and the delta error is negative then (NL)
- If the error is positive and the delta error is negative then (PM)
- If the error is negative and the delta error is positive then (NS)
- If the error is positive and the delta error is positive then (PL)

2.3 Aggregation, Type Reduction and Defuzzification

For the implementation of the controller the scheme shown in Fig. 3 is followed.

In Fuzzy logic general theory, exist many different ways of representing the union, intersection and complement of fuzzy sets. The union is represented by the t-conorms or s-norms, while the intersection is defined by the t-norms, these cover a wide range of set operators, allowing to choose the most adequate, according to the needs of the problem to be resolved and the design of the corresponding fuzzy inference system (Mendel) [5]. In engineering applications with fuzzy sets, local implications are normally used, since they show a cause-effect relation, because these are applicable to real systems where the behavior is variable through time. The most common combination in engineering is the minimum or the algebraic product for intersection, the maximum for union and the standard complement.

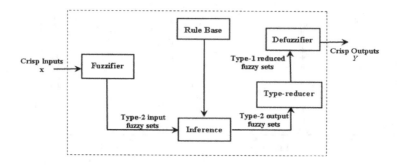

Fig. 3. Fuzzy controller scheme (Source: (Lynch *et al.*) [4] p. 349)

For the chosen application, the inference engine used was Mamdani (minimum implication and maximum for aggregation). The type reduction used was the EKM algorithm (Enhanced Karnik Mendel), which was a variation of the Karnik Mendel algorithm, this iterative method calculates the centroid intervals for an IT2-FS performing an exhaustive search over the domain of discourse of the function, allowing so to achieve a faster convergence than with the KM algorithm. Finally, the type singleton defuzzification was obtained, finding the output value as the average between the centroid of the upper and lower functions (Duran *et al.*) [1].

3   Algebra

In Fuzzy Logic theory, a crisp membership value is assigned for the expert knowledge-based Type 1 sets which can been from a Boolean structure where $I = ([0, 1], \leq)$. Nevertheless this model is unrealistic, due to its restrictions. To solve this problem an interval of values is determined $\{(a, b) : a, b \in [0, 1], a \leq b\}$ this allows a representation of the uncertainty in the data to describe, which can be expressed by means of four element algebra or Morgan algebra $I^2 = [0, 1]^2$ assigning two degrees of partial membership (u, v) (Nguyen *et al.*) [7].

Due to the characteristic isomorphism presented between Kleene and Morgan algebra, namely, that they share the same mathematical structure and the first

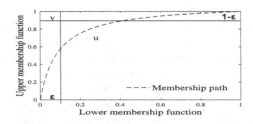

Fig. 4. Automorphism Morgan algebra with a trajectory of Type-2 fuzzy sets

can be mapped within the second; it is possible to process the proposed fuzzy sets for this particular case through three valued algebra, since its trajectories in automorphism (map within an algebraic structure within it self) in Morgan algebra only pass on a partial membership value, this is depicted in Fig. 4:

Kleene Algebra

The three valued algebra or Kleene algebra, is an algebra that consists of a set of data $0, 1$ and a third value u represented by a level of partial membership, that is defined as an interval $[\epsilon, 1 - \epsilon]$. The order relation is depicted in Eq. 3, where zero makes reference to a value with no membership, one for a value of membership of 100% to the set and u is an intermediate value in which may or may not exist membership.

$$0 \rightarrow u \rightarrow 1 \tag{3}$$

3.1   Design by Kleene Algebra

Based on the set of rules obtained in (Lynch *et al.*) [4], an FLC with an inference system based on the concretion based on Boolean relations (CBR) is proposed, which is an alternative for the implementation of FLCs for automation, as in the case of the initial study. The concept of inference systems based on Boolean relation lays its foundations in the segmentation of the universes with Boolean sets and in the monotone transition between Boolean regions (Espitia *et al.*) [6]. This concept is also used to carry out a Concretion Based on Boolean and Kleenean relations (CBKR) to achieve the translation of the linguistic relation in a truth table with Kleene algebra (Salazar) [8] (Table 1):

Table 1. Truth table for the output of the controller.

e	δ	NL	NS	PM	PL
0	0	1	0	0	0
0	u	u	u	0	0
0	1	0	1	0	0
u	1	0	u	0	u
1	1	0	0	0	1
1	u	0	0	u	u
1	0	0	0	1	0
u	u	u	u	u	u
u	0	u	0	u	0

To obtain the expressions that simplify the algebraic relations, the truth table was taken to regular form, namely, a way in which the output values can be reproduced by means of a formula. For this case the disjunctive normal form, in which it is only necessary to take into account the membership values one and u. Once the expressions are obtained for each of the outputs, these are grouped in a known formula as a simple function. A simple function is a function that can take a finite number of different values, in this manner a simple function can be expressed as a linear combination of indicator functions for the Boolean case (Eq. 4) and for the fuzzy sets it will be the union of all of the intersections between a constant or another fuzzy set with a membership function (Eq. 5) (Nguyen *et al.*) [7], depicted as follows:

$$\varphi(\omega) = \sum_{i=1}^{n} a_i I_{A_i}; a_i \in R \tag{4}$$

$$Q(\varphi) = \vee_{i=1}^{n}(a_i \wedge \mu(A_i)) \tag{5}$$

Where A_i must be measurable and discrete, namely, that the elements between sets does not exist. Given the Eq. 5, the simple function for the controller is defined as

$$V = NL(\bar{e} * \bar{d}) + NS(\bar{e} * d) + PM(e * \bar{d}) + PL(e * d) \tag{6}$$

Given the Eq. 6, two types of controllers are proposed, the first of them will take NL, NS, PM and PL as the centers of the output sets. For the second case a controller was developed where the indicator functions will not be constant but will be membership functions. Thus the output interval is obtained to which the type reduction can be applied, allowing so to compare the behavior with respect to the simple function and the Type-2 sets of conventional intervals. As a metric to develop a comparison between the different controllers, the squared normalized mean error will be used, since this measures the average of the squared errors, namely, the difference between the reference and the output of the control system. The expression of the MSE is:

$$MSE = \frac{1}{n} \sum_{i=1}^{N} (u - y)^2 \tag{7}$$

where u is the reference and y is the output of the system.

4   Results and Simulations

When a sweep over the inputs of the controller is executed, the control surface that was obtained is depicted in Fig. 5(a). Similarly, the same procedure was performed with the previously obtained expressions by three valued algebra, the surface depicted in Fig. 5(b):

It is observed in each of the surfaces the separation that exists for each of the established rules, moreover the Fig. 5(b) presents softer falls in the critical points, namely, near the origin and in the intervals where there is a change of rules. In this manner a similar behavior to the one proposed in (Lynch *et al.*) [4] is observed.

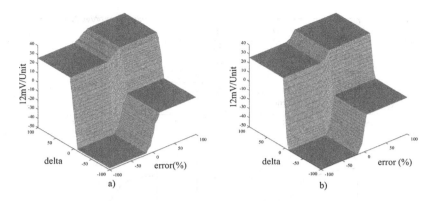

Fig. 5. (a) Control surface of Interval Type-2 controller, (b) Control surface of Interval Type-2 controller with algebra

4.1 Simulation

As depicted in Fig. 1, the open loop system cannot follow the proposed reference, since applying the reference velocity of 20 rad/s, the output is of 100 rad/s, thus, it is necessary to apply a control system that allows the system to reach the different references that the user wants to program. Similarly it is desired to obtain a response as in (Lynch *et al.*) [4], thus it was decided to control the angular velocity of the system, since the behavior of the velocity and the acceleration is similar to a motor behavior. Next, four different control schemes will be applied and their response will be analyzed.

Controller with Type-1 Sets. The controller with Type-1 sets was simulated as in (Lynch *et al.*) [4] with nine rules and three fuzzy sets for the input, a response was obtained as depicted in Fig. 6(a), where it is observed that it was not possible to obtain a stationary state error equal to zero, in addition it presents an oscillatory behavior. For this reason it is the generation of a limit cycle is inferred, this is verified by means of Fig. 6(c), where the system follow a trajectory towards a closed orbit. Likewise, a simulation adding noise sources to the input of the fuzzy system (PSE = 0.1), a mean square error equal to 16,669 was obtained, while having ideal inputs in the controller an MSE of 4,805 was obtained. With additional tests and modifying the initial conditions it was deduced that the system is asymptotically stable.

Controller with Type-2 Sets. Contrary to what happened in the previous case with the Type-1 sets, with the use of the Interval Type-2 sets, the quantity of rules was reduced from nine to four, besides it was possible to obtain a stationary state error equal to zero presenting permanent oscillations over the reference Fig. 6(b). Likewise in Fig. 6(d) it is depicted that the system has a limit cycle.

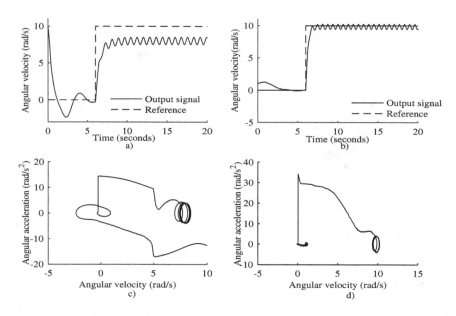

Fig. 6. (a) Output response of Type-1 FLC, (b) Output response of Type-2 FLC (conventional), (c) Phase plane Type-1 FLC, (d). Phase plane Type-2 FLC (conventional)

Type-2 Controller Implemented with Algebra. Once analyzed the controller of Type 2 fuzzy sets with Kleene algebra, it was depicted in Fig. 7(a) and (b) an improvement with respect to the amplitude of the oscillations present when arriving to the reference value, besides of that an improvement in the settling time of the system. Similarly the system continues to present a limit cycle as depicted in the graphics (c) and (d) of the Fig. 7 respectively.

Type-2 Controllers with Uncertainty Inputs. Figure 8 depicts the different responses obtained when adding sources of white noise to the inputs of the controllers, these are considered as uncertainty, due to the random perturbations to the inputs of the controller within a range of specific power density. Even though perturbation by white noise do not physically exist, these are theoretical approximation of noise with correlation close to zero with respect to the bandwidth of the system.

Table 2 and Fig. 9 shows the behavior of the different topologies of a Type-2 Fuzzy controller versus the increments in the density of power of white noise in the inputs, the error was evaluated by means of the Eq. 7 where it can be observed that the most sensible is the simulated through a simple function and the best response was obtained by the Interval Type-2 fuzzy sets. It can be remarked that an improvement is present by simulating the topology of the three valued algebra using the type reduction, which makes the system less affected by the increment in the power of the noise. In relation to the behavior of the controller

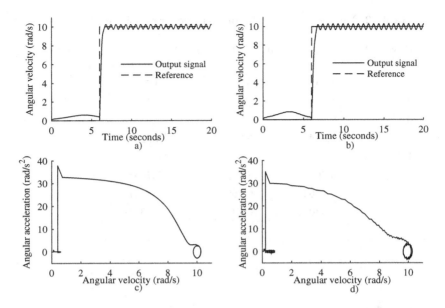

Fig. 7. (a) Output response of Type-2 FLC ( ), (b) Output response of Type-2 FLC (CBKR with Type reduction), (c) Phase plane Type-2 FLC (CBKR), (d) Phase plane Type-2 FLC (CBKR with Type reduction)

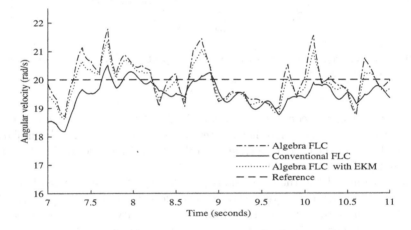

Fig. 8. System response with a Type-2 controller with uncertainty inputs

with Type-1 sets, it was observed that the sensibility concerning to noise, has a relation of approximately 16:1 in comparison to the Type-2 FLCs.

To perform a comparison regarding the computational complexity of the proposed methods, an analysis of the algorithms took place using the Bachmann-Landau (Big-O) notation, which characterizes the functions of the algorithms according to the growth rate, to give it order and represent an approximation of

Table 2. Mean square error for different power of noise in the input

Power (PSD)	Conventional	Algebra (CBKR)	Algebra (CBKR with type reduction)
–	1.44	0.5442	0.7541
0.1	1.5714	1.1991	1.1887
0.5	2.4698	3.4835	2.928
1	3.8843	5.6289	4.8251
1.5	5.2272	7.2574	6.4371
2	6.4078	8.5556	7.7685
2.5	7.4754	9.6591	8.8767
3	8.43002	10.6430	9.8354

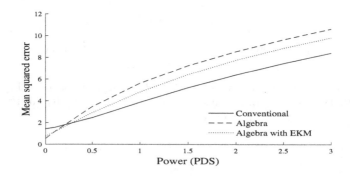

Fig. 9. Mean squared error with variation of the spectral power density for different topologies of Type-2 FLC

the upper limit of the computational complexity of the algorithm, being independent to the machine where it executes (Johnsonbaugh *et al.*) [3]. Similarly, additional data of the execution time was taken in the machine, under the same initial and performance conditions.

As shown in Table 3, the expressions that describe the different methods are approximated to the highest degree term. Therefore it can deduce that when the simulation is performed through algebra, the complexity is the smallest due to linear behavior. For the remaining cases, the computational complexity behavior

Table 3. Comparison of Computational complexity

Method	Big-O expression	Execution time(s)
Algebra	$137O(1) + 9O(n) \approx O(n)$	0.5708
Type-2 (Conventional)	$2065O(1) + 13O(n) + 24O(n^2) \approx O(n^2)$	0.7526
Algebra with EKM	$1100O(1) + 110O(n) + 32O(n^2) \approx O(n^2)$	0.9370

is quadratic, which implies that the computational cost increases during the algorithm execution. Furthermore it was validated through execution times that Big-O notation supplies an appropriate analysis of proposed algorithms.

5   Conclusion

Type-1 FLC was the most noise-sensitive controller in its inputs, because the MSE value increased 246.83% compared to the MSE with ideals inputs, for this specific situation the control objectives were not attained since the control action didn't exhibit a reference following as it was required. For the remaining cases where IT2 FLC was used, the control objectives were attained. Two additional designs were presented in addition to the conventional design of IT2 FLC. The first one using CBKR and the second one Using CBKR with Type reduction, an improvement in sensitivity of 0.94% was obtained in the second case concerning to the average of MSE with the variation of uncertainly inputs presented in the first case. However the computational complexity increases 64.5% in the second case concerning to the execution time, this was verified through Big-O notation where the second method presented a quadratic characteristic complexity. It was observed that the best behavior in relation to the sensitivity with noise inputs was the conventional design of IT2 FLC, because the average MSE was reduced 2.59% in relation to the FLC with CBKR and 1.78% in relation to the FLC with CBKR and Type reduction. Regarding to computational complexity the FLC with CBKR was the best due to its linear characteristic, obtaining an execution time of 0.5708.

For this particular system, limit cycles were presented in the responses of all designed controllers, which produced steady-state permanent oscillations in the output of the controlled system. For simulated controllers with Kleene algebra such oscillations were smaller than Type-1 and conventional Type-2 FLCs. The use of Kleene algebra and fuzzy inference methods like CBKR and CBKR with Type reduction was validated for Type-2 fuzzy logic controllers design.

References

1. Duran, L.K., Melgarejo, M.A.: Implementación hardware del algoritmo karnik-mendel mejorado basada en operadores cordic. Ingeniería y Competitividad **11**(2), 21–39 (2009)
2. Hernández, I., Ochoa, C.: Control difuso y construcción de un mecanismo capaz de golpear con distintos efectos una bola de billar (2012)
3. Johnsonbaugh, R., Osuna, M.G.: Matemáticas Discretas. Pearson Educación, Upper Saddle River (2005)
4. Lynch, C., Hagras, H., Callaghan, V.: Embedded type-2 FLC for real-time speed control of marine and traction diesel engines. In: The 2005 14th IEEE International Conference on Fuzzy Systems, FUZZ 2005, pp. 347–352. IEEE (2005)
5. Mendel, J.M.: Fuzzy logic systems for engineering: a tutorial. Proc. IEEE **83**(3), 345–377 (1995)

6. Méndez, J.J.S.: Diseño y simulación de un controlador difuso de temperatura emple-
   ando el concresor basado en relaciones Booleanas. Tecnura **16**(32), 29–40 (2012)
7. Nguyen, H.T., Walker, E.A.: A First Course in Fuzzy Logic. CRC Press, Boca Raton
   (2005)
8. Salazar, O.: Método de diseño y optimización de controladores difusos FIS-BBR
   cuasi-estándar por medio de lógicas clásica y trivalente de Kleene (2014)
9. Strogatz, S.H.: Nonlinear Dynamics and Chaos: With Applications to Physics, Biol-
   ogy, Chemistry, and Engineering. Westview press, Boulder (2014)

On Computing the Footprint of Uncertainty of an Interval Type-2 Fuzzy Set as Uncertainty Measure

Juan Carlos Figueroa-García[1]([⊠]), Germán Jairo Hernández-Pérez[2], and Yurilev Chalco-Cano[3]

[1] Universidad Distrital Francisco José de Caldas, Bogotá, Colombia
jcfigueroag@udistrital.edu.co
[2] Universidad Nacional de Colombia, Bogotá Campus, Bogotá, Colombia
gjhernandezp@gmail.com
[3] Instituto de Alta Investigación, Universidad de Tarapacá, Arica, Chile
yurichalco@gmail.com

Abstract. This paper presents a uncertainty measure of an Interval Type-2 fuzzy set based on its *Footprint of Uncertainty*. The proposed measure provides information about the amount of uncertainty contained into an Interval Type-2 fuzzy set. Some relationships between the proposed measure and other well known measures of an Interval Type-2 fuzzy set as the centroid, variance, cardinality, etc. are defined and illustrated through some application examples.

Keywords: Interval Type-2 fuzzy sets · Cardinality · Uncertainty measure

1 Introduction and Motivation

Classical fuzzy sets measure what a single expert perceives about a variable, and Interval Type-2 fuzzy sets (IT2FS) help to involve the perceptions of multiple experts into a single measure that represents human-like linguistic uncertainty. Its applicability to problems where no statistical information is available, is wide. IT2FSs have been applied to control (see Mendel, John and Liu [1], Sepúlveda et al. [2], Wu and Tan [3], Castillo et al. [4]), Linear programming (see Figueroa-García [5-7], Figueroa-García and Hernández [8,9]), and other topics (see Wu and Mendel [10], Hung and Yang [11], Zeng et al. [12], Figueroa-García [13, 14], Figueroa-García, Chalco-Cano and Román-Flores [15], Figueroa-García and Hernández [16,17]).

J.C. Figueroa-García—Assistant Professor at the Universidad Distrital Francisco José de Caldas, Bogotá - Colombia.

G.J. Hernández-Pérez—Associate Professor of the Engineering Department of the Universidad Nacional de Colombia, Bogotá Campus.

Y. Chalco-Cano—Full Time Professor of the Mathematics Department of the Universidad de Tarapacá, Arica - Chile.

© Springer International Publishing AG 2016
J.C. Figueroa-García et al. (Eds.): WEA 2016, CCIS 657, pp. 247–257, 2016.
DOI: 10.1007/978-3-319-50880-1_22

This paper focuses on some definitions for measuring the *Footprint of Uncertainty* (FOU) of an IT2FS using integration in the Lebesgue/Riemmann sense. The FOU of an IT2FS is barely defined as the area between their lower and upper boundaries. This way, we propose to compute the FOU of an IT2FS as a crisp measure of its linguistic uncertainty. Several uncertainty measures for IT2FSs have been defined before (see Wu and Mendel [18,19]), so we focus on the FOU of an IT2FS since it provides additional information about how much uncertainty is contained into it.

The paper is divided into five sections. Section 1 is an Introductory section. Section 2 presents some basics about Interval Type-2 fuzzy sets; in Sect. 3, some concepts the FOU of an IT2FS are introduced. Section 4 presents some application examples, and Sect. 5 presents the concluding remarks of the study.

2   Basics on Interval Type-2 Fuzzy Sets

Firstly, we establish basic notations. $\mathcal{P}(\mathbb{X})$ is the class of all crisp sets, $\mathcal{F}_1(\mathbb{X})$ is the class of all Type-1 fuzzy sets (T1FS), and $\mathcal{F}_2(\mathbb{X})$ is the class of all Type-2 fuzzy sets (T2FS) (see Mendel [20,21]). A T1FS is denoted by capital letters e.g. A with a membership function $\mu_A(x)$ while a T2FS is denoted by emphasized capital letters $\tilde{A}$ with a membership function $\mu_{\tilde{A}}(x)$. μ_A measures the affinity degree of a value $x \in X$ regarding the concept/word/label A:

$$A = \{(x, \mu_A(x)) \mid x \in X\}$$

A Type-2 fuzzy set $\mu_{\tilde{A}}(x)$ measures uncertainty of a value $x \in X$ regarding A, so $\tilde{A}$ is a uncertain set itself. A Type-2 fuzzy set can be defined as follows:

$$\tilde{A} = \{((x, u), \mu_{\tilde{A}}(x, u)) : x \in X,\ u \in J_x \subseteq [0, 1]\}$$

where A is a linguistic label (word), and $\tilde{A}$ represents uncertainty around A.

An IT2FS is a set in which $\mu_{\tilde{A}}(x, u) = 1$, and $\mu_{\tilde{A}}(x)$ is completely characterized by $J_x \subseteq [0, 1]$ using an *Upper* membership function $UMF(\tilde{A}) = \overline{\mu}_{\tilde{A}} \equiv \overline{A}$ and a *Lower* membership function $LMF(\tilde{A}) = \underline{\mu}_{\tilde{A}} \equiv \underline{A}$, as shown in Fig. 1.

In Fig. 1, $\tilde{A}$ is an IT2FS, the universe of discourse for the primary variable x is the set $x \in X$, the *support* of $\tilde{A}$, $supp(\tilde{A})$ is the interval $x \in [\overline{\tilde{x}}, \widehat{\overline{x}}]$ and $\mu_{\tilde{A}}$ is a triangular membership function with parameters $\overline{\tilde{x}}, \widehat{\overline{x}}, \underline{\tilde{x}}, \widehat{\underline{x}}$ and $\overline{x}$. $^\alpha \overline{\mu}_{\tilde{A}}(x)$ is the degree of membership of a value x regarding its UMF, $\overline{A}$; $^\alpha \underline{\mu}_{\tilde{A}}(x)$ is the degree of membership of a specific value x regarding its LMF, $\underline{A}$, and $u \in J_x = [0, 1]$.

In this paper, we do not make any distinction between definitions of Interval valued fuzzy sets and IT2FSs given by Mendel [20] since they are equivalent (see Mendel [22], Bustince [23], Bustince et al. [24], and Türksen [25]).

3   Measuring the Footprint of Uncertainty of an IT2FS

First, we present some uncertainty measures for IT2FSs introduced by Wu and Mendel [19] (centroid, variance, and cardinality) which we want to relate its FOU.

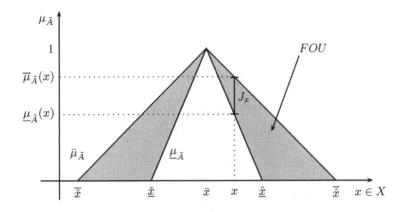

Fig. 1. Interval Type-2 Fuzzy set $\tilde{A}$

3.1 Uncertainty Measures for IT2FSs

On of the most important uncertainty measures of an IT2FS is its centroid $C(\tilde{A})$, which is the union of the centroids of all embedded T1FSs (A_e), i.e.:

$$C_{\tilde{A}} = \bigcup_{\forall A_e} c(A_e) = \left[c_l(\tilde{A}), c_r(\tilde{A}) \right], \tag{1}$$

The relative variance $v(\tilde{A})$ is the union of the relative variances of all embedded T1FSs (A_e):

$$V_{\tilde{A}} = \bigcup_{\forall A_e} v_{\tilde{A}}(A_e) = \left[v_l(\tilde{A}), v_r(\tilde{A}) \right], \tag{2}$$

The cardinality $P_{\tilde{A}}$ is the union of the cardinalities of all embedded T1FSs (A_e):

$$P_{\tilde{A}} = \bigcup_{\forall A_e} p(A_e) = \left[p_l(\tilde{A}), p_r(\tilde{A}) \right], \tag{3}$$

where

$$c_l(\tilde{A}) = \min_{\forall A_e} c(A_e),$$

$$c_r(\tilde{A}) = \max_{\forall A_e} c(A_e),$$

$$v_l(\tilde{A}) = \min_{\forall A_e} v_{\tilde{A}}(A_e),$$

$$v_r(\tilde{A}) = \max_{\forall A_e} v_{\tilde{A}}(A_e),$$

$$v_{\tilde{A}}(A_e) = \frac{\sum_{i=1}^{N} \left[x_i - c(\tilde{A}) \right]^2 \mu_{A_e}(x_i)}{\sum_{i=1}^{N} \mu_{A_e}(x_i)},$$

$$c(\tilde{A}) = \frac{c_l(\tilde{A}) + c_r(\tilde{A})}{2}.$$

$$p_l(\tilde{A}) = \min_{\forall A_e} p(A_e) = p(\underline{\mu}_{\tilde{A}}(x)),$$

$$p_r(\tilde{A}) = \max_{\forall A_e} p(A_e) = p(\overline{\mu}_{\tilde{A}}(x)).$$

Further details about the computation (with examples) of those uncertainty measures have been provided by Wu and Mendel [19], Burillo and Bustince [26], and Melgarejo [27,28].

3.2 Size of FOU($\tilde{A}$)

An IT2FS is characterized by its two membership functions: lower and upper where its FOU is simply composed by the area between them. The FOU of an IT2FS is then measurable only iff $\exists(J_x \forall x \in X)$ and $J_x \subseteq [0,1]$ is continuous. Then, the size of FOU($\tilde{A}$) is defined as a function that comprises its area:

$$\text{FOU}(\tilde{A}) : \tilde{A} \to \mathbb{R} \tag{4}$$

The above uncertainty measures have been defined to measure uncertainty regarding $x \in X$, and how large/small is FOU($\tilde{A}$) means how ambiguous the perceptions about $\tilde{A}$ are, and how uncertain the definition of a fuzzy set A can be. Now, a measure of the uncertainty contained into an IT2FS $\tilde{A}$ is its FOU($\tilde{A}$) which is defined as follows:

Definition 1. Let $\tilde{A} \in \mathcal{F}_2$ be an IT2FS. The size of the FOU (Footprint Of Uncertainty), $FOU_{\tilde{A}}$ is:

$$\text{FOU}_{\tilde{A}} = \int_{x \in X} \overline{\mu}_{\tilde{A}}(x)dx - \int_{x \in X} \underline{\mu}_{\tilde{A}}(x)dx \equiv p_r(\tilde{A}) - p_l(\tilde{A}) \tag{5}$$

in the continuous case, and

$$\text{FOU}_{\tilde{A}} = \triangle x_i \left[\sum_{i=i}^{n} \overline{\mu}_{\tilde{A}}(x_i) - \sum_{i=1}^{n} \underline{\mu}_{\tilde{A}}(x_i) \right] \equiv p_r(\tilde{A}) - p_l(\tilde{A}) \tag{6}$$

where $\triangle x_i$ is the delta step for Riemann integration, in the discrete case.

Different cases can contain small/large $\text{FOU}_{\tilde{A}}$ going from $0 \to \infty$. This leads us to think in the following measure to verify how uncertain $\tilde{A}$ is, as defined as follows.

Definition 2. *Let $\tilde{A} \in \mathcal{F}_2$ be an IT2FS. Its relative FOU, $FOU_r(\tilde{A})$ is:*

$$FOU_r(\tilde{A}) = 1 - \frac{p_l(\tilde{A})}{p_r(\tilde{A})}. \tag{7}$$

If $\text{FOU}_r(\tilde{A}) \to 0$ means that no uncertainty is involved since $p_l(\tilde{A}) = p_r(\tilde{A})$ (see Eq. (7)), and if $\text{FOU}_r(\tilde{A}) \to 1$ means that $\tilde{A}$ is fully uncertain since $p_l(\tilde{A}) > p_r(\tilde{A})$. This way, $\text{FOU}_{\tilde{A}}$ and $\text{FOU}_r(\tilde{A})$ show how ambiguous an IT2FS is, helping to see how uncertain $\tilde{A}$ is. It is clear that a classical fuzzy set A has no FOU, and more ambiguous IT2FSs would have a higher $FOU(\tilde{A})$.

Definition 3. *Let $\tilde{A}, \tilde{B} \in \mathcal{F}_2$ two IT2FSs whose FOU are defined in Definition 1, and its $FOU_r(\tilde{A})$ are defined in Definition 2, then the following properties hold:*

(i)   *If $FOU_r(\tilde{A}) \geqslant FOU_r(\tilde{B})$, then $\tilde{A}$ has more uncertainty than $\tilde{B}$*
(ii) *As $FOU_r(\tilde{A}) \to 0$, as $|c_r(\tilde{A}) - c_l(\tilde{A})| \to 0$*
(iii) *As $FOU_r(\tilde{A}) \to 0$, as $|v_r(\tilde{A}) - v_l(\tilde{A})| \to 0$*

Some examples are performed to see the applicability and meaning of our proposal.

4   Application Examples

Two application examples are presented in this section: a first simple example using triangular IT2FSs, and a second example using Gaussian IT2FSs.

Triangular example: We denote a triangular membership function as $T(a, b, c)$, so in this example we have $\overline{\mu}_{\tilde{A}} = T(\overline{a}, \overline{b}, \overline{c}) = T(3, 11, 22)$, $\underline{\mu}_{\tilde{A}} = T(\underline{a}, \underline{b}, \underline{c}) = T(6, 11, 15)$ as shown in Fig. 2.

Using Definition 1, $p_r(\tilde{A})$, $p_l(\tilde{A})$, $\text{FOU}_{\tilde{A}}$, and $\text{FOU}_r(\tilde{A})$ are obtained as follows:

$$p_r(\tilde{A}) = \frac{\overline{c} - \overline{a}}{2} = 15,$$

$$p_l(\tilde{A}) = \frac{\underline{c} - \underline{a}}{2} = 10,$$

$$\text{FOU}_{\tilde{A}} = p_r(\tilde{A}) - p_l(\tilde{A}) = 5,$$

$$\text{FOU}_r(\tilde{A}) = 1 - 10/15 = 1/3.$$

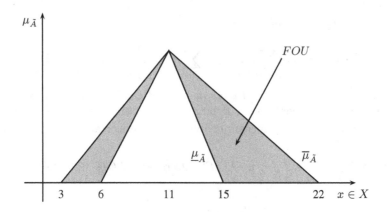

Fig. 2. Interval Type-2 Fuzzy set $\tilde{A}$

Now, consider a new fuzzy set $\tilde{B}$ characterized by $\bar{\mu}_{\tilde{A}} = T(\bar{a}, \bar{b}, \bar{c}) = T(2, 12, 25)$, $\underline{\mu}_{\tilde{A}} = T(\underline{a}, \underline{b}, \underline{c}) = T(5, 12, 20)$ as shown in Fig. 3.

Using Definition 1, $p_r(\tilde{B})$, $p_l(\tilde{B})$, $\text{FOU}_{\tilde{B}}$, and $\text{FOU}_r(\tilde{B})$ can be obtained in a closed form as shown as follows:

$$p_r(\tilde{B}) = \frac{\bar{c} - \bar{a}}{2} = 17.5,$$

$$p_l(\tilde{B}) = \frac{\underline{c} - \underline{a}}{2} = 13.5,$$

$$\text{FOU}_{\tilde{B}} = p_r(\tilde{B}) - p_l(\tilde{B}) = 4,$$

$$\text{FOU}_r(\tilde{B}) = 1 - 13.5/17.5 = 0.2286.$$

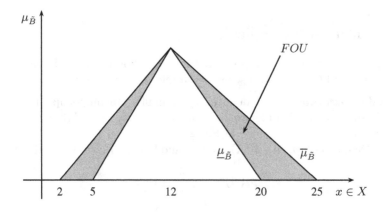

Fig. 3. Interval Type-2 Fuzzy set $\tilde{B}$

To compare $\tilde{A}$ to $\tilde{B}$ we have computed their centroids and variances, as shown as follows:

$$c_l(\tilde{A}) = 9.466; c_r(\tilde{A}) = 12.88; |c_l(\tilde{A}) - c_r(\tilde{A})| = 3.424; c(\tilde{A}) = 11.17$$
$$c_l(\tilde{B}) = 11.20; c_r(\tilde{B}) = 13.96; |c_l(\tilde{B}) - c_r(\tilde{B})| = 2.760; c(\tilde{B}) = 12.58$$
$$v_l(\tilde{A}) = 3.552; v_r(\tilde{A}) = 17.60; |v_l(\tilde{A}) - v_r(\tilde{A})| = 14.05; v(\tilde{A}) = 10.58$$
$$v_l(\tilde{B}) = 8.409; v_r(\tilde{B}) = 22.47; |v_l(\tilde{B}) - v_r(\tilde{B})| = 14.06; v(\tilde{B}) = 15.44$$

As shown in Definition 3 $C(\tilde{A})$ is bigger than $C(\tilde{B})$ as a result of $\text{FOU}_{\tilde{A}} > \text{FOU}_{\tilde{B}}$ and $\text{FOU}_r(\tilde{A}) > \text{FOU}_r(\tilde{B})$. In the case of $V(\tilde{A})$ and $V(\tilde{B})$ it is not clear whether $V(\tilde{A}) = V(\tilde{B})$ or not, but it is clear that

$$\sqrt{v_l(\tilde{A})} = 1.885; \sqrt{v_r(\tilde{A})} = 4.195; \left|\sqrt{v_l(\tilde{A})} - \sqrt{v_r(\tilde{A})}\right| = 2.311; \sqrt{v(\tilde{A})} = 3.040$$

$$\sqrt{v_l(\tilde{B})} = 2.899; \sqrt{v_r(\tilde{B})} = 4.739; \left|\sqrt{v_l(\tilde{B})} - \sqrt{v_r(\tilde{B})}\right| = 1.839; \sqrt{v(\tilde{B})} = 3.820$$

which means that deviation standard of $\tilde{A}$ is smaller than $\tilde{B}$, as we pointed out in Definition 3.

Wu and Mendel have pointed out that $\sqrt{v_l(\tilde{A})} \cdot \sqrt{v_r(\tilde{A})}$ indicates compactness, and $\sqrt{v_r(\tilde{A})} - \sqrt{v_l(\tilde{A})}$ indicates the size of $\text{FOU}_{\tilde{A}}$ (see [19]). In our example, we have obtained the following results:

$$\sqrt{v_l(\tilde{A})} \cdot \sqrt{v_r(\tilde{A})} = 7.906,$$
$$\sqrt{v_l(\tilde{B})} \cdot \sqrt{v_r(\tilde{B})} = 13.74$$

This means that $\tilde{A}$ is more compact than $\tilde{B}$ (less disperse) since $\sqrt{v_l(\tilde{A})} \cdot \sqrt{v_r(\tilde{A})} < \sqrt{v_l(\tilde{B})} \cdot \sqrt{v_r(\tilde{B})}$ while containing more linguistic uncertainty.

Gaussian example: Now, we compare two Gaussian IT2FSs $G(c, \underline{\delta}, \overline{\delta})$: $G(5, 2, 3)$ and $G(5, 1.5, 3.5)$ which are shown in Figs. 4 and 5.

Using Definition 1, $p_r(\tilde{A})$, $p_l(\tilde{A})$, $\text{FOU}_{\tilde{A}}$, and $\text{FOU}_r(\tilde{A})$ are obtained as follows:

$$p_r(\tilde{A}) = 7.519,$$
$$p_l(\tilde{A}) = 5.013,$$
$$\text{FOU}_{\tilde{A}} = p_r(\tilde{A}) - p_l(\tilde{A}) = 2.507,$$
$$\text{FOU}_r(\tilde{A}) = 1 - 5.013/7.519 = 1/3.$$

Now consider the set $\tilde{B}$ shown in Fig. 5.

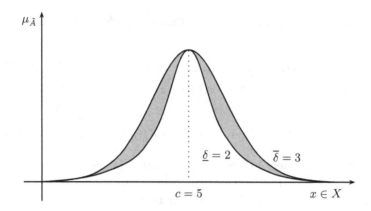

Fig. 4. Gaussian Interval Type-2 fuzzy set $\tilde{A}$.

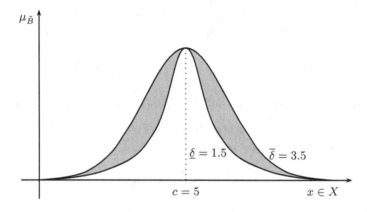

Fig. 5. Gaussian Interval Type-2 fuzzy set $\tilde{B}$.

Using Definition 1, $p_r(\tilde{B})$, $p_l(\tilde{B})$, $\text{FOU}_{\tilde{B}}$, and $\text{FOU}_r(\tilde{B})$ are obtained as follows:

$$p_r(\tilde{B}) = 8.773,$$
$$p_l(\tilde{B}) = 3.759,$$
$$\text{FOU}_{\tilde{B}} = p_r(\tilde{B}) - p_l(\tilde{B}) = 5.013,$$
$$\text{FOU}_r(\tilde{B}) = 1 - 8.773/3.759 = 0.5714.$$

To compare $\tilde{A}$ to $\tilde{B}$ we have computed their centroids and variances as follows:

$$c_l(\tilde{A}) = 4.3; c_r(\tilde{A}) = 5.7; |c_l(\tilde{A}) - c_r(\tilde{A})| = 1.4; c(\tilde{A}) = 5$$
$$c_l(\tilde{B}) = 3.5; c_r(\tilde{B}) = 6.5; |c_l(\tilde{B}) - c_r(\tilde{B})| = 3; c(\tilde{B}) = 5$$
$$v_l(\tilde{A}) = 8.41; v_r(\tilde{A}) = 3.61; |v_l(\tilde{A}) - v_r(\tilde{A})| = 4.8; v(\tilde{A}) = 6.010$$
$$v_l(\tilde{B}) = 12.25; v_r(\tilde{B}) = 1.96; |v_l(\tilde{B}) - v_r(\tilde{B})| = 10.29; v(\tilde{B}) = 7.105$$

Again, $C(\tilde{A})$ is bigger than $C(\tilde{B})$ as a result of $\text{FOU}_{\tilde{A}} > \text{FOU}_{\tilde{B}}$ and $\text{FOU}_r(\tilde{A}) > \text{FOU}_r(\tilde{B})$ (see Definition 3). For $V(\tilde{A})$ and $V(\tilde{B})$ it is not clear whether $V(\tilde{A}) = V(\tilde{B})$ or not, so it is clear that

$$\sqrt{v_l(\tilde{A})} = 1.9;\ \sqrt{v_r(\tilde{A})} = 2.9;\ \left|\sqrt{v_l(\tilde{A})} - \sqrt{v_r(\tilde{A})}\right| = 1.0;\ \sqrt{v(\tilde{A})} = 2.40$$

$$\sqrt{v_l(\tilde{B})} = 1.4;\ \sqrt{v_r(\tilde{B})} = 3.5;\ \left|\sqrt{v_l(\tilde{B})} - \sqrt{v_r(\tilde{B})}\right| = 2.1;\ \sqrt{v(\tilde{B})} = 2.45$$

$$\sqrt{v_l(\tilde{A})} \cdot \sqrt{v_r(\tilde{A})} = 5.51,$$

$$\sqrt{v_l(\tilde{B})} \cdot \sqrt{v_r(\tilde{B})} = 4.90$$

which means that deviation standard of $\tilde{A}$ is smaller than $\tilde{B}$, as we pointed out in Definition 3.

This also means that $\tilde{A}$ is more compact than $\tilde{B}$ (less disperse) since $\sqrt{v_l(\tilde{A})} \cdot \sqrt{v_r(\tilde{A})} < \sqrt{v_l(\tilde{B})} \cdot \sqrt{v_r(\tilde{B})}$ while containing more linguistic uncertainty.

5   Concluding Remarks

We have defined $\text{FOU}_{\tilde{A}}$ as a measure of information $\text{FOU}_r(\tilde{A})$. As larger $\text{FOU}_r(\tilde{A})$ as more uncertain $\tilde{A}$ is, which means that if $\text{FOU}_r(\tilde{A}) \to 0$ then $\tilde{A}$ is simply a classical fuzzy set with no uncertainty involved.

Some uncertainty measures defined by Wu and Mendel [19] and Burillo and Bustince [26] have been taken into consideration to see how larger values of $\text{FOU}_r(\tilde{A})$ lead to wider values of $C_{\tilde{A}}, V_{\tilde{A}}$ and $P_{\tilde{A}}$, which is what we expect from uncertain fuzzy sets.

Wu and Mendel [19] proposed some relationships for $V_{\tilde{A}}$ and $P_{\tilde{A}}$ defined as compactness, which finally does not necessarily mean that $\text{FOU}_r(\tilde{A}) > \text{FOU}_r(\tilde{B})$, and we could see that as larger $\text{FOU}_r(\tilde{A}) >$ as larger $C(\tilde{A})$ and $\sqrt{v(\tilde{A})}$ are.

Finally, we have defined the size of the FOU of $\tilde{A}$ as $\text{FOU}_{\tilde{A}}$, and we have seen some relationships between some well known uncertainty measures $C_{\tilde{A}}, V_{\tilde{A}}$ and $P_{\tilde{A}}$. As expected, the size of $\text{FOU}_{\tilde{A}}$ indicates dispersion over $C_{\tilde{A}}, V_{\tilde{A}}$ and $P_{\tilde{A}}$, and $\text{FOU}_r(\tilde{A})$ indicates how much uncertainty a fuzzy set $\tilde{A}$ has. Finally two sets $\tilde{A}$ and $\tilde{B}$ are comparable via $\text{FOU}_r(\tilde{A})$ and $\text{FOU}_r(\tilde{B})$ since it is a standardized measure of uncertainty.

Further Topics

The analysis of general Type-2 fuzzy sets based on the presented results is a potential application for the near future. Applications in optimization, decision making and type-reduction based on the presented results are interesting fields to be covered as well.

References

1. Mendel, J.M., John, R.I., Liu, F.: Interval type-2 fuzzy logic systems made simple. IEEE Trans. Fuzzy Syst. **14**, 808–821 (2006)
2. Sepúlveda, R., Castillo, O., Melin, P., Rodríguez-Díaz, A., Montiel, O.: Experimental study of intelligent controllers under uncertainty using type-1 and type-2 fuzzy logic. Inf. Sci. **177**, 2023–2048 (2007)
3. Wu, D., Tan, W.W.: Genetic learning and performance evaluation of interval type-2 fuzzy logic controllers. Eng. Appl. Artif. Intell. **19**, 829–841 (2006)
4. Castillo, O., Aguilar, L., Cázarez, N., Cárdenas, S.: Systematic design of a stable type-2 fuzzy logic controller. Appl. Soft Comput. **8**, 1274–1279 (2008)
5. Figueroa-García, J.C.: Solving fuzzy linear programming problems with interval type-2 RHS. In: Conference on Systems, Man and Cybernetics, pp. 1–6. IEEE (2009)
6. Figueroa-García, J.C.: Interval type-2 fuzzy linear programming: uncertain constraints. In: IEEE Symposium Series on Computational Intelligence, pp. 1–6. IEEE (2011)
7. Figueroa-García, J.C.: A general model for linear programming with interval type-2 fuzzy technological coefficients. In: Annual Meeting of the North American Fuzzy Information Processing Society (NAFIPS), pp. 1–6. IEEE (2012)
8. Figueroa-García, J.C., Hernández, G.: A method for solving linear programming models with interval type-2 fuzzy constraints. Pesquisa Operacional **34**, 73–89 (2014)
9. Figueroa-García, J.C., Hernández, G.: Linear programming with interval type-2 fuzzy constraints. In: Ceberio, M., Kreinovich, V. (eds.) Constraint Programming and Decision Making. SCI, vol. 539, pp. 19–34. Springer International Publishing, Cham (2014). doi:10.1007/978-3-319-04280-0_4
10. Wu, D., Mendel, J.M.: Uncertainty measures for interval type-2 fuzzy sets. Inf. Sci. **177**, 5378–5393 (2007)
11. Hung, W.L., Yang, M.S.: Similarity measures between type-2 fuzzy sets. Int. J. Uncertainty Fuzziness Knowl. Based Syst. **12**, 827–841 (2004)
12. Zheng, G., Wang, J., Zhou, W., Zhang, Y.: A similarity measure between interval type-2 fuzzy sets. In: IEEE International Conference on Mechatronics and Automation, pp. 191–195. IEEE (2010)
13. Figueroa-García, J.C.: Interval type-2 fuzzy markov chains: an approach. In: 2007 Annual Meeting of the North American Fuzzy Information Processing Society (NAFIPS), vol. 28, pp. 1–6 (2010)
14. Figueroa-García, J.C.: Interval type-2 fuzzy Markov Chains. In: Sadeghian, A., Mendel, J.M., Tahayori, H. (eds.) Advances in Type-2 Fuzzy Sets and Systems, vol. 301, pp. 49–64. Springer, New York (2013). doi:10.1007/978-1-4614-6666-6_4
15. Figueroa-García, J.C., Chalco-Cano, Y., Román-Flores, H.: Distance measures for interval type-2 fuzzy numbers. Discrete Appl. Math. **197**, 93–102 (2015)
16. Figueroa-García, J.C., Hernández-Pérez, G.J.: On the computation of the distance between interval type-2 fuzzy numbers using a-cuts. In: Annual Meeting of the North American Fuzzy Information Processing Society (NAFIPS), vol. 1, pp. 1–6. IEEE (2014)
17. Figueroa-García, J.C., Hernández, G.: A transportation model with interval type-2 fuzzy demands and supplies. In: Huang, D.-S., Jiang, C., Bevilacqua, V., Figueroa, J.C. (eds.) ICIC 2012. LNCS, vol. 7389, pp. 610–617. Springer, Heidelberg (2012). doi:10.1007/978-3-642-31588-6_78

18. Wu, D., Mendel, J.M.: A comparative study of ranking methods, similarity measures and uncertainty measures for interval type-2 fuzzy sets. Inf. Sci. **179**, 1169–1192 (2009)
19. Wu, D., Mendel, J.M.: Uncertainty measures for Interval type-2 fuzzy sets. Inf. Sci. **177**, 5378–5393 (2007)
20. Mendel, J.M.: Uncertain Rule-Based Fuzzy Logic Systems: Introduction and New Directions. Prentice Hall, Upper Saddle River (2001)
21. Mendel, J.M., Wu, D.: Perceptual Computing: Aiding People in Making Subjective Judgments. Wiley, Hoboken (2010)
22. Mendel, J.M.: Advances in type-2 fuzzy sets and systems. Inf. Sci. **177**, 84–110 (2007)
23. Bustince, H.: Interval-valued fuzzy sets in soft computing. Int. J. Comput. Intell. Syst. **3**, 215–222 (2010)
24. Bustince, H., Barrenechea, E., Pagola, M., Fernandez, J.: Interval-valued fuzzy sets constructed from matrices: application to edge detection. Fuzzy Sets Syst. **60**, 1819–1840 (2009)
25. Türksen, I.: Interval-valued fuzzy sets and compensatory AND. Fuzzy Sets Syst. **51**, 295–307 (1992)
26. Burillo, P., Bustince, H.: Entropy on intuitionistic fuzzy sets and on interval-valued fuzzy sets. Fuzzy Sets Syst. **78**, 305–316 (1996)
27. Melgarejo, M.A.: A fast recursive method to compute the generalized centroid of an interval type-2 fuzzy set. In: Annual Meeting of the North American Fuzzy Information Processing Society (NAFIPS), pp. 190–194. IEEE (2007)
28. Duran, K., Bernal, H., Melgarejo, M.: Improved iterative algorithm for computing the generalized centroid of an interval type-2 fuzzy set. In: 2008 Annual Meeting of the IEEE North American Fuzzy Information Processing Society (NAFIPS) (2008)

A Note About Sensitivity Analysis
for the Soft Constraints Model

Germán Jairo Hernández-Pérez[1] and Juan Carlos Figueroa-García[2($\boxtimes$)]

[1] Universidad Nacional de Colombia, Bogotá Campus, Bogotá, Colombia
gjhernandezp@gmail.com
[2] Universidad Distrital Francisco José de Caldas, Bogotá, Colombia
jcfigueroag@udistrital.edu.co

Abstract. In this paper we analyze some cases where the *Soft Constraints* of a fuzzy LP *Linear Programming* model can be changed, which is known as *Sensitivity* analysis. Other related properties are also glimpsed and discussed in order to see how this model is sensible to changes in the parameters in their constraints. Some examples are provided and the results are discussed.

Keywords: Sensitivity analysis · Fuzzy linear programming · Soft constraints

1 Introduction

The soft constraints model (Zimmermann [1], Zimmermann & Fullér [2]) is one of the most popular fuzzy optimization models due to its efficiency, simplicity and reliability. Its main scope is to incorporate imprecision coming from human perceptions into the constraints of an LP model though fuzzy sets. While other approaches to Fuzzy Linear Programming (FLP) problems have been presented in bibliography, Rommelfanger [3–6], Fiedler et al. [7], Ramík [8,9], Ramík and Řimánek [10], Gasimov & Yenilmez [11], we will focus on the self called Zimmermann soft constraints model.

Černý & Hladík [12], and Hladík [13] to two main families of fuzzy LPs: problems with fuzzy parameters and fuzzy constraints *(FLP)*, and problems with fuzzy parameters and crisp constraints. Hladík [13] has defined basic concepts of feasibility for interval valued equations which can be extended to FLPs, so we propose similar conditions over its constraints. To do so, we define the instances of FLPs over we can change their constraints $\tilde{b}$.

We complement the seminal work of Hamacher, Leberling & Zimmermann [14] by including changes over all the constraints of an FLP, which is different

---

G.J. Hernández-Pérez is Associate Professor of the Engineering Dept. of the Universidad Nacional de Colombia, Bogotá Campus.

J.C. Figueroa-García is Associate Professor of the Universidad Distrital Francisco José de Caldas, Bogotá - Colombia.

J.C. Figueroa-García et al. (Eds.): WEA 2016, CCIS 657, pp. 258–267, 2016.
DOI: 10.1007/978-3-319-50880-1_23

from their work. This way, the idea is to see how an FLP changes given different configurations over $\tilde{b}$. Its applicability on real scenarios is wide since it helps to decision makers to see the system's behavior in advance.

The paper is organized into 6 sections; Sect. 1 introduces the main problem; Sect. 2 presents basic notations; Sect. 3 presents the Zimermmann approach to FLPs; Sect. 4 presents the proposed sensitivity analysis over the constraints of an FLP; In Sect. 5, an example is presented and solved, and finally Sect. 6 presents some concluding remarks of the study.

2 Basic Notations

In this paper, we consider X as the powerset whose elements $x \in X$ are real numbers $\mathbb{P}(X) \in \mathbb{R}$, and $\mathcal{P}(X)$ is the class of all crisp sets. In a *crisp* set $A \in X$, an element x is either a member of the set or not. A set S is called singleton $\{S\}$ if has a single element $x \in \mathbb{R}$. In the real numbers $\mathbb{R}$, S is a constant. This implies that $\chi_S(x) = 1$, and $\chi_S(\cdot) = 0$ for every $x \notin S$.

A fuzzy set $\tilde{A}$ is a generalization of a *crisp* or boolean set. It is defined over a powerset X and is characterized by a *Membership Function* namely $\mu_{\tilde{A}}(x)$ that takes values in the interval [0,1], $\tilde{A} : X \rightarrow [0,1]$. A fuzzy set $\tilde{A}$ may be represented as a set of ordered pairs of an element x and its membership degree, $\mu_{\tilde{A}}(x)$, i.e.,

$$\tilde{A} = \{(x, \mu_A(x)) \mid x \in X\} \tag{1}$$

where $\mathcal{F}(\mathbb{R})$ is the class of all fuzzy sets.

Now, $\tilde{A}$ is contained into a family of fuzzy sets $\mathcal{F} = \{\tilde{A}_1, \tilde{A}_2, \cdots, \tilde{A}_m\}$, each one with a membership function $\{\mu_{\tilde{A}_1}(x), \mu_{\tilde{A}_2}(x); \cdots, \mu_{\tilde{A}_m}(x)\}$. The *support* of $\tilde{A}$, $supp(\tilde{A})$, is composed by all the elements of X that have nonzero membership in $\tilde{A}$, this is

$$supp(\tilde{A}) = \{x \mid \mu_{\tilde{A}}(x) > 0\} \; \forall \; x \in X \tag{2}$$

2.1 Fuzzy Decision Making

Bellman & Zadeh defined in their seminal paper [15] the concept of a fuzzy optimal solution as the values of $x \in X$ that maximizes the fuzzy decision set $\tilde{D}$ given $\tilde{G}_n$ goals and $\tilde{C}_m$ constraints:

$$\tilde{D} = \tilde{G}_1 \cap \cdots \tilde{G}_n \cap \tilde{C}_1 \cap \cdots \tilde{C}_m$$

whose optimal solution x^* is given by:

$$x^* = \sup_x \{\tilde{G}_1 \cap \cdots \tilde{G}_n \cap \tilde{C}_1 \cap \cdots \tilde{C}_m\}$$

Then, the idea is to find the values x^* that maximizes the membership degree of the set $\tilde{D}$. In LPs (or linear problems in general) whose constraints are defined with linear membership functions, the solution of x^* can be found via linear optimization methods, and some special cases of fuzzy LPs implies that its goal is a function of the constraints of the problem which is the case of the Zimmermann's soft constraints model.

3   The Soft Constraints Model

Fuzzy linear programming has been explored by Klir & Yuan [16], Klir & Folger [17], Y.J. Lai & C. Hwang [18], Timothy J. Ross [19], J. Kacprzyk & S.A. Orlovski [20], Tanaka & Asai [21] and Tanaka, Okuda & Asai [22] propose fuzzy solutions for FLP problems, among others, and Zimmermann [1,2] has defined the soft constraints model which is basically an LP model whose constraints are linear fuzzy sets. Its mathematical representation is as follows:

$$\underset{x}{\text{Max }} z = c'x + c_0$$
$$s.t.$$
$$Ax \lesssim \tilde{b} \qquad (3)$$
$$x \geqslant 0$$

where $x \in \mathbb{R}^n$, $c \in \mathbb{R}^n$, $c_0 \in \mathbb{R}$, $A \in \mathbb{R}^{n \times m}$. $\tilde{b}$ denotes the set of fuzzy constraints, where every of their elements $\tilde{b}_i$ is defined by two parameters $\check{b}_i$ and $\hat{b}_i$ (see Fig. 1).

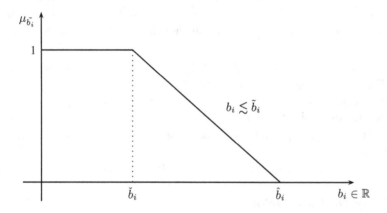

Fig. 1. Fuzzy set B_i

This approach assumes the Right Hand Side (RHS) parameters of an LP problem as a linear fuzzy set. To do so, Zimmermann designed an algorithm that solves this kind of problems through an α-cut approach, which consists on defining a set of solutions $\tilde{z}(x^*)$ to find a joint-optimal $\alpha - cut$ for $\tilde{z}(x^*)$ and $\tilde{b}$. The method is summarized next:

Algorithm 1

1. Calculate an inferior bound called z_{min}, ($\check{z}$) by using $\check{b}$ as a frontier of the model.
2. Calculate a superior bound called z_{max}, ($\hat{z}$) by using $\hat{b}$ as a frontier of the model.

3. Define a Fuzzy Set $\tilde{z}(x^*)$ with bounds $\check{z}$ and $\hat{z}$ and trapezoidal membership function. This set represents the degree that any feasible solution has regarding the optimization objective.
4. Create an auxiliary variable α and solve the following LP model

$$\text{Max } \{\alpha\}$$
$$s.t.$$
$$c'x + c_0 - \alpha(\hat{z} - \check{z}) = \check{z} \qquad (4)$$
$$Ax + \alpha(\hat{b} - \check{b}) \leqslant \hat{b}$$
$$x \geqslant 0$$

This method uses α as a decision variable that finds the max intersection among all fuzzy constraints. This means that α operates as an overall satisfaction degree of all fuzzy constraints, so also it represents a defuzzification degree that returns a fuzzy measure that reaches a crisp optimal solution of the global problem.

Hamacher, Leberling & Zimmermann [14] performed a sensitivity analysis for partial fuzzy LPs in which a fuzzy linear goal and fuzzy linear constraints are allowed to be violated in a permissible quantity. The problem we address here is the problem of analize the behavior of x^* regarding different changes on $\hat{b}$ and $\check{b}$ under the base that $\tilde{z}(x^*)$ comes from optimal solutions of $\hat{b}$ and $\check{b}$ as seen in Algorithm 1.

4   Sensitivity Analysis in FLPs

In this paper, we consider simultaneous changes over $\hat{b}$ and $\check{b}$ in two ways: changing $\hat{b}$ and $\check{b}$ at the same rate, and changing every element of $\hat{b}$ and $\check{b}$ at different rates.

Every set of changes lead to obtain different results, so we will give some considerations for every case. Our results are different (but related) to the results of Hamacher, Leberling & Zimmermann [14] since they kept $\check{b}$ constant and evaluated changes over $\hat{b}$ while we change both $\check{b}$ and $\hat{b}$ to see the behavior of $\tilde{z}(x^*)$.

For the sake of understanding, we define the following measure way to represent incremental changes over b:

$$\Delta\check{b} = \check{\lambda} \cdot \check{b}, \ \check{\lambda} > 1 \qquad (5)$$
$$\Delta\hat{b} = \hat{\lambda} \cdot b, \ \hat{\lambda} > 1 \qquad (6)$$

where $\check{\lambda}$ and $\hat{\lambda}$ are scale factors.

Both $\check{\lambda}$ and $\hat{\lambda}$ variables allow to handle changes over $\check{b}$ and $\hat{b}$ as a multiplier. All three proposed cases are discussed in the following sections.

4.1   Homogeneous Changes on both $\hat{b}$ and $\check{b}$

In this case we set $\check{\lambda} = \hat{\lambda}$ as λ. This means that we change $\tilde{b}$ in a fully homogeneous way i.e. by linear increments. Therefore, the model (3) changes its constraints to $Ax \lesssim \Delta\tilde{b}$. In other words:

$$
\begin{aligned}
&\underset{x}{\text{Max }} z = c'x + c_0 \\
&\quad \text{s.t.} \\
&\quad Ax \lesssim \lambda\tilde{b} \\
&\quad x \geqslant 0
\end{aligned}
\tag{7}
$$

which (by duality) is equivalent to say

$$
\begin{aligned}
&\underset{y}{\text{Min }} w = \lambda\tilde{b}'y \\
&\quad \text{s.t.} \\
&\quad A'y \gtrsim c \\
&\quad y \geqslant 0
\end{aligned}
\tag{8}
$$

This means that the solution of the primal problem when their constraints are incremented λ times is equivalent to the same problem in which their costs and variables x are incremented λ times in its dual (this is $y = \lambda x$). It is also equivalent to have the following model:

$$
\begin{aligned}
&\underset{x}{\text{Max }} z = \lambda(c'x + c_0) \\
&\quad \text{s.t.} \\
&\quad A\lambda x \lesssim \tilde{b} \\
&\quad x \geqslant 0
\end{aligned}
\tag{9}
$$

It also leads to have a new fuzzy decision set $\lambda \cdot \tilde{z}$ which can be obtained as follows:

$$
\begin{aligned}
&\text{Max } \{\alpha\} \\
&\quad \text{s.t.} \\
&c'x + c_0 - \lambda\alpha(\hat{z} - \check{z}) = \lambda\check{z} \\
&Ax + \lambda\alpha(\hat{b} - \check{b}) \leqslant \lambda\hat{b} \\
&\quad x \geqslant 0
\end{aligned}
\tag{10}
$$

Proposition 1. *Let* $\check{\lambda} = \hat{\lambda} = \lambda$, $\lambda \geqslant 1$ *be a linear increment over* $\tilde{b}$, *then the following relations hold:*

$$
\begin{aligned}
\lambda\check{b} &\rightarrow \lambda\check{z}, \lambda x^* \\
\lambda\hat{b} &\rightarrow \lambda\hat{z}, \lambda x^* \\
\lambda c, \lambda c_0, \check{b} &\rightarrow \lambda x^* \\
\lambda c, \lambda c_0, \hat{b} &\rightarrow \lambda x^* \\
\{\alpha | Ax, \tilde{b}, c, c_0\} &= \{\alpha | Ax, \lambda\tilde{b}, c, c_0\}
\end{aligned}
$$

which implies that α *remains constant.*

4.2   Heterogeneous Changes on both $\hat{b}$ and $\check{b}$

Now, we can consider the case in which $\check{\lambda} \neq \hat{\lambda}$. This means that we change $\tilde{b}$ in different ways for both $\check{b}$ and $\hat{b}$, which includes two cases: $\check{\lambda} \neq \hat{\lambda}$ or $\check{\lambda}_j \neq \hat{\lambda}_j$. The first case considers a single $\check{\lambda}$ for $\check{b}$ and a $\hat{\lambda}$ for $\hat{b}$, and the second case considers different λ for every constraint b_j.

This way, the model (3) can be decomposed as follows:

$$\text{Max}_{x} \; \check{z} = c'x + c_0$$
$$s.t.$$
$$Ax \lesssim \check{\lambda}\check{b} \qquad (11)$$
$$x \geqslant 0$$

and

$$\text{Max}_{x} \; \hat{z} = c'x + c_0$$
$$s.t.$$
$$Ax \lesssim \hat{\lambda}\hat{b} \qquad (12)$$
$$x \geqslant 0$$

The solution of this problem is nonlinear in the sense that the interaction among variables and different values of λ for every constraint cannot easily obtained from the original values of $\tilde{b}$, so both problems shown in Eqs. (11) and (12) have to be fully computed. This also leads to have a new fuzzy decision set $\Delta \cdot \tilde{z}$ which can be obtained as follows:

$$\text{Max} \; \{\alpha\}$$
$$s.t.$$
$$c'x + c_0 - \alpha(\hat{\lambda}\hat{z} - \check{\lambda}\check{z}) = \check{\lambda}\check{z} \qquad (13)$$
$$Ax + \alpha(\hat{\lambda}\hat{b} - \check{\lambda}\check{b}) \leqslant \hat{\lambda}\hat{b}$$
$$x \geqslant 0$$

Proposition 2. *Let $\check{\lambda} \geqslant 1, \hat{\lambda} \geqslant 1, \check{\lambda} \neq \hat{\lambda}$ be linear increments over $\check{b}, \hat{b}$, then the following relations hold:*

$$\begin{array}{ccc} \check{\lambda}\check{b} & \rightarrow & \check{\lambda}\check{z}, \check{\lambda}x^* \\ \hat{\lambda}\hat{b} & \rightarrow & \hat{\lambda}\hat{z}, \hat{\lambda}x^* \\ \check{\lambda} \neq \hat{\lambda} & \rightarrow & \Delta\hat{\alpha}, \Delta x^* \\ \multicolumn{3}{c}{\{\alpha | Ax, \tilde{b}, c, c_0\} \neq \{\Delta\alpha | Ax, \check{\lambda}\check{b}, \hat{\lambda}\hat{b}, c, c_0\}} \end{array}$$

where $\Delta\alpha \neq \alpha$ and $\Delta x^* \neq \{\check{\lambda}x^*, \hat{\lambda}x^*\}$ are differential changes of α and x^* given $\check{\lambda}, \hat{\lambda}$.

This also holds for the case $\check{\lambda}_j \; \forall \, j \in m$ and $\hat{\lambda}_j \; \forall \, j \in m$, $\check{\lambda}_j \neq \hat{\lambda}_j$.

5   Application Example

To illustrate the concepts presented here, we present some examples of how λ operates over the following base problem:

$$\text{Max } \check{z} = 3x_1 + 2x_2 + 3x_3$$

$$\text{s.t}$$

$$1x_1 + 2x_2 + 2x_3 \leqslant 12$$
$$3x_1 + 4x_2 + 2x_3 \leqslant 11$$
$$8x_1 + 11x_2 + 9x_3 \leqslant 36$$

and

$$\text{Max } \hat{z} = 3x_1 + 2x_2 + 3x_3$$

$$\text{s.t}$$

$$1x_1 + 2x_2 + 2x_3 \leqslant 17$$
$$3x_1 + 4x_2 + 2x_3 \leqslant 16$$
$$8x_1 + 11x_2 + 9x_3 \leqslant 42$$

whose results are shown as follows:

$$
\begin{array}{ll}
\check{z} = 12.82 & \hat{z} = 15.75 \\
x_1^* = 2.4545 & x_1^* = 5.25 \\
x_2^* = 0 & x_2^* = 0 \\
x_3^* = 1.8182 & x_3^* = 0 \\
C_1 = 6.091 & C_1 = 5.25 \\
C_2 = 11 & C_2 = 15.75 \\
C_3 = 36 & C_3 = 42
\end{array}
$$

Note that $\check{z} = 12.82$ has two binding constraints C_2 and C_3 while $\hat{z} = 15.75$ has only one binding constraint C_3. The resultant fuzzy LP (see Eq. (4)) provides an optimal $\alpha^* = 0.5057$, $x_1^* = 3.9373, x_2^* = 0, x_3^* = 0.8297$ with C_2, C_3 as binding constraints. This means that the set $\tilde{z}$ is defined by $\check{z}, \hat{z}$ which comes from their associated binding constraints.

5.1   Homogeneous Increments

Based on the Proposition 1 we can easily compute any linear increment over $\check{z}$ or $\hat{z}$. For instance if we select two values $\lambda = \{1.25, 1.5\}$ then the original problem turns into the following solution:

$$\lambda = 1.25 \qquad\qquad \lambda = 1.5$$

$\check{z} = 16.023$	$\hat{z} = 19.69$	$\check{z} = 19.227$	$\hat{z} = 23.625$
$x_1^* = 3.0681$	$x_1^* = 6.563$	$x_1^* = 3.6817$	$x_1^* = 5.25$
$x_2^* = 0$	$x_2^* = 0$	$x_2^* = 0$	$x_2^* = 0$
$x_3^* = 2.2728$	$x_3^* = 0$	$x_3^* = 2.7273$	$x_3^* = 0$
$C_1 = 7.614$	$C_1 = 6.563$	$C_1 = 9.136$	$C_1 = 7.875$
$C_2 = 13.75$	$C_2 = 19.69$	$C_2 = 16.5$	$C_2 = 23.63$
$C_3 = 45$	$C_3 = 52.5$	$C_3 = 54$	$C_3 = 63$

Note that this exemplifies all the results shown in Proposition 1. Also note that $\alpha^* = 0.5057$ holds for both $\lambda = \{1.25, 1.5\}$ and it multiplies x^*.

5.2 Heterogeneous Increments

In this example we hold $\check{b}$ that is $\check{\lambda} = 1$ and change $\hat{\lambda} = 1.3$ whose results are:

$\check{\lambda} = 1$	$\hat{\lambda} = 1.3$
$\check{z} = 12.82$	$\hat{z} = 20.48$
$x_1^* = 2.4545$	$x_1^* = 6.825$
$x_2^* = 0$	$x_2^* = 0$
$x_3^* = 1.8182$	$x_3^* = 0$
$C_1 = 6.091$	$C_1 = 6.825$
$C_2 = 11$	$C_2 = 20.475$
$C_3 = 36$	$C_3 = 54.6$

Note that even when $\check{b}$ has been changed to $\hat{\lambda} = 1.3$, the results of the optimization problem does not hold as shown in Proposition 2 since $\Delta\alpha = 0.5028$ which is different to the original $\alpha = 0.5057$, and the optimal variables x^* are also not linearly incremented for $\Delta\alpha = 0.5028$.

While the original FLP is reached by $\alpha = 0.5057, x_1^* = 3.9373, x_2^* = 0$, $x_3^* = 0.8297$, the heterogeneously increased problem does not show a linear relation between decision variables $\Delta\alpha = 0.5028, \Delta x_1^* = 4.7593, \Delta x_2^* = 0, \Delta x_3^* = 0.7968$ while keeping the same binding constraints. Also note that Δx^* cannot be obtained by $\check{\lambda} x^*$ or $\hat{\lambda} x^*$ which implies that heterogeneous increments over $\check{\lambda}, \hat{\lambda}$ lead to heterogeneous changes over α^* and x^*.

Finally, it is clear that for homogeneous changes λ over $\check{b}$ and $\hat{b}$ the problem (including the FLP) is homogeneously increased by λ, except for α which remains constant. For heterogeneous changes, it is clear that α and x^* change in a differential way.

6   Concluding Remarks

We have shown that linear increments on FLP problems does not lead to have changes on the maximum satisfaction degree α, obtained from the Zimmermann's method (see Algorithm 1). This means that while the constraints of the problem has been linearly incremented, its fuzzy solution holds as shown in Proposition 1.

In the case of heterogeneous changes over the constraints of the problem, the optimal satisfaction degree α changes to $\Delta\alpha$ in a nonlinear increment. This means that the entire problem changes in a nonlinear rate, as shown in as shown in Proposition 2.

Finally, we have shown that it is easy to compute homogeneous changes over $\breve{b}$ and $\hat{b}$ while we need to recompute the problem in the case of heterogeneous increments, which implies more computing resources. It is also important to note that the binding constraints on the original problems $\breve{b}$ and $\hat{b}$ hold as the binding constraints of the FLP, in the homogeneous case.

Further Topics

The analysis of Interval Type-2 fuzzy linear programming problems is a natural step in sensitivity analysis. Extensions of the presented results to the works of Figueroa-García & Hernández-Pérez [23,24] are interesting applications in the near future.

References

1. Zimmermann, H.J.: Fuzzy programming and Linear Programming with several objective functions. Fuzzy Sets Syst. **1**, 45–55 (1978)
2. Zimmermann, H.J., Fullér, R.: Fuzzy reasoning for solving fuzzy mathematical programming problems. Fuzzy Sets Syst. **60**, 121–133 (1993)
3. Rommelfanger, H.: Entscheiden bei UnschSrfe - Fuzzy Decision Support-Systeme, 2nd edn. Springer, Heidelberg (1994)
4. Rommelfanger, H.: A general concept for solving linear multicriteria programming problems with crisp, fuzzy or stochastic values. Fuzzy Sets Syst. **158**, 1892–1904 (2007)
5. Rommelfanger, H.: FULPAL - an interactive method for solving multiobjective fuzzylinear programming problems, pp. 279–299. Reidel, Dordrecht (1990)
6. Rommelfanger, H. In: FULP - A PC-supported procedure for solving multicriteria linear programming problems with fuzzy data. Springer-Verlag 154–167(1991)
7. Fiedler, M., Nedoma, J., Ramík, J., Rohn, J., Zimmermann, K.: Linear Optimization Problems with Inexact Data. Springer-Verlag (2006)
8. Ramík, J.: Optimal solutions in optimization problem with objective function depending on fuzzy parameters. Fuzzy Sets Syst. **158**, 1873–1881 (2007)
9. Ramík, J.: Soft computing: overview and recent developments in fuzzy optimization. Technical report, Institute for Research and Applications of Fuzzy Modeling (2001)
10. Řimánek, R.: k: inequality relation between fuzzy numbers and its use in fuzzy optimization. Fuzzy Sets Syst. **16**, 123–138 (1985)
11. Gasimov, R.N., Yenilmez, K.: Solving fuzzy linear programming problems with linear membership functions. Turk. J. Math. **26**, 375–396 (2002)
12. Černý, M., Hladík, M.: Optimization with uncertain, inexact or unstable data: linear programming and the interval approach. In: Němec, R., Zapletal, F. (eds.) Proceedings of the 10th International Conference on Strategic Management and its Support by Information Systems, pp. 35–43. VŠB - Technical University of Ostrava (2013)

13. Hladík, M.: Weak and strong solvability of interval linear systems of equations and inequalities. Linear Algebra Appl. **438**, 4156–4165 (2013)
14. Hamacher, H., Leberling, H., Zimmermann, H.-J.: Sensitivity analysis in fuzzy linear programming. Fuzzy Sets Syst. **1**, 269–281 (1979)
15. Bellman, R.E., Zadeh, L.A.: Decision-making in a fuzzy environment. Manag. Sci. **17**, 141–164 (1970)
16. Klir, G.J., Yuan, B.: Fuzzy Sets and Fuzzy Logic: Theory and Applications. Prentice Hall, Upper Saddle River (1995)
17. Klir, G.J., Folger, T.A.: Fuzzy Sets, Uncertainty and Information. Prentice Hall, Upper Saddle River (1992)
18. Lai, Y.J., Hwang, C.: Fuzzy Mathematical Programming. Springer, Heidelberg (1992)
19. Ross, T.J.: Fuzzy Logic with Engineering Applications. Mc Graw Hill, New York (1995)
20. Kacprzyk, J., Orlovski, S.A.: Optimization Models Using Fuzzy Sets and Possibility Theory. Kluwer Academic Press, Boston (1987)
21. Tanaka, H., Asai, K.: Fuzzy solution in fuzzy linear programming problems. IEEE Trans. Syst. Man Cybern. **14**, 325–328 (1984)
22. Tanaka, H., Asai, K., Okuda, T.: On fuzzy mathematical programming. J. Cybern. **3**, 37–46 (1974)
23. Figueroa-García, J.C., Hernández, G.: Linear Programming with Interval Type-2 fuzzy constraints. In: Ceberio, M., Kreinovich, V. (eds.) Constraint Programming and Decision Making. Studies in Computational Intelligence, vol. 539, pp. 19–34. Springer, Heidelberg (2014)
24. Figueroa-García, J.C., Hernández, G.: Behavior of the soft constraints method applied to interval type-2 fuzzy linear programming problems. In: Huang, D.-S., Jo, K.-H., Zhou, Y.-Q., Han, K. (eds.) ICIC 2013. LNCS, vol. 7996, pp. 101–109. Springer, Heidelberg (2013). doi:10.1007/978-3-642-39482-9_12

A Model for Fuzzy-Cost Travel Distribution Problems Using Entropy Measures

Jenny Paola León[1], Juan Carlos Figueroa-García[1]($^{(\boxtimes)}$),
and Héctor López-Ospina[2]

[1] Universidad Distrital Francisco José de Caldas, Bogotá, Colombia
jennyleo92@hotmail.com, jcfigueroag@udistrital.edu.co
[2] Pontificia Universidad Javeriana,
Bogotá, Colombia
hectorlopez@javeriana.edu.co

Abstract. This paper presents a model for solving probabilistic travel distribution problems that involves fuzzy uncertainty. Using entropy measures for interval-valued problems, we extend those results to a fuzzy environment via extension principle and nonlinear mathematical programming methods. An application example is solved using the proposed fuzzy entropy method in order to analyze their results.

Keywords: Travel distribution problems · Fuzzy sets · Entropy maximization

1 Introduction and Motivation

Transportation problems are among the most common in industry. Different approaches and methods can be applied to solve them, and different uncertainty sources can appear in different situations (see Klir & Yuan [1], Klir & Folger [2], Bazaraa [3], Wilson [4], Ortúzar & Willumsen [5]) and its handling can be a complex task. Different theories can be used to model uncertainty sources such as numerical, probabilistic, linguistic, etc. so the analyst needs to use different methods and algorithms.

The crisp urban travel distribution problem (see Ortúzar & Willumsen [5]) assumes crisp coefficients which are suitable for very stable problems. When probabilistic uncertainty (i.e. numerical uncertainty) is present into some parameters then either probabilistic or stochastic programming are suitable techniques to be used, and entropy maximization offers a more compact method for solving the problem (see Fang, Rajasekera & Tsao [6], Shannon [7]).

J.P. León is undergraduate student of the Industrial Engineering Dept. of the Universidad Distrital Francisco José de Caldas, Bogotá - Colombia.

J.C. Figueroa-García is Assistant Professor of the Universidad Distrital Francisco José de Caldas, Bogotá - Colombia.

H. López-Ospina is Associate Professor of the Pontificia Universidad Javeriana, Bogotá - Colombia.

© Springer International Publishing AG 2016
J.C. Figueroa-García et al. (Eds.): WEA 2016, CCIS 657, pp. 268–279, 2016.
DOI: 10.1007/978-3-319-50880-1_24

This paper focuses on solving a fuzzy-cost urban probabilistic travel distribution problem using interval methods, entropy measures, and the fuzzy extension principle. An application example is provided and its results are discussed. The paper is divided into six sections. Section 1 introduces the problem. In Sect. 2 some basics about entropy-based urban travel distribution problems are given; in Sect. 3, some concepts of fuzzy sets are presented. Section 4 shows an approach for solving fuzzy-cost urban travel distribution problem with probabilistic travel times; in Sect. 5, an application example is presented and solved, and the Sect. 6 presents the concluding remarks of the study.

2   Entropy Based Interval-Valued Urban Travel Distribution Problem

Classical transportation models are focused on sending a quantity x_{ij} of a specific product from the i_{th} source (supplier) $i \in \mathbb{R}_n$ to the j_{th} customer (demand) $j \in \mathbb{R}_m$ at a fixed cost c_{ij}. In this problem called crisp transportation problem, a single product is considered but the amount of travels is not considered in the analysis and its solution is provided by convex optimization methods. Another kind of transportation problems regard to the quantity of travels needed from the i_{th} source (supplier) $i \in \mathbb{R}_n$ to the j_{th} customer (demand) $j \in \mathbb{R}_m$ at a fixed cost c_{ij} which is known as the crisp travel distribution problem.

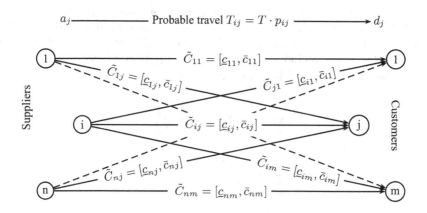

Fig. 1. Interval-costs, probabilistic travel problem

When probabilistic uncertainty is present over the amount of travels to do, then a combinatorial problem appears since there are (i, j) probable travels among a total of T travels (Fig. 1). Let p_{ij} be the probability of traveling between (i, j), $T_{ij} = T \cdot p_{ij}$ be the amount of travels to do from the i_{th} source (supplier) $i \in \mathbb{R}_n$ to the j_{th} customer (demand) $j \in \mathbb{R}_m$, then the most probable distribution of travels is given by maximizing the Wilson's equation (see Ortúzar & Willumsen [5]):

$$W(T_{ij}) = \frac{T!}{\prod_{(i,j)} T_{ij}!} \tag{1}$$

The idea of this problem is to maximize its entropy (Shannon's entropy) which leads to solve the problem $\ln W(T_{ij}) = \ln T! - \ln \prod_{(i,j)} T_{ij}!$ (which is equivalent to $\ln W(T_{ij}) = \ln T! - \sum_{(i,j)} \ln(T_{ij}!)$). Using the Stiriling's approximation $\log X! \approx X \cdot \log X - X$ (See Romik [8]) we can define the following optimization problem:

$$\underset{(i,j)}{\text{Max}} \left\{ -\sum_{i,j} T_{ij} \ln T_{ij} \right\}$$

$$s.t.$$

$$\sum_{i,j} T_{ij} = T$$

whose solution is a uniform distribution since it provides the biggest uncertainty.

At this point the problem seems to be very easy to solve, but in some cases additional information can leads to different optimal distributions. Such information includes demands, suppliers availability and uncertain costs which in practical applications come from users valuation of some attributes like travel time, waiting and transfer times. In particular, the interval-valued costs (ICTP) proposed by López-Ospina [9] is based on the model proposed by Ortúzar y Willumsen [5] which includes demands (O_i), suppliers availability (D_j), and interval costs $\tilde{C}_{ij} = [\underline{c}_{ij}, \bar{c}_{ij}]$ is defined as follows:

$$\underset{(i,j)}{\text{Max}} \left\{ -\sum_{i,j} T_{ij} \ln T_{ij} \right\}$$

$$s.t.$$

$$\sum_{i \in \mathbb{R}_n} T_{ij} = D_j, \ \forall \, j \in \mathbb{R}_m, \tag{2}$$

$$\sum_{j \in \mathbb{R}_m} T_{ij} = O_i, \ \forall \, i \in \mathbb{R}_n,$$

$$\sum_{i \in \mathbb{R}_n, j \in \mathbb{R}_m} \tilde{C}_{ij} \otimes T_{ij} = \tilde{C}.$$

where $\tilde{C} = [\underline{C}, \bar{C}]$ is the total distribution cost, $\otimes$ denotes interval-valued product, and $\tilde{C}$ comes from the following formulae:

$$\underline{C} = \sum_{i \in \mathbb{R}_n, j \in \mathbb{R}_m} \underline{c}_{ij} \cdot T_{ij}^o \qquad (3)$$

$$\bar{C} = \sum_{i \in \mathbb{R}_n, j \in \mathbb{R}_m} \bar{c}_{ij} \cdot T_{ij}^o \qquad (4)$$

where T_{ij}^o is an a priori travel distribution coming from historical information.

Now, the problem is now how to get a point in C which maximizes the entropy of the whole model. As C_{ij} is a continuous interval, then the complexity of the problem is highly increased, so the discrete method proposed by López-Ospina [9] is applied. The method uses a convex combination of every C_{ij} defined as:

$$c_{ij} = \lambda \cdot \bar{c}_{ij} + (1 - \lambda)\underline{c}_{ij}, \ \lambda \in [0, 1] \qquad (5)$$

where λ is divided into a finite amount of values $\lambda_k = k/l, \ k \in l$ which results into the following $l + 1$ problems to solve:

$$\underset{(i,j)}{\text{Max}} \left\{ -\sum_{i,j} T_{ij} \ln T_{ij} \right\}$$

$$s.t.$$

$$\sum_{i \in \mathbb{R}_n} T_{ij} = D_j, \ \forall \, j \in \mathbb{R}_m, \qquad (6)$$

$$\sum_{j \in \mathbb{R}_m} T_{ij} = O_i, \ \forall \, i \in \mathbb{R}_n,$$

$$\sum_{i \in \mathbb{R}_n, j \in \mathbb{R}_m} (\lambda \cdot \bar{c}_{ij} + (1 - \lambda)\underline{c}_{ij}) \cdot T_{ij} = \lambda \cdot \bar{C} + (1 - \lambda)\underline{C}.$$

at a fixed cost c_{ij}.

3   Basics on Fuzzy Sets

Let us start with some notations. $\mathcal{P}(\mathbb{X})$ is the class of all crisp sets of X, and $\mathcal{F}_1(\mathbb{X})$ is the class of all fuzzy sets. The concept of *membership* function generalizes the *indicator* function used in classical sets theory. A membership function $\mu_{\tilde{A}}(\cdot)$ is defined as:

$$\mu_{\tilde{A}}(\cdot) : X \rightarrow [0, 1] \qquad (7)$$

A fuzzy set is a generalization of a *Crisp* or Boolean set. It is defined on an universe of discourse X and is characterized by a *Membership Function* namely $\mu_{\tilde{A}}(x)$ that takes values in the interval [0,1]. A fuzzy set A may be represented as a set of ordered pairs of a generic element x and its grade of membership function, $\mu_{\tilde{A}}(x)$, i.e.,

$$\tilde{A} = \{(x, \mu_{\tilde{A}}(x)) \,|\, x \in X\} \qquad (8)$$

Now, $\tilde{A}$ is contained into a family of fuzzy sets $\mathcal{F}_1 = \{\tilde{A}_1, \tilde{A}_2, \cdots, \tilde{A}_m\}$, and A is a *Linguistic Label* that defines the sense of the fuzzy set through the concept A, and it is the way how an expert perceives X and the shape of $\tilde{A}$. Basically, a fuzzy set is a measure of imprecision of what an expert thinks about $x \in X$.

Henceforth we do not make any distinction between a membership function $\mu_{\tilde{A}}(\cdot)$ and $\tilde{A}$ when refer to a fuzzy set. The α-*cut* of $\mu_{\tilde{A}}(x)$ namely $^\alpha\tilde{A}$ represents the interval of all values of x which has a membership degree equal or greatest than α:

$$^\alpha\tilde{A} = \{x \mid \mu_{\tilde{A}}(x) \geqslant \alpha\} \; \forall \; x \in X \tag{9}$$

The interval of values which satisfies $^\alpha A$ is defined by

$$^\alpha\tilde{A} \in [\inf_x \; ^\alpha\mu_{\tilde{A}}(x), \; \sup_x \; ^\alpha\mu_{\tilde{A}}(x)] = [^\alpha\check{A}, \; ^\alpha\hat{A}] \tag{10}$$

A graphical display of a triangular fuzzy set is given in Fig. 2.

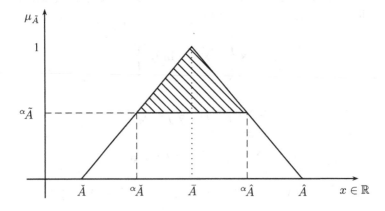

Fig. 2. Fuzzy set $\tilde{A}$

4   A Fuzzy-Cost Distribution Model Based on Entropy Maximization

Fuzzy costs $\tilde{C}_{ij}$ commonly come from experts opinions and/or perceptions, so imprecision appears as uncertainty source which can be modeled using interval-valued models. A fuzzy-cost urban travel distribution model based on entropy measures can be extended from (2) (see Fig. 2) to the following mathematical programming model:

$$\text{Max}_{(i,j)} \left\{ -\sum_{i,j} T_{ij} \ln T_{ij} \right\}$$

$$s.t.$$

$$\sum_{i \in \mathbb{R}_n} T_{ij} = D_j, \ \forall \, j \in \mathbb{R}_m, \tag{11}$$

$$\sum_{j \in \mathbb{R}_m} T_{ij} = O_i, \ \forall \, i \in \mathbb{R}_n, \tag{12}$$

$$\sum_{i \in \mathbb{R}_n, j \in \mathbb{R}_m} \tilde{C}_{ij} \cdot T_{ij} = \tilde{C}. \tag{13}$$

where $\tilde{C}$ is the fuzzy total distribution cost. Equation (11) envelops probabilistic uncertainty handled through Eq. (1), and (13) envelops fuzzy uncertainty over transportation costs.

Without lack of generality, we can rewrite (11), (12), and (13) as $h(\cdot)$ which results in the shorter model $z^* = \text{Max}_{(i,j)}\{-\sum_{i,j} T_{ij} \ln T_{ij} \,|\, h(\cdot)\}$. This way, we can use the extension principle to compose the set $\tilde{Z}$ of optimal solutions (costs), as follows:

$$f(\tilde{C}_{ij})(z^*) = \sup_{z^* = \text{Max}_{(i,j)}\{-\sum_{i,j} T_{ij} \ln T_{ij} \,|\, h(\cdot)\}} \min_{ij}\{\tilde{C}_{ij}(c_{ij})\} \tag{14}$$

So $\tilde{Z}$ can be recomposed via fuzzy extension principle, as follows:

$$\tilde{Z} := f(\tilde{C})(z^*) = \bigcup_{\alpha \in [0,1]} \alpha \cdot f(^{\alpha}\tilde{C})(z^*) \tag{15}$$

This representation leads to an NP-hard problem since every single point z^* in $\tilde{Z}$ can be computed from an infinite amount of combinations of T_{ij} and c_{ij}. To save computations, we use $^{\alpha}\tilde{C}_{ij}$ as an approximation of $\tilde{Z}$ which leads to the following model:

$$^{\alpha}\tilde{Z} = \text{Max}_{(i,j)} \left\{ -\sum_{i,j} T_{ij} \ln T_{ij} \right\}$$

$$s.t.$$

$$\sum_{i \in \mathbb{R}_n} T_{ij} = D_j, \ \forall \, j \in \mathbb{R}_m, \tag{16}$$

$$\sum_{j \in \mathbb{R}_m} T_{ij} = O_i, \ \forall \, i \in \mathbb{R}_n,$$

$$\sum_{i \in \mathbb{R}_n, j \in \mathbb{R}_m} {}^{\alpha}\tilde{C}_{ij} \cdot T_{ij} = {}^{\alpha}\tilde{C}.$$

where $\tilde{C}$ is the fuzzy total distribution cost.

Interval computations are useful in order to obtain solutions of a fuzzy model using α-cuts, so the model (6) is applied to find the solution of (16). To do so, we compute the boundaries of every interval provided by $^{\alpha}\check{C}_{ij}$ which leads to a two-sided problem. First, we define the boundaries of every α-cut of $\tilde{C}$:

$$^{\alpha}\check{C} = \sum_{i \in \mathbb{R}_n, j \in \mathbb{R}_m} {}^{\alpha}\check{C}_{ij} \cdot T^o_{ij} \tag{17}$$

$$^{\alpha}\hat{C} = \sum_{i \in \mathbb{R}_n, j \in \mathbb{R}_m} {}^{\alpha}\hat{C}_{ij} \cdot T^o_{ij} \tag{18}$$

where T^o_{ij} is an a priori travel distribution coming from historical information.

Now, the left boundary $^{\alpha}\check{z}^*$ is obtained as follows:

$$^{\alpha}\check{z}^* = \underset{(i,j)}{\text{Max}} \left\{ -\sum_{i,j} T_{ij} \ln T_{ij} \right\}$$

$$s.t.$$

$$\sum_{i \in \mathbb{R}_n} T_{ij} = D_j, \ \forall \, j \in \mathbb{R}_m, \tag{19}$$

$$\sum_{j \in \mathbb{R}_m} T_{ij} = O_i, \ \forall \, i \in \mathbb{R}_n,$$

$$\sum_{i \in \mathbb{R}_n, j \in \mathbb{R}_m} {}^{\alpha}\check{C}_{ij} \cdot T_{ij} = {}^{\alpha}\check{C}.$$

and its right boundary $^{\alpha}\hat{z}^*$ is obtained as follows:

$$^{\alpha}\hat{z}^* = \underset{(i,j)}{\text{Max}} \left\{ -\sum_{i,j} T_{ij} \ln T_{ij} \right\}$$

$$s.t.$$

$$\sum_{i \in \mathbb{R}_n} T_{ij} = D_j, \ \forall \, j \in \mathbb{R}_m, \tag{20}$$

$$\sum_{j \in \mathbb{R}_m} T_{ij} = O_i, \ \forall \, i \in \mathbb{R}_n,$$

$$\sum_{i \in \mathbb{R}_n, j \in \mathbb{R}_m} {}^{\alpha}\hat{C}_{ij} \cdot T_{ij} = {}^{\alpha}\hat{C}.$$

Basically, the above models approximate the shape of $\tilde{Z}$ using $\tilde{C}_{ij}$ and maximizes the uncertainty contained into T_{ij} per α-cut (see Fig. 3).

The proposed methodology addresses two uncertainty sources: entropy of travels T_{ij}, and fuzzy costs $\tilde{C}_{ij}$. While an interval-valued model maximizes the entropy of a single α-cut, the union of all α-cuts compose the fuzzy set of optimal solutions via Eq. (15), so we are obtaining a set of fuzzy-entropy optimal solutions. The model (16) must be ran α times, so as bigger the amount of α-cuts as better its approximation of $\tilde{Z}$.

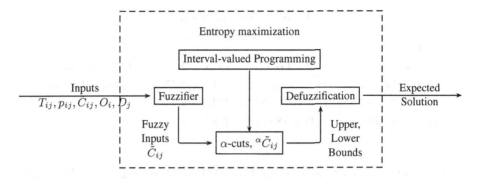

Fig. 3. Entropy-based fuzzy methodology

4.1 Expected Solution

In the proposal of López-Ospina [9] (see Eq. (2)) the expected value of the interval-valued problem is obtained by computing $\lambda = 0.5$ in the equation $\lambda \cdot \underline{c}_{ij} + (1 - \lambda)\bar{c}_{ij} \cdot T_{ij}$. In a fuzzy environment, expected value of a fuzzy set $\tilde{Z}$ can be computed using different measures such as the centroid $C(\tilde{Z})$ and Yager index rank $I(\tilde{Z})$ (see Klir & Yuan [2], and Yager [10]) which are shown as follows:

$$C(\tilde{Z}) = \frac{\sum_{i=1}^{n} x_i \cdot \tilde{Z}(x_i)}{\sum_{i=1}^{n} \tilde{Z}(x_i)}$$

$$I(\tilde{Z}) = \frac{1}{2} \sum_{i=1}^{n} (^{\alpha_i}\check{Z} + {}^{\alpha_i}\hat{Z})\Delta_{\alpha_i}$$

where $[^{\alpha}\check{A}, \,^{\alpha}\hat{A}]$, $\alpha \in [0, 1]$ is the α-cut of $\tilde{A}$, and Δ_{α_i} is a delta step on α.

Basically, $C(\tilde{Z}), I(\tilde{Z})$ are defuzzified central measures of the maximum entropy of the problem based on fuzzy costs, highly desired in decision making. As usual, analysts require a crisp measure of the average behavior of the problem, so the centroid and the Yager index are either easy-to-get and convex measures of central tendency of $\tilde{Z}$.

5 Application Example

In this example, we want to find the best travel distribution among four origins $m = 4$ and four destinations $n = 4$. The idea is to define travel costs using expert's judgements via fuzzy sets which do not depend on statistical and/or historical information, and combine them to a priori information about frequency of travels which are used to estimate the probability of sending a vehicle from a supplier to a customer. For simplicity, costs are defined as triangular fuzzy sets denoted by $T(\check{c}, \bar{c}, \hat{c})$ (see Table 1).

Table 1. Fuzzy costs $\tilde{C}_{ij}$

(i,j)	D_1	D_2	D_3	D_4
O_1	$T(2.5, 2.7, 3)$	$T(11, 11.6, 12)$	$T(18.5, 18.9, 19)$	$T(22, 22.4, 24)$
O_2	$T(12, 12.9, 13)$	$T(3, 3.7, 4)$	$T(13.5, 13.55, 14)$	$T(19.5, 19.95, 21)$
O_3	$T(15, 16.4, 17)$	$T(13.5, 14.25, 15)$	$T(4.5, 4.8, 5)$	$T(7, 7.9, 8)$
O_4	$T(24, 24.1, 25)$	$T(18.5, 18.9, 19)$	$T(8.5, 8.8, 10)$	$T(4.5, 4.7, 5)$

To compute the set $\tilde{C}$ we use Eqs. (17), (18), and the a priori travel distribution T_{ij}^o shown in Table 2. Every value $^{\alpha}\check{C}$ and $^{\alpha}\hat{C}$ needs to be updated for every $\alpha \in [0, 1]$ in order to compose the set of optimal solutions $\tilde{Z}$ (see Eq. (15)).

Table 2. A priori travel distribution T_{ij}^o

(i,j)	D_1	D_2	D_3	D_4
O_1	25	100	60	170
O_2	40	25	60	130
O_3	60	60	25	110
O_4	80	170	310	10

Now, we compute $^{\alpha}\check{Z}$ and $^{\alpha}\hat{Z}$ for 11 α-cuts using Eqs. (19) and (20), whose results are shown in Table 3.

Table 3. Results of optimization process

α	$^{\alpha}\check{Z}$	$^{\alpha}\hat{Z}$
0	−7888.63	−7869.62
0.1	−7887.36	−7870.22
0.2	−7886.12	−7870.81
0.3	−7884.82	−7871.4
0.4	−7883.56	−7871.99
0.5	−7882.24	−7872.59
0.6	−7880.95	−7873.18
0.7	−7879.59	−7873.77
0.8	−7878.28	−7874.37
0.9	−7876.90	−7884.96
1	−7885.55	−7885.55

Keep in mind that T_{ij}^o is an a priori matrix which comes from different sources such as historical, experts, etc. and it is used to compute p_{ij} which leads to T_{ij}. If T_{ij}^o changes then $\tilde{Z}$ will change as a result of a change in p_{ij}, $\tilde{C}_{ij}$ and $\tilde{C}$ as shown in Fig. 4.

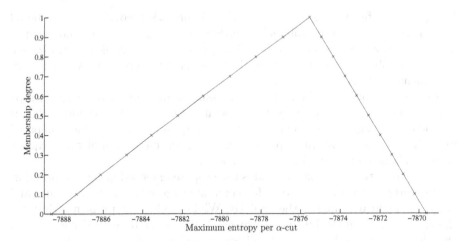

Fig. 4. Set $\tilde{Z}$ of optimal solutions

Finally the expected value of $\tilde{Z}$ i.e. $C(\tilde{Z})$ and $I(\tilde{Z})$ are shown as follows:

$$C(\tilde{Z}) = -7878,68$$
$$I(\tilde{Z}) = -7878,38$$

In this case $C(\tilde{Z})$ and $I(\tilde{Z})$ are very similar due to the symmetry of all fuzzy costs. The maximum entropy that can be expected is ≈ -7878 which means that this value maximizes probabilistic uncertainty over T_{ij} in average. The minimum and maximum entropy expectations are -7888.63 and -7869.62 which is the range over the system works, given the a priori travel distribution T_{ij}^o shown in Table 2. The most possible entropy value is $z^* = -7885.55$ (membership 1 in Fig. 4 and Table 2) which represents the most possible scenario given the perceptions of the experts about uncertain costs, at maximum entropy.

In this case, we have maximized the entropy of the information coming from Table 2 which is probabilistic a priori information about historical travel distribution. At the same time, we have involved fuzzy travel costs coming from linguistic uncertainty without historical information that comes from the experts of the system, so the solution presented here maximizes probabilistic information involving linguistic uncertainty via fuzzy costs.

Finally, decision making can use different scenarios: pessimistic scenario $\check{Z} = {}^\alpha\check{Z}$ for $\alpha = 0$, optimistic scenario $\hat{Z} = {}^\alpha\hat{Z}$ for $\alpha = 0$, most possible scenario $\bar{Z} = {}^\alpha\check{Z}$ for $\alpha = 1$, or expected scenarios $C(\tilde{Z})$ and $I(\tilde{Z})$. All remaining values

$^{\alpha}\check{Z}$, $^{\alpha}\hat{Z}$ for different values of α operates as different choices that decision makers can take at different uncertainty degrees, as desired.

6   Concluding Remarks

The proposed fuzzy solution $\tilde{Z}$ comprises information coming from interval decomposition of $\tilde{C}_{ij}$ and probabilistic uncertainty coming from T_{ij} into a single model via fuzzy extension principle. The proposal uses classical optimization models for solving a two-way uncertain transportation problem, which is very convenient for decision making.

Computationally speaking, finding a solution of a problem using entropy measures becomes a more complex task, so if fuzzy uncertainty is added then it depends on the amount of α-cuts used for decomposing $\tilde{C}_{ij}$; but when compared to an interval cost problem, it provides a better representation of what experts perceive about costs using fuzzy sets for words.

The application example illustrates the proposed method using a priori information interval entropy measures for combining probabilistic travel times and fuzzy costs which simplifies the analysis. While solving the problem using stochastic optimization can be an expensive task, the use of an α-cut decomposition and the fuzzy extension principle allows to find a good approximation of the whole solution.

Future Work

An extension of the presented results to a multiple people perceptions via Type-2 fuzzy sets can be done using the results of Figueroa-García [11], and Wu & Mendel [12] which allows to handle linguistic uncertainty.

References

1. Klir, G.J., Yuan, B.: Fuzzy Sets and Fuzzy Logic: Theory and Applications. Prentice Hall, Upper Saddle River (1995)
2. Klir, G.J., Folger, T.A.: Fuzzy Sets, Uncertainty and Information. Prentice Hall, Upper Saddle River (1992)
3. Bazaraa, M.S., Jarvis, J.J., Sherali, H.D.: Linear Programming and Networks Flow. Wiley, New York (1998)
4. Carlsson, C., Fedrizzi, M., Fullér, R.: Fuzzy Logic in Management, vol. 66. Springer, New York (2012)
5. Ortúzar, J., Willumsen, L.G.: Modelos de distribución zonal. Modelos de Transporte 1, 265–271 (2008)
6. Fang, S., Rajasekera, J., Tsao, H.: Entropy Optimization and Mathematical Programming. Operations Research & Management Science, vol. 8. Kluwer Academic Publishers, New York (1997)
7. Shannon, C.: A mathematical theory of communication. Bell Syst. Tech. J. **27**, 393 (1948)

8. Romik, D.: Stiriling's approximation for $n!$: the ultimate short proof? Am. Math. Monthly **107**, 556–567 (2000)
9. López-Ospina, H.: Modelo de maximización de la entropía y costos generalizados intervalares para la distribución de viajes urbanos. Ingeniería y Universidad **17**, 390–407 (2013)
10. Yager, R.: A procedure for ordering fuzzy subsets of the unit interval. Inf. Sci. **24**, 143–161 (1981)
11. Figueroa-García, J.C.: A general model for linear programming with interval type-2 fuzzy technological coefficients. In: 2012 Annual Meeting of the North American Fuzzy Information Processing Society (NAFIPS), pp. 1–6 (2012)
12. Wu, D., Mendel, J.M.: Uncertainty measures for interval type-2 fuzzy sets. Inf. Sci. **177**, 5378–5393 (2007)

Power Systems

Analysis THD and Power Factor for Luminaries Implemented in the Traffic Light System of Bogota

José Ignacio Rodríguez-Molano[✉], Hugo A. Serrato, and Carlos A. Parra

Universidad Distrital Francisco José de Caldas, Bogotá, Colombia
jirodriguez@udistrital.edu.co, hualseva@hotmail.com,
ingenieromartinez_electrico@hotmail.com

Abstract. Traffic lights costs 0.5% of the gross domestic product (GDP) of the city due to heavy traffic, so multiple actions are being carried out to reduce this indicator and mitigate its effects. However, although Bogotá currently has around 1.400 signalized intersections, the importance of traffic lights in mobility is still vital. Besides technological change, city policies, preventive and corrective maintenance of traffic lights, this paper presents a study of power quality and harmonics analysis in traffic lights focused on the quality of the devices used, not from phenomena coming from the electrical network. Full LED lights, turn arrows, pedestrian and green halogen lights are tested over a special module to measure harmonic distortion and power factor before recommending THD levels for them.

Keywords: Harmonic distortion · Power factor · Power quality · Traffic lights

1 Introduction

The city of Bogotá–Colombia has overpassed all growth and expansion predictions, not only in population but in air cargo and traffic of business passengers. As usual in Latin American governments, there have been some successes and mistakes in planning, so the Administrative Department of Planning (former Urban Planning Department) has been created in 1968 to perform city planning, and its related institutions have tried everything possible to project and legislate matters relating to the development of Bogotá (Decreto 3133: Por el cual se reforma la organización administrativa del distrito especial de Bogotá, 1968). To do so, a planning section was created and transformed by the District Planning Department with the participation of different actors [2] in 2006.

The progressive increase of cars, which according to figures from the National Transit Record "RUNT" reached 12 million vehicles in 2015 of which <10% were dedicated to public transportation [3]. This leads to a bottleneck effect in global transportation where a great amount of vehicles versus low rates of investment in infrastructure (road network) results in larger traffic jams, even if the traffic light system is not as developed as it should be[1], which becomes to a real problem in mobility.

---

[1] The traffic light system is an essential component to control the city traffic, which allows the organized and safe use of the space available for the movement of vehicles and pedestrians, in order to safeguard their transit in a controlled way.

© Springer International Publishing AG 2016
J.C. Figueroa-García et al. (Eds.): WEA 2016, CCIS 657, pp. 283–294, 2016.
DOI: 10.1007/978-3-319-50880-1_25

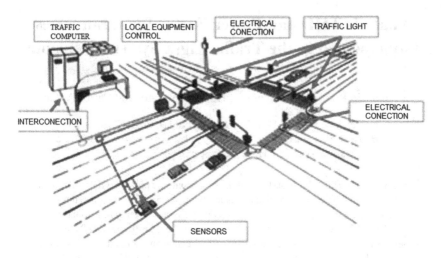

Fig. 1. Basic structure of a typical double signalized intersection [4] (Color figure online)

For example, the traffic light network of Bogotá in 2008 was more than 30 years old, and it did not allow any programming on timing for the traffic lights according to traffic flows, so in order to improve the mobility of vehicles during peak hours and to reduce both car drivers and pedestrians at traffic lights waiting times, the Traffic Secretariat of Bogota has been gradually installing an intelligent traffic light system while changing luminaires, lamps, and bulbs, which are a fundamental part of the traffic light system[2], so incandescent Light-Emitting Diode bulbs were replaced for LED lights.

Due to the rise of technological developments in the last years, this equipment has led to support electronic-based loads, which are susceptible to electromagnetic interference (see Fig. 2) such as harmonic distortion, fast voltage fluctuations (flicker), transients, sags, swell and others [5].

2   Power Quality

All those new technical and operational challenges affect the power supply network, as part of the basic structure of a signalized intersection. Figure 1 shows an intersection system where several sensors and control equipment interact in the crossing signals (traffic light). This equipment commonly uses power converters, essentially nonlinear loads, as new LED technology in traffic lights does. Although LED technology is more efficient, it also brings disturbances to the power grid. This means increasing operating costs, increased interconnections, system failures, reduced equipment life, and inner erratic operation, among many other issues (see harmonic distortion [6]).

---

[2] Traffic lights are signaling devices by which the movement of vehicles, bicycles and pedestrians on the road regulated by assigning the right of crossing both to vehicles and to pedestrians by a priority sequence, according to indicating lights: red, yellow and green, operated by an electronic control unit.

A *"clean"* power grid implies much less strain on equipment and increases its duration, which means lower maintenance costs and replacement of damaged equipment [6, 7]. Thus, to obtain a clean electric grid for the traffic light system in Bogotá, it is needed a measurement of the electromagnetic interference of the current system.

3   Interferences on Traffic Light System

Ramirez and Cano [6] defined the quality of electricity services as a term related to service continuity and quality of the voltage wave [8]. Service continuity has been traditional erred as reliability, but it is related to the number, duration, and average users affected by interruptions per year. Besides the quality of voltage (or voltage waveform) service continuity is a term used to describe the amount of disturbance or voltage fluctuations e.g. harmonics, transients, voltage fluctuations, and power factor as seen in Fig. 2, and pointed out in [9].

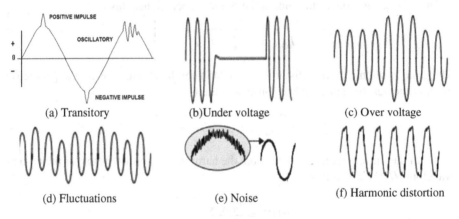

Fig. 2. Frequent types of electromagnetic disturbances in the voltage waveform on a grid [10]

The voltage supplied to a load (lamps and control devices) is characterized by the frequency, magnitude, wave shape, continuity and unbalance of the voltage waveform. Define the supply quality in terms of deviations of these parameters from their ideal values (reference) and maximum deviation in terms of what they can achieve without affecting the correct functioning of electrical equipment; which is equivalent to the definition of the Regulatory Commission for Energy and Gas, CREG, 080. It states that power quality related to deviations from the specified values for variables such as voltage and waveforms of voltage and current [11].

3.1   Harmonic Distortion

Harmonic distortion is a permanent phenomena to any electrical system. The concept of harmonic analysis comes from mathematical theorems developed by Jean Baptiste Joseph Fourier. He stated that any periodic function can be represented by an infinite series of sine and cosine multiples of the fundamental frequency called Fourier series. As he described, the aim of the Fourier series is to represent any periodic function as the sum of trigonometric sinus and cosines of the same period T, so for the kind of waves that we address in an electrical system (sinusoidal), the Fourier expansion can be defined as:

$$i(t) = a_n \sin(\omega t)\omega + b_n \cos(\omega t) \tag{1}$$

where

$$a_n = \frac{1}{\pi} \int_0^{2\pi} i(t) \sin(n\omega t) d(\omega t) \tag{2}$$

$$b_n = \frac{1}{\pi} \int_0^{2\pi} i(t) \cos(n\omega t) d(\omega t) \tag{3}$$

The *Root Mean Square (RMS)* of an amplitude-phase form of the Fourier series is equal to the square root of the sum of the squared coefficients, this is:

$$I_{RMS} = \sqrt{a_n^2 + b_n^2} \tag{4}$$

where the harmonic current distortion (in RMS) can be obtained using the geometric mean of the non-fundamental harmonics and Eq. (4),

$$I_{H-RMS} = \sqrt{I_{2RMS}^2 + I_{3RMS}^2 + \cdots + I_{nRMS}^2} \tag{5}$$

With this current harmonic distortion, the harmonic distortion factor for the current waveform HDF_I is as follows:

$$HDF_I = \frac{I_{H-RMS}}{I_{1RMS}} \tag{6}$$

Substituting Eqs. (5) in (6) as percentage, the rate of total harmonic distortion is:

$$\%THD_I = \frac{\sqrt{I_{2RMS}^2 + \cdots + I_{nRMS}^2}}{I_{1RMS}} \times 100 \tag{7}$$

A similar reasoning leads to find the *THD* in the voltage wave:

$$v(t) = a_n \sin(\omega t)\omega + b_n \cos(\omega t) \tag{8}$$

The fundamental component of voltage *(V1RMS) THD* of the voltage wave is:

$$\%THD_V = \frac{\sqrt{V_{2RMS}^2 + \cdots + V_{nRMS}^2}}{V_{1RMS}} \times 100 \tag{9}$$

The interest in measuring the *THD* is that power systems (including the traffic lights) are sensitive to non-linear loads and they can present a number of undesirable effects, including overheating and damage to electrical conductors, premature failure of transformers, line voltage distortion in feeders, and branch circuits fed from high impedance sources [8].

3.2 Power Factor

Given the negative impact of the harmonics in the power factor correction, a separate space is appropriate to model an electrical system. Figure 3a shows that the power factor is the dimensionless ratio of lag or displacement *cos(θ)* between the voltage and the current at the fundamental frequency, or equivalent to the active power (kW) regarding the apparent power (kVA) of the system or the load [12].

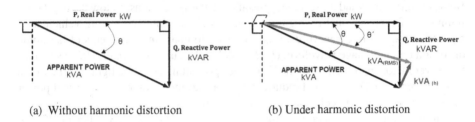

(a) Without harmonic distortion   (b) Under harmonic distortion

Fig. 3. Representation of the power triangle.

Now, the apparent power is defined according to Eq. (10) with active power P, reactive power Q, and apparent power S:

$$S = P + jQ = V.I^*$$ (10)

Using Euler's identity in Eq. (10), the active power factor is the magnitude of the apparent power $|S|$, multiplied by the cosine of the phase angle or displacement $θ$:

$$S = |S|.\cos θ + j|S|\mathrm{sen}θ$$ (11)

Alternatively, Eq. (10) explains the phase angle between the voltage and current, $θ_v - θ_i$, at the fundamental frequencies 50 Hz or 60 Hz, as appropriate.

$$S = VI \cos(θ_v - θ_i) + jVI \,\mathrm{sen}(θ_v - θ_i)$$ (12)

From Eqs. (11) and (12) the following equation of power factor pf is defined, which should be as close as possible to 1 (not greater than 1).

$$pf = \cos(θ_v - θ_i) = \cos θ = \frac{P}{|S|} = \frac{P}{V.I}$$ (13)

$$pf' = \cos θ' = \frac{P'}{|S'|} < fp = \cos θ = \frac{P}{|S|} = \frac{P'}{V' \cdot I'}$$ (14)

It is possible to associate the power factor *THD* of both voltage and current:

$$RPF = \frac{P'}{|S|} = \frac{P'}{V'.I'} = \frac{P}{V_{1RMS}I_{1RMS}\sqrt{1+(THD_V/100)^2}\sqrt{1+(THD_I/100)^2}} \tag{15}$$

where $RPF = fp' = \cos\theta'$.

The importance of maintaining absolute control harmonics in the electrical network traffic lights is given by Eq. (15), especially when as a mandatory rule the equipment used in the traffic light system (e.g. step luminaries and control equipments) require energy power to a specific voltage and active power.

4 Methodology

Both new luminaries and those already installed in the system must follow the regulatory framework for power quality, regardless their purpose (flares regulating vehicular or pedestrian traffic). In other words, it is necessary to make measurements of harmonic distortion on the voltage waveform (*LDLT*) and in the current wave (*THDI*), as well as the power factor (*pf* or *PF*) of all the luminaries present in the traffic light system. Some practical recommendations and requirements for harmonic control in electrical power systems are provided in technical regulation IEC 61000-3-2.

Moreover, under the theoretical foundations seen in Eqs. (7), (13), (19) and (20) to measure *THD* and its corresponding power factor, it is necessary to measure the electric power consumed in the system by any method. The measuring equipment PDF Everfine 9811 uses both the voltmeter and ammeter methods, the *THD* and power factor are measured by the method of voltmeter or power transformer (*PT*) and the ammeter or current transformer (*CT*). The information is transferred to a PC through a RS-232-C interface.

5 Results

Once everything is assembled using a voltage sweep of 80 V to 130 V in steps of two volts, with the measuring equipment Everfine PF 9811 for the full SIMSA LED type TRV-G08DR2R2 model built for an input of 65–140 V AC, a nominal operating frequency of 50 or 60 Hz, and 14.5 W. Table 1 shows some metrics where the first three columns characterizing the network, including the rating of the luminaries[3].

Before any data processing, the nature of the load should be established. The relation between the nominal voltage and the current ratio appears in Fig. 4. For a linear approximation to the dispersion data (values measured for voltage and current), R^2 is equal to 0.9694, while for a polynomial approximation of order 2, R^2 equals 0.9994. It is clear that a trend line is better when R^2 is close 1, so the relationship between the current and voltage values to full SIMSA LED luminaries is non-linear.

---

[3] All the values of voltage, current, and power are in RMS.

Table 1. Features of the network and measures of the power factor and THD-V-I for the full LED type light SIMSA

Voltage measured [V]	Nominal voltage [V]	Nominal current [A]	Nominal capacity [W]	Power factor	THD-V [%]	THD-I [%]
80	80,5	0,162	13,09	0,999	2,3	6,0
86	86,3	0,152	13,17	0,998	2,2	6,2
92	92,0	0,144	13,28	0,998	2,4	6,1
98	98,5	0,136	13,44	0,998	2,4	6,2
104	104,1	0,130	13,59	0,998	2,4	6,1
110	110,1	0,125	13,80	0,998	2,4	5,9
116	116,4	0,120	14,01	0,997	2,4	6,0
122	122,3	0,116	14,25	0,997	2,5	5,9
130	130,3	0,112	14,64	0,996	2,5	6,0

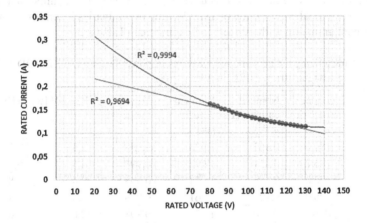

Fig. 4. Relation between nominal current and nominal voltage for SIMSA LED luminaries

In Fig. 5a and b it is possible to see the harmonic distortion, both for voltage and current. If (7) and (13) are considered (in ideal conditions) the relation between the harmonic distortion corresponding to the voltage wave and the current wave should be constant and close to zero as possible. However, in practice it is not the case, given the theoretical conditions already explained.

On the other hand, both values do not exceed 10% of THD, so using (20) it is possible to infer that the luminaries do not individually affect the power factor of the load (if there is a difference, it is mostly due to the THD-I). Hence, we can see that the first harmonic component of voltage and current is approximately 100% of the RMS wave value. Of course, it happens without considering an important number of luminaries simultaneously active at the same point of common coupling (*PCC*).

As expected there is a null input of the even harmonics for the first fifteen multiples of the fundamental frequency, the odd harmonics for the full SIMSA LED luminaries are the most critical, they are prone to wave harmonic current pollution, predominantly

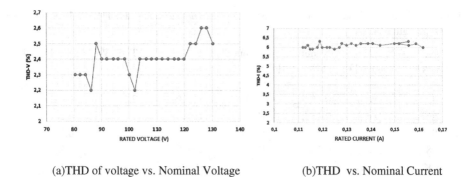

(a)THD of voltage vs. Nominal Voltage   (b)THD vs. Nominal Current

Fig. 5. Characterization of harmonic distortion for the full SIMSA LED luminaire

with third order harmonics; this is understandable do to the use of AC/DC converters with low power in the luminaries (less than 100 W). However, it is important to point out that the individual contribution of a single lamp or luminaries in terms of generating harmonic contamination in the system is insignificant (Table 2).

Table 2. Characterizing the network and measures of power factor and THD THD-V-I for the LED Luminaire with turn arrow SoBright type

Voltage measured [V]	Nominal voltage [V]	Nominal current [A]	Nominal capacity [W]	Power factor	THD-V [%]	THD-I [%]
80	80,0	0,165	13,23	0,998	2,5	7,3
86	86,2	0,151	12,92	0,998	2,3	6,9
92	92,0	0,138	12,74	0,998	2,4	6,8
98	98,0	0,128	12,61	0,998	2,5	6,8
104	104,2	0,120	12,55	0,998	2,6	7,0
110	110,0	0,114	12,52	0,998	2,4	7,0
116	116,2	0,107	12,50	0,998	2,5	7,1
122	122,3	0,102	12,46	0,997	2,6	6,7
130	130,4	0,095	12,46	0,997	2,6	6,5

The same procedure is followed for the LED luminaries with turning arrow SoBright, A10-G08THA117GC model with 84 LEDs; built for an input of 80–135 V AC, a nominal operating frequency of 50 or 60 Hz, and less than 15-Watts using an AC/DC low power converter power. Once again, the same happens for the LED Luminaries with turn arrow SoBright type, the load is not linear, R^2 equals to 0.9981 for a polynomial trend line of degree two; the graph is omitted. The same happens for the relation between voltage and nominal current vs. harmonic distortion (the performance in comparative terms with the full SIMSA LED luminaries remains).

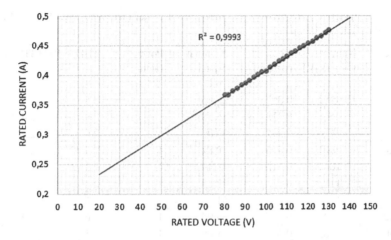

Fig. 6. Relation between nominal current vs. nominal voltage for a green module halogen luminaries (Color figure online)

Likewise, for the LED Luminaries for pedestrian crossing SoBright type, model P10-G08THA120RC with 76 LEDs; built for an input of 80–135 V AC; a nominal operating frequency of 50 or 60 Hz, and less than 15 W (using AC/DC low power converter). The following measures were obtained (Table 3):

Table 3. Characterization of the network and measures of power factor, THD-V and THD-I type LED luminaire for pedestrian SoBright

Voltage measured [V]	Nominal voltage [V]	Nominal current [A]	Nominal capacity [W]	Power factor	THD-V [%]	THD-I [%]
80	80,4	0,180	14,49	0,999	2,4	5,8
86	86,2	0,151	13,00	0,999	2,3	5,4
92	92,3	0,139	12,89	0,999	2,5	5,3
98	98,2	0,130	12,85	0,999	2,6	5,6
104	104,2	0,123	12,83	0,998	2,6	5,7
110	110,3	0,116	12,83	0,998	2,5	5,8
116	116,2	0,110	12,83	0,998	2,5	5,5
122	122,2	0,105	12,84	0,998	2,5	5,3
130	130,2	0,098	12,85	0,998	2,6	5,3

For the green module halogen luminaries, the load is linear while all other parameters remains the same, as seen on Fig. 6. The following measures were obtained (Table 4):

Table 4. Characterizing the network and measures of power factor and THD THD-V-I for the green module halogen luminaire

Voltage measured [V]	Nominal voltage [V]	Nominal current [A]	Nominal capacity [W]	Power factor	THD-V [%]	THD-I [%]
80	80,2	0,367	29,46	1	2,5	2,4
86	86,1	0,378	35,58	1	2,6	2,4
92	92,0	0,391	36,05	1	2,6	2,4
98	98,1	0,405	39,82	1	2,5	2,4
104	104,0	0,418	43,49	1	2,3	2,1
110	110,1	0,431	47,55	1	2,6	2,3
116	116,2	0,445	51,75	1	2,6	2,3
122	122,2	0,457	55,95	1	2,6	2,4
130	130,2	0,475	61,88	1	2,5	2,3

The contribution of harmonics to the power factor is small, depending on the measuring equipment (rounded up to 1) as seen in Fig. 6, with average values of total harmonic distortion of 2.55 for THD-V and 2.34 for THD-I.

It is expected that green module halogen luminaires with linear load do not add an important number of interfering harmonics in to the network, as seen in Fig. 7 where the percentages do not exceed 3% of THD for voltage and nominal current. Generally, the performance of full LED luminaries SIMSA type, pedestrian and turn arrow SoBright type, has similar power consumption (about 13 W), but not greater THD-I compared to THD-V, The dominance of the third harmonic remains.

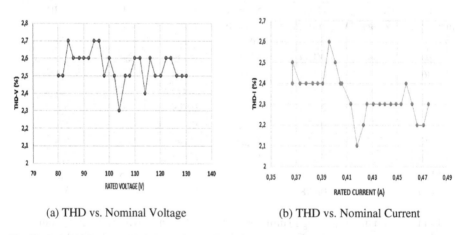

(a) THD vs. Nominal Voltage   (b) THD vs. Nominal Current

Fig. 7. Relation between current vs. voltage for the green module halogen luminaire (Color figure online)

The difference between the nominal capacities of each luminary type is high. The consumption of the halogen luminaries is 4x greater than of the LED ones. Thus, it is necessary to perform a technological change to fix related issues such as high THD when a significant number of LED lights are active simultaneously at the same PCC.

6 Conclusions

The electromagnetic interference that affects the grid of traffic lights, especially when using LED lights and low power converters (usually nonlinear) generate harmonics into the network. As a result, it is important to mitigate or eliminate (if possible) the harmful effects of electromagnetic interference on the power grid, if what it is expected is a major factor of power with voltage stability, lower losses on the network, no resonance problems, and amplification of electrical disturbances.

It is said the any equipment, luminary or bulb is considered as Class A, if it keeps limits on THD-I as follows: for the third harmonic of 2.30%, for the fifth of 1.14%, for the seventh of 0.77%, for the ninth of 0.40%, for the eleventh of 0.33%, for the thirteenth of 0.21%, and those contained between the fifteenth and the thirty-ninth harmonic of $0.15 \times 15/n$, where n equals the number of the harmonic. We have shown that the full LED luminary SIMSA type as well as the LED Luminaries for pedestrians and with turn arrow SoBright are class A.

Comparing the LED type luminaries to the green module halogen luminaries, the power consumption of LEDs is lower in a 300%. This difference in consumption shows the need for a technological replacement to fix high THD when a significant number of LED lights are simultaneously active at the same PCC.

In general, the behavior of LED luminaries, either full SIMSA with turn arrow and pedestrian SoBright has similar power consumption (about 13 W), but not higher THD-I compared to THD-V; there is a predominance of the third harmonic. Also, for the LED and halogen luminaries, the dispersion does not exceed the 10% of THD, then, reviewing (20), it follows that individual luminaries do not affect the power factor of the load.

Therefore, it is clear that the first harmonic component of voltage and current is about 100% RMS value of the wave; which is to say that it has an insignificant participation in the harmonics (>1) in the wave distortion.

References

1. Colombian decree law 3133 December 26, 1968. Por el cual se reforma la organización administrativa del distrito especial de Bogotá
2. Bogotá council. Agreement 257 November 3, 2009. Por el cual se dictan normas básicas sobre la estructura, organización, y funcionamiento de los organismos y las entidades de Bogotá D.C. y se expiden otras disposiciones
3. Méndez, A.V.:Desarrollo de una metodologia para el control de la señalización del trafico y el sistema de semaforizacion, Bogotá (2009)
4. Abreu, A.: Calidad de potencia eléctrica en redes de distribución, Maracaibo (2005)
5. Guerrero, R., Martínez, I.: Calidad de energía Factor de potencia y filtrado de armónicos. McGraw-Hill Educación (2012)
6. Ramírez, S., Cano, E.: Calidad del servicio de energía eléctrica. Publicaciones Universidad Nacional de Colombia, sede Manizales (2006)

7. Monzón, M.: Calidad de suministro eléctrico: Huecos de tensión, mitigación de sus efectos en las plantas industriales. Publicaciones Universidad Carlos III de Madrid, Madrid (2013)
8. American Power Conversion. Seven kinds of problems in electric power supply. APC publications, Rhode Island (2005)
9. Kosmák, J., Misak, S., Proko, L.: Power quality dependence on connected appliances in an off-grid system. In: 16th International Scientific Conference on Electrical Power Engineering (EPE) (2015). Kouty and Desnou Eds.
10. Islam, M., Chowdhury, N., Sakil, A., Khandakar, A., Abu-Rub, H.: Power quality effect of using incandescent, fluorescent, CFL and LED lamps on utility grid. In: First Workshop on Smart Grid and Renewable Energy: SGRE 2015, Doha (2015)
11. IEEE standar 1159. The IEEE standards association (2009)
12. Colombian ministry of transportation resolution 1050 May, 2004. Por la cual se adopta el Manual de Señalización para calles, carreteras y ciclo rutas de Colombia

On-line Visualization and Long-Term Monitoring of a Single-Phase Photovoltaic Generator Using SCADA

Oswaldo Lopez-Santos[✉], Jhon S. Arango-Buitrago,
and David F. González-Morales

Program of Electronics Engineering, Universidad de Ibagué, Ibagué, Colombia
oswaldo.lopez@unibague.edu.co

Abstract. This paper describes the design and implementation of a Supervisory, Control & Data Acquisition (SCADA) system dedicated to realize on-line visualization and long-term monitoring of the performance of a single-phase single-module photovoltaic grid-connected installation. The main objective of this development is to ensure continuous monitoring of the efficiency and relevant power quality indicators of a two-stage microinverter providing a comprehensive treatment of the electrical variables. The system consists of a software component developed in LabVIEW and a hardware component including specialized sensors and analogue electronics. Both components communicate synchronously through an acquisition card, which enhances visualization and accuracy of computations. The mathematical expressions employed to obtain variables and indicators are listed, explained and verified by means of simulated results.

Keywords: SCADA · Photovoltaic generators · Two-stage microinverter · Grid-connected installation · Power quality

1 Introduction

SOLAR microinverters are a promising technology of power conversion which has allowed the modularization of the photovoltaic installations and in consequence the accessibility of the solar energy for a higher number of users [1–3]. Today, the power installed in rooftop stations is comparable with centralized installations and show a less incipient contribution when compared with other renewable energy generation alternatives [4, 5]. The application of photovoltaic energy in distributed installation is growth in Colombia, in part because these systems are increasingly reliable by the absence of batteries. Sustainability of this trend implies challenges such as recognize advantages, drawbacks and particular electrical and environmental conditions [6].

Microinverter devices are developed by a fair number of manufacturers and commercialized around the world. Technical specification of some of these products is summarized in [7]. Currently, the efforts to improve its capabilities, performance and reliability remain latent as an open problem in the academic and industrial research focused in power electronics and control [8, 9]. Among existing architectures of

© Springer International Publishing AG 2016
J.C. Figueroa-García et al. (Eds.): WEA 2016, CCIS 657, pp. 295–307, 2016.
DOI: 10.1007/978-3-319-50880-1_26

microinverters, the two-stage microinverters has been intensely studied in last years because of they have demonstrated simplicity, low-cost and higher dynamic performance, among other advantages [10, 11]. The study and analysis of the device variables along the time is facilitated thanks to its configuration, which can be exploited by means of monitoring system continuously verifying the evolution of the variables, indicators and generating long-term information to detect weaknesses susceptible to improvement. A way to contribute with this objective is to evaluate the static a dynamic behavior of solar microinverters taken real-time measurement of the relevant electrical variables and processing that information to obtain key indicators. Figure 1 represents the power connections of a single-phase single-module two-stage microinverter differentiating the main variables of three connection points:

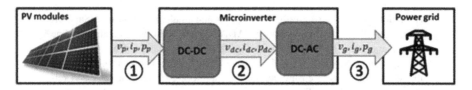

Fig. 1. Block diagram of the proposed two-stage solar microinverter

1. PV module side: v_p, i_p, p_p
2. DC-link: v_{dc}, i_{dc}, p_{dc}
3. AC side: v_g, i_g, p_g

Total Harmonic Distortion (THD), Power Factor (PF), Displacement Power Factor (DPF), Maximum Power Point Tracking (MPPT) efficiency, converter stage efficiency and global efficiency have been selected as supervised indicators. The system also determines and visualizes the measured average power in the three selected points, and the apparent, real, reactive and distortive power at the AC side. The SCADA system proposed in this paper takes into account some ideas of other developments have been reported promoting the use of smart monitoring applied in power quality analysis and more recently in renewable energy systems. In general, this work retains similarities in some functions such as acquisition, measurement, visualization, supervision, local and remote monitoring, fault detection, diagnostic, historic registration, power quality analysis, and performance analysis [12–21]. However, in comparison with other proposed SCADA system developed in LabVIEW [22–25], the potentialities of this application are extended from conventional measurement and monitoring of power generation to long-term supervision and performance analysis. The system is evaluated working with a two-stage photovoltaic installation, but it can be used to study other industrialized microinverters in the same way introduced in [26].

The rest of the paper is organized as follows: Sect. 2 has a general description of the SCADA system decomposing hardware and software components. After that, in Sect. 3, the mathematical expressions involved in discrete-time computation of power quality and performance indicators are derived. These expressions are verified and compared with continuous time measurement and computations by means of simulated results in Sect. 4. Finally, some conclusions and future work are presented in Sect. 5.

2   General Description of the System

The proposed system is composed by a software module developed in LabVIEW and a
hardware module which uses sensors and analogue electronics. Both modules communicate through an acquisition card which synchronizes the execution of the algorithm with the power grid be means of a PLL-based circuit. Figure 2 shows a
descriptive block diagram of the system and its components. Four fundamental blocks
can be identified: (a) the power stage, composed by the PV module, and the solar
microinverter; (b) the measurement, conditioning and synchronization circuit; (c) the
acquisition card; and (d) the computation application. The first three blocks will be
described hereinafter as the hardware module whereas the last block will be treated as
the software module.

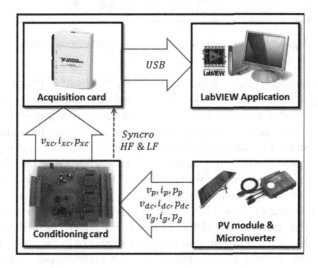

Fig. 2. Descriptive block diagram of the proposed system

2.1   Hardware Component

The hardware module is completely integrated in the Printed Circuit Board
(PCB) depicted in Fig. 3. The circuit is integrated by a set of current and voltage
sensors, a synchronization circuit and some conditioning electronics interconnected
with the computer application by means of the acquisition card DAQ NI USB-6210.
One voltage sensor and one current sensor are used to obtain measurements in each of
the three defined connection points. Voltages are measured by using LV-20P isolated
closed-loop hall-effect transducers and currents are measured by using CAS 6-NP and
CAS-15-NP isolated closed-loop hall-effect transducers. All signals are conditioned by
means of active filters and arithmetical operators using analogue electronics. Integrated
circuits and sensors are fed by internal power sources implemented with DC-DC
converters PTN04050C and PTN04050A providing ± 15 VDC from an external source
of 5 VDC.

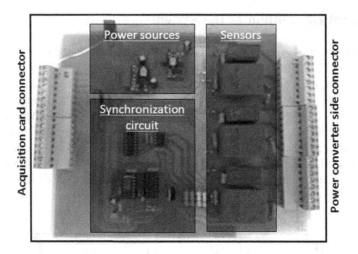

Fig. 3. Measurement, conditioning and synchronization PCB

The synchronization circuit, which was recently presented in [27], was developed using the Integrated Circuit (IC) CD4046 as PLL and the CD4040 as frequency divider. Among the main advantages of this synchronized acquisition it must be highlighted establishment of a constant number of samples per grid period facilitating and simplifying the compute of averages, RMS values, Fourier decomposition and in general mathematical expressions involving integrals defined for intervals related by an integral value with the grid frequency. In this particular application, the system acquires 1024 samples per period or what is equivalent operates at a sampling frequency of 61.440 Hz when the grid frequency is 60 Hz. A uniform quantization of ten bits is used for analogic to digital conversion (ADC). This synchronization method incorporates a component in the SCADA system generating the trigger of the signal acquisition and the waveform visualization which is one of the main contributions of the work.

2.2 Software Module

The software module of the system can be described by means of the component diagram in Fig. 4 which was created using the Unified Modeling Language (UML). As it is depicted, the SCADA system is composed by nine components. The synchronization component defines the sample frequency of the current and voltage signals acquisition component and defines the number of samples to calculate the power quality and performance indicators whereas defines the trigger of the Graphical User Interfaces (GUI) to visualize the waveforms and computed indicators in real time. Both GUIs can be remotely accessed by means of the WEB publishing component. A permanent data set of variables and indicators evolution is registered in two databases which provide information to the report generation component.

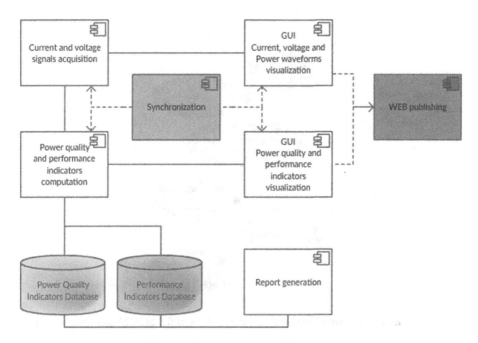

Fig. 4. Component diagram of the SCADA capabilities

In Fig. 5, a use case diagram is depicted listing the on-line function provided to users of the SCADA application through the GUI. These interfaces allows to access different functions such as visualization, configuration, report printing, remote access.

3 Computed Variables and Indicators

The synchronization circuit provides a high frequency signal 1024 higher than the grid frequency. Then, each signal is acquired and processed considering an exact number N of 1024 samples per period and a scalar quantization of ten bits. Considering this, mathematical expressions derived and employed to obtain the desired values are detailed below.

3.1 Computations at the PV Module Side

The system acquires the voltage and current waveforms of the PV side as $v_p(k) = v_{pk}$ and $i_p(k) = i_{pk}$ for $k = 1, 2, \ldots, N$ and stores N samples of both variables in the $1xN$ vectors $\mathbf{V_p} = \left[v_{p1}, v_{p2}, \ldots, v_{pN}\right]$ and $\mathbf{I_p} = \left[i_{p1}, i_{p2}, \ldots, i_{pN}\right]$ respectively. Average voltage and current are computed as follows:

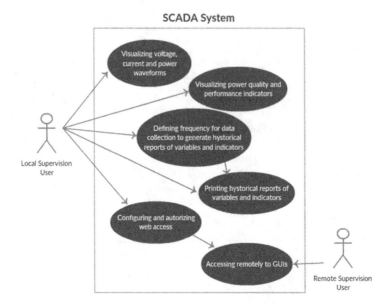

Fig. 5. Diagram of the on-line user functions of the SCADA system.

$$V_{P_{avg}} = \frac{1}{N} \sum_{k=1}^{N} v_{pk} \tag{1}$$

$$I_{P_{avg}} = \frac{1}{N} \sum_{k=1}^{N} i_{pk} \tag{2}$$

The instantaneous input power can be computed as the following dot product:

$$P_p = V_p \cdot I_p = [p_{p1}, p_{p2}, \ldots, p_{pN}] \tag{3}$$

From this, average power can be computed as:

$$P_{P_{avg}} = \frac{1}{N} \sum_{k=1}^{N} p_{pk} \tag{4}$$

Also, the maximum available power for a grid period is obtained as the maximum value p_{pk} of the vector P_p:

$$P_{P_{max}} = \max(P_p) \tag{5}$$

Then, this last result allows computing the per grid-cycle MPPT efficiency as:

$$\eta_{MPPT} = \frac{P_{P_{avg}}}{P_{P_{max}}} \tag{6}$$

3.2   Computations at the DC-Link

The system acquires the voltage waveform of the DC-link as $v_{dc}(k) = v_{dck}$ and a filtered version of the input current of the DC-AC stage as $i_{dc}(k) = i_{dck}$ for $k = 1, 2, \ldots, N$ and stores the N samples for both variables in the vectors $V_{dc} = [v_{dc1}, v_{dc2}, \ldots, v_{dcN}]$ and $I_{dc} = [i_{dc1}, i_{dc2}, \ldots, i_{dcN}]$. Average voltage and current at the DC-link are:

$$V_{dc_{avg}} = \frac{1}{N} \sum_{k=1}^{N} V_{dc} \tag{7}$$

$$I_{dc_{avg}} = \frac{1}{N} \sum_{k=1}^{N} I_{dc} \tag{8}$$

The RMS value of the DC-link voltage is obtained as:

$$V_{dc_{RMS}} = \sqrt{\frac{1}{N} \sum_{k=1}^{N} (V_{dc} \cdot V_{dc})} \tag{9}$$

Consequently, the Ripple Factor (RF) is:

$$RF_{dc} = \frac{V_{dc_{AC}}}{V_{dc_{avg}}} = \frac{\sqrt{V_{dc_{RMS}}^2 - V_{dc_{avg}}^2}}{V_{dc_{avg}}} \tag{10}$$

From this, average power can be computed as:

$$P_{dc_{avg}} = V_{dc_{avg}} I_{dc_{avg}} \tag{11}$$

3.3   Computations at the AC Side

The computation of powers, efficiency and performance indicators at the AC side are developed taken as basis the pnciples of electrical power in the presence of harmonic content [29, 30]. Figure 6 shows the vectors of the power components discriminated as real power, reactive power and distortive power using the standard conventions.

The system acquires the voltage and current waveforms of the grid side as $v_g(k)$ and $i_g(k)$ for $k = 1, 2, \ldots, N$ and stores the N samples for both variables in the vectors $V_g = [v_{g1}, v_{g2}, \ldots, v_{gN}]$ and $I_g = [i_{g1}, i_{g2}, \ldots, i_{gN}]$. RMS values of voltage and current are determined as:

$$V_{g_{RMS}} = \sqrt{\frac{1}{N} \sum_{k=1}^{N} (V_g \cdot V_g)} \tag{12}$$

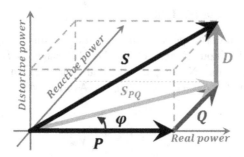

Fig. 6. Graphic representation of the power components vectors

$$I_{g_{RMS}} = \sqrt{\frac{1}{N}\sum_{k=1}^{N}\left(\mathbf{I_g}\cdot\mathbf{I_g}\right)} \tag{13}$$

Defining the vectors $\mathbf{S_s}$ and $\mathbf{C_s}$ as a sine and a cosine waveforms sampled for N elements respectively, RMS values of the fundamental components of current and voltage are obtained from the Fourier series expansion using expressions:

$$V_{g_1} = \frac{1}{N}\sqrt{\frac{1}{2}\left[\left(\sum_{k=1}^{N}\mathbf{V_g S_s}\right)^2 + \left(\sum_{k=1}^{N}\mathbf{V_g C_s}\right)^2\right]} \tag{14}$$

$$I_{g_1} = \frac{1}{N}\sqrt{\frac{1}{2}\left[\left(\sum_{k=1}^{N}\mathbf{I_g S_s}\right)^2 + \left(\sum_{k=1}^{N}\mathbf{I_g C_s}\right)^2\right]} \tag{15}$$

RMS value of the harmonic components of current and voltage are given by:

$$V_{g_h} = \sqrt{V_{g_{RMS}}^2 - V_{g_1}^2} \tag{16}$$

$$I_{g_h} = \sqrt{I_{g_{RMS}}^2 - I_{g_1}^2} \tag{17}$$

From this, apparent power is easily computed as:

$$S_g = V_{g_{RMS}} I_{g_{RMS}} \tag{18}$$

The instantaneous output power is computed as follows:

$$P_g = \mathbf{V_g}\cdot\mathbf{I_g} \tag{19}$$

From which, real power can be computed as:

$$P_{g_{avg}} = \frac{1}{N} \sum_{k=1}^{N} P_g \tag{20}$$

Therefore, the distortive power is obtained as:

$$D_g = \sqrt{V_{g_1}^2 I_{g_h}^2 + V_{g_h}^2 I_{g_{RMS}}^2} \tag{21}$$

Finally, the reactive power can be computed using the trigonometric representation in Fig. 5 as:

$$Q_g = \sqrt{S_g^2 - P_g^2 - D_g^2} \tag{22}$$

The Total Harmonic Distortion with respect to the Root Mean Square values (THD-R) of the output current and voltage are:

$$THD_v = \frac{V_{g_h}}{V_{g_{RMS}}} \tag{23}$$

$$THD_i = \frac{I_{g_h}}{I_{g_{RMS}}} \tag{24}$$

Then, the Power Factor (PF) is obtained as:

$$PF_g = \frac{P_g}{S_g} \tag{25}$$

and the Displacement Power Factor (DPF) is obtained as:

$$DPF_g = \cos\left[\text{atan}\left(\frac{Q_g}{P_g}\right)\right] \tag{26}$$

3.4   Computation Related with the Overall Performance

The efficiency of each conversion stage is computed using (27) and (28) whereas the global efficiency is computed using (29). Then, all the desired evaluation indicators are defined.

$$\eta_{DC-DC} = \frac{P_{dc}}{P_p} \tag{27}$$

$$\eta_{DC-AC} = \frac{P_g}{P_{dc}} \tag{28}$$

$$\eta_o = \frac{P_g}{P_p} = \eta_{DC-DC}\,\eta_{DC-AC} \tag{29}$$

4 Simulated Results

In order to evaluate the effect of quantization and sampling in the accuracy of measurements and computations, simulated waveforms were obtained for the two-stage solar microinverter presented in [28]. Table 1 summarizes variables and indicators directly obtained from simulations compared with results considering 10 bits and 61.440 Hz sampled measurements. The cut-off frequency of the low-pass filter used to obtain the low frequency components of the current at the DC-link is settled to 600 Hz. Defining the continuous time measurement of all variables as the term x_{cont} and the sampled measurement of all variables as the term x_{sample}, the deviation error can be computed as:

Table 1. Comparison between continuous time and discrete time values for measurements, computed variables and indicators.

Variable Indicator	Continuous time Measurement	Sampled Measurement	Error
$V_{p_{avg}}$	21.05 V	21.02 V	0.14%
$I_{p_{avg}}$	5.64 A	5.64 A	0.01%
$P_{p_{max}}$	118.94 W	118.94 W	0.01%
$P_{p_{avg}}$	118.78 W	118.60 W	0.13%
η_{MPPT}	99.86%	99.71%	0.15%
$V_{dc_{avg}}$	400.03 V	399.79 V	0.69%
$V_{dc_{RMS}}$	400.16 V	399.92 V	0.05%
RF_{dc}	2.55%	2.55%	0.01%
$I_{dc_{avg}}$	0.2997 A	0.2914 A	2.77%
η_o	98.13%	97.42%	0.72%
$P_{dc_{avg}}$	116.71 W	116.84 W	0.11%
$V_{g_{RMS}}$	220.617 V	220.614 V	0.00%
$I_{g_{RMS}}$	0.5292 A	0.5290 A	0.03%
THD_i	5.41%	5.51%	1.85%
S_g	116.75 VA	116.72 VA	0.02%
$P_{g_{avg}}$	116.58 W	116.54 W	0.03%
PF_g	0.99851	0.99850	0.00%
η_{DC-DC}	98.25%	97.67%	0.59%
η_{DC-AC}	99.88%	99.74%	0.14%

$$Error_x = \left| \frac{x_{cont} - x_{sample}}{x_{cont}} \right| \tag{30}$$

As it can be observed from data in Table 1, the resulting error is negligible which confirms the expected accuracy of the system computing variables and indicators. Computational cost of each mathematical operation implemented by means of different alternatives has been also evaluated but is not presented in this paper.

5 Conclusions and Future Work

The design and development of a SCADA system to evaluate single phase photovoltaic generators was detailed showing the advantages to synchronize the sampling of the measured variables with the grid frequency. Effect of discretization in measurement has been taken into account in validating the system design. Currently, experimental test are applied to the system in order to validate its functionality using a Fluke 43B Power Quality Analyzer as measuring pattern.

Acknowledgements. This work has been developed with the partial support of the Gobernación del Tolima under Convenio de cooperación 1026 - 2013 - Scientific Culture Project. The results presented in this paper have been obtained with the assistance of students from the Research Hotbed on Power Electronic Conversion (SICEP), Research Group D+TEC, Universidad de Ibagué, Ibagué-Colombia.

References

1. Sher, H.A., Addoweesh, K.E.: Micro-inverters - promising solutions in solar photovoltaics. Energy. Sustain. Dev. **16**, 389–400 (2012)
2. Blaabjerg, F., Chen, Z., Kjaer, S.B.: Power electronics as efficient interface in dispersed power generation systems. IEEE Trans. Power Electron. **5**, 1184–1194 (2004)
3. Xue, Y., Chang, L., Kjaer, S.B., Bordonau, J., Shimizu, T.: Topologies of single-phase inverters for small distributed power generators: an overview. IEEE Trans. Power Electron. **5**, 1305–1314 (2004)
4. Arup Ltda: Five minutes guide Rooftop Solar PV. http://www.arup.com/ ~ /media/ Publications/Files/Publications/F/5min_guide_to_solar_Arup.ashx
5. Gagnon, P., Margolis, R., Meluis, J., Philips, C., Elmore, R.: Rooftop Solar Photovoltaic Technical Potential in the United States: A Detailed Assessment. In: National Renewable Energy Laboratory (NREL), Technical report (2016)
6. Gaona, E.E., Trujillo, C.L., Guacaneme, J.A.: Rural microgrids and its potential application in Colombia. Renew. Sustain. Energy Rev. **51**, 125–137 (2015)
7. Lopez-Santos, O.: Contribution to the DC-AC conversion in photovoltaic systems: module oriented converters, Doctoral dissertation, INSA de Toulouse, pp. 1–248 (2015)
8. Edwin, F.F., Weidong, X., Khadkikar, V.: Dynamic modeling and control of interleaved flyback module-integrated converter for PV power applications. IEEE Trans. Ind. Electron. **61**(3), 1377–1388 (2014)

9. Sukesh, N., Pahlevaninezhad, M., Jain, P.K.: Analysis and implementation of a single-stage flyback PV microinverter with soft switching. IEEE Trans. Ind. Electron. **61**(4), 1819–1833 (2014)

10. Lopez-Santos, O., Martinez-Salamero, L., Garcia, G., Valderrama-Blavi, H.: Sliding-mode control of a transformer-less dual-stage grid-connected photovoltaic micro-inverter. In: Proceedings of the 10th International Multi-Conference on Systems, Signals & Devices (SSD) 2013, pp. 1–6 (2013)

11. Dominic, J.C.: Comparison and Design of High Efficiency Microinverters for Photovoltaic Applications. Master thesis, Virginia Polytechnic Institute and State University, pp. 1–109 (2014)

12. Drews, A., de Keizer, A.C., Beyer, H.G., Lorenz, E., Betcke, J., van Sark, W.G.J.H.M., Heydenreich, W., Wiemken, E., Stettler, S., Toggweiler, P., Bofinger, S., Schneider, M., Heilscher, G., Heinemann, D.: Monitoring and remote failure detection of grid-connected PV systems based on satellite observations. Sol. Energy **81**(4), 548–564 (2007)

13. Polo, F.A.O., del Rosario, J.J.A., García, G.C.: Supervisory control and automatic failure detection in grid-connected photovoltaic systems. In: Proceedings of the International Conference on Industrial, Engineering and Other Applications of Applied Intelligent Systems, pp. 458–467 (2010)

14. Bayrak, G., Kabalci, E., Cebeci, M.: Real time power flow monitoring in a PLL inverter based PV distributed generation system. In: Proceedings of the 16th International Power Electronics and Motion Control Conference and Exposition (PEMC), pp. 1035–1040 (2014)

15. Mujumdar, U.B., Tutkane, D.R.: Development of integrated hardware set up for solar photovoltaic system monitoring. In: Proceedings of the Annual IEEE India Conference (INDICON) (2013)

16. Won, D.J., Chung, I.Y., Kim, J.M., Moon, S.I., Seo, J.C., Choe, J.W.: Development of power quality monitoring system with central processing scheme. In: Proceedings of the IEEE Power Engineering Society Summer Meeting, vol. 2, pp. 915–919 (2002)

17. Abidullah, N.A., Abdullah, A.R., Shamsudin, N.H., Ahmad, N.H.T.H., Jopri, M.H.: Real-time power quality signals monitoring system. In: Proceedings of the IEEE Student Conference on Research and Development (SCOReD), pp. 433–438 (2013)

18. Yingkayun, K., Premrudeepreechacharn, S.: A power quality monitoring system for real-time detection of power fluctuations. In: Proceedings of the 40th North American Power Symposium (NAPS), pp. 1–5 (2008)

19. Chouder, A., Silvestre, S.: Automatic supervision and fault detection of PV systems based on power losses analysis, energy conversion and management. Energy Convers. Manage. **51** (10), 1929–1937 (2010)

20. Zhang, M., Li, K.: A power quality monitoring system over the internet. In: Proceedings of the 1st International Conference on Information Science and Engineering (ICISE), pp. 1577–1580 (2009)

21. Ben Belghith, O., Sbita, L.: Remote GSM module monitoring and Photovoltaic system control. In: Proceedings of the International Conference Green Energy, pp. 188–192 (2014)

22. Bayrak, G., Cebeci, M.: Monitoring a grid connected PV power generation system with Labview. In: International Conference on Renewable Energy Research and Applications (ICRERA), pp. 562–567, 20–23 (2013)

23. Padhee, S., Singh, Y.: Data logging and supervisory control of process using LabVIEW. In: Students' Technology Symposium (TechSym), pp. 329–334, 14–16 (2011)

24. Vergura, S., Natangelo, E.: Labview interface for data analysis of PV. In: International Conference Clean Electrical Power, pp. 236–241 (2009)

25. Kaminský, D., Bilik, P., Hula, J.: Desarrollo de una plataforma completa de análisis de calidad de energía utilizando NI CompactRIO. http://sine.ni.com/cs/app/doc/p/id/cs-14588#

26. Van Dyk, E.E., Meyer, E.L., Vorster, F.J., Leitch, A.W.R.: Long-term monitoring of photovoltaic devices. Renew. Energy **25**(2), 183–197 (2002)
27. Lopez-Santos, O., Garcia, G., Avila-Martinez, J.C., Gonzalez-Morales, D.F., Toro-Zuluaga, C.: A simple digital sinusoidal reference generator for grid-synchronized power electronics applications. In: IEEE Workshop on Power Electronics and Power Quality Applications (PEPQA), pp. 1–6 (2015)
28. Lopez-Santos, O., Garcia, G., Martinez-Salamero, L., Cortes-Torres, L.: Suppressing the effect of the DC-link voltage ripple on the current control of a sliding-mode controlled microinverter. In: Proceedings of the CHILEAN Conference on Electrical, Electronics Engineering, Information and Communication Technologies (CHILECON), Santiago, pp. 447–452 (2015)
29. Shaffer, R.A.: Fundamentals of Power Electronics with MATLAB. Charles River Media, Boston (2007)
30. Akagi, H., Watanabe, E.H., Aredes, M.: Instantaneous Power Theory and Applications to Power Conditioning, pp. 1–379. John Wiley & Sons, Hoboken (2007)

Overvoltage Protection for Distributed Maximum Power Point Tracking Converters in Series Connection

Carlos Andrés Ramos-Paja[✉] and Andrés Julián Saavedra-Montes

Departamento de Energía Eléctrica y Automática,
Universidad Nacional de Colombia, Medellín, Colombia
{caramosp,ajsaaved}@unal.edu.co

Abstract. Distributed maximum power point tracking (DMPPT) circuits are useful to improve the power production of photovoltaic (PV) systems operating under mismatched conditions such as partial shading. The main option to implement DMPPT circuits is the series connection of PV systems based on dc/dc converters, however those converters are subjected to overvoltage conditions that could damage the circuit. This paper proposes a sliding-mode control technique to avoid overvoltage conditions, which ensures the circuit operation in a safe operating point.

Keywords: Safety · Sliding-mode · Granular MPPT · Grid connection

1   Introduction

Urban photovoltaic (PV) systems are one of the most promising clean energy sources [1]. In this way, PV systems are commonly installed on rooftops, parking lots and streets, which improve the profitability of those spaces. However, urban environments exhibit obstacles that produce partial shadings over the PV panels [1–3], e.g. buildings, trees. This condition is illustrated in Fig. 1(a), in which a commercial PV installation is subjected to multiple partial shades. Moreover, the shading patter changes along the day, hence a PV panel could be subjected to multiple shading conditions varying the percentage of covered area.

Those operating conditions are the main cause of the mismatching phenomenon on PV systems [2,3], which significantly reduces the power production of the PV installation. Such power drop is caused by the activation of bypass diodes to protect the PV panels from hot-spot phenomena, which leads to overheating conditions that degrade, or even destroy, the PV array [2,3]. However, the activation of the bypass diodes produce multiple maximum power points (MPP) in the power-vs-voltage curve of the PV array, hence classical MPPT algorithms could be trapped in a local MPP (LMPP), which reduces even more the power production [4].

Several solutions have been proposed to mitigate the impact of this phenomenon [4]: multi-maximum power point tracking algorithms, electrical reconfiguration and distributed maximum power point tracking (DMPPT) circuits. The

© Springer International Publishing AG 2016
J.C. Figueroa-García et al. (Eds.): WEA 2016, CCIS 657, pp. 308–319, 2016.
DOI: 10.1007/978-3-319-50880-1_27

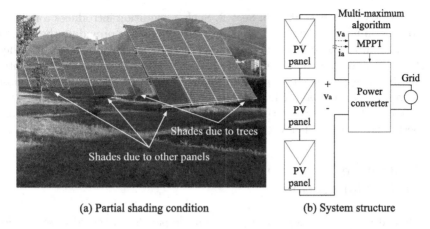

(a) Partial shading condition   (b) System structure

Fig. 1. Partial shading on a commercial PV installation with centralized structure.

multi-maximum power point tracking algorithms [4] are aimed at detecting the global maximum power point (GMPP) in mismatched PV arrays based on the classical centralized structure presented in Fig. 1(b). That solution considers the series-connection of the PV panels to provide the high-voltage required at the input port of the power converter. In this case the MPPT algorithm does not keep trapped in a LMPP, which enables to produce the highest power for the particular shading patter and electrical connection. However, since some bypass diodes are active, the bypassed PV panels do not produce power, which in turns reduces the power production as will be described in Sect. 2.

The electrical reconfiguration consists in changing the electrical connections between the PV panels to construct the PV array with the highest GMPP. This process demands a very high computational effort due to the large amount of possibilities, and nowadays there is not reported a solution to perform this process in real-time. Finally, this solution is also based on the centralized architecture, hence in mismatched conditions some PV panels will be bypassed [3,4].

DMPPT circuits replace the bypass diodes with dc/dc converters, which enable to perform MPPT operations in each PV module independently [2] even under mismatching conditions. Therefore, when a PV array is subjected to partial shading, the DMPPT solution always produce a higher power in comparison with any centralized solution. The main approaches for DMPPT systems are based on parallel and series connection of the dc/dc converters, where the series connection, presented in Fig. 3, is preferable to implement grid-connected PV systems [5]. This is due to the series-connection of the output ports of the dc/dc converters require a lower boosting factor in comparison with the parallel connection, which in turns improves the efficiency of the power stage [6].

The series-connection of the converters output ports imposes the same current i_a to the output capacitors. Moreover, the grid-connected power converter (inverter) regulates the dc voltage v_a at its input terminals, hence the output voltage of each dc/dc converter depends on the power balance between all the converters as will be described in Sect. 2. Such a condition introduces a reliability problem: in mismatched conditions the dc/dc converter providing the highest power will exhibit the highest output voltage, and depending on the mismatched profile, such a voltage could be higher than the rating of the output capacitor and MOSFET, which produces a circuit failure. Therefore, Sects. 3 and 4 propose an overvoltage protection for DMPPT systems in series connection. Finally, the performance of the proposed solution is evaluated in Sect. 5 using simulations and Sect. 6 closes the paper with the conclusions.

2 Distributed Maximum Power Point Tracking in Series-Connection

Commercial PV systems are formed by multiple panels connected in series. For example, Fig. 2 shows the current-vs-voltage and power-vs-voltage curves of two sets of three Kyocera KD300-80 panels, PV1 and PV2 respectively. In this figure PV1 (red line) is fully irradiated at $1000\,W/m^2$, while PV2 (blue line) is partially shaded with an equivalent irradiance of $500\,W/m^2$. Connecting both sets in a series array, as in Fig. 1(b), produces the current and power curves given in the dashed black line of Fig. 2: the mismatched array exhibits two LMPP due to the activation of the bypass diode associated to the shaded set PV2, where the global maximum power point, or GMPP, is the one at the right.

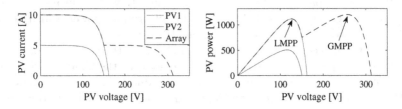

Fig. 2. Current and power curves of PV1, PV2 and the series-connected array. (Color figure online)

Then, if the mismatched PV array is forced to work at the first LMPP it produces 1115 W at 126.6 V, which is the same power produced by PV1 because PV2 is bypassed. Instead, if the PV array works at the GMPP it produces 1199 W at 257.3 V because PV2 produces power, but not the maximum one. However, if both PV1 and PV2 are able to work at their respective MPP, the PV system will produce 1621.7 W. That is the principle of the DMPPT approach.

2.1 DMPPT Circuit in Series-Connection

Figure 3 presents a DMPPT circuit based on the PV sets PV1 and PV2 and considering boost converters, which are widely used in DMPPT solutions [4, 5, 7].

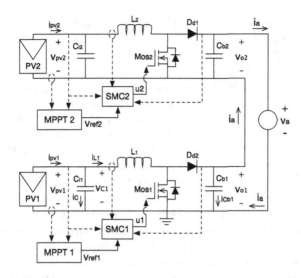

Fig. 3. DMPPT circuit for PV1 and PV2 based on boost converters.

The circuit includes two control loops for each PV set: an inner sliding-mode controller (SMC) to regulate the PV voltage and a cascade MPPT algorithm. The SMC has the objective of rejecting environmental and load perturbations to ensure the tracking of the MPPT reference, while the MPPT algorithm provides the voltage reference to reach the MPP. In this solution the sliding-mode control technique was adopted to ensure global stability and robustness to changes in the operation conditions, which are common problems in PV systems [8]. The MPPT algorithm adopted in this work is the perturb and observe (P&O), which is widely adopted due to its high efficiency and reduced cost [5,8].

In the circuit, the current i_a circulating by the output capacitors C_{b1} and C_{b2} is the same. Moreover, grid connected inverters regulate the dc voltage v_a at the input terminals, hence it is modeled using the voltage source v_a as proposed in [5]. This means that the sum of all the converters output voltages must be equal to v_a. In addition, since the current is the same for all the output capacitors, the output voltage of each converter is proportional to the output power of that converter. Those electrical conditions impose the output voltages for the dc/dc converters reported in (1), where N is the number of converters.

$$v_{oi} = \frac{P_{PVi}}{\sum_{j=1}^{N} P_{PVj}} \cdot v_a \qquad (1)$$

2.2 Overvoltage Condition in Mismatched Operation

In uniform conditions all the PV sets produce the same maximum power, hence from expression (1) it is concluded that the output voltages of the associated dc/dc converters is the same. This condition enables to define the voltage rating for the output capacitor and MOSFET, which could be set with a safe margin over the nominal value to account for transients. e.g. between 20% and 30%. For example, the DMPPT circuit in Fig. 3 consider $v_a = 400$ V, hence in uniform conditions the output voltages are $v_{o1} = v_{o2} = 200$ V. This means that the output capacitors and MOSFETs used to construct the circuit could be selected with voltage ratings of $V_{MAX} = 260$ V (30% safe margin).

However, from expression (1) is also concluded that, under mismatching conditions, the output voltages are not the same, in fact, they are proportional to the delivered power. For example, considering the operation conditions for PV1 and PV2 given in Fig. 2, the output voltage of the converter associated to PV1 is 275 V, which will destroy its components. Subsequently, the second converter must to support all the output voltage and it will be also damaged.

This overvoltage problem was firstly analyzed by Femia et al. in [5], where the authors demonstrate that under mismatching conditions some PV sets must not operate at the MPP to avoid damages. To illustrate this concept, the left side of Fig. 4 presents the possible operation conditions of the DMPPT circuit in Fig. 3 under the mismatched conditions given in Fig. 2: the optimal condition is defined by $v_{PV1} = 126.6$ V and $v_{PV2} = 115.7$ V, which produces 1621.7 W (GMPP without restrictions). However, that operating point will impose an output voltage $v_{o1} = 275$ V that damages the dc/dc converter associated to PV1. Therefore, the feasible operating conditions, which prevent damages in both dc/dc converters, must to exclude the operating points with overvoltages in v_{o1} or v_{o2}. The right side of Fig. 4 includes the overvoltage restrictions, which put in evidence the existence of new optimal conditions (GMPP with restrictions) that produce 1344.6 W. Therefore, the DMPPT system must to operate in some of those conditions to provided the highest power without damaging the circuit.

This problem was addressed in [7], where two independent linear controllers were designed to regulate the PV and output voltages. However, that solution is not able to ensure global stability, which reduces the PV system safety [8].

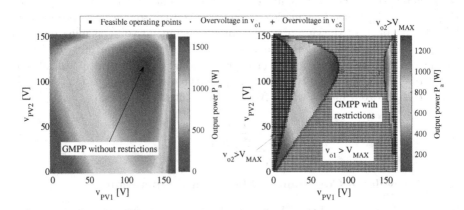

Fig. 4. Operation conditions of the DMPPT circuit in Fig. 3 under the mismatched conditions given in Fig. 2.

Therefore, the following section proposes a non-linear controller based on the sliding-mode technique to overcome those problems.

3   Sliding-Mode Controller

The design of the SMC is aimed at providing two control actions: tracking the reference provided by the MPPT algorithm and ensure the limitation of the output voltage of the dc/dc converter. However, those actions are exclusive since the output voltage limitation requires to diverge from the MPP condition as presented in Fig. 4. Therefore the following control objectives are defined: (1) without overvoltage condition the PV voltage must be controlled to follow the reference provided by the MPPT algorithm; (2) under overvoltage the output voltage must be controlled to a safe value near the feasible frontier.

To implement both actions in a single control circuit, the sliding function Ψ given in (2) and surface $\Phi = \{\Psi = 0\}$ are defined. In that surface k_{PV} and k_o are parameters that must be designed to impose a desired performance, while OV is the signal detecting the overvoltage condition, which could be generated using a comparator as described in Sect. 4.

$$\Psi = i_L - k_{PV} \cdot (v_{pv} - v_{ref}) \cdot (1 - OV) - k_o \cdot (v_o - V_{MAX}) \cdot (OV) \qquad (2)$$

The operation of Ψ and Φ are characterized for the two control objectives:

- MPPT mode $(OV = 0)$:

$$\Psi_{MPPT} = i_L - k_{PV} \cdot (v_{pv} - v_{ref}) \quad \wedge \quad \Phi_{MPPT} = \{\Psi_{MPPT} = 0\} \qquad (3)$$

- Overvoltage mode $(OV = 1)$:

$$\Psi_{OV} = i_L - k_o \cdot (v_o - V_{MAX}) \quad \wedge \quad \Phi_{OV} = \{\Psi_{OV} = 0\} \qquad (4)$$

Finally, from the DMPPT circuit in Fig. 3, the switched differential equations modeling the converter operation are given in (5), (6) and (7), where i_L represents the inductor current and u represents the MOSFET control signal.

$$\frac{d\, v_{pv}}{dt} = \frac{i_{pv} - i_L}{C_i} \qquad (5)$$

$$\frac{d\, v_o}{dt} = \frac{i_L \cdot (1 - u) - i_a}{C_b} \qquad (6)$$

$$\frac{d\, i_L}{dt} = \frac{v_{pv} - v_o \cdot (1 - u)}{L} \qquad (7)$$

3.1   MPPT Mode

The stability of the SMC depends on three conditions: transversality, reachability and equivalent control, which are described in detail in [8]. The transversality condition evaluates the ability of the controller to affect the system trajectory, i.e. the system controlability. The reachability conditions analyze the ability of the system to reach the surface. Finally, the equivalent control analyzes the saturation of the control signal. To implement a stable SMC those conditions must be fulfilled.

Transversality Condition is evaluated from expression (8) [8]. In that way, the derivative of Ψ_{MPPT} is given in (9), which considers constant the MPPT command. Finally, the transversality condition for this mode is verified in (10).

$$\frac{d}{du}\left(\frac{d\,\Psi_{MPPT}}{dt}\right) \neq 0 \quad (8)$$

$$\frac{d\,\Psi_{MPPT}}{dt} = \frac{d\,i_L}{dt} - k_{PV} \cdot \frac{d\,v_{pv}}{dt} = \frac{v_{pv} - v_o \cdot (1 - u)}{L} - k_{PV} \cdot \frac{i_{pv} - i_L}{C_i} \quad (9)$$

$$\frac{d}{du}\left(\frac{d\,\Psi_{MPPT}}{dt}\right) = \frac{v_o}{L} > 0 \quad (10)$$

Reachability Conditions are evaluated by verifying the correct sign of the switching function derivative in both sides of the surface [8]. Since in this operation mode the transversality is positive (10) the following inequalities must be fulfilled [8]:

$$\lim_{\Psi_{MPPT} \to 0^-} \frac{\Psi_{MPPT}}{dt}\bigg|_{u=1} > 0 \quad \wedge \quad \lim_{\Psi_{MPPT} \to 0^+} \frac{\Psi_{MPPT}}{dt}\bigg|_{u=0} < 0 \quad (11)$$

Replacing (9) into (11) leads to (12) and (13). Those expressions take into account the charge balance principle [6], which ensures a null steady state current in the input capacitor, hence in steady-state $i_{pv} = i_L$. Therefore, expressions (12) and (13) verify the reachability conditions because in a boost converter $v_{pv} < v_o$.

$$\lim_{\Psi_{MPPT} \to 0^-} \frac{\Psi_{MPPT}}{dt}\bigg|_{u=1} = \frac{v_{pv}}{L} > 0 \quad (12)$$

$$\lim_{\Psi_{MPPT} \to 0^+} \frac{\Psi_{MPPT}}{dt}\bigg|_{u=0} = \frac{v_{pv} - v_o}{L} < 0 \quad (13)$$

Equivalent Control Condition is verified by analyzing the range of the average value u_{eq} of the control signal u, which in dc/dc converters corresponds to the duty cycle. Hence, the equivalent control condition is given in (14).

$$0 < u_{eq} < 1 \quad (14)$$

The expression for u_{eq} is obtained by considering the existence of the sliding-mode [8], which means that the system is within the sliding surface and with a trajectory parallel to the surface. Those conditions are formalized as follows:

$$\Psi_{MPPT} = 0 \quad \wedge \quad \frac{d\,\Psi_{MPPT}}{dt} = 0 \quad (15)$$

From (15), the value of $u_{eq,MPPT}$ for this operation mode is given in (16). Then, evaluating the equivalent control condition (14) for (16) leads to the same inequalities (12) and (13) previously obtained in the reachability analysis.

$$u_{eq,MPPT} = 1 - \frac{v_{pv}}{v_o} \quad (16)$$

Equivalent Sliding-Mode Dynamics provide information about the closed-loop behavior of the system, which is useful to design the parameter k_{PV}. In this mode the surface (3) imposes the control law $i_L = k_{PV} \cdot (v_{pv} - v_{ref})$, which interacts with the differential equation of the PV voltage (5). The Laplace representation of (5) including the control law is given in (17).

$$v_{pv} = \frac{\frac{1}{k_{PV}}}{\frac{C_i}{k_{PV}} \cdot s + 1} \cdot i_{pv} + \frac{1}{\frac{C_i}{k_{PV}} \cdot s + 1} \cdot v_{ref} \tag{17}$$

From expression (17) it is noted that k_{PV} must be positive to ensure global stability. Moreover, the SMC provides null steady-state error with respect to the reference v_{ref}, however there exists a voltage deviation equal to $\frac{i_{pv}}{k_{PV}}$. Those conditions provide the guidelines to design k_{PV} as given in (18), where $\max(i_{pv})$ is to the maximum PV current, i.e. the short-circuit current, and Δv_{MPPT} is the acceptable voltage error, e.g. the voltage ripple or the MPPT resolution.

$$k_{PV} = \frac{\max(i_{pv})}{\Delta v_{MPPT}} > 0 \tag{18}$$

In any case, it must be noted that the cascade MPPT algorithm behaves as an integrator, hence the error Δv_{MPPT} will be compensated.

For the DMPPT circuit in Fig. 3, the maximum currents for both PV sets is $\max(i_{pv}) = 10\,\text{A}$ and the MPPT resolution will be set to 0.5 V, hence $\Delta v_{MPPT} = 0.5\,\text{V}$. Therefore, for that example, $k_{PV} = 20\,\text{A/V}$.

3.2   Overvoltage Mode

Transversality Condition is evaluated from expression (19) [8], where the derivative of Ψ_{OV} is given in (20) and the transversality is given in (21).

$$\frac{d}{du}\left(\frac{d\,\Psi_{OV}}{dt}\right) \neq 0 \tag{19}$$

$$\frac{d\,\Psi_{OV}}{dt} = \frac{d\,i_L}{dt} - k_o \cdot \frac{d\,v_o}{dt} = \frac{v_{pv} - v_o \cdot (1-u)}{L} - k_o \cdot \frac{i_L \cdot (1-u) - i_o}{C_b} \tag{20}$$

$$\frac{d}{du}\left(\frac{d\,\Psi_{OV}}{dt}\right) = \frac{v_o}{L} + \frac{k_o}{C_b} \cdot i_L > 0 \tag{21}$$

To ensure a single circuital implementation of both components of Ψ (2), both MPPT and Overvoltage modes must to have the same transversality sign. Moreover, in the subsections below is demonstrate that k_o must be negative to ensure global stability. Therefore, applying those constraints to expression (21) leads to (22), which limit the magnitude of k_o for a positive transversality.

$$|k_o| < \frac{C_b \cdot V_{MAX}}{L \cdot \max(i_{pv})} \tag{22}$$

Reachability Conditions in this operation mode account for a positive transversality (21), therefore the following inequalities must be fulfilled [8]:

$$\lim_{\Psi_{OV} \to 0^-} \frac{\Psi_{OV}}{dt}\bigg|_{u=1} > 0 \quad \wedge \quad \lim_{\Psi_{OV} \to 0^+} \frac{\Psi_{OV}}{dt}\bigg|_{u=0} < 0 \tag{23}$$

Replacing (20) into (23) leads to (24) and (25). Using the charge and flux balances in the capacitors and inductor [6], which provide the steady-state relations $i_{pv} = i_L$, $i_a = i_L \cdot d'$ and $v_{pv} = v_o \cdot d'$, it is demonstrated that expressions (24) and (25) are equivalent to (22).

$$\lim_{\Psi_{OV} \to 0^-} \frac{\Psi_{OV}}{dt}\bigg|_{u=1} = \frac{v_{pv}}{L} + k_o \cdot \frac{i_a}{C_b} > 0 \tag{24}$$

$$\lim_{\Psi_{OV} \to 0^+} \frac{\Psi_{OV}}{dt}\bigg|_{u=0} = \frac{v_{pv} - v_o}{L} - k_o \cdot \frac{i_L - i_a}{C_b} < 0 \tag{25}$$

Equivalent Control Condition is given in (14), and the analysis of u_{eq} is performed in the following conditions:

$$\Psi_{OV} = 0 \quad \wedge \quad \frac{d\,\Psi_{OV}}{dt} = 0 \tag{26}$$

From (26), the value of $u_{eq,OV}$ for this operation mode is given in (27). Then, evaluating the equivalent control condition (14) for (27) leads to the same inequalities (24) and (25) previously obtained in the reachability analysis.

$$u_{eq,OV} = 1 - \frac{\frac{v_{pv}}{L} + k_o \cdot \frac{i_a}{C_b}}{\frac{v_o}{L} + k_o \cdot \frac{i_L}{C_b}} \tag{27}$$

Equivalent Sliding-Mode Dynamics are based on the surface (4) that imposes the control law $i_L = k_o \cdot (v_o - V_{MAX})$, which interacts with the differential equation of the output voltage (6). The Laplace representation of the system is:

$$v_o = \frac{\frac{1}{k_o \cdot d'}}{-\frac{C_b}{k_o \cdot d'} \cdot s + 1} \cdot i_a + \frac{1}{-\frac{C_b}{k_o \cdot d'} \cdot s + 1} \cdot V_{MAX} \tag{28}$$

From expression (28) it is noted that k_o must be negative to ensure global stability. Moreover, the SMC provides null steady-state error with respect to the reference V_{MAX}, however there exists a voltage deviation equal to $\frac{i_a}{k_o \cdot d'} < 0$, which is negative since the converter always deliver power, i.e. $i_a > 0$. Those conditions provide the guidelines to design k_o as given in (29), where $\max(i_{pv})$ is the maximum PV current, i.e. short-circuit current, and Δv_o is the acceptable voltage error. This expression was calculated taking into account the steady-state relations $i_{pv} = i_L$ and $i_a = i_L \cdot d'$.

$$k_o = -\frac{\max(i_{pv})}{\Delta v_o} < 0 \tag{29}$$

In any case, it must be noted that the error Δv_o introduces an additional safety magnitude under the destruction limit V_{MAX}.

For the DMPPT circuit in Fig. 3 max $(i_{pv}) = 10$ A and the error magnitude was set to $\Delta v_o = 1$ V. Therefore, for that example, $k_o = -10$ A/V. Moreover, the example considers $L = 410 \ \mu H$ and $C_b = 200 \ \mu F$, hence the evaluation of (22) is $|k_o| < 12.6829$ A/V, which fulfills all the stability conditions.

4 Controller Implementation

To limit the switching frequency of the SMC, the controller is implemented using an hysteresis comparator as reported in [8]. Figure 5 shows the implementation of the hysteresis comparator in the power electronics simulator PSIM, which in this case imposes a hysteresis band of 0.2 A. The figure also presents the calculation of the switching function and the switches used to implement the transition between the MPPT and Overvoltage operating modes.

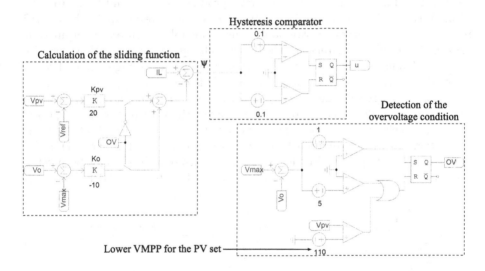

Fig. 5. Implementation of the proposed controller in PSIM.

The circuit to detect the overvoltage condition is also based on an hysteresis comparator to avoid chattering around V_{MAX}. The Overvoltage mode is triggered, using the signal OV, when the output voltage is 1 V higher than V_{MAX}, hence V_{MAX} must be, at least, 1 V under the destruction limit. Moreover, to finalize the Overvoltage mode, i.e. enter on MPPT mode, the circuit has two possible conditions: an output voltage 5 V lower than V_{MAX} or a PV voltage equal to the lower MPP voltage for that PV set. The last condition is introduced to avoid a large PV voltage disturbance.

Finally, the P&O algorithm was modified to include a new input OV, which stops the algorithm when the system is in Overvoltage mode. In this way the MPPT algorithm do not diverges far from the MPP zone in Overvoltage mode.

5 Simulation Results

The DMPPT system of Fig. 3 was implemented in PSIM. The simulation considers three environmental conditions: it starts with both PV1 and PV2 operating at $1000\,W/m^2$, which corresponds to the red curves in Fig. 2. Then, at 10 ms, PV2 suffers a partial shade that reduces the effective irradiance to $500\,W/m^2$, which corresponds to the mismatched conditions analyzed in Fig. 4. At 30 ms, PV1 is subjected to the same shade applied to PV1 ($500\,W/m^2$), hence both PV sets operate at the same irradiance and the system is in uniform conditions.

The results are presented in Fig. 6, where the output voltages of both dc/dc converters, v_{o1} and v_{o2}, are equal to 200 V up to 10 ms due to the uniform conditions ($1000\,W/m^2$). During this period the controller operates in MPPT mode, hence the PV voltages v_{pv1} and v_{pv2} follow the MPPT commands to drive the system to the GMPP: each PV set produces 1115 W, hence the DMPPT power is 2230 W. From 10 ms the MPPT controller of PV2 tracks the new MPP for $500\,W/m^2$, which is reached at 16 ms: PV1 produces 1115 W and PV2 produces 506.7 W (DMPPT power equal to 1621.7 W), which corresponds to the GMPP reported in Fig. 4 without restrictions. This is possible because the output voltages of the dc/dc converters are within the safe operation limit. However, due to the difference in the power production, the output voltage v_{o1} of PV1 is increasing while the output voltage v_{o2} of PV2 is decreasing.

At 22 ms v_{o1} reaches 261 V and the controller of PV1 enters in Overvoltage mode: the controller forces to operate in the GMPP with restrictions reported in Fig. 4, which effectively prevents the converter destruction and, at the same time, produces the maximum achievable power in that condition, i.e. a DMPPT power equal to 1344.6 W. Finally, at 30 ms the irradiance reaching both set is the same ($500\,W/m^2$), hence the controller of PV1 switches to MPPT mode.

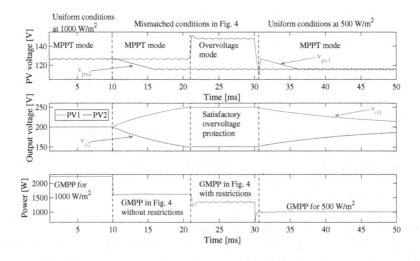

Fig. 6. Simulation of the proposed DMPPT solution in PSIM.

6   Conclusion

The safe operation conditions to extract the maximum power in a series-connected DMPPT circuit have been analyzed. Such information has been used to design a SMC able to protect the DMPPT circuit from overvoltage conditions.

The design equations of the SMC are applicable to any DMPPT circuit based on boost converters. Moreover, the concepts and controller are extendible to any number of dc/dc converters because the design process is modular: this means that, independent of the number of converters, each controller will protect the associated converter from overvoltage conditions.

Finally, the proposed structure could be also extended to other dc/dc converter topologies, such as buck or buck-boost, which are used in step-down and step-up/down applications, e.g. battery chargers, optimizers in micro-inverters.

Acknowledgments. This work was supported by the Universidad Nacional de Colombia and Colciencias (Fondo nacional de financiamiento para ciencia, la tecnología y la innovación Francisco José de Caldas) under the projects MicroRENIZ-25439 (Code 1118-669-46197) and DIGEMICRO-30773 and under the doctoral scholarship 095-2005.

References

1. Kabir, M.N., Mishra, Y., Ledwich, G., Dong, Z.Y., Wong, K.P.: Coordinated control of grid-connected photovoltaic reactive power and battery energy storage systems to improve the voltage profile of a residential distribution feeder. IEEE Trans. Ind. Inform. **10**(2), 967–977 (2014)
2. Romero-Cadaval, E., Spagnuolo, G., Franquelo, L.G., Ramos-Paja, C.A., Suntio, T., Xiao, W.M.: Grid-connected photovoltaic generation plants: components and operation. IEEE Ind. Electron. Mag. **7**(3), 6–20 (2013)
3. Spagnuolo, G., Petrone, G., Lehman, B., Ramos-Paja, C.A., Zhao, Y., Orozco, M.L.: Control of photovoltaic arrays: dynamical reconfiguration for fighting mismatched conditions and meeting load requests. IEEE Ind. Electron. Mag. **9**(1), 62–76 (2015)
4. Bastidas-Rodriguez, J.D., Franco, E., Petrone, G., Ramos-Paja, C.A., Spagnuolo, G.: Maximum power point tracking architectures for photovoltaic systems in mismatching conditions: a review. IET Power Electron. **7**(6), 1396–1413 (2014)
5. Femia, N., Lisi, G., Petrone, G., Spagnuolo, G., Vitelli, M.: Distributed maximum power point tracking of photovoltaic arrays: novel approach and system analysis. IEEE Trans. Ind. Electron. **55**(7), 2610–2621 (2008)
6. Erickson, R.W., Maksimovic, D.: Fundamentals of power electronics. Springer Science & Business Media (2007)
7. Ramos-Paja, C., Saavedra-Montes, A., Vitelli, M.: Distributed maximum power point tracking with overvoltage protection for pv systems. DYNA **80**(178), 141–150 (2013)
8. Gonzales, D., Ramos-Paja, C.A., Giral, R.: Improved design of sliding-mode controllers based on the requirements of mppt techniques. IEEE Trans. Power Electron. **31**(1), 235–247 (2016)

Discrete Time Nested-Loop Controller for the Output Stage of a Photovoltaic Microinverter

Oswaldo Lopez-Santos[✉], Luis Cortes-Torres, and Sebastián Tilaguy-Lezama

Program of Electronics Engineering, Universidad de Ibagué, Ibagué, Colombia
oswaldo.lopez@unibague.edu.co

Abstract. This paper presents a comprehensive study of the digital implementation of the control requirements of the output stage of a two-stage solar microinverter. This approach uses a synchronized nested-loop controller which ensures the tracking of an internally generated high-quality current reference, the estimation and cancelation of the effect of the DC-link voltage ripple in the control loops and the regulation of the average value of the DC-link voltage. The proposed control architecture is validated by means of simulation results comparing operation of the inverter using continuous time, quasi-discrete time and discrete time implementations.

Keywords: Microinverter · Two-stage microinverter · Cascade control · Nested-loop controller

1 Introduction

The output stage of a two-stage solar microinverter is a DC-AC grid-connected converter responsible for the conversion of the power obtained from the photovoltaic (PV) module through a DC-DC converter named as input stage. This last converter boosts the low-voltage of the PV module to an admissible level to feed the DC-AC converter named output stage. This two-stage architecture allows splitting the control functions of the microinverter facilitating its implementation and increasing the general performances [1–5]. Normally, the input stage integrates the Maximum Power Point Tracking (MPPT) function which implies a regulation of the input variables and some freedom of the output variables. For this reason, in addition to the function to provide a high-quality output current to be injected into the grid, the output stage is responsible for the power balance between both stages. This means that the amount of power injected into the grid corresponds accurately to the power produced by the PV module taken into account the power losses. This balance is established by means of the voltage regulation in the connection point between DC-DC and DC-AC stages named as DC-link or DC bus [6, 7]. Figure 1 represents a two-stage solar microinverter, identifying the conversion stages, the PV module, the grid and the DC-link connection point.

Recently, in [8], it have been proposed a continuous time control method for the output stage of a transformer-less two-stage solar microinverter [9], which uses a nested-loop controller in which the internal loop is developed using a sliding-mode current

J.C. Figueroa-García et al. (Eds.): WEA 2016, CCIS 657, pp. 320–331, 2016.
DOI: 10.1007/978-3-319-50880-1_28

controller and the outer loop uses a PI controller regulating the voltage at the DC-link. The performance of that controller was verified by means of simulation and experimental results. Subsequent to that work, a proposal suppressing the effect of the DC-link voltage ripple in the control loops was developed in [10] contributing increasing the power quality of the delivered energy and also allowing the size reduction of the coupling capacitor. One of the key aspects of the resulting control architecture is the generation of high-quality waveforms to obtain the current reference and the estimation of the mentioned voltage ripple. To cover this requirement a synchronization system was developed and presented in [11], allowing a simple generation of the required waveforms into a digital device. However, no results were reported hitherto translating the control problem to the discrete time in order to facilitate its real implementation in a single digital device. Hence, some efforts must be dedicated to disclose the effect of the digital implementation of this control over its static and dynamic performances.

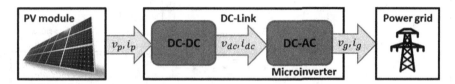

Fig. 1. Block diagram of the studied two-stage solar microinverter

Other works about microinverters reported implementation of the control in digital devices such as Digital Signal Processors (DSP) [12, 13], but nevertheless, only few of them clarify the discrete time concerns of that implementations [14]. The aim of this work is to present a complete understanding of the control of the output stage of a solar microinverter focused on its digital implementation and compare the obtained performance with the one obtained in continuous time. Three possibilities are analyzed: (a) all the control operating in continuous time suggesting implementation with analogue electronics, (b) current controller operating in continuous time and other functions in discrete time, and (c) all the control operating in discrete time suggesting a fully digital implementation. The rest of the paper is organized as follows: Sect. 2 present the general description of the control system separating the main functions. After that, in Sect. 3, discretization of the nested-loop controller is explained using partial simulation results. Section 4 is dedicated to give simulation results comparing continuous time, quasi-discrete time and fully discrete time versions of the overall control. Conclusions are presented in Sect. 5.

2   General Description of the Control System

In Fig. 2, a block diagram of the overall control including digitalization elements is depicted. The circuit diagram of the output stage of the studied solar microinverter is shown with the only purpose to relate the variables of the control system with the variables of the power converter. The control system can be decomposed in five key functions identified in Fig. 2.

1. Phase Locked Loop (PLL).
2. Sine-wave reference generator.
3. Hysteresis current controller.
4. DC-link voltage ripple estimator.
5. DC-link voltage controller.

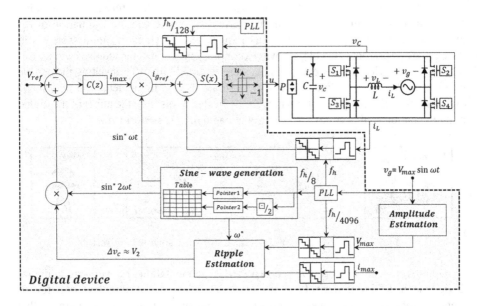

Fig. 2. Block diagram of the complete control system including discrete time elements

A measurement of the grid voltage v_g is used to obtain synchronization in frequency and phase through the use of a PLL ensuring unitary power factor. PLL generates square waves with frequencies 2^N multiple of the grid frequency in order to synchronize all the control functions. Internal configuration of the PLL is not presented in this paper.

The current and voltage controllers configure a nested-loop in which the DC-link voltage v_c is the slower variable. The inner loop (current controller) enforces the tracking of the current reference $i_{g_{ref}}$ over the inductor current i_L by means of a simple hysteresis comparator which can be implemented in both analogue and digital form. The main difference between these implementations is the delay effect introduced by the Analogue to Digital Acquisition (DAC) which accentuates chattering beyond the desired hysteresis band.

Because of the AC component in the DC-link voltage, we have introduced an estimation of this ripple to eliminate its effect in the control loops. This estimation requires the computation of the amplitude and also the generation of a sine waveform at the double frequency of the grid with null phase shift. Then, the DC-link voltage regulator eliminates the error using a reduced sampling rate. Figure 3 shows generated waveforms besides the generated sample frequencies.

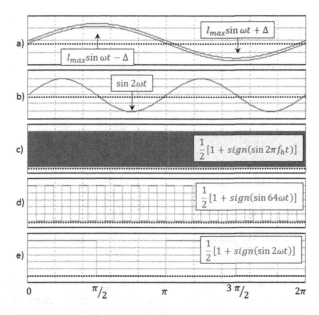

Fig. 3. Simulated waveforms: (a) hysteresis band around the current reference; (b) DC-link ripple waveform; (c) main PLL frequency; (d) sample frequency of the voltage regulator; (e) sample frequency of the ripple amplitude estimation.

3 Discretization of the Control Functions

The proposed control has been studied applying concepts of the general discrete time control theory [15], and also using particular characteristic of the digital control applied in power converters [16, 17]. Discretization of the reference generation and the nested loop controller are detailed below.

3.1 Generation of Discretized Sinusoidal References

Two sinusoidal normalized waveforms are required to cover the control requirements. The first one is the shape of the reference of the inner controller which must have the same frequency and phase of the grid voltage; and the second is the fundamental component of the DC-link voltage ripple which is used to cancel the ripple effect in controllers. In order to obtain a high level of power quality, the output current reference should be as similar as possible to the expression:

$$i_{g_{ref}}(t) = I_{max} \sin \omega t \tag{1}$$

Digital generation implies the presence of small steps in the signal due to the sampling and quantization effects. This corresponds to data losses which increases the THD of the generated signal. In order to have a high-quality reference, a minimum number of samples per period must be ensured. Table 1 shows a simple analysis of the

THD of a sine waveform using quantization of 8 bits for different sampling frequencies obtained as 2^N multiple of the grid frequency.

Table 1. THD of a sine waveform for differet sampling frequencies

Sampling frequency	THD
$4 f_g$	48.3%
$8 f_g$	23.0%
$16 f_g$	11.4%
$32 f_g$	5.71%
$64 f_g$	2.90%
$128 f_g$	1.55%
$256 f_g$	0.95%
$512 f_g$	0.07%
$1024 f_g$	0.06%

The presence of ripple content in the DC-link voltage measurement introduces undesirable harmonic content because the amplitude of the current reference is defined by the output of the voltage regulator in which the ripple reflects despite of the low-pass frequency response of the controller. Cancelation of that component in measurement is accomplished generating a sinusoidal waveform with double grid frequency whose amplitude is estimated as a function of the produced power with the expression:

$$v_{C_2}(t) = \Delta_{v_C} \sin 2\omega t \tag{2}$$

where Δ_{v_C} is defined as:

$$\Delta_{v_C} = \frac{\sqrt{\left(\omega L I_{max}^2\right)^2 + \left(V_{max} I_{max}\right)^2}}{4 C V_{dc} \omega} \tag{3}$$

where V_{max} and I_{max} use a sampling frequency of $f_h/4096$ (equivalent to the double grid frequency). The value of ω indicated in Fig. 2 is obtained from the input of the Voltage Controlled Oscillator (VCO) of the PLL an updated at the f_h clock frequency. Values of V_{dc}, C and L are considered as constants. As happens with the current reference, the accuracy generating the waveform can increase or decrease power quality considerably.

The proposed digital implementation uses an off-line sampled sine waveform stored in a table in order to obtain both references. Reproduction of the values in the table depends on the clock frequency given by the PLL. As it can be observed in Fig. 2, the voltage ripple reference is obtained by means of a reproduction of the table values at a sampling frequency of $f_h/8$ whereas the current reference uses a frequency of $f_h/16$. 512 samples per period are obtained for both references considering an acceptable trade-off between quality and memory occupation.

3.2 Discretization of the Current Loop

The sliding-mode approach can be successfully employed in the tracking of time-varying references in power converters [18–20]. The theoretical concept of sliding motion defines an infinite frequency to commute between the different dynamic structures of the system; however, the imposition of a finite switching frequency in power converters allows attaining the desired surface as the average of the resulting chattering. A variable switching frequency can be employed to implement this kind of control, but nonetheless, this requires of hysteresis comparators based in analogue electronics. The use of a Pulse Width Modulator (PWM), in fact, implies a discretization at the frequency of the carrier signal.

Some recent works have studied the effect of discretization in sliding-mode based current controllers of DC-DC converters but these approaches cannot be directly employ in the DC-AC case [21, 22]. In order to remain with the same spirit of the hysteresis comparator implementation in discrete time, some consideration must be taken into account:

- Discretization introduces a delay in the measurement of the current signal which will be reflected in the uniformity of the current ripple.
- Synchronization of the current measurement acquisition with the other control loops facilitates the design, analysis and implementation of the control system.
- Some constraints will appear related with computational limitations of the digital device and the desired range of switching frequency.

The approach developed in this paper uses a high frequency f_h generated by the PLL in order to synchronize the current control loop. This frequency is selected as 8192 times higher than the grid frequency in order to ensure that acquisition time of the digital device is covered even for the maximum admissible grid frequency. Having a switching frequency varying below 50 kHz, at least 10 samples per switching period will be obtained.

3.3 Discretization of the DC-Link Voltage Regulator

From [8], the ideal sliding dynamic of the DC-link voltage is defined by the following expression in frequency domain:

$$V_c(s) = -\frac{LI_{max}s + V_{max}}{2CV_{ref}s}I_{max}(s) + \frac{1}{CV_{ref}s}P(s) \tag{4}$$

From which, the DC-link voltage to output current transfer function (5) can be obtained assuming no power disturbances and neglecting the zero effect.

$$G_v(s) = \frac{V_c(s)}{I_{max}(s)} = -\frac{LI_{max}s + V_{max}}{2CV_{ref}s}I_{max}(s) \tag{5}$$

On the other hand, by adding the Zero Order Hold characteristic to the voltage controller, we have

$$C(s) = -\left(\frac{1 - e^{Ts}}{s}\right)\frac{K_c(T_c s + 1)}{s(T_f s + 1)}, \quad K_c, T_c, T_f > 0 \tag{6}$$

Then, the pulse transfer-function $C(z)$ in (7) is obtained from (6) by applying the Z transform:

$$C(z) = -K_c(1 - z^{-1})\mathcal{Z}\left\{\frac{T_c s + 1}{s^2(T_f s + 1)}\right\}$$

$$C(z) = K_c\left(\frac{T_a + (T_s - T_a)(1 + e^{-\alpha})z^{-1} - T_a e^{-\alpha}z^{-2}}{1 - (1 + e^{-\alpha})z^{-1} - e^{-\alpha}z^{-2}}\right) \tag{7}$$

where $\alpha = \dfrac{T_s}{T_f}$ and $T_a = T_c - T_f$.

As it was described before, the sampling frequency is selected in order to have a stable and robust behavior of this control loop, similar with the one found for implementation in continuous time. Therefore, a 2^N multiple of the grid frequency must be selected to maintain synchronization of all control loops. As it is illustrated in Fig. 4, the location of the poles into the unitary circle depends on the sampling frequency more than the injected current.

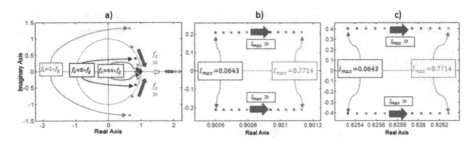

Fig. 4. Locus of the closed-loop system considering different sampling frequencies and different values of the output current amplitude.

Using a higher sampling frequency, the poles of the controller are located near to the point $(-1,0)$ which is difficult to implement without increase the computational cost because of the use of more digits to the right of the decimal place. On the other hand, reducing the sampling frequency can lead the system to instability. A sampling frequency between 8 and 64 times the grid frequency is adequate to preserve stability ensuring an accurate implementation. Also, Fig. 4 shows that the effect of the uncertainty in the amplitude of the injected current in the root location is negligible.

Figure 5 shows simulated results comparing the response of both continuous and discrete time implementations of the control when increasing and decreasing power disturbances are applied. Parameters of simulations are listed in Table 2. Graphics show

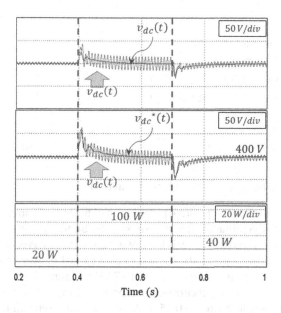

Fig. 5. Transient responses of the DC-link voltage regulation loop coping with power disturbances at 0.4 and 0.7 s.

simultaneously the simulation of the circuit with the corresponding simulation of the model (continuous and discrete). As it can be note, no important differenced appears as effect of discretization confirming an adequate selection of the sampling frequency of this loop.

4 Simulated Results

In order to verify the correct operation of the output stage of the microinverter using the proposed discrete time implementation, several simulations have been realized obtaining a comparison between two operation conditions of the converter: fully continuous time and fully discrete time. Parameters of the converter in Table 2 are used in all simulations. The continuous time controller is given by the transfer function:

$$C(s) = \frac{0.02418(0.06\,s + 1)}{s(0.005\,s + 1)} \tag{8}$$

Conversely, the discrete time controller is given by the impulse transfer function (9) using a sampling frequency of 16 times the grid frequency.

$$C(z) = \frac{0.003244z^{-1} + 0.003177z^{-2}}{1 - 1.779z^{-1} + 0.7788z^{-2}} \tag{9}$$

Table 2. Converter and control parameters

Converter parameters			
Parameter	Symbol	Value	Units
Nominal grid voltage	V_g	220	V
Nominal grid frequency	f_g	50	Hz
DC-link voltage	V_{ref}	400	V
DC-link capacitor	C	27	µF
Coupling Inductor	L	10	mH

4.1 Steady State Behavior of the Output Current

Figure 6a shows a detail of the positive peak region of the output current when converter operates with a fully continuous time control system. Simulation uses a reference with an amplitude of 0.65 A, and a hysteresis band of ±0.25 A. As observed in the enlargement of the current waveform below, the current is constrained between the desired limits establishing a switching frequency of around 17 kHz. Figure 6b shows a detail of the positive peak region of the output current corresponding to a reference with an amplitude of 0.65 A, and a hysteresis band of ±0.25 A. As observed, discretization of measurement introduces overflow of the current outside of the hysteresis band. This behavior reduce the switching frequency to 15 kHz because the on and off intervals are slightly longer. Also, the ripple of the current lengthens until 0.1 A (40% of Δ).

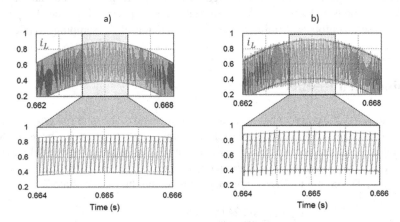

Fig. 6. Output current waveform in the peak region: (a) continuous time current control, detail of 6 ms (top) and detail of 2 ms (bottom), (b) discrete time current control, detail of 6 ms (top) and detail of 2 ms (bottom).

4.2 Transient Response to Power Disturbances

In order to evaluate the dynamic behavior of the converter variables using continuous time and discrete time control implementations, different test with increasing and decreasing power disturbances were applied. Figures 7 and 8 depict current and voltage waveforms of the DC-AC stage of the microinverter operating with continuous time and discrete time respectively. The input power starts in 20 W at 0.2 s until 0.4 s when the power increases to 100 W. After that, in 0.7 s, the power decreases to 40 W. As observed, converter shows a stable operation and an optimum transient response despite the magnitude of the applied disturbances. There are no notable differences between both versions of the control beyond an increment of 20 V in the voltage overshoot (5%). The capture at the right-side of Figs. 7 and 8 shows the correspondence in the steady-state behaviors of both types of control.

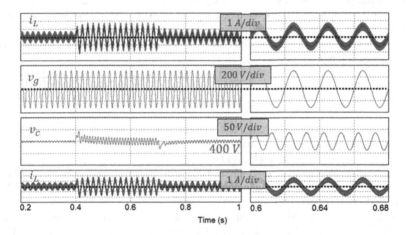

Fig. 7. Transient responses of the DC-AC converter variables for converter operating with continuous time control.

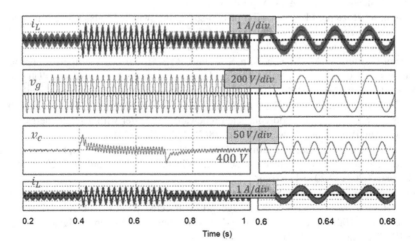

Fig. 8. Transient responses of the DC-AC converter variables for converter operating with digital control.

5 Conclusions

A fully digital implementation of the control of the output stage of a solar microinverter has been presented evaluating its performance in comparison with the continuous time version of the same control. Evaluation of the THD has shown that the digitalization information losses do not introduce significant negative effects, showing the advantages to integrate the control in a digital device. It has been confirmed that the proposed implementation shows good static and dynamic performance which merits the effort to develop experimental version to completely validate the approach.

Acknowledgements. This research is being developed with the partial support of the Gobernación del Tolima under Convenio de cooperación 1026 - 2013 - Research Culture. The results presented in this paper have been obtained with the assistance of students from the Research Hotbed on Power Electronic Conversion (SICEP), Research Group D+TEC, Universidad de Ibagué, Ibagué-Colombia.

References

1. Jiang, S., Cao, D., Li, Y., Peng, F.Z.: Grid-connected boost-half-bridge photovoltaic microinverter system using repetitive current control and maximum power point tracking. IEEE Trans. Power Electron. **27**(1), 4711–4722 (2012)
2. Patrao, I., Figueres, E., González-Espín, F., Garcerá, G.: Transformerless topologies for grid-connected single-phase photovoltaic inverters. Renew. Sustain. Energy Rev. **15**(7), 3423–3431 (2011)
3. Ahmed, M.E.S., Orabi, M., Abdelrahim, O.M.: Two-stage micro-grid inverter with high-voltage gain for photovoltaic applications. IET Power Electron. **6**(9), 1812–1821 (2013)
4. Gazoli, J.R., Villalva, M.G., Siqueira, T.G., Ruppert, E.: Micro-inverter for integrated grid-tie PV module using resonant controller. In: Proceedings IEEE Power and Energy Society General Meeting, San Diego, CA, pp. 1–8 (2012)
5. Zengin, S., Boztepe, M.: Evaluation of two-stage soft-switched flyback micro-inverter for photovoltaic applications. In: Proceedings 8th International Conference on Electrical and Electronics Engineering (ELECO), Bursa, pp. 92–96 (2013)
6. Karimi-Ghartemani, M., Khajehoddin, S.A., Jain, P., Bakhshai, A.: A systematic approach to DC-bus control design in single-phase grid-connected renewable converters. IEEE Trans. Power Electron. **28**(7), 3158–3166 (2013)
7. Khajehoddin, S.A., Karimi-Ghartemani, M., Jain, P.K., Bakhshai, A.: DC-bus design and control for a single-phase grid-connected renewable converter with a small energy storage component. IEEE Trans. Power Electron. **28**(7), 3245–3254 (2013)
8. Lopez-Santos, O., Garcia, G., Martinez-Salamero, L., Avila-Martinez, J.C., Seguier, L.: Non-linear control of the output stage of a solar microinverter. Intl. J. Control, 1–20 (2015). doi: 10.1080/00207179.2015.1116126
9. Lopez-Santos, O., Martinez-Salamero, L., Garcia, G., Valderrama-Blavi, H.: Sliding-mode control of a transformer-less dual-stage grid-connected photovoltaic micro-inverter. In: Proceedings 10th IEEE International Multi-Conference on Systems, Signals & Devices (SSD), Tunisia, pp. 1–6 (2013)

10. Lopez-Santos, O., Garcia, G., Martinez-Salamero, L., Cortes-Torres, L.: Suppressing the effect of the DC-link voltage ripple on the current control of a sliding-mode controlled microinverter. In: Proceedings Chilean Conference on Electrical, Electronics Engineering, Information and Communication Technologies (CHILECON), pp. 447–452 (2015)
11. Lopez-Santos, O., Garcia, G., Avila-Martinez, J.C., Gonzalez-Morales, D.F., Toro-Zuluaga, C.: A simple digital sinusoidal reference generator for grid-synchronized power electronics applications. In: Proceedings IEEE Workshop on Power Electronics and Power Quality Applications (PEPQA), pp. 1–6 (2015)
12. Lai, W.F., Chen, S.M., Liang, T.J., Lee, K.W., Ioinovici, A.: Design and implementation of grid connection photovoltaic micro inverter. In: IEEE Energy Conversion Congress and Exposition (ECCE), Raleigh, NC, pp. 2426–2432 (2012)
13. AN1338, Application Note.: Grid-Connected Solar Microinverter Reference Design Using a dsPIC® Digital Signal Controller. Microchip Technology Inc., pp. 1–56 (2011)
14. Jiang, S., Cao, D., Li, Y., Peng, F.Z.: Grid-connected boost-half-bridge photovoltaic microinverter system using repetitive current control and maximum power point tracking. IEEE Trans. Power Electron. **27**(11), 4711–4722 (2012)
15. Ogata, K.: Discrete-Time Control Systems, 2nd edn, pp. 1–994. Prentice Hall, Englewood Cliffs (1995)
16. Buso, S., Mattavelli, P.: Digital control in power electronics. In: Lectures on Power Electronics, pp. 1–158. Morgan & Claypool Publishers (2006)
17. Emadi, A., Khaligh, A., Nie, Z., Lee, Y.J.: Integrated Power Electronic Converters and Digital Control, pp. 1–350. CRC Press (2009)
18. Jiabing, H., Zhu, Z.Q., Nian, H., Shang, L., He, L.: Sliding mode current control of grid-connected voltage source converter. In: Proceedings of the IEEE Energy Conversion Congress and Exposition (ECCE), pp. 912–919 (2010)
19. Kim, I.-S.: Sliding mode controller for the single-phase grid-connected photovoltaic system. Appl. Energy **83**, 1101–1115 (2006)
20. Flores-Bahamonde, F., Valderrama-Blavi, H., Bosque-Moncusi, J.M., García, G., Martínez-Salamero, L.: Using the sliding-mode control approach for analysis and design of the boost inverter. IET Power Electron. **9**(8), 1625–1634 (2016)
21. Marcos-Pastor, A., Vidal-Idiarte, E., Cid-Pastor, A., Martinez-Salamero, L.: Interleaved digital power factor correction based on the sliding-mode approach. IEEE Trans. Power Electron. **31**(6), 4641–4653 (2016)
22. Vidal-Idiarte, E., Carrejo, C.E., Calvente, J., Martinez-Salamero, L.: Two-loop digital sliding mode control of DC–DC power converters based on predictive interpolation. IEEE Trans. Industr. Electron. **58**(6), 2491–2501 (2011).

Comparative Study of Optical Filtering Schemes for Convergent Access Network

Oscar Julian Castiblanco-Pardo, Joan Camilo Valencia-Montaña, and Gustavo Adolfo Puerto-Leguizamón[✉]

Universidad Distrital Francisco José de Caldas, Bogotá, Colombia
{ojcastiblancop,
jcvalenciam}@correo.udistrital.edu.co,
gapuerto@udistrital.edu.co

Abstract. Searching for solutions to cope with the increasing demand of bandwidth in communications networks, the approach of sending Radio Frequency (RF) signals through optical fiber has raised as a potential solution to this issue. Such architecture is known as radio over fiber system (RoF). In order to enhance these kinds of systems, it is necessary to improve the optical reception to efficiently detect both signals (baseband and RF). This paper presents the summarized results of the comparative study of three optical filtering schemes: Fabry-Perot filter, Fiber Bragg Gratings (FBG) and Sagnac interferometer through the analysis of the Bit Error Rate (BER) obtained by simulations.

Keywords: Optical fibers · Fabry-Perot · Bragg gratings · Sagnac interferometers · Birefringence

1 Introduction

Second generation of optical networks are the evolution of optical data networks that besides they make a simple point to point transmission, they include tasks of routing and switching and include some functions related to control, management and network protection as well. At the same time it provides a mean for saving equipment and optoelectronics conversion, therefore, the concept of optical layer is introduced.

For the development of RF systems operating at Extremely High Frequencies (EHF), it is shown issues like the equipment's cost of electronic used, increased number of base stations, and increased power required for the transmission of data in the wireless environment, these problems in implementation can be solved through RoF technology, since the optical fiber has high immunity to electromagnetic interference, high transmission capacity and propagation losses independent of the frequency with values ranging between 0.2 and 0.5 dB/km [1, 2].

That is why convergence of wireless communications with the fiber optic systems are presented as a technical solution to improve wireless services distribution due to the need of flexibility and mobility of users and the increasing bandwidth consumption [1, 3]. This paper evaluates the use of optical filters in a RoF communication system by

J.C. Figueroa-García et al. (Eds.): WEA 2016, CCIS 657, pp. 332–342, 2016.
DOI: 10.1007/978-3-319-50880-1_29

adding filtering modules before optical detection of the combined baseband and RF signals. While the baseband was conveyed on 1550 nm, this work evaluates the separation of RF signals ranging from 1 GHz to 60 GHz.

2 Optical Filters

2.1 Fabry-Perot Filter

The Fabry-Perot interferometer (or multibeam), is a cavity formed by two highly reflective mirrors located in parallel one beside the other (see Fig. 1). It is extensively used today due to the fact that beside being an electro-optical device of high resolution power, it is used also as resonant cavity in lasers or as tunable optical filters [4].

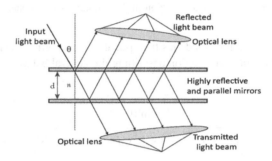

Fig. 1. Fabry-Perot interferometer. Taken from [5]

Its basic operation consists of a light beam that enters the filter through the first reflecting surface, the filter output is the light beam exiting from the second surface, the reflected rays pass through the first surface again and through lenses are combined to obtain a single signal [6].

Considering that the mirrors are manufactured using the same material and can be considered identical, the transfer function of energy of Fabry-Perot filter is (see [6]):

$$T_{FP}(f) = \frac{\left(1 - \frac{A}{1-R}\right)^2}{\left(1 + \left(\frac{2\sqrt{R}}{1-R}\sin(2\pi f \tau)\right)^2\right)} \qquad (1)$$

where A indicates the absorption loss of each mirror, which means, the fraction of incident light that is absorbed by the mirror, R indicates the reflectivity of each mirror (which should be identical), the reflectivity is defined as the fraction of incident light that is reflected by the mirror, τ is the one-way propagation delay through the cavity, the refractive index of the cavity is denoted by n and the length by l, and $\tau = nl = C$, where C is the speed of light in vacuum.

2.2   Fiber Bragg Gratings (FBG)

The Fiber Bragg grating filter consists of periodic perturbations in the optical fiber, such perturbation is done through exposure of the core to a pattern of rays or beams of ultraviolet light as seen in Fig. 2.

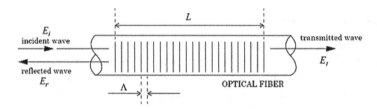

Fig. 2. FBG with constant periodic variation in the refractive index change. Taken from [8]

When the ultraviolet light irradiates the optical fiber, its refractive index is changed permanently [7]. The transfer function describing the general behavior of the fiber FBG is given by [8]:

$$T(f) = \frac{k \cdot \sinh\left(\sqrt{k^2 - \xi^2}\right)}{\xi \cdot \sinh\left(\sqrt{k^2 - \xi^2}\right) + j\left(\sqrt{k^2 - \xi^2}\right) \cdot \cosh\left(\sqrt{k^2 - \xi^2}\right)} \tag{2}$$

where k defines the coupling factor between fields counter-propagated, that is, the waves E_i and E_r, and ξ represents the normalized frequency offset of the central frequency of filter.

We can also find k as the maximum reflectivity of the FBG fiber and it is given by:

$$R_{max} = jE_r = E_{ij}$$

The magnitude of change in the refractive index Δn depends on several factors such as irradiation conditions, the intensity, the dose of light irradiation and also factors such as the composition of the fiber core and some process before writing of the grid in the fiber to be used as filter [9]. The purpose of the refractive index modulation is the phase matching in the core of the fiber, so that, within the signal is counter-spread with its counterpart to generate a strong reflection in the stopband [8].

2.3   Sagnac Interferometer

A Sagnac interferometer is a fiber loop connected to a fiber optic directional coupler of four ports, the coupler has a division ratio of wave amplitude α as seen in Fig. 3.

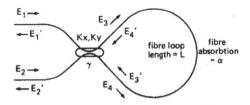

Fig. 3. General diagram of a Sagnac interferometer. Taken from [10]

The transfer function of the Sagnac interferometer can be expressed as [10]:

$$\begin{pmatrix} E_{3n} \\ E_{4n} \end{pmatrix} = (1 - \gamma)^{1/2} \begin{pmatrix} (1 - K_n)^{1/2} & jK_n^{1/2} \\ jK_n^{1/2} & (1 - K_n)^{1/2} \end{pmatrix} \begin{pmatrix} E_{1n} \\ E_{2n} \end{pmatrix} \tag{3}$$

where E_{mn} with (m = 1, 2, 3, 4 and n = x, y) are the field complex amplitudes, K_n is the field intensity of coupling for polarization in x and y, and γ represents the excess losses of the coupler.

When the incident light beam arrives at the coupler, it enters port 1 and is divided to exit through the port 3 and 4 in the main loop, the light beam exiting the port 3 rotates clockwise and the port 4 in anticlockwise direction. When both signals return to the coupler the physical phenomenon of interference occurs. α constant is usually 0.5, so fifty percent of the input signals travels clockwise and the other fifty percent anti-clockwise. Light that passes through the coupler and travels through the waveguide experiences a phase delay of $\pi/2$ with respect to the other beam. The transmitted light intensity on port 2 is equal to the sum of the signal anti-clockwise with phase $\pi/2$, the clock signal with relative phase equal to π and both of equal amplitude [11].

3   System Description

A RoF communication model in which both baseband and RF signals are combined and transported over an optical fiber link is proposed. Prior to the signal detection, optical filtering of the combined signal is carried out so that each one enters a section for independent detection. The modeling system is depicted in Fig. 4. Introducing optical filtering into the detection process improves the system performance and reduces the BER values in convergent networks based on RoF because the carrier suppression effect that occurs with direct detection of the optical field is eliminated [12, 13]. The transmitter delivers a baseband with a Pseudorandom Bit Sequence (PRBS), Non Return to Zero (NRZ) encoded at 1.25 Gb/s and a RF signal featuring the same codification but transmitted at 625 Mb/s onto subcarriers values from 1 GHz to 60 GHz. Specific details of the RoF transmitter for convergent access networks can be found in [14].

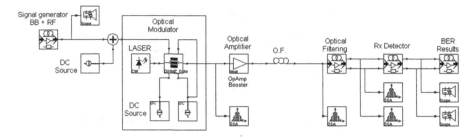

Fig. 4. Layout of the system for the evaluation of filtering techniques in RoF access networks

Every filtering scheme (Fabry-Perot, FBG and Sagnac interferometer) were modeled in the Virtual Photonics Inc. simulation tool where relevant parameters of each filtering technique were parameterized in order to assess the performance for the proper filtering of baseband and RF signals.

It is important to point out that while both Fabry-Perot and FBG filters have pre-defined modules in the simulation tool, the Sagnac interferometer does not have a representational module that implement its functionality. Therefore, a scheme based on the physical theory and its transfer function was developed as seen in Fig. 5. Thus, two loops of birefringent optical fiber were overlapped and linked together using a directional coupler; two polarization controllers were added in order to emulate the birefringence of the fiber.

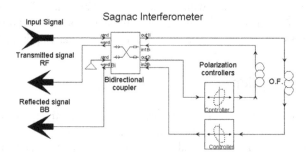

Fig. 5. Scheme developed for a Sagnac Interferometer-based filtering

4   Results

After performing the conducted simulations by varying the RF frequency signal between 1 and 60 GHz and also the link length from 5 km to 100 km, the BER for the transported signals were computed for each filtering scheme. The obtained with the Fabry-Perot filter are shown in Fig. 6, the parameters used for this filter are FSR of 60 GHz and a mirror transmission coefficient equal to 0.1. Figure 6(a) shows the BER performance for the baseband and RF signal at different link lengths where red area represents the BER's optimal values (between 7.893×10^{-28} and 2.933×10^{-9}).

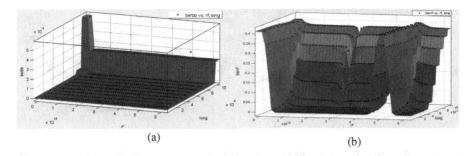

(a)   (b)

Fig. 6. BER performance using Fabry-Perot filters. (a) Baseband signal. (b) RF signal. X-axis: RF frequency [Hz], Y-axis: link length [km], Z-axis: BER level. (Color figure online)

Note that in blue and yellow areas, the obtained BER exceeded the optimal reference level (1×10^{-7}). It is noted that the filtering of the baseband signal is not affected by variations on the link length or RF signal. In Fig. 6(b) the BER performance for RF signal is analyzed, it can be seen that most of the surface area represents high levels of BER. However, in the red area minimum values are found between 5 and 30 km of the link length and two spams of frequencies, one from 9 GHz to 41 GHz and the other from 59 GHz to 60 GHz.

To identify the combination of RF frequency and link length at which the BER level is optimum, a data filtering was performed and relevant results are shown in Fig. 7. Figure 7(a) shows the points that represent a BER value lower than 1×10^{-7} for RF and baseband signals. Figure 7(b) represents in three dimensions the BER behavior and the BER level that represent each point. Is important to clarify that the yellow area contains no data, it is simply a graphic tool connecting points across the surface.

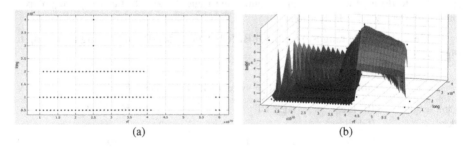

(a)   (b)

Fig. 7. Optimum BER values for RF and baseband using Fabry-Perot filters. (a) Obtained data with optimal BER. (b) BER level for each optimum point value. X-axis: RF frequency [Hz], Y-axis: link length [km], Z-axis: BER level.

As far as the FBG filtering system is concerned, the parameterization included the grating length that was analyzed from 5 cm to 25 cm, a Blackman apodization profile and a delta n parameter equal to $12e^{-5}$, the BER obtained in baseband signal is shown in Fig. 8(a). This graph shows that most of the BER values obtained are lower than 1×10^{-7} (red area, bottom of the graph), i.e., the baseband signal is not affected and two points have high error rates in the yellow area featuring BER values of 12 and 1×10^{-6}.

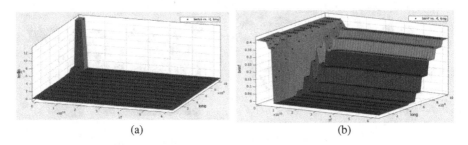

(a)   (b)

Fig. 8. BER performance using FBG filters. (a) Baseband signal. (b) RF signal. X-axis: RF frequency [Hz], Y-axis: link length [km], Z-axis: BER level. (Color figure online)

BER performance for RF signal is shown in Fig. 8(b), the red area at the bottom of the graph contains lower levels of BER in which the FBG filtering works properly. In Fig. 9(a), the values of this area have leaked and present a BER levellower than 1×10^{-7} and in Fig. 9(b) the BER level is represented for each one of the points.

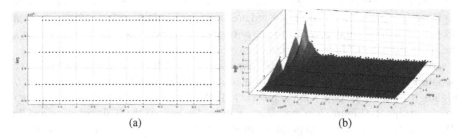

(a)   (b)

Fig. 9. Optimum BER values for RF and baseband using FBG filters. (a) Obtained data with optimal BER. (b) BER level for each optimum point value. X-axis: RF frequency [Hz], Y-axis: link length [km], Z-axis: BER level.

Table 1 shows the ranges of optimal BER for the Fabry-Perot filtering according to Figs. 7, 8 and 9.

Table 1. Optimal BER of system with Fabry-Perot filtering

Link length [km]	RF Freq. [GHz]	BER RF	BER baseband
5	9 to 41	2.52×10^{-28} to 3.73×10^{-8}	5.62×10^{-28} to 7.28×10^{-28}
5	59 to 60	7.67×10^{-10} to 3.21×10^{-8}	5.84×10^{-28} to 6.03×10^{-28}
10	10 to 41	1.32×10^{-26} to 8.52×10^{-8}	6.03×10^{-28} to 7.80×10^{-28}
10	59	2.94×10^{-9} to 7.23×10^{-8}	6.47×10^{-28} to 6.27×10^{-28}
20	60	8.59×10^{-21} to 8.26×10^{-8}	1.27×10^{-27} to 1.08×10^{-27}
30	25	6.971×10^{-14}	5.515×10^{-27}
40	25	2.983×10^{-8}	1.579×10^{-25}

Table 2. Optimal BER of system with FBG filtering

Link length [km]	RF Freq. [GHz]	BER RF	BER BB
5	8 to 60	4.13×10^{-37} to 2.25×10^{-10}	6.07×10^{-86} to 7.77×10^{-83}
10	8 to 60	2.93×10^{-30} to 1.23×10^{-8}	3.35×10^{-87} to 4.30×10^{-84}
20	9 to 60	1.28×10^{-17} to 2.10×10^{-8}	1.54×10^{-87} to 7.15×10^{-86}
30	10 to 60	3.19×10^{-9} to 7.06×10^{-8}	2.18×10^{-87} to 1.09×10^{-86}

Table 2 shows the ranges in which optimal BER of the FBG filtering system are specified according to data discussed above.

Finally, the results for a placement of a Sagnac interferometer with an inner loop length of 5 m and an external loop length of 20 m before the detection module are shown in Fig. 10. Figure 10(a) shows the results obtained for the baseband signal. The Sagnac interferometer presents optimal BER values in the red area. However, it is necessary to analyze the BER optimal level for the RF signal to better define the working range. In Fig. 10(b), the Sagnac filter response is shown. Similarly to the response of the previous filters analyzed, a curve of BER values is observed where some bit error values are optimal in the red area for the RF signal detection.

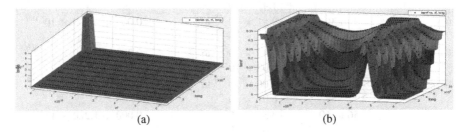

(a)   (b)

Fig. 10. BER performance using a Sagnac interferometer filter. (a) Baseband signal. (b) RF signal. X-axis: RF frequency [Hz], Y-axis: link length [km], Z-axis: BER level. (Color figure online)

Since not all the values of the red area are optimal for a correct detection, a more selective graph where only BER values lower than or equal to 1×10^{-7} are shown in Fig. 11. Thus, it can be determined that the amount of possible system configurations having an optimum BER level occurs at low link lengths (5 to 30 km), Fig. 11(a) shows that the Sagnac filter works at regular intervals while Fig. 11(b) shows their BER levels. It should be clarified that blue and yellow area does not have values.

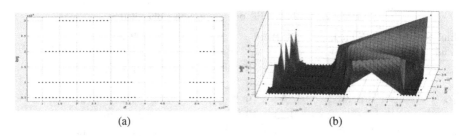

(a)   (b)

Fig. 11. Optimum BER values for RF and baseband using a Sagnac interferometer filter. (a) Baseband signal. (b) BER values. X-axis: RF frequency [Hz], Y-axis: link length [km], Z-axis: BER level. (Color figure online)

Table 3 shows the ranges in which optimal BER of the Sagnac filtering system are specified, according to data discussed above.

Table 3. Optimal BER of system with Sagnac filtering

Linking length [km]	RF Freq. [GHz]	BER RF Rank	BER BB Rank
5	8 to 37	5.95×10^{-44} to 6.50×10^{-8}	0.000 to 5.680×10^{-186}
5	53 to 60	1.07×10^{-32} to 1.45×10^{-9}	0.000 to 2.150×10^{-294}
10	9 to 36	9.51×10^{-35} to 4.41×10^{-9}	0.000 to 4.900×10^{-189}
10	53 to 60	4.44×10^{-25} to 6.03×10^{-8}	0.000 to 4.210×10^{-299}
20	11 to 34	1.06×10^{-19} to 6.01×10^{-8}	0.000 to 1.300×10^{-192}
20	56 to 60	3.38×10^{-13} to 2.64×10^{-8}	0.000 to 1.220×10^{-301}
30	15 to 29	6.01×10^{-11} to 6.40×10^{-8}	2.3×10^{-297} to 1.17×10^{-191}
30	60	9.440×10^{-8}	7.040×10^{-294}

5 Conclusions

The response of optical filters proposed in this study is favorable for separating baseband and RF signals in convergent networks because they allow obtaining optimal bit error rates for both signals transmitted by a single thread of optical fiber.

With the use of FBG filters in the optical system, an improved detection is performed as BER values lower than 1×10^{-7} are feasible for RF frequencies between 8 and 60 GHz and link lengths of up to 30 km. This type of filter allows greater applicability in convergent RoF networks.

Moreover, the system with Fabry-Perot filter presents a BER range lower than the FBG filtering scheme, however, it achieves an optimal BER value at 25 GHz and at a link length of 40 km.

The system based on a Sagnac interferometers obtained a similar performance as the Fabry-Perot filter featuring a maximum link length of 30 km and a more dynamic range of optimal BER values. The advantage of this type of filter is its selectivity and finesse since it allows for precise tuning of the frequency required for filtering. Based on this work, it was determined that by having a ring with a length longer than the other, for example 70 m and 7 m, the filter is more selective, i.e. it has a lower bandwidth. If the two rings have similar lengths, it can filter multiple signals at the same time as it reduces its free spectral range.

Based on the study of each filter, it can be determined that the performance of the FBG filter depends on the length of the Bragg gratings, as the longest this length, more selective is the filter. Also, it is necessary the use of an apodization profile to allow that the filtered signal has a rejection level higher than 20 dB.

The use of optical filters before the signal detection module is not only useful to improve this process, but also simplifies the signal reception since the need of a RF oscillator to perform the down conversion of the RF signal is avoided.

References

1. Varghese, A.T., Mohammed, E., Lajos, H.: Performance improvement and cost reduction techniques for radio over fiber communications. IEEE Commun. Surv. Tutorials **17**(2), 627–670 (2015)
2. López, E.: Estudio Teórico y Simulación de un OTDR para Sistemas de Comunicaciones por Fibra Óptica. Universidad Politécnica de Madrid (2013)
3. Jianxin, M., Yanjie, L.: A full-duplex multiband access radio-over-fiber link with frequency multiplying millimeter-wave generation and wavelength reuse for upstream signal. Opt. Commun. **334**, 22–26 (2015)
4. Ruiz, M.A.: Diseño de un Analizador de Espectros Ópticos Basado en un Filtro Sintonizable Fabry-Perot (2004)
5. Suliman, T., Subramaniam, S.: Fabry Perot Filter Analysis and Simulation Using Matlab (2012)
6. Ramaswami, R., Sivarajan, K., Sasaki, G.: Optical Networks: a Practical Perspective. Morgan Kaufmann, Burlington (2010)
7. Erdogan, T., Mizrahi, V., Lemaire, P., Monroe, D.: Decay of ultraviolet-induced fiber bragg gratings. J. Appl. Phys. **76**(1), 73–80 (1994)
8. VPI Systems: Photonic Modules Reference Manual, p. 1577 (2002)
9. Hill, K.O., Meltz, G.: Fiber bragg grating technology fundamentals and overview. J. Lightwave Technol. **15**(8), 1263–1276 (1997)
10. Mortimore, D.B.: Fiber loop reflectors. J. Lightwave Technol. **6**(7), 1217–1224 (1988)
11. Estudillo-Ayala, J., Kuzin, E., Ibarra-Escamilla, B., Rojas-Laguna, R.: Teoría del Interferómetro de Sagnac de Fibra de Baja Birrefringencia y Torcida. Rev. Mex. Fís. **47**(3), 271–274 (2001)
12. Xinying, L., Jiangnan, X., Yuming, X., Jianjun, Y.: QPSK vector signal generation based on photonic heterodyne beating and optical carrier suppression. IEEE Photonics J. **7**(5) (2015)

13. Puerto, G., Ortega, B., Capmany, J., Suárez, C.: Architecture and performance of optical packet switching router architecture for future Internet networks. Rev. Fac. Ing. Univ. Antioquia **55** (2010)
14. Puerto, G., Suárez, C.: Analytical model of signal generation for radio over fiber systems. DYNA **81**(188), 26–33 (2014)

Miscellaneous Applications

Design of a Telemedicine Ubiquitous Architecture Based on the Smart Device mHealth Arduino 4G

Yair E. Rivera-Julio[✉]

Systems Engineering Department, Universidad Simón Bolivar, Barranquilla, Colombia
yrivera2@unisimonbolivar.edu.co

Abstract. The paper focuses on the design of an open telematics architecture for telemedicine linked to a mobile ubiquitous device, a standalone device with direct connection to the cellular data network LTE (Long Term Evolution). The device when developed allows a multiplexing of biometric readings through adaptation of specialized Sensors and distributed in different parts of the body, which allow mapping the vitals signal: level of glycemia, Body Temperature Sensor, Blood Pressure Sensor, Pulse and Oxygen in Blood Sensor (SPO2), Airflow Sensor (Breathing), Galvanic Skin Response Sensor (GSR - Sweating), Electrocardiogram Sensor (ECG) and Electromyography Sensor (EMG). The system's modem (TELIT Le910) allows obtaining geo positioning signal of each patient in real time through GPS positioning GLONASS system. This set of data is sent and stored to a geographic health information system, where there is a specialized middleware for a geo-referencing related in real time with those specialized health services and their physical infrastructures. A whole technological system that allows to take advantage of the services 4g and the geographic information systems of health monitoring care of patients with chronic diseases in Colombia, where there are some remote areas and difficult access.

Keywords: LTE · Arduino · ECG · EMG · SPO2 · GPS · GLONASS

1 Introduction

Currently a wide range of services has been tested and implemented on closed systems solutions to an increasing extent in wireless transmission systems for the health; this is largely due to massive increase in mobile technologies in remote and difficult areas access, where multiple accesses to a data network through mobile devices was almost impossible. According to the quarterly newsletter of ICT in Colombia, during the fourth trimester of 2014, the total number of mobile users was (5565663), comprised of 3G users (3,751,593), users 4G (1,134,987) and finally 2G users (679,083) [1]. This massive increase in users is accompanied by the development of emerging technologies in the field of telemedicine and telemetry, which have enabled the implementation of ubiquitous services, implemented in medical high-end devices under a closed developed services, making it inflexible to implement changes, and are only affordable by large medical companies with a high price on the market [2]. On the other hand, it is necessary to optimize this type of mobile technologies oriented to telemedicine to access remote areas

© Springer International Publishing AG 2016
J.C. Figueroa-García et al. (Eds.): WEA 2016, CCIS 657, pp. 345–356, 2016.
DOI: 10.1007/978-3-319-50880-1_30

and difficult accessibility as it is the case of those departments of southern Colombia, near the Amazon, which aims to improve the health system in communities in particular: control of pregnancy, diagnosis and support in the treatment of chronic diseases as well as diseases and epidemics, training of health workers, and data collection remote by health system [3]. Based on the above, it wants to show a design of an open source architecture, centered on a modular design based on Arduino for telemedicine, which makes it flexible and easily adaptable to changes; An intelligent device, equipped with an autonomous and wireless connection to a cellular data network 4G via transmitter MODEM TELIT Le910. The device enables a real-time biometric census for the monitoring of the vital signs of each patient through specialized interfaces: level of glycemia, Body Temperature Sensor, Blood Pressure Sensor, Pulse and Oxygen in Blood Sensor (SPO2), Airflow Sensor (Breathing), Galvanic Skin Response Sensor (GSR - Sweating), Electrocardiogram Sensor (ECG) and Electromyography Sensor (EMG). While the modem (Telit 910) attached to the device obtains the geographic positioning of each patient, the whole data is sent over data network of the cellular network 4G and finally it is stored in a geographic information system of health on line. That would allow to maximize services and accented medical resources in fixed or mobile hospital infrastructures in a given time; equally important would be a connectivity for taking advantage of the logical resources of some medical specialists in remote areas.

In the section of related work shows a short description of the current technologies on mobile health apps. In the section of the platform and modeling development, it is intended to describe the architecture, components, and communication protocols used as well as the modeling of diagram platform, and the type of network communication data, which highlights the autonomy and ubiquity Connection of the device for patient monitoring. In the technological criteria selection section, a comparison of different wireless communication standards regarding LTE is established, At last, the health module results in the mobile application and data display are described.

2 Related Work

Currently the medical devices have raised some applications in telemedicine to monitor biometric signals wirelessly based on the concept of medical care, IE in the census and data storage without human intervention. Applications such as HeartMapp developed under Android, allow to have a constant reading of the cardiac signals and store the data locally or remotely, depending on whether it is connected to a data network or not; at this point the relevant data of each patient is related to define some significant trend [4]. With the foregoing, the mobile application depends on an ECG sensor for heart reading, which communicates via Bluetooth with the mobile device, making the architecture much more complex, as there is a point in the communication. Other similar technologies as the PATRIOT are functional in the cloud and try to show real-time readings doing synchronization services through the HTTP protocol, like the HeartMapp is involved 3-point communication, the signal processor for sensometria, the device Mobile (cell-phone), in which is taken as an extension or router for wireless communication via Bluetooth and finally the application server that stores data on the web [5]. All these solutions make relevance in an extension of communication for the census rather than an independent and direct connection device to the mobile data network; which makes the biometric sensor rely on an intermediate device in communication, so is added an additional and necessary delay in communication, and that also does not take into account the geo location of the patient as solution parameter [6]. The proposed architecture aims to show the sensometria directly connected to the data network, a range of direct connection with the LTE cellular network, which allows more data readings in the shortest time with minimum delay in transmission of data and a maximum yield of energy, thanks to the low power working this network [7].

3   Platform and Modeling Development

Through the new telematics, architecture is intended to provide a foundation for specialized services, which require high data transference with a minimal transmission delay, taking into account the mobility and Geo patient positioning. These services would be supported by technologies 4G LTE cellular network, which provides a high data transmission transference, 100 Mbps at moving and 1 Gbps at rest, to permit to establish a connection point-to-point and identified by a miniSIMCARD. The connectivity of all these mobile services would be based on an architecture designed in the IP protocol for both voice transfers as a for video and data, that makes easier potentiate the services associated with QoS (Quality of Service) [8], thus optimizing the transfers of information wirelessly. The development would be totally modular and flexible programmed under the open source Arduino controller, ensuring full connectivity and mobility in the Colombian territory or inaccessible areas [9].

3.1   Architecture of the m-Health Device

The modular development would be programmed in Arduino, a simplified version of C++, that lets you add open source libraries specialized according to the selected work modules, the Arduino one contains a master microcontroller ATmega328, able to perform tasks of high performance through 23 lines of general purpose, additionally has 32 records with 3 timers mode comparison, equipped with 54 digital inputs/outputs for values either digital or analog. Also contains a 16 MHz crystal oscillator crystal, making possible to obtain the values coded synchronously with other modules, for this particular case there would be the capture and coding of biometric signals; then, this data captures values that are necessary to check the vital state in all patients remotely through the modular e-Health Sensor plate PlatforV2.0 [10].

This synchronization is done directly between the 2 platforms through the port SPI (Serial Peripheral Interface), which is a serial communication standard for exchanging digital signals. Finally the synchronization between these two platforms is given dependently, a type of configuration (master/slave) between these modules establishes a multiplexed data for the collection and shipment of these encoded signals, which allows you to run a code for the census of several biometric signals with different sensors, and this communication would be regulated through 4 basic signals: SCLK (clock) synchronization bits, SS/Select: Select type of communication master/slave, MOSI (Master Output Slave Input): Output bit master and slave input bits and finally the signal the MISO (Master input Slave Output): output and input bits of the slave bit to master [11, 12].

3.2 Census and Transmission of Biometric Data

The signals captured by the biometric sensors are encoded and multiplexed by the e-Health Platform V2.0; an entire platform designed for adaptation of specialized sensors in the human body, the monitoring is realized through sensors: blood pressure (sphygmomanometer), patient position (accelerometer) and muscle/eletromyography sensor (EMG), pulse, oxygen in blood (SPO2), airflow (breathing), body temperature, electrocardiogram (ECG), glucometer, galvanic skin response (GSR - sweating). The census data is taken in real time and the encoded data are sent for processing via SPI communication port. From the coding of this type of biometric signal, the motherboard can get these values for making data vectors; The vectors are transformed to be sent and stored in a data base server on the web along with the geographical location of each patient [13]. For the data transmission is established a Wireless communication of low power through the TELIT Le910 4G modem, which allows a direct connection to the TCP/IP data network of the LTE cellular network; the technology allows the speed of up to 100 Mbps downstream moving and 1 Gbps at rest, 50 Mbps data raise and a bandwidth of 20 MHz, this significant increase in rate transmission is due to the implementation of the modulation (64 QAM) joint a new techniques set in antennas for sending and receiving multiple signals MIMO (multiple Input multiple Output), a specialized configuration that promotes the implementation of multiple antennas for sending and receiving data [14].

On the other hand the modem to the main controller M-health is connected via a standardized interface XBEE, by which compatible with the transmission of HSPA data (High Speed Packet Access) and UMTS (Universal Mobile Telecommunication System), a technology that minimizes costs of access to the data network of cellular technology LTE [15]. For geo positioning of the patient, the module can be connected directly to a satellite positioning system. The operating range of the modem is of 1.65 V to 5.5 V, which facilitates portability and efficient energy management, unlike others modulars connection type modem as the sim908, whose operation requires an additional consumption of up to 7 V for synchronization in the communication, the latter is only compatible with the system GPS [16].

The GPS link occurs through a technology of media access, that establishes a multiplexed communication by code division (CDMA), that is, all users share the same space radio frequency, but each signal is identified through a code; finally the increased of data rate in the modem is due to the BPSK modulation system used, or phase-shift keying, and determines greater performance in bandwidth due to its configuration and implementation of symbols in the communication [17].

3.3 Modeling System

For a better organized design view, technology and its integration to their servers and data terminals, it is necessary to perform a modeling between different actors and the way they interact with the platform, i.e., a specification the logic of specialized areas based on diagram, and so to determine the components of the system [24] (As an example see Fig. 1).

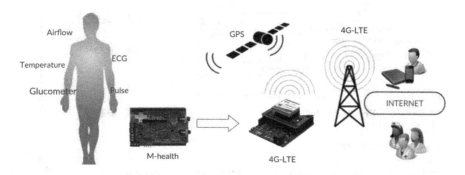

Fig. 1. Technical diagram, system platform

Within the modeling system there is a module with a unique relationship with each patient, it is physically composed by an international identification SIMCARD module, which identifies each patient and is associated to an ID number international IMSI (International Mobile Subscriber Identity), a number conformed principally by the country code, the operator of the data network and finally by the MSIN (mobile subscription identification number). From this module SIMCARD a secure communication through a security protocol is established; This protocol is based on an authentication method supported on a temporary key t of 64-bit of authentication, which is adopted by cryptographic algorithms, the first algorithm A3 is for subcripstor authentication, A8 for key generation and A5 for a radio encryption in the electromagnetic spectrum, [18]; thanks to this type of coding a secure communication based on fair non-repudiation is established. This technique permits an exchange data between two entities in such way that neither of the parties can deny having participated in the transaction. This is crucial in the context of next generation e-Health systems, as it forges a non-repudiable audit trail and thus allows for data subjects (that is, the patient who the data is about) to be able to trace where their data has travelled to and thus detect potential data breaches/ misuse of personal data [19, 20]. Specifically, in terms of technological infrastructure for data storage, technology has a roaming open source system installed and configured as application server, that takes of the census data sent by the mobile device through the ubiquitous protocol HTTPS, which contains the GET function, necessary for identification and the sent of data on the web in the form of vector [21]. From the application server online, anyone previously identified by the system can query the data stored, from any mobile device connected to the data network and a mobile application installed and pre-configured, this exchange of information is standard and transparent to the user (As an example see Fig. 2).

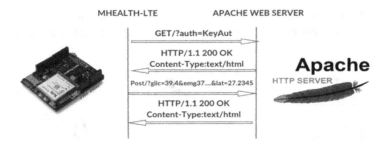

Fig. 2. Exchange of messages between mHealth and server

3.4 Data Visualization

Given that the system can record the Geo-referencing the patient through consultations specialized data, and relate it simultaneously with the identifiable physical infrastructure of health (hospitals, clinics, ambulances or health points). For this reason multilayer architecture services are implemented; these components help to define an application layer functional optimal and necessary for requirements of exchange of data through web [22]. Spatial queries geo related to a number of enhanced functions for mapping and space, IE, a number of services of geo code are provided and defined, theses queries takes input parameter geospatial coordinates of each patient, and the same time are correlated with each one of the geographical coordinates of each hospitals infrastructures and others specialized medical services, A whole this set of elements can generate intelligent queries based on a Geographic information system. Alternatively the health services are trying to integrate of the Geo referenced services. [23], For viewing the data layer, it interacts directly with the remote services offered through Google Maps Java-Script API, using these resources and data types geospatial provides a unified view of services natively established through the web. All this guarantees a specialized architecture for representing and analyzing the spatial data extension [24]. It is necessary to have a server database PostgreSQL engine and a spatial data in PostGIS for storing information. Latter it has the functionality of supporting geographic queries on the web from any device that connects to the Internet through browser, here it is located all System middleware. Finally, the system can provide excellent spatial indexing mechanisms, especially on the stored data of the patient, their environment concerning medical and hospital resources [25] (As an example see Fig. 3).

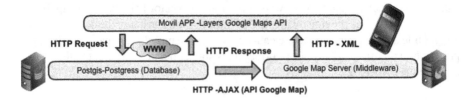

Fig. 3. Unified service layer

3.5 Telematics Architecture

This architecture is conditioned in such a way that the device that initiates the communication of data can be multiplexed taking the signals from different biometric sensors for later sending to modem communication serial the encoded data via the SPI port, this allows an autonomous sent and data storage, via an encrypted HTTPS communication managed from the Apache server channel, a feature that handles a confidentiality and authentication at each end of the communication, through native support SSL (Secure Socket Layer) as is the mod_ssl module, implemented in the Apache server and setting TCP/IP private sockets [26]. To level network layer could work through the protocol TCP or UDP communication, this according to the type of communication you want to implement.

On the other hand, the system has access immediately to mobile services, MSM messaging (Short Message Service) and CBS (Cell Broadcast service), this last is a kind of instant message directed massively to devices associated with a specific selected area, and can be given repetitively between 2 s and 32 min, ideal for Emergency Alerting with fast delivery, this due to this system implements a dedicated signaling, independent of channels voice and data, thus allowing a QoS (quality of service) dedicated in real time, which guarantees more reliable alert message delivery [27] (As an example see Fig. 4).

Fig. 4. LTE architecture for telemedicine

4   Selection Criteria and Technology

For the development of the platform communication a criteria based in providing converged services was established; an infrastructure of fixed and wireless broadband, focusing on coverage and patient mobility; especially in those rural and inaccessible areas in the Colombian geography. For this the following parameters were considered: Potency, coverage, mobility and bandwidth [28]. This significant advantage in LTE or 4G technology is achieved through incrementals optimizations of access technologies in the radio RNC (Radio Network Controller) and BSC (Base Station Controller), with a support service delivery to the BTS (Base Transceiver Station), by which applies a new technique of spectral efficiency based on orthogonal frequency division multiple users OFDMA (orthogonal frequency-division multiple Access) to DOWNLINK, and

SC-FDMA (Single Carrier frequency Division multiple Access) for UPLINK [29, 30], This hardware architecture allows a much faster data transference with a time of 30 ms access, being that the LTE technology uses a band of 700 MHz, thus taking advantage of better coverage and spectral efficiency, suitable for multipath effects; greatly reducing communication delays until a total of 10 ms. Thanks to the spectral efficiency, a greater coverage is allowed. It can go to 100 km and reduce time in communicating with low power. Each final device obtains a greater use of energy and power, thus obtaining a battery with more hours of data transmission in the time, so that LTE offers us the ability to meet those needs telemetry that for technical reasons are very difficult to cover with other wireless communication standards such as Wi-Fi, or 3G Bluetooth [31] (As an example see Fig. 5).

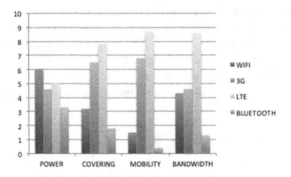

Fig. 5. Selection criteria mobile technology

In relation to the technical specifications, it's possible to make a comparison between the current market technologies for wireless data transmission and the Proposed, the design main criterion is to establish an architecture telematics allowing a bandwidth stable with low delay in data transmission, a development transmission with low power energy and an excellent coverage in wireless communication (As an example see Table 1).

Table 1. Comparison among transmission technologies.

Parameter	ZigBee	Bluetooth	802.11b	802.11g	LTE standard
Throughput (Mbps)	0.03	1–3	11	54	200
Max. Range (ft)	75	30	200	200	328084
Bandwidth (MHz)	0.6	1	22	20	5–20
Price (USD)	2.0	3.0	5.0	12	130

5   Results

From any mobile device connected to the Internet, information of each patient with the values of the most important biometric readings is observed, between these: Glucose sensor, body temperature sensor, blood pressure sensor (sphygmomanometer), pulse and oxygen in blood sensor (SPO2), airflow sensor (Breathing), galvanic skin response sensor (GSR - Sweating), electrocardiogram (ECG), and Electromyography (EMG) sensors. The values of these data are updated almost in real time and directly from the sensors to the data system on line; The Android-based mobile application allows you to monitor the patient's vital signs given its geo positioning; however, the device could associate preventive medical alarms based on critical reading data from sensors and linked to a number of triggers, which could activate a priority communication in real time and independent of LTE data network, where the device generates a series of type SMS messages unidirectional or CBS messages. On the other hand the doctor in charge has the ability to review the medical history of each patient, since the application has a direct connection to the database of the computer system of health, which allows to execute SQL statements (Structured Query Language) to generate specialized reports, thus every doctor in Colombia and even outside the country could analyze the clinical evolution of each patient (Fig. 6).

Fig. 6. Biometrics ECG and blood sugar levels

To perform measures, the device is adapted to the corresponding sensors in order to begin the biometrics; in this proof were performed measurements of glucose in the blood (see Fig. 7). The app developed on Android and located on any mobile device is connected to the LTE data network to perform a reading almost in real time on the stream of data of each patient, where each biometric signal was mapped from the biomedical device to web service.

For data storage, the device has a direct connection and autonomy with the information system, which allows you to store different types of data depending on the sensor or sensors configured. This information is related directly to each patient information, also it is consulted the clinical history, based on all this information and applying modern techniques of data processing as specialized algorithms, it is possible to detect abnormalities in the patient [32]. Through the app some tracking of biometric variable is made, for this option the glucose level in the blood is related with each patient in her medical records system, in essence this value would be consulted in near real time from the web. Finally given the measurement of most such signals tends to recur over time, it could be set averaging techniques, These techniques allow to summarization of a set of events, where through intelligent algorithms may be classified the behavior of the signal in order to identify a corresponding pattern in function time or in their respective frequencies.

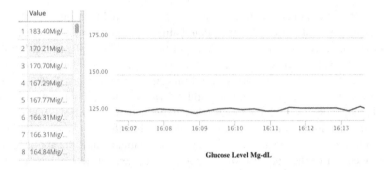

Fig. 7. Visualization glucose in the blood Mid/dl

6   Conclusions and Future Work

The design of an open source architecture based on Arduino able to take a census of biometric signals multiplex and track vital signs of each patient is established, in order to encode these values and send them along with their geographical location through data network wireless and supported by LTE technology, with a connectivity IP protocol. At the other end of the communication, the value is stored in a geographic information system database of health located on the web, whose functionality is related with the geographic information of each patient in relation with the physical infrastructure of hospital services and health electronic record system to generate an integration that allows a unified view. The sum of all this technological infrastructure aims to the concept of a geographical information open source system health, including an extension of specialist consultations in real time, thanks to the autonomous connection with the device and a bandwidth defined up 1 GB in digital data transference with low power cellular network for LTE, accompanied by a ubiquitous wireless transmission with minimal delays and better transmission times. The prototype system does track patients with extreme care in postoperative state, where each vital sign or biometric signals are monitored constantly through specialized algorithms, which when detecting an abnormality proceed immediately to send SMS messages or BCD of so instant, depending on the type of reading detected. All this infrastructure connectivity allows to implement a strategy for optimizing the health services, where specialists from different areas and located in different countries, exchanging concepts and criteria to track real-time to each patient in remote areas and difficult to access.

References

1. Ministerio de tecnologias de la informacion y las comunicaciones de colombia (2015) Boletin Trimestral de las TIC-Colombia, Cifras Cuarto Trimestre de 2014, 8–9
2. Silva, L.A.B., Costa, C., Oliveira, J.L.: An agile framework to support distributed medical imaging scenarios. In: 2013 IEEE International Conference on Healthcare Informatics, pp. 345–350. IEEE (2013)

3. Lancheros-Cuesta, D.J., Tumialan, A., Giovanni, J., et al.: Telemedicine platform for monitoring diabetic retinopathy. In: 2014 9th Iberian Conference on Information Systems and Technologies, pp. 1–6. IEEE (2014)
4. Sano, M.D., Perez, A., Miguel, A., Giovannetti, F.: Demonstration paper: HeartMapp: a mobile application to improve CHF outcomes and reduce hospital readmissions. In: Proceedings of the Conference on Wireless Health, WH 2015, pp. 81–92 (2015)
5. Antoniou, A., Valchinov, E.S., Chatzigiannakis, I., et al.: Patriot: delivering instant heart observation with a miniature wearable ECG and cloud platform. In: Proceedings of the 19th Panhellenic Conference on Informatics, PCI 2015, pp. 177–182 (2015)
6. Abiola, S.O.: Node view: a mHealth real-time infectious disease interface disease interface - 2014 Ebola outbreak case study. In: UBICOMP/ISWC 2015, Adjunct, Osaka, Japan, pp. 297–300, 7–11 September 2015
7. Tamilselvan, S., Prabakar, D.: LTE approach for real time applications in telemedicine using FMC. Int. J. Eng. Res. Technol. 2, 1917–1924 (2013)
8. Técnica, E., Comillas, P.: Universidad SDI, Redes móviles terrestres: 4g, pp. 1–12 (2010)
9. Purusothaman, S.R.R.D., Rajesh, R., Bajaj, K.K., Vijayaraghavan, V.: Implementation of arduino-based multi-agent system for rural Indian microgrids. In: 2013 IEEE Innovative Smart Grid Technologies-Asia, ISGT Asia 2013, pp. 1–5 (2013)
10. Julio, Y.E.R.: Development of a prototype arduino-mobile in area of telemedicine for remote monitoring diabetic people. In: 2015 Asia-Pacific Conference on Comput Aided System Engineering (APCASE), pp. 36–40 (2015)
11. Brama, R., Tundo, P., Ducata Della, A., Malvasi, A.: An inter-device communication protocol for modular smart-objects. In: 2014 IEEE World Forum Internet Things, pp. 422–427. IEEE (2014)
12. Rao, A.T., et al.: Real time ECG signal transmission for remote monitoring, 348–354
13. Al-Kuwari, A.M.A.H., Ortega-Sanchez, C., Sharif, A., Potdar, V.: User friendly smart home infrastructure: BeeHouse. In: 5th IEEE International Conference on Digital Ecosystems and Technologies (IEEE DEST 2011), pp. 257–262. IEEE (2011)
14. Mahjabeen, D., Ahmed, A., Rafique, S.: Use of LTE for the interoperability between different generations of wireless communication. Int. J. Commun. Netw. Syst. Sci. 4, 424–429 (2011)
15. Mai, Y.-T., Chen, J.-Y.: IP multimedia relay architectures with Multi-RAT support in LTE-Advanced wireless network. In: 2013 7th Asia Modelling Symposium, pp. 283–288. IEEE (2013)
16. Campillo, D., Torres, H., González, R., et al.: Computing in cardiology, pp. 1077–1080 (2014)
17. Benprom, P., Pinthong, C., Kanprachar, S.: Analysis of convolutional coded direct sequence spread spectrum CDMA system with a BPSK jamming signal. In: 8th Electrical Engineering/Electronics, Computer, Telecommunications and Information Technology Association of Thailand-Conference, pp. 268–271. IEEE (2011)
18. Lee, C.-C., Hwang, M.-S., Yang, W.-P.: Extension of authentication protocol for GSM. IEE Proc. Commun. 150, 91 (2003)
19. Vermesan, O., Friess, P.: Building the Hyperconnected Society. River Publishers (2015)
20. Paulin, A., Welzer, T.: A universal system for fair non-repudiable certified e-mail without a trusted third party. Comput. Secur. 32, 207–218 (2013)
21. Turau, V.: HTTPExplorer. ACM SIGCSE Bull. 35, 198–201 (2003)
22. Boulos, M.N.K.: Web GIS in practice III: creating a simple interactive map of England's strategic health authorities using google maps API, google Earth KML, and MSN virtual Earth map control. Int. J. Health Geogr. 4, 22 (2005)

23. Yang, C.-T., Chu, Y.-Y., Tsaur, S.-C.: Notice of retraction implementation of a medical information service on Android mobile devices. In: 4th International Conference on New Trends in Information Science and Service Science (NISS), pp. 72–77 (2010)
24. Cao, Y., Zhao, Z., Huaiyu, X., et al.: An instant messaging system based on google map. In: 2010 2nd International Conference on Advanced Computer Control, pp. 21–24. IEEE (2010)
25. Nutanong, S., Adelfio, M.D., Samet, H.: An efficient layout method for a large collection of geographic data entries. In: Proceedings of the 16th International Conference on Extending Database Technology - EDBT 2013, p. 717. ACM Press, New York (2013)
26. Li, G., Zheng, H., Li, G.: Building a secure web server based on OpenSSL and apache. In: Proceedings of the International Conference on E-Business and E-Government, ICEE 2010, pp. 1307–1310 (2010)
27. Song, M., Jun, K., Chang, S.: An efficient multiplexing method of T-DMB and cell broadcast service in emergency alert systems. IEEE Trans. Consum. Electron. **60**, 549–557 (2014)
28. Eul, H.: Complexity challenges towards 4th generation communication solutions. In: Proceedings of the 5th IEEE/ACM International Conference on Hardware/Software Codesign and System Synthesis - CODES+ISSS 2007, p. 123. ACM Press, New York (2007)
29. Raghunath, K., Chockalingam, A.: SC-FDMA versus OFDMA: sensitivity to large carrier frequency and timing offsets on the uplink. In: GLOBECOM - IEEE Global Telecommunications Conference, pp. 1–6 (2009)
30. Jimaa, S., Alfadhl, Y.: LTE-A an overview and future research areas. In: 2011 IEEE 7th International Conference on Wireless and Mobile Computing, Networking and Communications, pp. 395–399. IEEE (2011)
31. Zaki, Y., Weerawardane, T., Gorg, C., Timm-Giel, A.: Multi-QoS-aware fair scheduling for LTE. In: IEEE 73rd Vehicular Technology Conference (VTC Spring), pp. 1–5 (2011). Institute of Communications Networks, Hamburg University of Technology
32. Sain, M., Lee, H., Chung, W.Y.: Personal healthcare information system. In: NCM 2009 - 5th International Joint Conference on INC, IMS, IDC, vol. 1, pp. 1540–1545 (2009)

Study of Factors Affecting the Choice Modal of Transportation in an Urban Environment Using Analytic Hierarchy Process

Alberto Fraile[1,2], Juan Antonio Sicilia[1,2(✉)], Rubén González[1,2], and Alfonso González[1,2]

[1] Universidad Internacional de La Rioja (UNIR), Av. Gran Vía Rey Juan Carlos I, 41, 26002 Logroño, La Rioja, Spain
{juanantonio.sicilia,ruben.gonzalez,alfonso.gonzalezbarrios}@unir.net
[2] Department of Mechanical Engineering, Universidad de Zaragoza, María Luna 3, 50018 Zaragoza, Spain
afrailep@unizar.es

Abstract. In modern economies it is essential a proper system of transport that enables population mobility and consequent accessibility to services. However, its current configuration is causing strong negative externalities and generates much of the problems of environmental, social and energetic sustainability. The changes required by the current unsustainable configuration have to be based on a new vision of transport and on the development of theoretical and empirical criteria that enable the creation of sustainable transport systems.

The purpose of this study is to analyse the most important factors of urban mobility in its current configuration, but not only the mobility of passengers but of all the elements of mobility in urban environments. Externalities caused by transport have been analysed, and the necessary principles to develop a model to aid decision-making regarding the modal split in a city have been developed.

From a holistic view, it has been developed an analytical model based on methodological support obtained from the technique of multi-criteria analysis AHP (Analytic Hierarchy Process), with the aim of achieving user satisfaction, sustainable growth and energetic and environmental efficiency. The construction of the model has allowed to analyse the sensitivity and robustness of the AHP, so as to obtain the classification of attributes with respect to an ideal situation, but also the most appropriate modal split of alternatives with respect to the various evaluation criteria. As operation check of the functioning made by the model, a methodology in a case study with different characteristics has been applied.

Keywords: Urban transport · Urban mobility · AHP methodology · Sustainability · Energy efficiency

© Springer International Publishing AG 2016
J.C. Figueroa-García et al. (Eds.): WEA 2016, CCIS 657, pp. 357–367, 2016.
DOI: 10.1007/978-3-319-50880-1_31

1   Introduction

A vast number of problems from Applied Science including engineering can be brought by means of solving a nonlinear equation using mathematical modeling [2,3,13,14]. One of that problems, in concrete the choice modal of transportation in urban environments, is studied in this paper.

In recent decades there have been profound social, economic and technological changes have led to a new model of urban mobility. That model, which tends to be implemented globally, is characterized by the increase in average distances travelled, changes in the grounds for the displacements and changes in the location of production activities. In modern economies is essential that suitable transport that enables the population mobility and the consequent accessibility to services. However, its current configuration is causing strong negative externalities and generates much of the problems of environmental, social and energy sustainability. The changes required by the current unsustainable configuration should be based on a new vision of transportation and the development of theoretical and empirical criteria that enable the creation of sustainable transport systems. Such a system must be based on the principle of multimodal transport. The purpose of this paper is to analyze the most important factors of urban mobility in its current configuration, analyze the negative externalities caused by the transportation, and develop the principles necessary to develop a model in which the modal distribution is optimized in a city in a way that is sustainable, both in terms of passengers and freight. Previously, in other works as [4–8,10–12,16,19] using different methodologies, the factors affecting modal choice in different countries are analyzed, success stories in sustainable mobility are described and traffic optimization indicators are described. To do this, in the Decision Theory, it has been selected Analytic Hierarchy Process (AHP) technique to support different stages of the proposed methodology. This technique allows by building a hierarchical model, efficiently and graphically, organizes information about a problem, break it down and analyze it by parts in different matrix, visualize the effects of changes in levels and synthesize.

2   Objectives

The main objectives sought in this article are:

- Analyze key factors of urban mobility in the current situation of cities, taking into account all the elements involved in mobility in urban environments (technological advances, new regulations, influence the economic attitude, changes in urban planning,...) and study their behavior.
- From here, develop the principles necessary to develop a model to aid decision-making for action, in order to meet three overall objectives, customer satisfaction, sustainable growth and energy and environmental efficiency.

Similarly, secondary objectives are:

- Develop a model of analysis to study mobility in an urban environment taking into account the influence of factors affecting transport for best modal split.
- Deep generating all the necessary knowledge of the problems existing urban mobility today from a holistic view, as well as factors critical to your organization.
- Justify, within the theory of decision, the selection of AHP technique to support various stages of the proposed methodology.
- Building the analysis model, in collaboration with a group of experts in the field.
- Define all elements of the model (criteria, sub-criteria, attributes and alternatives), and develop the AHP. Also, an analysis of sensitivity and consistency of the model.

3   Methodology

The proposed methodology is based on the Analytic Hierarchy Process (AHP), method appearing through Professor Thomas L. Saaty, 1977, in the Journal of Mathematical Psychology [17]. The AHP is a method of organizing information and reasoning used in making decisions. The AHP contributes to solving complex problems structuring a hierarchy of criteria, stakes and results, extracting trials to develop priorities. In short, the AHP is a general approach to defining problems, set priorities and make decisions. The AHP involves all aspects of the decision-making process, and modeling the problem through a hierarchical structure and uses a priority scale to synthesize and deliver judgments ordering or ranking of the alternatives according to the weights obtained (priorities).

This methodology proposes a way to sort analytical thinking which include three basic principles:

1. The principle of building hierarchies
2. The principle of prioritizing
3. The principle of logical consistency

To promote consistency of judgments Saaty proposes the fundamental scale that bears his name [18]. This scale is structured according to the intensity of importance of some judgments about others with the values 1, 3, 5, 7 or 9, from low to high importance (see Table 1).

To determine the best decision, in a generic way, the AHP method requires follow these steps: define the problem; choose the actors; structuring the decision problem in order to build a model of hierarchy; select the feasible alternatives; build the hierarchical model; login judgments; summary of results; and validation of the decision.

Therefore, the system of the AHP of the establishment of a goal, criteria and alternative structure, as you can see in Fig. 1.

Table 1. Fundamental scale of judgments Saaty

Intensity of importance	Definition	Explanation
1	Equal importance	Two activities contribute equally to the objective(s)
3	Weak importance	Experience and judgment slightly favour one activity over another
5	Essential or strong importance	Experience and judgment strongly favour one activity over another
7	Demonstrated importance	An activity is strongly favour one activity over another
9	Absolute importance	The evidence favouring one activity over another is of highest possible order of affirmation
2, 4, 6, 8	Intermediate values between the two adjacent judgements	Where compromise is needed
Reciprocals of the nonzero	If activity i has one of the above nonzero numbers assigned to it when compared with activity j, then j has the reciprocal value when compared with i	

The priority of the alternatives with respect to the goal, which was the objective sought is obtained according to the objective function:

$$W_{A_i}^{MI} = \sum_{j=1}^{M} \sum_{k=1}^{M} W_{A_i}^{C_{jk}} W_{C_{jk}}^{C_j} W_{C_j}^{MI} \tag{1}$$

To learn how priority values are obtained from the assessments carried out by the actors in the AHP, it must repeat the following three steps as many times as there are elements influenced in the hierarchy:

(1) It is building a Reciprocal Matrix Binary Comparisons $[A]$ (of order n, which equals the number of elements that are assessing their influence) from valuations $a_{ij}(i = 1, ..., n; j = 1, ..., n)$ made by the evaluator actor and/or decision maker. For this, each a_{ij} corresponds to a numeric value of the fundamental Saaty scale.

$$[A] = \begin{vmatrix} 1 & a_{12} & ... & a_{1n} \\ \frac{1}{a_{12}} & 1 & ... & a_{2n} \\ ... & ... & ... & ... \\ \frac{1}{a_{1n}} & \frac{1}{a_{2n}} & ... & 1 \end{vmatrix}$$

(2) The next step is the calculation of local priorities. The mathematical procedure is followed in obtaining the principal eigenvector method to the

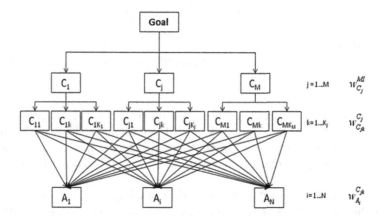

Fig. 1. Structure of AHP (goal, criteria and alternatives)

right [17]. This method, based on the Perron-Frobenius theorem provides local priorities solving the system of equations:

$$AW = \lambda_{max}W \tag{2}$$

where $A = (a_{ij})$ is the Reciprocal Matrix Binary Comparisons, λ_{max} the principal eigenvalue of A, y $W = (W_1, W_2, \ldots, W_n)$ the vector of local priorities ratio scale measures and normalized to have unity. In this case, normalization has applied the so called distributive $(\sum_j W_j = 1)$.

In practice, the solution W is obtained (power method) by raising the matrix judgments on a sufficiently large power, adding rows and normalizing these values by dividing the sum of each row for the total amount. The process ends when the difference between two consecutive powers is small. The priority vector w represents the relative importance of the criteria or sub compared in each pairwise comparison matrices.

(3) For the analysis of consistency, it is estimated the maximum eigenvalue associated λ_{max} with $[A]$ and the consistency index (CI) is obtained:

$$CI = \frac{\lambda_{max} - n}{n - 1} \tag{3}$$

where n is the orden of the matrix.

If the reason for inconsistency (CR), where the random index (RI) is obtained from Table 2, is less than 10 % then states that the valuations are consistent and the values $W_i(i = 1, ..., n)$ of the eigenvector W are accepted as good. If not, the decision maker is asked to redo the valuations of the Reciprocal Matrix Binary Comparisons:

$$CR = \frac{CI}{RI} \tag{4}$$

Table 2. Table of random values (Saaty) [1]

Matrix size	1	2	3	4	5	6	7	8	9	10
RI	0	0	0.525	0.882	1.115	1.252	1.341	1.404	1.452	1.484

The role of an expert group has been instrumental in the development of this work as it has intervened at various stages of development of the model and its view reflects the wide range of different approaches to representing each. The group was composed of experts in urban transport and multi-criteria decision making.

When meeting the expert group has been changing the structure and composition of that hierarchy, and are the group of experts who have decided to have the final structure, after many meetings and considerations.

A team approach can produce better solutions to complex problems [20]. These experts selected the most relevant attributes and structured as a four-level hierarchy: goal, criteria, sub-criteria, attributes and alternatives, working in context of group decision making. In this framework multiactor experts operate as a group, looking for a single decision based on the principle of seeking consensus. In the Fig. 2 can be seen the three phases of the process.

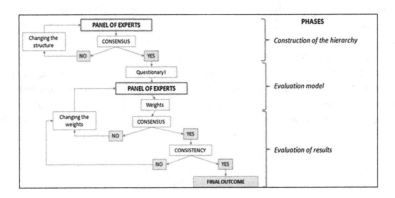

Fig. 2. Three phases of the process for the preparation of the AHP structure)

Finally in this paper, the AHP model structure is composed of the goal, 2 criterias (C_i), 13 sub-criterias (SC_{ij}), 24 attributes (Q_i) y 6 alternatives A_i.

- Goal: Efficiency in the modal split in urban environments
- Criterias:
    - C_1: Actors
    - C_2: Factors

- Subcriterias:

    $SC_{1,1}$: Users
    $SC_{1,2}$: Regulator and administrator
    $SC_{1,3}$: Urban population centres of attraction
    $SC_{1,4}$: Suppliers of technological innovation
    $SC_{1,5}$: Business mobility and distribution services
    $SC_{2,1}$: Accessibility
    $SC_{2,2}$: Quality of service
    $SC_{2,3}$: Comfort
    $SC_{2,4}$: Efficiency
    $SC_{2,5}$: Security
    $SC_{2,6}$: Technology
    $SC_{2,7}$: Environmental impact
    $SC_{2,8}$: Organization of the urban environment
- Attributes:

    Q_1: Design of Access roads suitable to use
    Q_2: Good organization of circulation
    Q_3: Existence of stops proportion to population density
    Q_4: Location appropriate car park
    Q_5: Balanced distribution of loading and unloading areas
    Q_6: Sufficient capacity
    Q_7: Low journey
    Q_8: High frequency
    Q_9: High rate flexibility
    Q_{10}: Comfort
    Q_{11}: Good computer interactive service
    Q_{12}: Low path length
    Q_{13}: Difficult terrain
    Q_{14}: Bad weather
    Q_{15}: Low costs in use
    Q_{16}: Low energy consumption
    Q_{17}: Low accident
    Q_{18}: Adequate traffic control
    Q_{19}: Technology vehicular updated
    Q_{20}: Existence of information and communications technology
    Q_{21}: Low emissions
    Q_{22}: Complete rules-use regulation
    Q_{23}: Existence of mobility plan
    Q_{24}: Complex morphology
- Alternatives:

    A_1: Pedestrian mobility
    A_2: Transportation by private vehicle
    A_3: Collective transport
    A_4: Goods transport vehicle
    A_5: Mobility nonmotorized vehicle
    A_6: New modes of mobility

In short, it structured decision making from the most general to the most specific thanks to the knowledge of the expert group. These experts have also been responsible for analyzing the model through 505 judgments (40 matrixes). In this phase of the methodology incorporates judgments based on the information obtained or the perception of the actors in the process. Therefore, once it has well defined and structured hierarchy, the operations described continues after systematic: the reciprocal matrix of binary relationships is obtained, the reason inconsistency and, if this is less than 10 %, eigenvector accept the right of the Reciprocal Matrix Binary Comparisons as a measure of local priority.

After making the 40 matrixes generated it is established the AHP model ranking of results. It is noted (see Tables 3 and 4) that there are four slots in the rankings. With respect to the attributes of the model, the low accident rate (Q_{17}) and high frequency (Q_8) are the ones that have greater weight and followed by the later group (Q_{16}, Q_{12} and Q_{23}). After a group of thirteen intermediate attributes, and finally a group with very low values ($Q_3, Q_4, Q_{14}, Q_5, Q_{13}$ and Q_{24}).

Table 3. Ranking of attributes

Attributes	Q_{17}	Q_8	Q_{16}	Q_{12}	Q_{23}	Q_{21}	Q_{22}	Q_7	Q_{11}	Q_2	Q_{10}	Q_{15}
% global	11,2	10,4	7	6,4	6,2	5,5	5,5	4,8	4,6	4,44	4	3,6

Table 4. Ranking of attributes

Attributes	Q_1	Q_9	Q_6	Q_{18}	Q_{19}	Q_{20}	Q_3	Q_4	Q_{14}	Q_5	Q_{13}	Q_{24}
% global	3,44	3,4	2,8	2,8	2,5	2,5	1,64	1,64	1,6	1,44	1,4	1,2

After analyzing the ranking has been obtained from the various elements of the model, it got to the end of the methodologies, where the assessment of alternatives is obtained (see Table 5).

Table 5. Ranking of alternatives

Alternatives	%
A_1	26,00
A_2	12,81
A_3	22,96
A_4	12,40
A_5	14,04
A_6	11,79

It can see that pedestrian mobility and collective transport accounts for nearly 50 % of the total. This corresponds to lines that are making sustainability in recent years from the EU.

Finally applying a sensitivity analysis allowed to verify the robustness and stability of the model is performed, examining the change that occurs in the systematic variations results when performed in a range of interest on one or more input parameters.

4   Case of Study

In this chapter if the aim is to test the validity and study the elaborate model, see how the factors affect in different types of cities. To perform this evaluation included the collaboration of a group of experts on issues related to transportation, government agencies, research centers, representatives of users, industry experts, etc., among which there were five people from each of the cities. It was developed a new questionnaire for these groups to assess their city with respect to the attributes of the AHP model developed in this paper.

To define an urban environment is required any analysis of it from four points: topography, geography, topology and size. Similarly, the numbers of inhabitants, population density, tourist attraction or existing means of transport are data that complement the characterization of a city. For this work, we selected several different scenarios, including the city of Teruel, Spain. This city is small, compressed town, with a small population and low population density.

As for the methodology of evaluation of each city it has used the Likert scale. This scale, also called the method of summary assessments, is named for R. Likert, who in 1932 published a report describing its use. Likert was the first to introduce this type of scale, taking them techniques personality measures [15]. It is a psychometric scale commonly used in questionnaires and is the most widely used scale survey research. Responding to a question from a questionnaire prepared by the technique of Likert, the level of agreement or disagreement with a statement (element, item, reactive or question) is specified. The final attitude that is assigned is the average of the scores given to each of the questionnaire items [9].

For this case of Teruel, note that the factors that are relevant with respect to each of the alternatives were obtained. On the Table 6 are ranked in order of importance, the three most influential attributes to this city for each alternative. More weight attributes are: the low accident rate (for pedestrian mobility), the

Table 6. Most influential attributes in each of the alternatives in the city of Teruel

	A_1	A_2	A_3	A_4	A_5	A_6
1	Q_{17}	Q_{23}	Q_8	Q_{11}	Q_{16}	Q_{10}
2	Q_{16}	Q_{12}	Q_7	Q_{17}	Q_{21}	Q_{12}
3	Q_{21}	Q_{22}	Q_{17}	Q_{12}	Q_{17}	Q_{22}

existence of mobility plan (for transport by private car), high frequency (for public transport), good interactive computer service (for transport goods vehicle), the low energy consumption (for mobility with no motor vehicle) and comfort (for new modes of mobility).

5   Conclusions

Progress has been made in the use of techniques covered in the Decision Theory for modeling complex systems. In particular, it discussed a new approach of using the AHP which allows taking into account the influence of factors interacting in deciding which mode of transport used for each shift and achieve the objective of meeting the needs of the user, sustainable growth of the city and improving the energy and environmental efficiency, which results in a certain modal split. This way you can have a holistic view of behavior in urban environments.

The development and proposal of a model analysis using a methodology to assess the influence of a set of related attributes, defined by experts from different fields and that takes into account different aspects of transport that are related to each other, regarding the mission to achieve efficiency in the modal split.

There are few jobs that advance the use of this technique of analysis for large cases such as transport problems and less focusing the analysis model from a global perspective in which agents interact with each other as is done in this project, unlike the widespread use of AHP to solve decision-making problems.

It has been proposed a method that through the results of the application of AHP allows assessment of the modal split in different settings, and can serve as a comparison for future decision-making, i.e., has established a framework of comparison.

Acknowledgments. This research was supported by Universidad Internacional de La Rioja (UNIR, http://www.unir.net), under the Plan Propio de Investigación, Desarrollo e Innovación 3 [2015–2017]. Research group: Modelación matemática aplicada a la ingeniería (MOMAIN).

References

1. Aguarón, J., Moreno-Jiménez, J.M.: The geometric consistency index: approximated thresholds. Eur. J. Oper. Res. **147**, 137–145 (2003)
2. Argyros, I.K., González, D.: Local convergence for an improved jarratt-type method in banach space. Int. J. Artif. Intell. Interact. Multimedia **3**(4) (2015). ISSN 1989-1660
3. Argyros, I.K., Magreñán, A.: On the convergence of an optimal fourth-order family of methods and its dynamics. Appl. Math. Comput. **252**, 336–346 (2015)
4. Black, J.A., Paez, A., Suthanaya, P.A.: Sustainable urban transportation: performance indicators and some analytical approaches. J. Urban Plan. Devel. **138**(4), 184–209 (2002)
5. Buehler, R.: Determinants of transport mode choice: a comparison of Germany and the USA. J. Transp. Geogr. **19**(4), 644–657 (2011)

6. Fraile, A., Muerza, M.V., Ponce, D., Larrodé, E. Análisis de los factores influyentes en el reparto modal de los desplazamientos diarios. Caso de estudio Zaragoza. In: IX Congreso de Ingeniería del Transporte, Madrid, pp. 1999–2009 (2010)

7. Fraile, A., Larrodé, E., Magreñán, A., Sicilia, J.A.: Decision model for siting transport and logistic facilities in urban environments: a methodological approach. J. Comput. Appl. Math. **290**, 100–120 (2015)

8. Gallego, J., Larrodé, E., Sicilia, J.A., Royo, B., Fraile, A.: Optimization and sizing methodology of necessary infraestructure for the incorporation of hydrogen to the transportation sector. DYNA - Ingeniería e Ind. **89**, 405–412 (2014)

9. Guil, M.: Escala mixta Likert-Thurstone. Rev. Andaluza Cien. Sociales **5**, 81–95 (2006)

10. Huapu, L. Influencing factors, challenges and approach for sustainable urban mobility in China. Tsinghua University (2007)

11. Larrodé, E., Gallego, J., Fraile, A.: Optimización de redes de transporte. Revista Lychnos VI, Cuadernos de la Fundación General CSIC (2011)

12. Litman, T.: Sustainable transportation indicators. A recommended research program for developing sustainable transportation indicators and data. In: Transportation Research Board Annual Meeting (2009)

13. Magreñán, A.: Different anomalies in a Jarratt family of iterative root-finding methods. Appl. Math. Comput. **233**, 29–38 (2014)

14. Magreñán, A., Cordero, A., Gutiérrez, J.M., Torregrosa, J.R.: Real qualitative behavior of a fourth-order family of iterative methods by using the convergence plane. Math. Comput. Simul. **105**, 49–61 (2014)

15. Morales, P.: Medición de actitudes en psicología y educación: construcción de escalas y problemas metodológicos, 2nd edn. journal. Universidad Pontificia Comillas, Madrid (2006)

16. Murphy, E.: Excess commuting and modal choice. Transp. Res. Part A. Policy Pract. **43**(8), 735–743 (2009)

17. Saaty, T.L.: The Analytic Hierarchy Process. McGraw-Hill, New York (1980)

18. Saaty, T.L.: The legitimacy of rank reversal. Omega **12**, 513–516 (1984)

19. Sicilia, J.A., Royo, B., Quemada, C., Oliveros, M.J., Larrode, E.: An decision support system to long haul freight transportation by means of ant colony optimization. DYNA - Ingeniería e Ind. **90**, 105–113 (2015)

20. Xu, J., Wu, Z.: A discrete consensus support model for multiple attribute group decision making. Knowl.-Based Syst. **24**(8), 1196–1202 (2011)

Model Driven Architecture Software and Interaction Flow Modelling Language for Tourism Data Acquisition in Colombia

Vanessa Nieto[1], Veronica Castro[1(✉)], Fernando Lopez[1],
Roberto Ferro[1], and Claudio Gonzalez[2]

[1] Corporacion Unificada Nacional de Educacion Superior CUN,
Bogotá, Colombia
yurivane89@hotmail.com, {veronica_castro,
jose_lopezq, roberto_ferro}@cun.edu.co
[2] Universidad Nacional Abierta y a Distancia, Bogotá, Colombia
claudio.gonzalez@unad.edu.co

Abstract. The rise of the software development methodology known as Model-Driven Engineering, has allowed the many advantages of its use to be observed, while meeting the main objective of increasing a company's profitability through an effort in software development. In the short-term it increases productivity by raising the value of first software artefacts; long-term it helps to avoid the obsolescence of primary objects of the software [1]. This way, compatibility between systems increases, the design process is simplified and communication, both among individuals and among teams working within the system, is fostered. It is for this reason that the development of a web application named OcioColombia, under the Model Driven Architecture (MDA) methodology, has been carried out. By doing this, the objectives achieved in each of the architecture's stages can be shown; the benefits offered by the methodology can be exposed and finally, different software tools are able to be orchestrated into an application that allows the user to search for entertainment events and tourist locations available in Colombia.

Keywords: Model Driven Engineering · Interaction flow modeling language · Ontological model · Business Process Modeling · Business rules

1 Introduction

Since the beginning of the software development era, various difficulties have arisen though one that stands out has been the complexity of meeting all of the requirements specified for an application or information system, in the computing environment known as 'machine language' [2]. In order to mitigate this kind of difficulty, different types of programming languages are used which specific syntaxes and structures have focused on the construction and execution of distinct processes. The importance of inventing different translators and compilers cannot be stressed enough [2]; these serve the function of allowing communication between the programmer and the machine by means of a graphical interface that is user-friendly both for the programmer and the end

© Springer International Publishing AG 2016
J.C. Figueroa-García et al. (Eds.): WEA 2016, CCIS 657, pp. 368–379, 2016.
DOI: 10.1007/978-3-319-50880-1_32

user. This interface comes complete with default functions and procedures that can be added or included within a block of code, therefore saving the programmer from having to create full sentences without any assistance or help. Furthermore, the use of translators or compilers allows for real-time testing of the effectiveness of blocks of code as they are built, thereby enabling the programmer to more easily identify possible syntax errors. They can also display the partial and final results of a software project, which is quite useful in the development of web applications.

Another significant breakthrough, which provided developers with the opportunity to express their designs using graphical representations, was the development or invention of CASE (Computer Aided Software Engineering) [2]. This tool allowed for a detailed analysis and synthesis of each program built. Although this tool was innovative, the flaws that could arise meant that it was unable to make greater contributions to the development of software; among the most significant being the limitation that existed for migrating developed programs to different platforms, or the development of more complex systems than those permitted by it.

Currently we face a digital revolution and purchasing power for technology is increasing. Most of the population has a noticeable preference for the use of mobile devices or smartphones for the sending, checking or processing of information, due to uninhibited access to unlimited information at any time of day, anywhere.

A significant advantage of using smartphones is the access provided to mobile applications installed, by default, on these devices as well as the possibility of acquiring other free and paid applications that meet specific functions or user needs. A functional feature worthy of mention is the ability to display a mobile version of all the elements that make up the graphical interface of a suitable web application. Because of the versatility of consulting and processing information through mobile applications, these have been implemented in different economic sectors of the market.

The tourism sector has long been one of the sectors which has benefited most from the use of these new technologies due to the fact that the use of mobile applications (Apps) has several advantages for the promotion of tourism businesses and their products and services. This has been possible thanks to technological innovation.

For its fauna, flora and ethnic diversity, foreigners consider Colombia as one of the most desired tourist destinations. It is well known that, in order to publicize diversity and cultural richness of a place on a global scale, the use of tools to promote and publicize said qualities should be encouraged. To raise awareness of ethnic and cultural diversity in Colombia, the development of a mobile application called OcioColombia, under the Model Driven Architecture (MDA) methodology, was carried out. By doing this, the objectives achieved in each stage of the architecture can be shown; the benefits offered by the methodology can be exposed and, finally, different software tools may be orchestrated into an application that allows the user to search for entertainment events and tourist locations available in Colombia.

Interaction Flow Modelling Language (IFML) was used, which supports the presentation layer of applications regardless of the technological intricacies implied for their realization. This language is based on OMG Model-Driven Architecture Framework standards to ensure its integration with the specifications of other software system layers [2].

First of all the Model driven architecture is explained, then there is a description of Service oriented mobile apps where Default Applications, Server-Connected Applications and Similar Applications Developed in Colombia are specified, subsequently there is a description of Modeling under IFML and Defining an ontological model, finally Conclusions and future work.

2 Model Driven Engineering

Despite important contributions made possible through the invention and implementation of languages, translators, compilers, and CASE in software development, they have failed to fully mitigate the complexity of complying with all of the requirements that may arise in software development. As time goes on, the creation and implementation of new tools has been possible: one of which is Model-Driven Engineering (MDE).

MDE software development methodology is based on the creation of models or abstractions throughout the life cycle of the software, which aim to analyse the most relevant aspects of a system. Hence, the use of this methodology enables the construction of a system of models with sufficient detail that it allows for the generation of a complete application system made up of these same models. In fact it can be stated that 'the model is the code', i.e. the focus is on modelling and the code is generated mechanically from models [2]. The many advantages of its use have been observed. The main objective of increasing the profitability of a company derived from software development effort is met; an increase in productivity in the short-term raises the value of the first artefacts, while long-term, avoidance of the obsolescence of primary software objects leads to increases in compatibility between systems, a simplified design process and the fostering of communication, both among individuals as well as among teams working within the system [2].

Model Driven Engineering technology offers a promising approach to address the inability of third generation languages to alleviate the complexity of platforms and express domain concepts effectively [3]. Amongst various objectives within MDE is the ability to generate new software from models, thereby supporting the productivity levels of software developers.

It is noteworthy that one of the most attractive aspects for developers is the possibility of making any adjustment or modification, specifically in models that support the development of software without having to locate the lines on which the adjustment must be made within endless blocks of code.

This aspect implies a notable optimization of time, which, as a result, minimizes the effort exerted by developers and increases the profitability of a company deriving from software development effort. This benefit comes in two basic forms through enhancing developers' productivity [4]: in the short-term, the value of first software artefacts is increased; long-term, rapid obsolescence of the primary software objects is avoided.

3   Service Oriented Mobile Apps

Mobile applications have been gaining momentum in the current age of the digital revolution. In today's market, a great variety of apps can be found, all with different architectures and built on different technologies. All have a specific aim: to meet the requirements or needs the customer or end user requires. These apps could be divided into two broad categories: default applications and applications connected to the server.

3.1   Default Applications

These applications are installed by default on mobile devices and can be executed with or without a network connection, a main component found inside the mobile phone. These applications can be classified into three types: native applications, those designed on a mobile platform and widgets [5].

- Native Applications: a native application is one designed to run on the computing environment (machine language and OS). It is written in programming languages compiled in C and C++ [6].
- Designed on Mobile Platform: an application based on a mobile platform is one specifically designed and developed to run on a mobile device with a specific operating system (Android, iOS, Windows Phone, etc.) [5]. A remarkable feature these Apps have is there is no possibility of fully migrating an App from one operating system to another. For example, applications developed for the iPhone only run on Apple devices with an iOS operating system [5].
- Widgets: These applications are usually light in terms of execution time; they complete routines or specific tasks, in most cases recurrent tasks assigned by the end user, whilst providing a friendly graphical user interface built under different programming languages, including HTML, CSS, JavaScript and XML [5], amongst others.

3.2   Server- Connected Applications

These applications are divided into Web mobile applications and HTML5 versions, which rely heavily on Web servers. As a matter of fact, mobile applications have been migrating to advanced programming languages such as HTML5, CSS3 and JQuery, now that these technologies include new features that represent a considerable improvement to the architecture of mobile apps, as well as to their graphical interface in comparison to previous languages or technologies used (HTML4, CSS and JavaScript) [5].

- Web Mobile Applications: This type of apps has specific functions embedded for the processing of information, since they can be executed remotely on the Web server. The three-layer architecture [7] is one of the most popular in the design of web applications and consists of a client layer (mobile devices), an application layer (Web server) and a database layer [5].
- HTML5 Applications: The W3C consortium currently regulates this markup language. In 2008, the first version of HTML5 was completed, which enabled the

creation of a standard consisting of a set of advanced features that can handle all the tasks that current technologies can (e.g. Adobe Flash System, Apple QuickTime and Oracle Java FX). In addition, HTML5 is compatible with the latest mobile technologies.

3.3   Similar Applications Developed in Colombia

Several applications that promote tourism in Colombia already exist. The most relevant of these are shown in Table 1 and Fig. 1.

Table 1. Input information

Name	Developer	Updated	Downloads (thousands)	Current Version	Reputation (out of 5)
Colombia	ProColombia	Jan. 21, 2015	10–50	1.19	3.4
Turismo Colombia	ITO Soft. SAS	Mar. 11, 2014	5–10	1.3	4.1
Gurú Viajero	Publicar	Dec. 17, 2014	1–5	1.0.6	4.5
Welcome to Colombia	Assist card	Jan. 8, 2015	0.5–1	2.0	4.1
Buceo Colombia	ProColombia	May. 19, 2015	1–5	1.0.3	4
Airbnb	Airbnb, Inc	Oct. 2, 2015	5000–10000	Vary	4.3

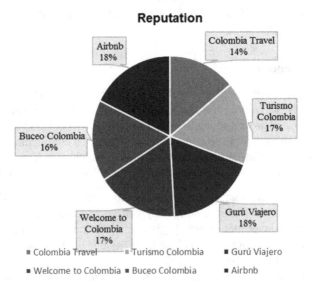

Fig. 1. Reputation of different applications

Some description about those apps is shown next.

- Colombia Travel: A creation by Proexport Colombia that contains detailed information of 26 tourism products in areas such as nature, adventure, beach and culture, museums, embassies and currency exchange offices, transportation and restaurants across the country.
- Tursimo Colombia: This is an initiative by Colombia's Ministry of Commerce, Industry and Tourism. The app shares a wide variety of tourist attractions in the country providing access to key information about the sites available to visit. This application makes it easy to locate physical tourist information points through maps that guide the user so that he or she can get help from trained personnel. It shares information with friends using social networks and provides the possibility of using the camera on your device to take photos of the available places and share them with other users of the application. (Photos must be approved by the MINCIT for publication).
- Guru Viajero: This Publicar app includes items such as itineraries, maps, a calendar of events, augmented reality, coupons and a tourism directory with dining offers, attractions, entertainment, shopping, transportation and currency exchange offices. Mobile guides are free and no internet connection is required once downloaded.
- Welcome to Colombia: This app was designed by AssistCard, with the support of the Colombian Association of Travel and Tourism (ANATO) and Proexport. The app provides assistance during a person's stay in the country. It has a chat function that operates 24 h a day and provides advice on transfers, recovery of lost objects and information about hospitals and medical services. The first three days of medical care are free of charge.
- Buceo Colombia: This is an application recommended for professional and amateur divers, and for those interested in exploring the Colombian marine world. It also allows for the sharing of photos on social media (Fig. 2).

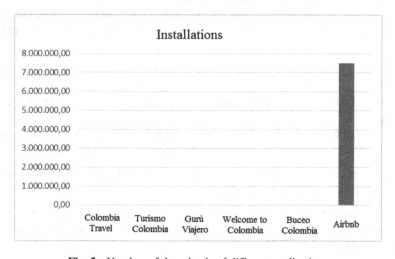

Fig. 2. Number of downloads of different applications

OcioColombia, the proposed application, is unlike those mentioned above in the sense that it allows for the addition of leisure activities, so that an event or location can be created and then shared.

In addition to this, the app was modeled with Interaction Flow Modelling Language (IFML) given that this generalizes the application from the web domain to a generic domain. This way, the front end of the mobile application can be represented in such a way that a clearer vision of the final product can more easily be seen.

4   Modeling Under IFML

Interaction Flow Modelling Language (IFML) was used for the development of the mobile application OcioColombia. It supports the presentation layer of applications regardless of the technological intricacies implied for their realization. This language is based on OMG Model-Driven Architecture Framework standards, which ensures its integration with the specification of the other layers of the software system. The developed application has the following characteristics:

The application was made on the Android platform, since this is a free software platform based on Linux and Java (Android) and most of it is open source.

It has a datasheet for each leisure activity and tourism event in Colombia; it also has multimedia content (images and text) obtained from tourist attractions.

The application has an administrator user performing the respective basic operations (create, query, modify, delete an event, categories and websites of interest). The use of social networks will be available to connect to Facebook.

The end user has the capability to make suggestions about an event, carry out searches for places of interest, rate a scheduled event or make a query thereof.

The construction process involves many tools and processes that generate intermediate files on the way to producing an .apk file. It is a very flexible process so that is useful, however, to understand what is happening behind the scenes - given that much of the construction process is configurable and extensible - the official Android IDE to develop applications was selected. Other command line tools used for this purpose were:

- Androide: Creates and updates Android projects and creates, moves and deletes AVDs.
- Android Emulator: Executes Android applications on an emulated Android platform.
- Android Debugging Bridge: Acts as an interface for the emulator or the connected device (Installs applications, bombards the device, runs commands, etc.).

In addition to the tools included with the SDK, named above, the following open source and third party tools are needed:

- Gradle: Compiles and builds Android projects in an installable .apk file.
- Keytool: Generates a keystore and a private password used to sign the .apk file. Keytool is part of the JDK.

- Jarsigner (or similar tools): Used to sign the .apk file with a private password generated by Keytool. Jarsigner is part of the JDK.
- Facebook Login for Android: Facebook SDK for Android enables people to access the application with a Facebook Login. When people log into their application with Facebook, they may grant permissions, so that information can be retrieved or the app can perform actions on Facebook on the user's behalf. Facebook App - Configured and linked to the application, with a single sign-in enabled. Facebook SDK - Added to the Facebook Android SDK project.
- Facebook App ID - To configure and link this to the Android application. Android Hash Key - To generate this and add it into a developer profile.
- Facebook Activity - Included in AndroidManifest.xml.

This project will not make use of SQLite, even though it is a very popular database engine currently offering such interesting features as: a small size, no server need, limited configuration requirement, use as a transactional means and, of course, being open source. Android comes as standard with all the necessary tools for the creation and management of SQLite databases, amongst which includes a full API to easily perform all necessary tasks.

Nevertheless, the project will communicate with a database hosted on web hosting mounted on MySQL, which is manageable through PHPM and Admin. The interconnection between systems and infrastructure is achieved via WebServices in PHP hosted on a remote server. Android contains the libraries and protocols necessary to send and receive POST and GET data, among others.

5 Defining an Ontological Model

An ontological model is an important foundation needed to represent the real world [8]. The term has grown in the field of computer science [9–11].

Through a collection of key concepts and their interrelation, it gives rise to the creation and use of ontology in order to create and present an abstract view of the application [13]. In order to represent the application taxonomy, an ontological open source editor [12] called Protege is used (Fig. 3).

A class diagram is a graphical representation used to show the structure of a system that will be implemented using an object-oriented language. Prior to the carrying out of class diagrams it is necessary to complete the requirements phase (Fig. 4).

Table 2 shows some of the most important business rules used for managing some of the most important events considered in the proposed app.

The main objective of the domain model is the specification of the relevant information, which is the domain of the application, in a formal and comprehensible manner. UMLDesigner was used for this purpose (Fig. 5).

5.1 Business Process Modeling

This is a graphical notation for modeling Standardized Business Processes that emerged from the Business Process Modeling Initiative (BPMI). BPMN defines the

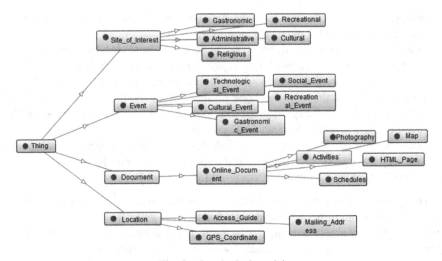

Fig. 3. Ontological model

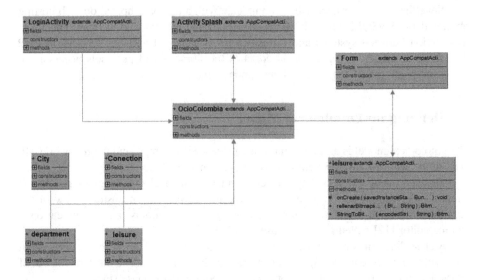

Fig. 4. Class diagram

creation of Business Process Models from the identification and disposal activities order, they are undertaken by the organization [6]. In addition, in BPMN participants are identified to perform the activities, interactions between these members, and the documents that are exchanged during Workflow [7]. Luna - Eclipse was used for this flap (Fig. 6).

Table 2. Business rules

Rule #	Decision point name	Description	Source for rule discovery	Current state of automation	Rule owner sme	Depend of rule
RN_1	Social networks	Facebook will be the only valid application to perform the authentication process	Cases of Use	Initial	App Admin	–
RN_2	Access conditions for data entry	The user must log into a social network to enter new events or sites of interest in the application	Cases of Use	Initial	App Admin	RN_1
RN_3	Event scheduling	The user's geographical position must be determined to validate the events corresponding to the national territory	Cases of Use	Initial	App Admin	RN_2
RN_4	Recommending Sites of Interest	Access is allowed only to the event types defined by a category	Cases of Use	Initial	App Admin	RN_2
RN_5	Event Category	The categories offered by the app for sorting are 1. Social Event, 2. Cultural Event, 3. Recreational Event, 4. Technological Event	Cases of Use	Initial	App Admin	–
RN_6	Sites of Interest Category	The categories offered by the app for sorting are 1. Religious, 2. Gastronomic, 3. Cultural, 4. Recreational 5. Administrative	Cases of Use	Initial	App Admin	–
RN_7	Event Type	Access is allowed only to the types of event defined by a category	Cases of Use	Initial	App Admin	RN_5
RN_8	Type of Sites of Interest	Access is allowed only to the types of sites of interest defined by a category	Cases of Use	Initial	App Admin	RN_6

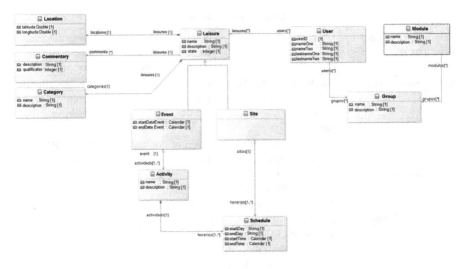

Fig. 5. Domain model

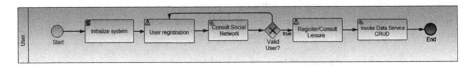

Fig. 6. Business Process Model

6   Conclusions and Future Work

All forms of engineering are based on computer systems models of the real world. Model-Driven Engineering is a methodology that offers multiple benefits, such as: an increase in productivity, the simplification of the design process, the compatibility between systems and the fostering of communication between members of the development team. The life cycle of the software is guaranteed through its power of adaptability, which in turn is facilitated by using business rules engines that minimize maintenance efforts and update business logic, through the uncoupling of both the rules and business logic. Thus, the useful life of the software is increased.

While modelling of the architecture of the application, it was observed that the defining of rules permits the expression of the abstraction of different business processes, as well as the terms and facts related to each rule.

In relation to the execution environment, applications can significantly increase their customization capabilities and adaptability, making organizations adjust their processes and business rules in response to dynamic business conditions.

References

1. Brambilla, M.: Interaction flow modeling language – Model-Driven UI Engineering of Web and Mobile Apps with IFML. Object Management Group (2015)
2. Ledgard, J., Trejo, T., David, A., Robles, E.: Conceptos fundamentales de Ingeniería dirigida por Modelos y Modelos de Dominio Específico 6(2), 9–19 (2010)
3. Schmidt, D.C.: Engineering. IEEE Comput. Sci. 39, 25–31 (2006)
4. Metamodeling, A.: Model-driven development: a metamodeling foundation. IEEE Softw. 20, 36–41 (2003)
5. Huy, N.P.: Developing Apps for Mobile Phones. Computing and Convergence Technology (ICCCT), pp. 907–912 (2012)
6. Chehimi, F., Coulton P., Edwards, R.: C++ optimizations for mobile applications. In: 10th International Symposium on Consumer Electronics (2006)
7. Hammer, J., Zhang, J., Khushraj, A.: Three-tier Architecture for Ubiquitous Data Access, pp. 177–180 (2001)
8. Jin, L., Liu, L.: An Ontology Definition Metamodel based Ripple-Effect Analysis Method for Ontology Evolution, Computer Supported Cooperative Work in Design, pp. 1–6 (2006)
9. Koutero, A., Fujita, S., Sugawara, K.: Design of an Assisting Agent Using a Dynamic Ontology. Computer and Information Science (ICIS), pp. 611–616 (2010)
10. Maedche, A., Staab, S.: Ontology Learning for the Semantic Web Ontologies for the Semantic Web. Working paper (2001)
11. Busagala, L.S.P., Ohyama, W., Wakabayash, T.I, Kimura, F.: Improving automatic text classification by integrated feature analysis. IEICE Trans. 91(4), 1101–1109 (2008)
12. Hogeboom, M., Esmahi, L.: Constructing knowledge bases for e-learning using protege 2000 and web services. In: 19th International Conference on Advanced Information Networking and Applications, 1, pp. 215–220 (2005)
13. Ferro, R., Nieto, Y., Montenegro, C.: Ontological knowledge model to engineering project integration based on PMS. Int. J. Inform. Process. Manage. 6, 1–11 (2015)

Towards the ICT Development in Colombia Through the Gartner Hyper Cycle

Michael S. Parra[✉], Vanessa Nieto, and Fernando Lopez

System Engineering, Corporación Unificada Nacional de Educación Superior CUN,
Bogotá, Colombia
{michael.parra,yuri_nieto,jose_lopezq}@cun.edu.co

Abstract. This paper describes a way to measure the development and evolution
of technologies implemented and managed by the Ministry of Information and
Communication Technologies in Colombia, through the use of tools of a quantitative nature where the process that a technology has had in years and how profitable it was for that administration is represented in graphs of analytical use, as
well as the different comparisons that can be made with different countries by
technology developers, technology consumers and/or emerging countries. At the
local level, this analysis is made on the basis of different reports of implementation
of technology produced by the different government reporting entities.

Keywords: Hypercube of gartner · Information and Communication
Technologies (ICT) · Hyper cycle · PETIC · MINTIC

1 Introduction

Technology, in addition to its evolution and development, has given ways to measure
its growth in a quantitative way, to observe in a scientific and analytical manner the
development and evolution that each technology has experienced, and in the same way
measure whether that technological progress was in the process of development and
implementation, or if it finally managed to establish itself and become a trend and a
necessity in the evolution of a process.

The first section of the article begins with a conceptualization of aspects contained
in the Gartner Hype Cycle (Method of measuring cycles of technology development)
[1], the phases of the cycle and the different criteria to be taken into account to measure
the development of a technology. This is followed by definitions of each of its phases.

With regard to the evaluation of the method and its application to the measurement
of ICT (Information and Communication Technologies) [2], this work looks closely at
the flow or cycle of leading technologies in the different governmental and commercial
and/or industrial areas in which they are used. This is followed by a detailed description
of the different ICT in use and the appropriation of ICT [3]. Is also included a briefly
history and description of concepts and guidelines of the ICT in Colombia.

The second section gives a brief overview of the evolution of ICT and its operation
in matters of the appropriation of ICT according to PETIC (Strategic Technology Plan)

© Springer International Publishing AG 2016
J.C. Figueroa-García et al. (Eds.): WEA 2016, CCIS 657, pp. 380–391, 2016.
DOI: 10.1007/978-3-319-50880-1_33

[4] in Colombia under the administration of the MINTIC (Ministry of Information and Communication Technologies in Colombia). The section explains the way in which the processes of the study, bidding, implementation and appropriation of a new technology under the administration of the MINTIC in its period of evolution works and how, according to national government reports there have been the most significant changes in technology and the PETIC in this century; changes that have happened in the past 10 years where there have been demonstrable transformations in terms of the appropriation of ICT in the country, prioritizing its cities, its people, local businesses and foreign investors.

The last section shows the study methodology of the investigation, and how the Hype Cycle was applied to identify the different stages of individual ICT in Colombia from its arrival in the country until its decline or success and appropriation in the country. Thus, the technologies that were taken on and those that were not will also be identified. These examples and comparisons implemented on the model of the Gartner Hype Cycle serve to find the strengths and weaknesses in the stages of the study, development and production of new ICT, compare levels of knowledge and proceed analytically to the decision-making stage.

2   What is the Gartner Cycle?

2.1   Gartner Hype Cycle

The Hype Cycle characterizes the typical progression of an emerging technology by representing its passage through different phases or stages called cycles in the Gartner Cycle. In that cycle the importance given to emerging technologies and the role that they play in a market or technological domain can be shown.

This cycle was first established in Gartner, located in Stanford, United States, an analysis and investigation center which provides opinions, advice and different business engineering data on information technology. This cycle that bears the name of Gartner has been a useful tool in company and governmental decision-making, on how an investment may positively or negatively affect productivity or the economy according to the need to possess a new technology that contributes to the development of a specific task. Similarly, it allows for measurements or comparisons about the level of techno-logical advancement in certain sectors in comparison to the cycle offered by Gartner, giving an annual report about the performance of each technological innovation and the stage in which it is compared to the previous year. To give an example, in the first quarter of 2016, the Gartner Cycle for 2015 was released, which clearly showed the progress, setbacks or total loss for the year (Fig. 1).

2.2   Phases of the Gartner Hype Cycle

The Hype Cycle is measured in five phases [5], which can be seen in Graph 1. These five phases represent the processes of change and evolution of a technology which governments, companies and shareholders see and take into account to decide whether or not to invest in a technology, according to its criteria, interpretation and analysis,

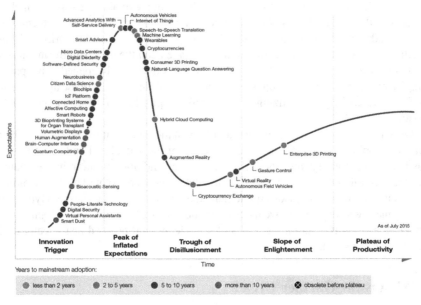

Fig. 1. Technology processes per stage. Source: Gartner, Inc.

whether to invest or purchase due to the advertising boom that a technology experiences at the peak of its expectations or if such technology should be ignored simply because it is not complying with the basic principles of expectation and is still currently in the development phase.

1. Technology Trigger: On the way to the peak of expectations, at which articles and means of communication explain the technology, how it works and discuss its potential impact on business and society. It is in this stage where technology begins to emerge through generations 1, 2, 3, 4 etc. To position itself in this stage the technology must be highly a specialized product or extremely difficult to use at that time due to still being in the study and development phases of usability, usefulness and user adaptation.

2. Peak of Inflated-Expectations: Advertising plays an important role in this phase of the cycle, since if the technology does not yet generate expectations by itself or by what it does, the advertising and focus on the cases of success could act as the trigger to launch the product to fame and expectation. The number of suppliers that offer the technology increases with the peak of expectations. These suppliers are mainly companies and smaller vendors who attempt to use the increasing amount of demand for the product to benefit their marketing.

3. Trough of Disillusionment: The technology ceases to be an urgent target for companies and the communication media lowers expectations of the product by means of complaints and negative reviews. Unlike during the launch and ascent to the peak of expectations, this phase discredits the product and sends it quickly towards the

trough of disillusionment; as is the case of some products or technologies that were still in the process of testing and passed very quickly to the peak of expectations where they ended up being a total failure because they were not given enough space for their development. In other cases, technologies had such flaws in their advertising campaigns that they were not known well enough to prevail.

4. Slope of Enlightenment: Due to the new advances in the technology, it begins to justify its need and extensive analyses are conducted on how the innovation and development of this technology could benefit businesses, their functioning and the way corporate processes are supported. It is easier to understand and adapt, given that there is already sufficient documentation in that regard. This is no longer a development stage of the product as such, it is the stage of development and adaptation to the specific needs of each client, who tests it and is documented based on the successful cases and experiences of different sectors of the corporate world. This technology is becoming continually more diverse and more understandable in its applicability, the risks at the time of use decrease and on the contrary the benefits increase.

5. Plateau of Productivity: The plateau represents the principle of conventional adoption of a technology, when the real benefits of the technology are proven and accepted. These technologies are appropriate and are much more useful than previously thought in the development of solutions to a specific need. This technology, being more mature, incites businesses to reduce costs of the study and increase costs in the innovation of this technology and the culture of appropriation. As this technology matures and becomes high profile, an "ecosystem" often evolves around it.

2.3 Information and Communication Technologies

Information and Communication Technologies or ICT [6] correspond and relate to all the technologies that in one way or another interfere and mediate in the informational and communicative processes between human beings, and can be understood as a set of technological resources integrated among themselves, that provide, by means of facilities of hardware, software, and telecommunications, the semi-automation and communication of processes related to business, scientific research, teaching, learning, matters of daily life, as well as fields such as agriculture, medicine and communications. These are the technologies of information and communication that we use in everyday and ordinary surroundings, but that to a certain extent provide added value to each task that is performed or desired to be done.

The importance of the use of ICT is that whether adopted or implemented, it is there, being more productive, and also being able to complete a greater number of tasks in the same time at a reduced cost through the use of equipment that helps us to deal with large amounts of information and process it quickly. Depending on the type of ICT that use, the ability to transmit and receive information almost immediately means that transfers of messages, data or information can be made from any part of the world in a matter of minutes. It could certainly be said that the development and the popularization of the Internet is mainly responsible for the growth and empowerment of ICT in the various fields.

2.4 ICT Appropriation by the General Public

This refers to the knowledge, practices and indispensable use of ICT tools implemented by citizens when faced with the developments and computing resources present in the 21st century, contributing to the closure of the digital gap from access to the Internet or other ICT resources [7].

The appropriation of information and communication technologies, is understood as the process by which an actor meets their needs in any given context in a timely and convenient manner, through the use of technology. For the process of appropriation to be successful, most importantly of all in society, conditions must be provided that favor him in all of the above. That is, actions of public appropriation will be more efficient in a context of promotion via organizational and governmental appropriation.

For example, when a citizen can easily and quickly gain access to applications from his home that allow him to avoid lengthy procedures for issuing documents, making payments or submitting applications before the government, this requires that they have adopted information technologies favorably, these technologies being relevant to the user at the time in which they perceive that their needs are met in a timely manner with technology and, consequently, feel the need to appropriate them.

The work of appropriation on the part of the Government and of public and private organizations makes sense to the extent that its ultimate aim is society. Today it is a reality that tablets are used in schools and, as these tablets are complemented by applications that promote their use in relation to productivity, well-being, quality of life and other social objectives, the appropriation will be successful.

3 ITC Strategies in Colombia

During their administration, the mission of the ministries or departments of ICT that exist in the government of each country is to offer best practices or appropriation techniques and implementation of ICT in the country, cities, small towns and local companies or companies with foreign investment. By doing this they seek to provide the best results in innovation, development, research and effective production on issues of technology or communications, always looking for constant improvements in innovation to stay on the cutting edge of technology as far as their strategic plan for technology and the investment by the government permits.

3.1 MINTIC and Its Strategy

In Colombia, the Ministry of Information and Communications Technologies (MINTIC) was founded on 30 June 2009; protected by law 134[8]1, the Communications Ministry went on to become the new MINTIC transforming with its creation technology in the history of the country, which in the past 5 years has managed to connect more citizens.

It has multiplied the connections of homes and businesses in figures which years ago and during previous government administrations in Colombia would have seemed unfathomable. One of the major achievements of the MINTIC has been go from having 2 million internet connections to approximately 8.8 million in the year 2014 and with the predictions and plans to double the figure by the year 2017. All of this has been thanks to several projects that the MINTIC manages on issues of the appropriation of ICT to support and stimulate the development of the technology sector in the country.

The MINTIC, as head of the technological sector in Colombia and leader of policy in the field of information and communication technologies, developed the Sectoral and Institutional Strategic Plan known as "Plan Live Digital", which is a product of a participatory process involving the contribution of the entities that are part of the administrative sector, companies representing different industries, the education sector represented by several universities and interested members of the public. The quantitative part of the companies, industries, education sector and the public is difficult to indicate due to the fact that it would relate to particular times of the process of strategic direction, and the lifetimes of the government.

The Information and Communication Technologies sector is composed of manufacturing, commercial and services industries whose products collect, process, create, transmit or display data and information electronically [8].

For manufacturing industries, products must be designed to fulfill the function of treatment of information and communication, including transmission and presentation, and must use electronic processing to detect, measure and/or register physical phenomena or to control a physical process.

For service industries, products must be designed to allow the function of information treatment and communication by electronic means, without negatively affecting the environment." [9].

However, the way that companies may make proposals to the MINTIC are framed by their participation in the exercise of planning, referred to in the previous point, and participation in the realization of agreements to the proposals put forward through the mechanisms of objective selection. In the latter, it is not necessary that they be companies in the ICT sector, but that they comply with the requirements of each process in particular.

3.2   Categorization in Investment Projects of MINTIC

The categorization of investment projects in the MINTIC is done according to Decree 841 [4]. Investment projects can be in five categories:

1. Projects that generate direct or indirect benefits in the form of goods or services.
2. Projects that have the function of recuperating a direct benefit generating capacity, such as: literacy activities; training; nutrition and the eradication of diseases; vaccination; attention to women, children or the elderly.
3. Projects that do not generate direct or indirect benefits, but allow future projects to be identified. These are basic or research studies.
4. Projects that serve the purpose of providing credit, financing projects from the categories above during the course of the year of execution. For these, global amounts are approved and it is the responsibility of the organism or executing agency to define the projects that are financed in this way.

In exceptional circumstances, the monies destined to the payment of guarantees granted by the Nation in relation to third party loans may be registered as investment projects, which are made effective only when these loan agreements were completed prior to December 31 1991 (Fig. 2).

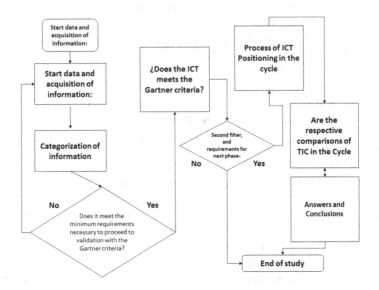

Fig. 2. Case-based work flow

4   Development of the Study Through the Gartner Cycle

4.1   Proposed Methodology

Gartner has made about 5 studies annually on ICT in different environments and continental models, in which there are countries with a high value of investment as well as others where ICT is so far just an emerging term [11]. It is from these analyses, graphs or reports that comparisons of the state of ICT in Colombia can be drawn; how close it is to becoming a technological power like India or how far behind it is when compared to emerging countries such as some on the African continent.

The investigation was made in several stages according to chart 3 which represents workflow. It was segmented in the following way:

1. Start data and acquisition of information: The information is taken from different sources, both Gartner techniques or criteria as well as annual, quarterly, semi-annual MINTIC reports and other reports from the OCyT, SIUST and articles related to ICT, the appropriation of ICT, Gartner and the Gartner Cycle.
2. Categorization of information: The information is adopted and categorized according to its type, be that an ICT based on E-commerce, Security, CRM, Work 3.0, Networks, Cloud Computing, Hardware, etc.
3. Does it meet the nminimun requirements?: whether such information is collected has dates, reports of advances in technology, press boom (articles in technology magazines or adverts).

4. Does the ICT meets the Gartner criteria?: The ICT that meets the requirements and of which there is information are taken, though this does not mean that the others are not taken into account, it only means that the technology is not yet mature enough or well known in the specific sector in which measurement is desired, in this case, Colombia and MINTIC.

5. Second filter, and requirements for next phase: In this case, the now mature technologies go on to be considered as state-of-the-art technologies or have a certain level of importance or recognition in the MINTIC or in the appropriation of ICT in Colombia, be that in private or public enterprises as well as in society.

6. The ICT is positioned in the cycle according to criteria: Taking into account the ICT criteria, they are positioned according to their characteristics, such as time in the market, investment levels, projection, number of companies that provide support to such technology and knowledge and appropriation of the ICT.

7. The respective comparisons of ICT in the cycle are made: The positions that the ICT achieves in the cycle are validated and compared with each other; observations or comparisons can be carried out of ICT with other countries and with the Gartner annual report of emerging technologies.

8. Answers and Conclusions: According to the answers that the curve throws up and the comparisons that were made, it can be determined which technologies are still not 100% developed and represent fertile ground for investment or research; one can also detect whether the lack of technological advancement affects others positively or negatively. Further studies may also be carried out.

9. End of study.

5   Results

Taking into account these graphic resources and ICT management reports, a comprehensive analysis was carried out of the operation of the Gartner study, the techniques to identify the progress in technologies, the positioning criteria of each technology in each one of its stages, and also the time identification icons that can be assigned to each of these technologies.

In the case of Colombia, an assessment was made according to the different reports of the MINTIC, its adjustment to PETIC, weekly, monthly and quarterly progress reports of investment in technology, as well as the different reports of the Colombian Observatory of Science and Technology (OCyT) according to their science and technology indicators in Colombia from 2015 (ICT) [12]. The different technologies implemented in Colombia were adjusted in the Gartner Hype Cycle chart.

In the study on the global scale, the implementation of initiatives such as the IOT [14] (Internet of Things) in India could be seen to be in the peak of the expectations, while here in Colombia it is still is in the launch phase. Not because it has not yet been a part of innovation, but rather because the concept and what that means is not yet clear for the population and even more seriously, in some technology companies it remains an overwhelming concept.

A case in which Colombia has technology in the peak of expectations (and can be said to already be going through the trough of disillusionment to be strengthened in the slope of enlightenment and plateau of productivity) is Cloud Computing and the structure of data centers [15]. This is reflected in the latest yearly reports of other emerging countries by Gartner (Fig. 3).

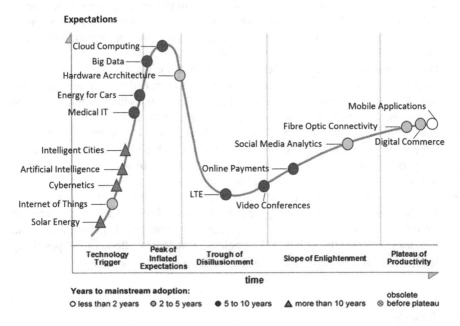

Fig. 3. Gartner Hype Cycle, ICT in Colombia.

For the dates of time or projections of how long it will take a technology to be implemented, the different reports and records of the impact of advertising at technological and corporate level were taken into account, where reference was made to those new technologies, such as the case of the entry of Big Data into Colombia, where their first appearances in technology date from 2013 [13], while in other countries they date many more years back.

It can be seen how investments and research in technology have been strategically implemented and are in the process of appropriation. According to the descriptions above, it is clear how each technology developing in Colombia is a key, so each one is supported by the others. Colombia is an emerging country with high progress and development in telecommunications technologies, where ICT has been its priority and, more still, the connectivity of the country. Colombia has adopted, as a priority, connectivity to all areas of the country, with the aim that research and development start to take first place, thereby increasing the percentage of investment in the various MINTIC research projects, which will be reflected in the medium term in the reports of the OCyT.

In comparison to other countries and the evolution of their technologies in 2015, Colombia is in an intermediate position, being consistent and taking into account one of the benchmarks for Latin America in technology, and an emerging country with projections of development and fertile ground for new investors in technology who are already advancing with agreements and negotiations under the protection of the Chancellery and the supervision of the MINTIC.

According to the development in some technologies like cloud computing, Colombia is at levels similar to India in relation to the levels of support and assistance on site, but India leads in both Data Center infrastructure and connectivity, that is to say that although there is good Cloud and Data Center service, there is still a need for better performance and support in transfer speed and connectivity.

It is in this area that the management of resources can be highlighted since several technologies have not yet reached the peak of expectations due to the failures in connectivity that occur in Colombia, the majority of which the MINTIC has promised to correct for the 2018 period.

Because the only way that Colombia can be compared with the outstanding competitiveness in technology of other countries is when it has a connectivity of over 90%, currently it can only be compared with emerging countries, such as those of Africa and some of the members of the Cooperation Council for the Arab States of the Gulf. These are countries that are also working hard on appropriation of ICT and, as a means of that appropriation, the implementation of connectivity, countries with the necessary knowledge developed in ICT, but still scarce of tools. Colombia can be classified in this way.

6 Conclusions

In the case of Big Data [16], which in other countries with greater investment in the development of technologies spends approximately 5 to 10 years in the process of the trough of disillusionment before reaching the plateau of productivity, in Colombia still requires 2 to 5 years to reach the peak of expectations.

Considering these data and reports of the Hype Cycle of different countries and continents, it becomes possible to take into account the development reports of MINTIC, articles from magazines that specialize in ICT development in Colombia, and other reports of some independent research and development companies, and thereby make a report similar to the Gartner Hype Cycle regarding ICT development in Colombia directed by the MINTIC.

The development of new technologies in Colombia can be appreciated by bearing in mind that the budget for research and development is on average 1% of the annual national budget, and that useful and bio-sustainable technologies such as solar energy are up until now still in the release process, given that there are very few companies and organizations who dare to invest in these types of technologies.

This is even more the case when they are so new in a country that they may lead to high research and maintenance costs, according to the description of the phase in which they are located. But it can also be appreciated that Colombia, in digital technologies, has demonstrated great advancement with analytical strategies and social media, web marketing and mobile applications that are close (on average 0 to 2 years) to the plateau of productivity with some huge progress being made on issues of development and research for the development of software.

One of the technologies that are in the trough of disillusionment is 4G LTE technology since, according to reports of Asomovil, some members of the public still hold beliefs about diseases, pests and harm regarding the installation of antennas for mobile communication.

According to the presidential draft for 2018, the number of connections should double, leaving more than 20 million citizens connected on average. However, due to the different problems in the installation of antennas, for example in the case of 4G LTE connectivity because there is no great difference between a 3.5G HDSPA and a 3.75G that feigns to be a real 4G LTE, it is difficult to achieve that goal.

The development of cloud computing can be seen in Colombia, where different supporting companies have been formed aimed by multiple sectors of the industry that require such technology. It can also be observed in the clinics that are implementing technologies for the administration of medicine by means of medical information technology. It is further apparent in the agricultural industries, where the cloud is used to bring administrative documentation from the city to rural areas. This information and access to information is possible thanks to the use of fiber optic connectivity, technology that is on the verge of passing into the plateau of productivity.

References

1. Linden, A., Fenn, J.: The Gartner Strategic Analysis Report. Understanding Gartner's Hype Cycles, R-20-1971 (2003)
2. Leal, E.T., Fenn, J.: Revista de Universidad y Sociedad del Conocimiento. Las tecnologías de la información y comunicaciones (TIC) y la brecha digital: su impacto en la sociedad de México, pp. 1–8 (2008)
3. Montes, J., Ochoa, S.: Acta Colombiana de Psicología. Apropiación de las tecnologías de la información y comunicación en cursos universitarios 9, 2 (2006)
4. Mejia, M.I., Bejarano, J.F.: Arquitectura TI Colombiana. Guía Cómo Estructurar el Plan Estratégico de Tecnologías de la Información - PETI (Versión 1.0) (2016)
5. Sondergaart, P.: Inside Gartner Research. How the art, science and rigor behind our research process and proprietary methodologies help you make the right decisions, every day. Versión 1.0, pp. 7–15 (2015)
6. Echeverria, J.: Revista iberoamericana de ciencia tecnología y sociedad. Apropiación social de las tecnologías de la información y la comunicación, pp. 171–182 (2016)
7. Macau, R.: Revista de Universidad y Sociedad del Conocimiento. TIC: ¿PARA QUÉ? (Funciones de las tecnologías de la información y la comunicación en las organizaciones), pp. 1–12 (2004)
8. Chandler, N., Hostmann, B., Rayner, N., Herschel, G.: Gartner's Business Analytics Framework. Processes and platforms that need to be integrated and aligned to take a more strategic approach to business intelligence (BI) (2011)
9. LeHong, H., Fenn, J.: Gartner's Research. Hype Cycle for Emerging Technologies (2011)
10. Barnekow, H.: EMC Forum Survey 2013 Results. Transforming IT study survey results 2013 (2013)

11. Evans, D.: Cisco Informe Técnico - Internet de las cosas (2011)
12. Smith, D., Petri, G.: Gartner's Research. Predicts 2014: Cloud Computing Affects All Aspects of IT (2013)
13. Sanou, B.: ITU Measuring the Information Society Report. Measuring the Information Society Report 2014 (2014)

A Proposed Architecture for the Development of a Cluster for Graduates of Higher Education Institutions

Alejandra Peña-Mosquera, Katherin Flórez-Vargas[✉],
and José Ignacio Rodríguez-Molano

Universidad Distrital Francisco José de Caldas, Bogotá, Colombia
{alpenam,kflorezv}@correo.udistrital.edu.co,
jirodriguezmolano@gmail.com

Abstract. This article discusses the needs and requirements of a mobile application oriented to the graduates from higher education institutions, taking into account the communication established so far in these institutions, the benefits offered by the special applications development for the interaction of between the different communities and the interests that may have the graduates of universities related to their alma mater. For this, there will be a preliminary outline about the architecture that implementation would require for their development, taking into account the needs of users and the viability of infrastructure resources; next to this improvements may be possible about the graduates quality of life and opportunities to develop in the future new utilities in this application.

Keywords: Mobile application · Graduates · Systems architecture · Higher education

1 Introduction

With the outcome of the smart-phones, the market of mobile telephony has revolutionized the way we communicate and keep ourselves informed <always online>. From this, the use of mobile applications takes a leading role and gives a real sense of the use of these devices.

Mobile Technologies offer the opportunity to create tools for assertive communication, besides facilitating other social dynamics that can benefit the academic community. Keeping in touch with the graduates, for example, is crucial given that as the universities as the graduates need a permanent bond that allows a mutual benefit; for the graduates it provides new job opportunities, job agencies affiliations, affiliations for graduates associations and in many cases they can still count with some of the benefits they had got as students. On the other side, universities can track the movements and dynamics of the human resources market to enhance their academic quality and find new opportunities to improve.

Nowadays new possibilities are explored in front of mobile applications design and development in order to ease the communication in the academy and that works as a sensor

© Springer International Publishing AG 2016
J.C. Figueroa-García et al. (Eds.): WEA 2016, CCIS 657, pp. 392–402, 2016.
DOI: 10.1007/978-3-319-50880-1_34

that can store information, so that it can be used in a model of BigData for academic information analysis. All this looking for a constant feedback to improve the quality of the universities, in the face of the labor guarantees that can be provided to the graduates.

For the understanding of this work, it is shown first a justification for it including the importance of IT in any 2016 university and explaining the need of developing the concept of the application and the infrastructure associated; secondly, it is shown a brief background of mobile technologies in the life style and life quality of people nowadays and how this has change the way people gets involved with the market. Then there is the development stage, where the viability of the idea of the application is studied by a review of the current state of TI's over the different universities relative to their graduates in Bogota, Colombia. In the Methodology section we develop the proposal through the architecture diagramming and a class diagram so the technologic viability could be explored; after this, we summarize our proposal for the application concept and finally we present as result a proposal about how to evaluate properly the prototype of an application.

2   Justification

Considering the rise of the concept of portability that currently exists, the growing trend in the use of mobile applications and looking for the benefits of the Alumni Association, it aims to do a proposal of infrastructure for mobile applications focused on graduates from the institutions of higher education, which helps to maintain a permanent bond with the university, promoting personal professional and social development, for the alumni, in addition to promote a sense of belonging and university integration.

It is intended that this analysis and application design, can serve as a basis for the creation of a mobile App that aims in maintaining the bond between the graduates of the universities, in addition to publicizing all benefits, academic programs and in general any activity that can be made by the graduates.

In addition to this, the information obtained from the application will be useful for the universities to be able to perform the tracking; in what fields and how the graduates of the university perform academic and occupationally, so that at the same time, these can design strategies and tools in the different academic programs to enforce those fields that are at the cutting edge in the labor sphere, and review those fields that are in decline.

This application would work within the university context, focused on a specific community; this in the Apps stores in the nowadays has a high usage because approximately 20% of the available applications are focused on communities, within the most important are those whose profits are reading news, radio, or weather forecasting, those are the ones that generally have more relevance within the day to day of a community [1]. In the particular case of application for universities the most important topics for the target group would be: news, jobs, benefits, events and forums. All this, of course relative to the academic affairs of the institutions.

For the conceptual development of an application such as the one required in this case were taken into account the criteria raised by the model TAMM (Technology Acceptance Model by Mobile Services) that include: ease of use, the value perceived by the user and the reliability of the information provided by the application [2]. This is considered to be because of the fact that although it can be thought a functional application without taking into account these variables, for an application to really represent a benefit over time to a user, this must be attractive, easy to use in the free time and that its reliability has relevance in the decisions that a potential user takes in their daily lives.

The technological tools designed for the well-being of the users as it is this indirectly, require a fundamental characteristic and that is that they should invite the user to modify their behavior toward one more profitable, in this case, the application looks forward to ease the decision-making of the users with respect to their working life or academic and in some cases economic; to achieve this, the use of the application must generate 'engagement' in the user and give sufficient information to support the new decisions by using intervention methods as a notification system, informative functionalities and all this with the ability to customize the tasks and information management to optimize the interpretation of the data and improve the understanding across a query [2].

3   Background

In the last ten years in Latin America mobile telephony has had a large increase; thanks to the reduction of costs in the equipment and the evolution of mobile technologies, has grown the number of users and the transfer speeds of information have increased [3].

Parallel to the growth of the use of mobile devices, the evolution of the same, has led to the integration of various technologies to these devices, technologies such as WiFi, Bluetooth, GPS, infrared, touchscreen and USB, among others, has allowed that the mobile phone is compatible with a wide range of devices and can be synchronized with other computers to exchange information [4]. This is the case, as usually arise on the smartphone, an intelligent device that combines the functions of a mobile phone with a PDA., which also offers substantial advantages, not only because it avoids the need to carry multiple portable devices, but because they offer a real integration of voice and data applications in a single device [3].

The first smartphone was designed by IBM in 1992, it was called Simon. This device was exposed in that year in the expo COMDEX as a product concept, but until 1993 was released to the public and marketed by BellSouth. Simon, apart from being a mobile phone, it contained calendar, address book, World Clock, Calculator, notebook, e-mail, sent and received fax and included games. Had no physical buttons to dial. Instead used a touch screen to select the contacts with your finger or to create facsimiles and memos with an optional stylus. The text was entered with a predictive keyboard included in the screen.

From the hand of the Smartphones it's been created in people the demand for the use of new services. Services that are based on these technologies to solve specific problems in the business area (m-business), commercial (m-commerce), academic (m-learning), health (m-health) and social (social networks like: Facebook, Twitter, Skype, Instagram, among others). That is how mobile applications are born and developed in order to supply the demand for these mobile services. The trend toward the use of mobile applications has had a high growth in the last ten years, the mobile platforms continue refining their perform-ance, and the need of users for a wide variety of mobile applications is increasing.

In 2015 the worldwide growth and penetration of the smartphones maintained its growth and it is estimated that by the end of 2016 46% of the world population will be using a smartphone; this represents almost 4.8 billion users who consume mobile applications. A market where day-to-day new needs arise, and thousands of offers are presented.

According to a study done by the company of analytical data, Flurry, the average time that people spend on their mobile phones and tablets every day is 158 min. Of these 158 min, 127 are invested in searches of browser and only 31 are invested by browsing or by visiting web pages. In the case of the smartphones and tablets, the different ways to find out products and research through mobile applications have increased rapidly so that joining this trend can be very advantageous for the entire organization with the interest in improving its accessibility.

4   Development

The development of a mobile application parts from the need generated by the absence of a way of effective communication between universities and their graduates to allow a reliable feedback upon the real impact of the services provided by the institution itself. It is here where the need arises to create a method that encourages constant communication between the University community and graduates.

Currently Colombia counts with 288 institutions registered by the Ministry of National Education, some of them with a presence in multiple cities around the country from which we chose two sets to evaluate as a reference. Analyzing the sector at Bogotá's level, we took the 19 public universities that has the capital of the country and the 14 universities currently cataloged currently as high quality (Table 1).

3 attributes in those universities were observed:

- If they have a web page with a special space dedicated to graduates.
- If they have any official profile for graduates in Facebook social network.
- If they have a special mobile application for graduates of the university.

These attributes were analyzed in order to detect the relationship between the university and its graduates. The analysis of these institutions found that 76% of these have a web page to contact the graduates, only 39% have an official profile focused on graduates on Facebook and none has developed a mobile application that promotes the link between graduates and their university.

Under these statistics we highlight the importance of the relationship that must be maintained between graduates and university, because this bond helps to:

- Know the quality of the education at the university, taking as a basis the opinion of the graduates about their own education.
- Analyze the impact that has the academy in the society.
- Provide information to support decision-making in the academic institutions to meet the labor existing demand.

Table 1. Reference Universities

Bogotá's Public Universities
Military Education Center – Cemil
National Directorate of Schools
School of Military Engineers
School of intelligence and counterintelligence Brigadier General Ricardo Charry Solano
School of Logistics
School of Postgraduate Courses of the Colombian Air Force Captain José Edmundo Sandoval - Epfac
Military Cadet School General Jose Maria Cordova
Higher School of Administration Publica-Esap-
Higher School of War
Technological School Central Technical Institute
Caro y Cuervo Institute
Technological Institute of Electronics and Comunicaciones-Itec-
National Service of Aprendizaje-Sena-
University Distrital-Francisco José de Caldas
University Militar-Nueva Granada
National University OPEN AND DISTANCE Unad
National University of Colombia
National Pedagogical University
Universidad-Colegio Greater of Cundinamarca
Bogotá's high quality Universities
College of Higher Studies of Administración-Cesa-
College of Our Lady of the Rosary
National Directorate of Schools
Colombian School of Engineering Julio Garavito
Foundation University of Bogota - Jorge Tadeo Lozano
Pontificia Universidad Javeriana
De La Salle University
University of The Andes
University Ean
Universidad Externado de Colombia
University Militar-Nueva Granada
National University of Colombia
University Santo Tomas
University Sergio Arboleda

5 Methodology

To consider the development of this application the hardware and software resources with which this is going to work should be checked, for this, an architecture was established taking into account the functional components of the application and the

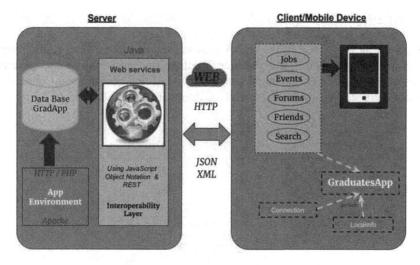

Fig. 1. Architecture of the application

infrastructure that it would bear. For the design of this architecture we pursue make a minimal use of physical resources because they have a higher costs compared to the infrastructure provided by the web. In this case, we propose to locate the information base in a cloud, which in this case will be filled initially from a support database to ensure the integrity of the official information in case of a security attack.

In Fig. 1 we can see the architecture suggested for the development of the mobile application. This uses the PHP language (Personal Home Page), and HTML (Hyper Text Markup Language. This is cataloged as easy learning by its flexibility and great similarity in syntax to languages such as C, Java or Perl.

One of the most interesting features of PHP is its easy to connect to system database managers such as MySQL, which has generated a major use to build dynamic applications [5].

Figure 1 shows the architecture of the application for the graduates, which has 2 main components:

1. *Server,* where is developed the integration with the data base; the initial information that parts from the data of graduates.
2. *Client/Mobile device*, where we present the proposed mobile application and its different classes.

The infrastructure connects with the application thanks to a set of web services, which works as a form of communication between the data base and the mobile application.

The web service that is defined as a set of protocols and standards that are used for exchanging data, enters the main resources of the Moodle (jobs, events, forums, friends and searchs) to receive each request by the user, this to recover and/or treat the data necessary to adequately respond to the request made.

The user in turn interacts on the application according to the proposed design in each interface; each of these screens is controlled thanks to Java classes responsible for each action that you want to execute, in this case the GraduatesApp class is responsible for the communication between all the classes, acting as home.

Figure 2 shows the use of the class GraduatesApp and its modules (jobs, events, forums, friends and searchs) and at the same time their connection with the administering classes of the database on the mobile device, the classes: LocalInfo and Connection, responsible for storing and pulling out all the information for each user.

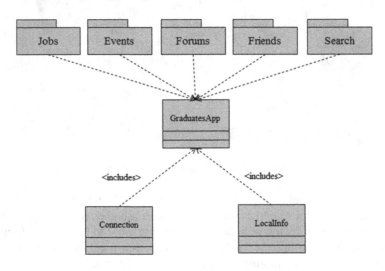

Fig. 2. View of the user. Built by the authors.

Figure 3 at the same time, shows the functionality of the server part, mainly the interaction of the web services infrastructure of the application with the classes.

Web services use a pattern of Project Data Access Object (DAO) to access and manipulate all the information that contains the database of Moodle. For each type of data that you plan to use, creates a DAO interface that indicates the operations that can be performed with this type; and at the same time in order to increase the flexibility of the application, the DAO classes are not created directly by the web services; instead, it is used a factory for the construction of the DAO classes [6]. That is to say, thanks to these web services users can access all of the resources of the Moodle.

Once defined the functional part of the interface, decisions must be made of aesthetics of the application taking into account the brand identity of each university, the perception of the graduates and the concept of the application in case there is one and apply to the interface the colors, fonts, proportions etc., that have been decided about the concept of aesthetics.

For the approach of an application we must take into account that in the applications, users can have several types of interaction, which can be classified in a general way as informational/utilitarian or experiential/entertainment. Informational type applications are those in which the user has a clear purpose of use to enter, as in the case of banking applications or online purchases and its purpose is clearly utilitarian and on the other

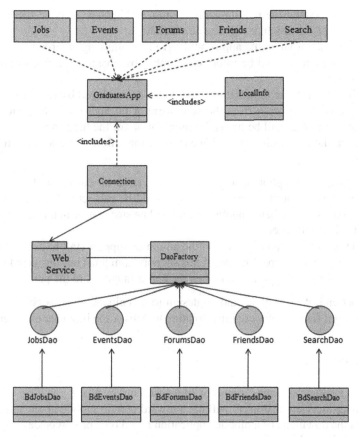

Fig. 3. View of the server. Built by the authors.

side are the experiential applications as chat rooms or video games that have as their main objective the entertainment or recreation of the user [7].

For the proposal of this application was taken into account that mostly this should be informational, but to integrate the forums section a space was opened for the exploration of the content in a free way by adding an experiential component, which favors the 'engagement' of the user with the brand, in this case the university.

At the end of this phase of architectural design of the application we could move to the next phase of the process, the interface design and development.

6 Proposal

The proposed infrastructure was design to support an app with several features which are supposed to give a sense of satisfaction with the university to the graduates. It is because of that that it need a strong support in two senses, firstly, holding the Data Base that contains the basic information of the users and finally, keep the traffic which will be generated by the interactions and the general use of the app.

To fully understand the requirements for this architecture, it is needed to have a preliminar idea of the task that will be done with it.

To have a general view, the app should have the following environments to allow the graduates no interact and be informed about: Jobs, Events, Forums, Contacts and Personal Profile.

A timeline with all the information should also be displayed by feeding the mobile device with new information from the administrator through the web services to the "Connection" class that will be fixing the information for the final user.

In addition the application could have a space that allows access to the following possibilities:

3. *Create Item:* This option would allow us to create an entry, as "Employment", "Forum", "event" or "benefit", entry that should be subject to the approval of the administrators before being published and will be stored now in the server so it can be shown to all the users.
4. *Help:* This section would contact to the admin or support staff to ask questions or solve technical problems. The use of this support team must be considered to set the access to the system information when the app is launched to the public.

The front-end of this app should be design to be enjoyable and sophisticated as it needs to be light for the software infrastructure to deliver the best user experience.

7 Results

For a proper evaluation of the proposal we suggest a survey where you use 6 criteria for understanding the view that users will have toward certain mobile application and its decision on the download of a mobile application based on a prototype developed. The criteria would be (a) Is it Attractive to engage during the user experience? (b) How good is the Perceived Value by the user? (c) Has it Ease of use? (d) Has it Reliability/Credibility from the user's experience? (e) Is there Fun and excitement in the experience? (f) How likely is that a user recommend the mobile app? (Diffusivity).

These six criteria are based on the concept of usability, which in the case of mobile applications is used to define how easy to use they can be and multiple aspects must be measure taking into account the interaction man-system. These attributes allow you to make evaluations and comparisons of the usability of different systems. Next, they are presented in summary:

- *Ease of Learning (Learnability):* How easy it is for users to accomplish basic tasks the first time they are faced with the app [8]. It's usually measured by the time spent with the system until they are be able to perform certain tasks in less of a given time (the time commonly used by expert users).
- *Efficiency:* The number of transactions per unit of time that the user can perform using the system. What is sought is the maximum speed to finish different tasks by the user. The greater the usability of a system, the faster the user to use it, and the work is done more quickly.

- *Quality to be Remembered (Memorability):* When users return to use the design after a period of non-use, how long does it take to return to acquire the necessary knowledge to use it efficiently? [8].
- *Errors:* Any system must be designed to prevent users from making mistakes in their use, trying to minimize their number. In addition, the system itself must facilitate the recovery in case the user commits errors [8].
- *Satisfaction:* Refers to the subjective impression of the user on the system. How much the users liked the various attributes of the system?

In general terms we can affirm the mobile applications are dependent on both the physical attributes of the Smartphone, as the terminals and features that have been programed into the application. For your design is vital to take into account the needs and preferences of the target user, it will be its satisfaction of use what will define mainly the level of usability of the application and, in good part, its success.

References

1. Xu, Q., Erman, J., Gerber, A., Mao, Z., Pang, J., Venkataraman, S.: Identifying diverse usage behaviors of smartphone apps. In: Proceedings of the 2011 ACM SIGCOMM Conference on Internet Measurement Conference, pp. 329–344. ACM (2011)
2. Chang, T.R., Kaasinen, E., Kaipainen. K.: What influences users' decisions to take apps into use? A framework for evaluating persuasive and engaging design in mobile Apps for wellbeing. In: Proceedings of the 11th International Conference on Mobile and Ubiquitous Multimedia, p. 2. ACM (2012)
3. Casar, J.R.: Tecnologías y Servicios para la Sociedad de la Información. Universidad Politécnica de Madrid (2005)
4. Mantilla, M.C.G., Ariza, L.L.C., Delgado, B.M.: Metodología para el desarrollo de aplicaciones móviles. Revista Tecnura **18**(40), 20–35 (2014)
5. Zapata, A.F., Rodríguez, J.: Diseño y desarrollo de una aplicación WEB para el consultorio empresarial que controle las prácticas de los estudiantes de la Universidad Libre Seccional Pereira, 2011. Doctoral dissertation, Universidad Libre de Pereira (2011)
6. Clunie, G.T., Crespo, S., Riley, J., Gómez, B., Rodríguez, K., Barraza, O.: Arquitectura para la configuración de escenarios de aprendizaje móvil, con el uso de la plataforma Moodle, vol. 10. Universidad Tecnológica de Panamá (2012)
7. Bellman, S., Potter, R.F., Treleaven-Hassard, S., Robinson, J.A., Varan, D.: The effectiveness of branded mobile phone apps. J. Interact. Mark. **25**(4), 191–200 (2011)
8. Cepeda, F.J.D.: Actualización docente en tecnologías educativas y aprendizaje móvil: Desarrollo de un programa institucional. Revista de Formación e Innovación Educativa Universitaria **7**(4), 211–226 (2014)
9. Ruiz, F.J., Belmonte, A.M.: Young people as users of branded applications on mobile devices. Media Educ. Res. J. Comunicar **22**(43), 73–81 (2014)
10. Piñeiro, T., Rodríguez, J.J.: La participación de los oyentes en las radio APPs españolas. Prácticas convencionales en la era de la portabilidad. adComunica **5**, 67–89 (2013)
11. Molina, A., Chirino, V.: Mejores prácticas de aprendizaje móvil para el desarrollo de competencias en la educación superior. IEEE-RITA **4**(4), 175–183 (2010)
12. Ibarrola, M.: Hacia una reconceptualización de las relaciones entre el mundo de la educación y el mundo del trabajo en América Latina. Revista Latinoamericana de Estudios Educativos (México) **18**(2), 9–63 (1988)

13. Sarmiento, S.A., Boada, H., Diaz, E.: Propuesta para impulsar el desarrollo de aplicaciones convergentes en colombia. Revista GTI **11**(30) (2013)
14. Aldana, G.: Características de los egresados del programa de Mercadeo Publicidad y Ventas de la Fundación Universitaria del Área Andina sede Bogotá. Teoría y Praxis Investigativa, **1**(2) (2006)
15. Becerra, G., González, F., Reyes, J., Camargo, F., Alfonso, A.: Seguimiento a egresados. Su importancia para las instituciones de educación superior. Teoría y praxis investigativa **3**(2), 61–65 (2008)
16. Cabrera, A., Weerts, D., Zulick, B.: Encuestas a egresados: tres fundamentos conceptuales en el seguimiento de egresados universitarios. Métodos de análisis de la inserción laboral de los universitarios, **55** (2003)
17. Romo, Z., Espinosa, R.: Apps como una posibilidad más de comunicación entre la marca y su público: un análisis basado en la valoración de los usuarios/Apps as an additonal possibility for the communication between brand and his audience: An analysis based on the users rating. Pensar la publicidad **6**(1), 81 (2012)
18. Okazaki, S., Mendez, F.: Exploring convenience in mobile commerce: moderating effects of gender. Comput. Hum. Behav. **29**(3), 1234–1242 (2013)
19. Taylor, D.G., Voelker, T.A., Pentina, I.: Mobile application adoption by young adults: a social network perspective, pp. 60–70. Sacred Heart University (2011)
20. Kaasinen. E.: Usability challenges in agent-based services. In: Zuidweg, H., Campolargo, M., Delgado, J. (eds.) IS&N 1999. LNCS, vol. 1597, pp 131–142. Springer, Heidelberg (1999)
21. The Open Group "ArchiMate® 2.1 Specification" 2012–2013

Specific Growth Rate Estimation in Fed-Batch Bioreactor Using Super Twisting Sliding Mode Observer

María Clara Salazar$^{(\boxtimes)}$ and Héctor Botero

Facultad de Minas, Departamento de Energía Eléctrica y Automática,
Universidad Nacional de Colombia, Medellín, Colombia
{mcsalazar1,habotero}@unal.edu.co
http://www.unal.edu.co

Abstract. This paper presents the application of a second order sliding mode observer based on the classic super twisting algorithm in order to estimate the specific growth rate in a model of fed-batch bioprocess. This observer estimates the specific growth rate without assuming a specific model (such as Monod or Haldane), using the biomass concentration measurement. The observer allows the fixed time estimation of the specific growth rate, and provides robustness against uncertainty and parametric changes.

Keywords: Bioprocess · Finite time convergence · Sliding mode observer · Specific growth rate estimation

1 Introduction

Bioprocess models are characterized by complex dynamic behavior and the difficulty of measuring some important variables. For example, in some applications, the biomass concentration can be directly measured, while others related to kinetics cannot be monitored due to modeling uncertainty and external disturbances. Thus, some authors have proposed robust observers which do not require a previous knowledge about the kinetic structure and some process parameters [1,2,5].

This way, some authors have estimated the specific growth rate by means of the product concentration measurement, using a second order sliding mode observer which allows finite time estimation [3]. On the other hand, observers have been proposed in order to estimate the specific growth rate according to the most popular kinetic models such as Monod and Haldane [4–7]. Some of these works are based on the high gain concept, which are comparable with the proposed observer in this article. However, few sliding mode observers presented in the literature hold properties such as fixed time and disturbance rejection.

From the background described, this article presents the application of a second order sliding mode observer based on classic Super Twisting algorithm structure, with stronger fixed time convergence characteristics, for estimation of

© Springer International Publishing AG 2016
J.C. Figueroa-García et al. (Eds.): WEA 2016, CCIS 657, pp. 403–411, 2016.
DOI: 10.1007/978-3-319-50880-1_35

specific growth rate in a model of fed-batch process through the measurement of biomass concentration, and it is also compared with the high gain Luenberger observer and a second order sliding mode observer using kinetic models (Monod and Haldane). The observer presented is applied to the model used in [5,6].

This article is distributed as follows: in Sect. 2, we present the bioprocess model as well as proposed models for specific growth rate. In the third section, we describe some observers reported in the literature for this type of processes, the results of these are used to compare in the results section. Then, the SOSMO is presented. In Sect. 4, the simulation performance of each of the observers used in this article are shown and the ITAE table to compare numerical error among them.

2   Bioprocess Model

Population growth dynamic behavior in bioprocess can be modeled by balance equations in the reactor which describe biomass and substrate accumulation, and volume culture variation. A model for this concept is shown in Eq. (1) (see [4]).

$$\frac{d(Vx)}{dt} = \mu V x - F_{out} x \tag{1}$$

$$\frac{d(Vs)}{dt} = -k_1 \mu V x + F_{in} s_{in} - F_{out} s \tag{2}$$

$$\frac{dV}{dt} = F_{in} - F_{out} \tag{3}$$

where x refers to biomass concentration, s substrate concentration in the reactor, s_{in} the input substrate concentration, F_{in}, F_{out} input and output fluxes, respectively. Also, μ is the specific growth rate, k_1 the yield coefficient due to the consumption of substrate by the biomass and V the volume of the culture medium.

In this paper the following simplifications has been considered:

- Initially the bioreactor contains an amount of biomass and substrate, and fills up progressively with the input substrate.
- The bioreactor is considered Fed-batch, then $F_{in} \neq 0$ y $F_{out} = 0$.
- The dilution rate is defined as $D = \frac{F_{in}}{V}$ and depends on biomass concentration and time.

Therefore, the following simplified model is obtained:

$$\dot{x} = (\mu(s) - D(x,t))x \tag{4}$$
$$\dot{s} = -k_1 \mu(s)x + D(s_{in} - s)x \tag{5}$$

In several references a simplified model is also used to prove observers [5]:

$$\dot{x} = (\mu - D(x,t))x \tag{6}$$
$$\dot{\mu} = \rho(x, \mu, t)x \tag{7}$$

In these models the specific growth rate can be a monotonic or non monotonic function substrate concentration dependent and it is commonly modeled by Monod equation or Haldane equation [2,4]. For example, Monod model expresses the dependence of μ with substrate concentration and it is shown in Eq. (8), where μ_{max} is the maximum value of the specific growth rate and K_M is the Michaelis-Menten constant which is valid when substrate concentration is greater than enzyme concentration. Furthermore, this model does not consider substrate inhibition in high substrate concentration.

$$\mu(s) = \mu_{max} \frac{s}{k_M + s} \tag{8}$$

Likewise, Haldane model describes substrate inhibition with the parameter k_I in Eq. (9). This specific growth rate representation is an example of a non monotonic function with substrate inhibition [2].

$$\mu(s) = \mu_0 \frac{s}{K_M + s + \frac{s^2}{K_I}} \tag{9}$$

Also, μ_0 can be described as

$$\mu_0 = \mu_{max}(1 + \sqrt{\frac{K_M}{K_I}}) \tag{10}$$

This way, if substrate inhibition is omitted, Haldane equation is reduced to Monod equation.

3 Kinetics Observers for Bioprocess

In this section three observers are described in order to estimate the kinetics in the bioprocess: High gain Luenberger observer, Sliding mode observer and the SOSMO.

3.1 Reported Observers

High Gain Luenberger Observer. This observer is composed by a replication of the bioprocess model and a correction factor that depends on biomass measure error. The correction factor contains tuning constants ζ y ω, as shown in Eq. (11).

$$\dot{\hat{x}} = (\hat{\mu} - D(x,t) + 2\zeta\omega(x - \hat{x}))x \tag{11}$$

$$\dot{\hat{\mu}} = \omega^2(x - \hat{x})x \tag{12}$$

This is characterized by the asymptotic convergence, i.e. the estimation error tends to zero when time tends to infinity. Thus, it achieves a bounded error under the assumption that the specific growth rate is bounded time derivative [5]. Furthermore, some authors propose an alternative to select the observer's poles with damping factor $\zeta = 0.7$ in order to improve the observer convergence with small overshoot [8,9].

Second Order Sliding Mode Observer. This observer has finite time convergence feature since it uses a Super-Twisting algorithm [5]. The observer structure is shown in Eq. (13).

$$\dot{\hat{x}} = (\hat{\mu} - D(x,t) + 2\beta(\bar{\rho}\,|x - \hat{x}|)^{\frac{1}{2}}\,sign(x - \hat{x}))x \tag{13}$$

$$\dot{\hat{\mu}} = \alpha\bar{\rho}\,\text{sign}(x - \hat{x})x \tag{14}$$

where the observer includes a discontinue structure due to *sign* function. This structure depends on the measure variable error which, by means of appropriate gains tuning α, β and ρ give finite time convergence and robustness characteristics. To verify the observer convergence a proof is presented in [6] using Lyapunov approach, so there are adjustable values of the gains to make it stable. Finally, this proof ensures that the error is zero in finite time, achieving convergence and robustness features.

3.2   SOSMO Applied to the Bioprocess

Taking in account the second order sliding mode observer presented before, this algorithm presents stronger characteristics such as fixed time convergence independent of initial conditions and robustness to process uncertainty [6,10].

Observer Structure. The structure is based on the classic Super Twisting algorithm and it requires the structure of the plant to be a second order system (see Eq. (15)). This structure also takes into account both the model uncertainty (δ) as the terms of non linearity (f_2). In this sense, to determine the convergence, Lyapunov equations have been applied to these algorithms allowing to analyze robustness to uncertainty and disturbances for convergence [11,12].

$$\dot{x}_1 = f_1(y, u) + b(t, u, y)x_2 \tag{15}$$

$$\dot{x}_2 = f_2(y, u) + \delta(t, x, u, w) \tag{16}$$

$$y = x_1 \tag{17}$$

where $x_{1,2} \in \mathbb{R}$ are the states, $u \in \mathbb{R}^m$ is a known input and $y \in \mathbb{R}$ is the measured output. Also, f_1 is a known continue function and f_2 refers to a discontinuous term from a multivalued function and finally, the bounded and positive function b is $0 \leq b_m \leq b(t, u, y) \leq b_M$ [6].

In this case, it is intended to estimate the state x_2 from the measure of x_1, therefore the general expression of the observer is shown in Eq. (18):

$$\dot{\hat{x}}_1 = -l_1(t)\phi_1(e_1) + f_1(y, u) + b(t, u, y)\hat{x}_2 \tag{18}$$

$$\dot{\hat{x}}_2 = -l_2\phi_2(e_1) + f_2(y, u) \tag{19}$$

where $e_{1,2} = x_{1,2} - \hat{x}_{1,2}$ are the estimation errors and the gains $l_{1,2}$ must be tuned correctly to assure the observer convergence. In addition, the nonlinear terms $\phi_1(e_1)$ and $\phi_2(e_1)$ have the form:

$$\phi_1(e_1) = \mu_1\sqrt{|e_1|}\mathrm{sign}(e_1) + \mu_2\,|e_1|^q\,\mathrm{sign}(e_1) \tag{20}$$

$$\phi_2(e_1) = \frac{\mu_1^2}{2}\mathrm{sign}(e_1) + \mu_1\mu_2\left(q + \frac{1}{2}\right)|e_1|^{q-\frac{1}{2}}\,\mathrm{sign}(e_1) \tag{21}$$

$$+ \mu_2^2\,|e_1|^{2q-1}\,\mathrm{sign}(e_1) \tag{22}$$

where $\mu_{1,2} > 0$ and $q > \frac{1}{2} \in \mathbb{R}$ are positive constants. Also, ϕ_1 and ϕ_2 are related as $\phi_2(e_1) = \phi_1'(e_1)\phi_1(e_1)$ and in this sense, ϕ_1 is continuous while ϕ_2 is discontinuous in $e_1 = 0$ when $\mu_1 > 0$. In this case, the state estimation errors satisfy the differential equation presented below.

$$\dot{e}_1 = -l_1(t)\phi_1(e_1) + b(t,u,y)e_2 \tag{23}$$
$$\dot{e}_2 = -l_2\phi_2(e_1) - \delta(t,x,u,w) \tag{24}$$

Taking into account that in Eq. (23) the disturbance error has an upper bound $|\delta(t,x,u,w)| \leq \Gamma$, $\Gamma > 0$ for $t \geq 0$. The convergence proof is in [6].

SOSMO Applied to the Growth Rate Estimation. This observer is based on the classic generalized Super Twisting algorithm as follows:

$$\dot{\hat{x}} = (\hat{\mu} - D(x,t) + k_1\phi_1)x \tag{25}$$
$$\dot{\hat{\mu}} = k_2\phi_2 x \tag{26}$$

with $\phi_{1,2}$ as shown in Eq. (27).

$$\phi_1 = \sqrt{|e_1|}\mathrm{sign}(e_1) + \mu((|e_1|)^{3/2})\mathrm{sign}(e_1) \tag{27}$$
$$\phi_2 = 0.5\mathrm{sign}(e_1) + 2\mu e_1 + 1.5\mu^2 e_1^2\mathrm{sign}(e_1) \tag{28}$$

The form of the proposed estimation structure in this work was described in Eq. (25). In this sense, with the conditions given in the convergence proof, tuned gains are taken as $k_1 = k_2 = 1.5$, $\mu_1 = 1$, $\mu_2 = 0.5$ and the power $q = 1.5$.

4   Results

In order to test the observers performance, this section presents the numerical simulation results of the proposed estimation structure. The simulations parameters were:

- Biomass concentration is measured (x) and the specific growth rate is estimated (μ).
- The biomass sensor has random noise with variance $v = 0,01[kg/m^3]$.
- Simulation time is $60\,h$.
- A parametric change in μ has been made in $t = 30\,h$, taking its maximum value as $\mu_m = 0,22h^{-1}$ at the beginning and then $\mu_m = 0,3h^{-1}$. This change remains in all the simulations.

– The nominal initial conditions of the model are $x(0) = 2,054[kg/m^3]$ and $s(0) = 0,893[kg/m^3]$.
– The nominal initial conditions of the observer are $\hat{x}(0) = 2,054[kg/m^3]$ and $\hat{\mu}(0) = 0,1902h^{-1}$.
– The dilution rate is defined as $D = \lambda x$.
– The input signal λ, is a square signal with period $10\,h$, mean value $0,0125$ and amplitude $0,005$.

Figures 1 and 2 represent the Luenberger observer results when the specific growth rate follows the Monod equation. Analogously, Figs. 3 and 4 represent the measured and estimated variables when there exist substrate inhibition, i.e. using the Haldane equation. Then, the second order sliding mode observer results are presented in Figs. 5, 6, 7 and 8 and the proposed observer simulation results are shown in Figs. 9, 10, 11 and 12.

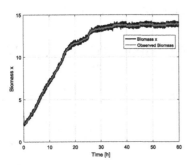

Fig. 1. Biomass concentration - Monod

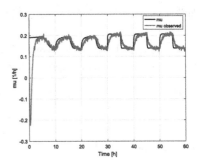

Fig. 2. Specific growth rate estimation - Monod

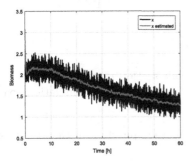

Fig. 3. Biomass concentration - Haldane

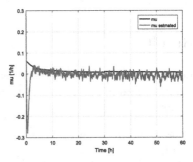

Fig. 4. Specific growth rate estimation - Haldane

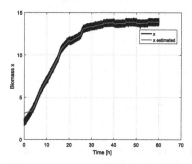

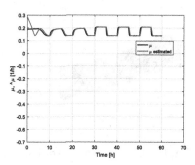

Fig. 5. Biomass concentration - Monod

Fig. 6. Specific growth rate estimation - Monod

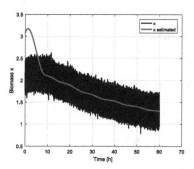

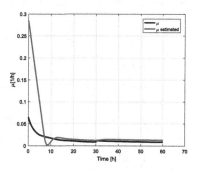

Fig. 7. Biomass concentration - Haldane

Fig. 8. Specific growth rate estimation - Haldane

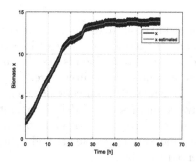

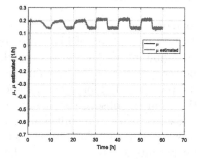

Fig. 9. Biomass concentration - Monod

Fig. 10. Specific growth rate estimation - Monod

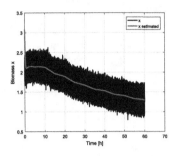
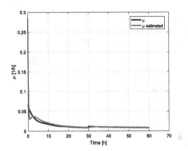
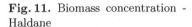

Fig. 11. Biomass concentration - Haldane

Fig. 12. Specific growth rate estimation - Haldane

In this case, the settling time and error have smaller values than the Luenberger observer and sliding mode observer. Table 1 shows the comparison among scenarios for the error measure ITAE.

Table 1. ITAE comparison

Numerical error comparison (ITAE)			
ITAE	Luenberger	Second order SMO	SMO proposed
Monod			
$ITAE_x$	51.02	16.67	3.399
$ITAE_\mu$	19.05	8.131	6.196
Haldane			
$ITAE_x$	21.03	26.89	12.27
$ITAE_\mu$	32.01	9.289	1.739

5   Conclusions

A second order sliding mode observer was applied in order to estimate the specific growth rate in a model of bioreactor by means of the measurement of biomass concentration in two cases: Monod and Haldane equations. The results obtained had better performance than some observers presented in the literature.

The proper tuning of gains is important to achieve the convergence characteristics from the observer structure and give robustness to model uncertainty. This task is still very difficult and there are no rules to achieve it in an optimal way. However filtering characteristics from the measured variable are highlighted since it permits a better quality of the observed variable.

As future work it is necessary to investigate and to propose observers that consider delayed measurements because sometimes the biomass concentration is obtained by means of laboratory test, therefore the information is delayed. Some papers related to this topic has been published recently (see [13,14]).

References

1. Dochain, D.: State and parameter estimation in chemical and biochemical processes: a tutorial. J. Process Control **13**(8), 801–818 (2003)
2. De Battista, H., Picó, J., Picó-Marco, E.: Globally stabilizing control of fed-batch processes with Haldane kinetics using growth rate estimation feedback. J. Process Control **16**(8), 865–875 (2006)
3. Nuñez, S., Garelli, F., De Battista, H.: Product-based sliding mode observer for biomass and growth rate estimation in Luedeking-Piret like processes. Chem. Eng. Res. Des. **105**, 24–30 (2016)
4. Bastin, G., Dochain, D.: On-line estimation of microbial specific growth rates. Automatica **22**(6), 705–709 (1986)
5. De Battista, H., Picó, J., Garelli, F., Vignoni, A.: Specific growth rate estimation in (fed-)batch bioreactors using second-order sliding observers. J. Process Control **21**(7), 1049–1055 (2011)
6. Moreno, J., Mendoza, I.: Application of Super-twisting-like observers for bioprocesses. In: 2014 13th International Workshop on Variable Structure Systems (VSS), pp. 1–6, June 2014
7. Picó, J., De Battista, H., Garelli, F.: Smooth sliding-mode observers for specific growth rate and substrate from biomass measurement. J. Process Control **19**(8), 1314–1323 (2009)
8. Oliveira, R., Ferreira, E.C.: Feyo de Azevedo, S.: Stability, dynamics of convergence and tuning of observer-based kinetics estimators. J. Process Control **12**(2), 311–323 (2002)
9. Perrier, M., de Azevedo, S.F., Ferreira, E.C., Dochain, D.: Tuning of observer-based estimators: theory and application to the on-line estimation of kinetic parameters. Control Eng. Prac. **8**(4), 377–388 (2000)
10. Moreno, J.: A linear framework for the robust stability analysis of a Generalized Super-Twisting Algorithm. In: 2009 6th International Conference on Electrical Engineering, Computing Science and Automatic Control, CCE, pp. 1–6, January 2009
11. Cruz-Zavala, E., Moreno, J., Fridman, L.: Uniform robust exact differentiator. IEEE Trans. Autom. Control **56**(11), 2727–2733 (2011)
12. Levant, A.: Robust exact differentiation via sliding mode technique. Automatica **34**(3), 379–384 (1998)
13. Mohd Ali, J., Ha Hoang, N., Hussain, M.A., Dochain, D.: Review and classification of recent observers applied in chemical process systems. Comput. Chem. Eng. **76**, 27–41 (2015)
14. Zhao, L., Wang, J., Yu, T., Chen, K., Liu, T.: Nonlinear state estimation for fermentation process using cubature Kalman filter to incorporate delayed measurements. Chin. J. Chem. Eng. **23**(11), 1801–1810 (2015)

Author Index

Printed in the United States
By Bookmasters